William Faulkner:

FOUR DECADES OF CRITICISM

William
Faulkner

FOUR DECADES OF CRITICISM

Edited by

LINDA WELSHIMER WAGNER

Michigan State University Press

1973

Copyright © 1973
Michigan State University Press
Library of Congress Card Catalog Number: 72–92455
ISBN 0–98013–176–1
Manufactured in the United States of America

PS
3511
A86
Z9852

★
　　★
　★
　　★

　　★

Contents

Introduction

WILLIAM FAULKNER would be pleased with current criticism of his writing. He was never in any hurry. He knew it would all be worth it, and that a good bit of his writing would last. The most that he asked from critics was "Saneness. . . . Live and let live; criticise with taste for a criterion."[1] Establishing the criteria for modern literature has taken perhaps too long, but now that more uniform standards of judgment exist, Faulkner is receiving the highest acclaim. As Jay B. Hubbell recently wrote, "No American writer of the twentieth century is now so highly praised as Faulkner."[2]

In the past fifteen years alone, approximately seven hundred essays on Faulkner's work have been published. A 1971 checklist of criticism on a single Faulkner novel, *The Sound and the Fury,* lists over 240 essays and reviews; a similar listing on *Light in August* includes 200 items.[3] Dissertations both completed and in progress indicate that the number of Faulkner authorities is only increasing.

Because so much good criticism has appeared since the 1960 edition of these essays *(William Faulkner: Three Decades of Criticism),* many changes in the table of contents have been necessary. Available for the first time since 1960, the essays of Part I describe Faulkner's background for writing, his development from poet to novelist, and some of his aesthetic principles. This emphasis on Faulkner as writer, and the novels which he wrote, is maintained through the collection; studies which deal with history, sociology, geography, and politics are represented only as they have direct bearing on Faulkner's writing itself.

Part II surveys Faulkner's writing generally, but each essay is rich in perceptive comments about individual works (an index has been added to this edition for easier cross-reference). Because Faulkner's technical virtuosity is sometimes difficult to appreciate on a first reading, the essays in Part III offer explanations for aspects of his structure and style; while Part IV contains interpretive essays focused on single novels or several related books.

The essays included here date from 1939 to 1971. Two of them were first published in 1939; they appear again in 1973 not for reasons of sentiment but because they have never been bettered. Compared to much of the bombast that greeted Faulkner's writing in the twenties and thirties, the essays of Conrad

1

Aiken, George Marion O'Donnell, and—in 1941—Warren Beck are particularly notable. With Faulkner, critics seemed slow in coming to their usually balanced stance. What passed for criticism was sometimes chauvinistic reaction to this supposedly uneducated, Southern writer, or moralistic condemnation of the alleged point of a novel. The real province of criticism—to give the work an interested and informed reading—often went ignored. And, perhaps more important to Faulkner's work, ignored also were the processes of criticism: first, deciding what the author is trying to do; second, deciding how well he has accomplished his aim; and only third, deciding whether his aim was worth achieving in the first place. With Faulkner, many critics began in reverse.

One important difference between comparatively early criticism of Faulkner's work and current comment is that the scholars who write about Faulkner now are likely to be conversant with all of his writing, rather than being expert on only selected novels. Faulkner's work, and not only in the Yoknapatawpha stories, interrelates closely. The best definition of "sanctuary" occurs, for example, not in the novel of that name but in the later *Light in August* and *Requiem for a Nun*. The full weight of Faulkner's insistence on man's ability to endure cannot be realized until one has read *The Mansion* (1959) even though he seemingly gave ample illustration of endurance in *The Sound and the Fury*, thirty years before. In current criticism the mosaic of Faulkner's belief is finally being studied as just that, a mosaic, a pattern of concrete scenes and images flashed brilliantly (and solidly) on the reader's consciousness, but seldom—anywhere—summarized or paraphrased. The best readers today have reconciled themselves to Faulkner's demanding techniques, and are interpreting single books and stories in light of the ethic of the whole canon.

Critics have also begun taking all of Faulkner's writing seriously. During the fifties, interest centered on the five major novels, those written from 1929 to approximately 1942. More recently the Snopes trilogy (and related stories) has been added to the central work. Increasingly now, interest is moving to those non-Yoknapatawpha County books like *Pylon* and *Wild Palms*, although few readers yet seem to appreciate fully what Stanley Tick calls the "blend" tales like *Knight's Gambit*, *Go Down, Moses* (all of it), and *The Unvanquished*. The earlier story collections have received little attention, as have the earliest novels and *The Fable*. There yet remains much work to be done.

Another recent shift in critical views of Faulkner has been that from seeing him as an iconoclastic Southern writer who knew very little about literature to recognizing him as a man very much in the mainstream of modern writing. Each of the essays in Part I, Faulkner's Development, contains new information about his formative reading, his extra-literary interests, and his theory. The reader will find further information in such books as H. Edward Richardson's *William Faulkner: The Journey to Self-Discovery* and Joseph Blotner's *Faulkner, A Biography*.

Seeing Faulkner as the conscious craftsman that he was has also sharpened critical opinion as to the reasons he wrote as he did. The multiple narrative perspectives in *Absalom, Absalom!* accordingly became intriguing in their own right, with the differences in the stories of Rosa Coldfield, Mr. Compson, Shreve, and Quentin becoming not "mistakes" by Faulkner but rather ways of characterizing the respective story teller. The fact that he returned to Temple Drake's story in the 1951 *Requiem for a Nun* is no longer considered poor strategy, the mark of an exhausted novelist, but rather a great writer's attempt to present another well-told story about the human comprehension of justice and honor, as well as a means of enriching the earlier *Sanctuary* and "That Evening Sun Go Down." This present keen interest in Faulkner as craftsman has also given us such helpful collations of early manuscript versions and published novels as *Faulkner's Revisions of Absalom, Absalom!* and *Sanctuary,* both compiled by Gerald Langland.

Faulkner scholarship has also taken new perspectives. In his formalist *Modern Fiction* (1971) William J. Handy bases Faulkner's supremacy on his meshing of form and content. Walter Brylowski's *Faulkner's Olympian Laugh* (1968) was the first myth-oriented interpretation. Glenn Sandstrom's essay "Identify Diffusion: Joe Christmas and Quentin Compson" (1967) incorporates third force psychology into an analysis of two important protagonists. Floyd Watkins' *The Flesh and the Word* studies Faulkner's writing in the company of that of T. S. Eliot and Hemingway, as does Jean Weisgerber compare Faulkner with Dostoievski (1968); James Guetti (in *The Limits of Metaphor,* 1967) puts Faulkner in the context of Melville and Conrad. All of these books are stylistic studies, Guetti analyzing the uses of metaphor, Watkins tracing the implementation of the concrete. Richard Poirier's *A World Elsewhere, The Place of Style in American Literature* (1966) also attempts to locate Faulkner's work in terms of its style, and Morris Beja's *Epiphany in the Modern Novel* (1971) is another comparative study of methods. Richard Hauck's *A Cheerful Nihilism* (1971) does much to explain the genuine comic elements of Faulkner's writing.

This past decade has also seen the appearance of the best-executed studies of Faulkner's work as a whole. Cleanth Brooks' *William Faulkner: The Yoknapatawpha Country* (1963) offers important correlations within the novels, and gives any reader an excellent sense of Faulkner as writer. In 1966 Michael Millgate published his second study of the author, this one titled *The Achievement of William Faulkner*. Millgate has combined factual information with insightful reading. Both books are very important contributions, generally in agreement—seeing Faulkner as both a great moralist and a great craftsman. In agreement with their general position are two other critics, Warren Beck (*Man in Motion: Faulkner's Trilogy*, 1961) and John W. Hunt (*William Faulkner: Art in Theological Tension*, 1965).

Aside from the many single essays and book-length critical studies, much material has been published to aid Faulkner scholars. To begin with, Faulkner's own last novel, *The Reivers*, appeared in 1962, amid noisy and mixed critical reaction. Valuable comments by Faulkner himself have been preserved in *Faulkner in the University*, edited by Frederick L. Gwynn and Joseph Blotner, and *Faulkner at West Point*, edited by Joseph L. Fant and Robert Ashley, published in 1959 and 1964 respectively. Particularly helpful is the 1968 *Lion in the Garden*, interviews with Faulkner from 1926 to 1962, edited by James B. Meriwether and Michael Millgate. The collection also includes the texts of Faulkner's Nagano Seminars.

Also available since 1960 are *Early Prose and Poetry*, edited by Carvel Collins (1962); *Essays, Speeches & Public Letters by William Faulkner*, edited by James B. Meriwether (1966); *The Faulkner-Cowley File* (1966); and *New Orleans Sketches*, edited by Carvel Collins (1968).

A great deal of recent activity has also centered on materials which help to understand the man Faulkner and his milieu. *Old Times in the Faulkner Country* consists largely of John Cullen's reminiscences as written by Floyd C. Watkins (1961); *William Faulkner of Oxford* (1965) is a compilation of anecdotes about Faulkner by friends and townspeople, edited by James W. Webb and A. Wigfall Green. Elizabeth M. Kerr's *Yoknapatawpha* (1969) is the most complete sociological study of Faulkner's Mississippi environs; and Martin J. Dain's photographic study *Faulkner's County: Yoknapatawpha* (1964) also provides useful information.

Since Faulkner's unexpected death on July 6, 1962, there has been much interest in his biography. Two books by his brothers helped to fill the need: in 1963 *My Brother Bill* by John Faulkner, and in 1967 *The Falkners of Mississippi* by Murry C. Falkner; both books are engaging if non-literary studies. Most recently, Joseph Blotner's *Faulkner, a Biography* has been published; and its accuracy and warm, informative style make it a fine resource for readers as well as a high tribute to Faulkner.

Because of the excellent bibliographies now in print, I have chosen to omit any bibliography from this edition. Instead, see Maurice Beebe's "Criticism of William Faulkner: A Selected Checklist" in *Modern Fiction Studies,* Spring, 1967; and the listings in the 1971 Spring and Fall *Resources for American Literary Study.* Of great help for any reader is James B. Meriwether's bibliographical essay on Faulkner in *Fifteen Modern American Authors,* edited by Jackson R. Bryer, 1969. Soon to be released is David Pownall's six-volume annotated bibliography of criticism published during the past fifteen years concerning all twentieth century writers, including 700 essays on Faulkner's work. Irene Lynn Sleeth's 1962 checklist, *William Faulkner: A Bibliography of Criticism* also includes a brief listing of essays in foreign journals, as does Olga Vickery's bibliography for *William Faulkner: Three Decades of Criticism.* The collected essays of Maurice Coindreau, Faulkner's French translator, provide some insight into Faulkner's reputation in France (*The Time of William Faulkner,* 1971), and Gordon Price-Stephens' essay "The British Reception of William Faulkner, 1929–1962" is also helpful.

Although the definitive bibliography of published work by Faulkner has not appeared, there are two partial listings. James Meriwether's *The Literary Career of William Faulkner: A Bibliographical Study* was published in 1961; and in 1968 came *William Faulkner, Man Working, 1919–1962,* by Linton R. Massey, the catalogue of the University of Virginia Faulkner collection at that time.

These are all important contributions toward making Faulkner scholarship both more accurate and more balanced. Scholars are still handicapped by not having a complete bibliography and the publication of more primary materials (particularly Faulkner's letters), but they are much better equipped in the 1970's than they were in the 1950's and 1960's.

Faced with a real wealth of critical insight, I have included here what seemed to be the strongest, best-substantiated essays available. Because collections of essays on single novels have recently been published, I have included criticism on as many novels as space permitted rather than using three or four essays about a single book, no matter how great the novel is considered to be. My thanks to my colleagues at Michigan State University, Clyde Henson, Victor Hoar, Virgil Scott, Joseph Waldmeir, Mary Josephs, and particularly Russell B. Nye; and to my editors Lyle Blair and Jean Busfield.

LINDA W. WAGNER
East Lansing, Michigan

1. "On Criticism," *Double Dealer,* VII (January-February, 1925), 83–84.
2. *Who Are the Major American Writers?* (Durham, N.C.: Duke University Press, 1972), 284.
3. John E. Bassett, "William Faulkner's *The Sound and The Fury:* An Annotated Checklist of Criticism," *Resources for American Literary Study,* I, No. 2 (Autumn 1971), 217–246 and M. Thomas Inge, "William Faulkner's *Light in August:* An Annotated Checklist of Criticism," *Ibid.,* I, No. 1 (Spring 1971), 30–57.

I. Faulkner: The Development of the Writer

THE APPRENTICESHIP OF WILLIAM FAULKNER

RICHARD P. ADAMS

THERE SHOULD BE no need for special emphasis on the obvious fact that Faulkner's apprenticeship involved an enormous amount of reading, intelligently chosen from the best literature available in Western civilization. But the scholarship on this point is such—or is so scanty—that this same obvious fact is what most needs to be emphasized. No general survey of Faulkner's reading has ever been published. Various people have suggested that Faulkner may have read this book or that; Faulkner himself has been questioned about many books in various interviews; and some influences have been pretty clearly pointed out. Enough work has been done to show that a great deal more can be done with profit, and that we need not be deterred—as people may have been in the past—by Faulkner's "I'm-just-an-ignorant-farmer-not-a-literary-man" propaganda.

It is true that Faulkner was provincial, and that in some ways the province in which he was born and reared and educated, and lived almost the whole of his life, is one of the less civilized parts of the Western world. But to conclude from these premises, as some appear to have done, that Faulkner was culturally isolated, that he was an ignorant genius, born in a manger, miraculously visited by the muses, and receiving inspiration for masterpiece after masterpiece out of the air without any teaching or learning, is to be guilty of incredible nonsense. There can be no royal road to the kind of work Faulkner did between 1928 and 1942. Certainly the man who could do it was a genius, but not even he could have done it without the hardest kind of study, thought, and labor. What came out of him in those fertile years had to come in part from an enormous amount of written matter previously absorbed into him. Granted, he was provincial. But he was also a highly sophisticated young man, who, living far from the capital, could not take his culture for granted but had

Reprinted with permission from *Tulane Studies in English*, XII (1962), 113–156.

to sweat for it, and who succeeded in educating himself more thoroughly, and in some ways more systematically, than most college graduates are educated.

Nor did he do so without encouragement and competent help. Oxford, Mississippi, is a college town, and Faulkner's father was an official of the University. During the school year 1919–1920, Faulkner, enrolled as a special student, made two A's in French and contributed a short story and twelve poems to the campus newspaper, *The Mississippian*. Four of the poems were translations from the French Verlaine. For the next two years he continued to publish poems in the paper, and also in the yearbook, and he wrote several reviews and critical essays for the paper's literary page. Presumably he spent a good bit of time on the campus; probably the library was not unknown to him or unvisited by him; and he must have been stimulated by his associations with at least some of his acquaintance among students and faculty members.

His most useful teacher was probably his friend Phil Stone, a young lawyer in town who had graduated from Yale and frequented the Brick Row Bookshop, where he had bought many volumes of modern poetry, particularly Eliot and the Imagists. Stone subscribed to the leading little magazines, including *Poetry, The Egoist, The Little Review,* and *The Dial,* and he was also interested in a number of French poets, whose works he owned, some in the original and some in translation. He made these materials, along with some critical and philosophical works, freely available to Faulkner, who devoured them in quantity.

For ten or more years before the spring of 1925, Faulkner evidently thought of himself, and was thought of by others, as being primarily a poet; and his serious reading seems to have been in poetry rather than in prose fiction. In an essay entitled "Verse Old and Nascent: A Pilgrimage," published in *The Double Dealer* for April, 1925,[1] he gave some account of his development during this period. "At the age of sixteen," he begins, "I discovered Swinburne. Or rather, Swinburne discovered me, springing from some tortured undergrowth of my adolescence, like a highwayman, making me his slave. . . . It was years later that I found in him much more than bright and bitter sound, more than a satisfying tinsel of blood and death and gold and the inevitable sea." Unfortunately he does not say what the "more" consisted of. He also "dipped into Shelley and Keats . . . but they did not move me." After the war his interest in poetry became more active and more serious. For a time, "With no background whatever I joined the pack belling loudly after contemporary poets." But apparently this enthusiasm, though intense, was soon exhausted. "That page," he says, "is closed to me forever. I read Robinson and Frost with pleasure, and Aldington; Conrad Aiken's minor music still echoes in my heart; but beyond these, that period might have never been. I no longer try to read the others at all."

He blames his disenchantment on Housman. "It was 'The Shropshire Lad' which closed the period. I found a paperbound copy in a bookshop and when I opened it I discovered there the secret after which the moderns course howling like curs on a cold trail in a dark wood, giving off, it is true, an occasional note clear with beauty, but curs just the same. Here was the reason for being born into a fantastic world: discovering the splendor of fortitude, the beauty of being of the soil like a tree about which fools might howl and which winds of disillusion and death and despair might strip, leaving it bleak, without bitterness; beautiful in sadness." The effect was to send him back to the older poets. "Shakespeare I read, and Spenser, and the Elizabethans, and Shelley and Keats." Keats now moved him. "I read 'Thou still unravished bride of quietness' and found a still water withal strong and potent, quiet with its own strength, and satisfying as bread. That beautiful awareness, so sure of its own power that it is not necessary to create the illusion of force by frenzy and motion. Take the odes to a Nightingale, to a Grecian urn, 'Music to hear,' etc.; here is the spiritual beauty which the moderns strive vainly for with trickery, and yet beneath it one knows are entrails; masculinity."

Evidence of Faulkner's relative lack of respect for the avantgarde appears as early as 1921, in a review of Conrad Aiken's *Turns and Movies* published in *The Mississippian* for 26 February.[2] The encounter with Housman may already have occurred, for the review begins by saying, "In the fog generated by the mental puberty of contemporary American versifiers while writing inferior Keats or sobbing over the Middle West, appears one rift of heaven sent blue—the poems of Conrad Aiken. He, alone of the entire yelping pack, seems to have a definite goal in mind. The others," Faulkner says, with "perhaps half a dozen exceptions," whom he does not name, "are so many loud sounds lost in a single depth of privet hedge. . . . the British nightingales, Mr. Vachel Lindsay with his tin pan and iron spoon, Mr. Kreymborg with his lithographic water coloring, and Mr. Carl Sandburg with his sentimental Chicago propaganda are so many puppets fumbling in a windy darkness." In general, the most radical experimenters in modern poetic modes and techniques seem to be the ones Faulkner shows least interest in. Ezra Pound and William Carlos Williams are barely mentioned, Williams only in one of Faulkner's interviews and Pound in an interview and one early essay. I find no reference anywhere in Faulkner's thus far published literary remains to Hart Crane, Marianne Moore, E. E. Cummings, Robinson Jeffers, or Wallace Stevens, and little indication that he was deeply interested in any of them.

The situation is different, and evidently more complicated, with T. S. Eliot. His name does not occur anywhere in Faulkner's works, and it crops up only twice in interviews, both times being mentioned first by questioners and neither time evoking any significant comment by Faulkner. Yet, as Frederick L. Gwynn has pointed out,[3] three of the poems in Faulkner's *A Green Bough* contain close parallels with early Elliot poems, and *Mosquitoes* and *Pylon* plainly refer to "The Love Song of J. Alfred Prufrock" and *The Waste Land*. Many other parallels can be added to these. In the prose sketch "Home," published in the New Orleans *Times-Picayune* for 22 February, 1925, Faulkner echoes "Prufrock" in describing a mood of hesitation: "His decision he could still revoke . . . there was yet time," and again, "To decide, to act. . . . it was not too late! There was still time."[4] In *Sartoris* "patches of woodland newly green and splashed with dogwood and judas trees" remind us of Eliot's paraphrase of *The Education of Henry Adams* in "Gerontion": "In depraved May, dogwood and chestnut, flowering judas. . . ." In *The Sound and the Fury* Quentin Compson imagines himself and his sister Caddy *"walled by the clean flame"* like Guido da Montefeltro in the passage from Dante's *Inferno* used by Eliot as the epigraph to "The Love Song of J. Alfred Prufrock." Quentin also uses the work *"philoprogenitive,"* which recalls the "Polyphiloprogenitive" of "Mr. Eliot's Sunday Morning Service." And he remembers saying to Caddy, "tell me what you're thinking about tell me," much as the woman in *The Waste Land* says " 'What are you think of? What thinking? What?' " His death by drowning, which he anticipates in terms that strongly suggest the "Death by Water" theme in Eliot, is a result of his impotence. The phrase "hothouse grapes," which occurs in "Sweeney among the Nightingales," also occurs in *Sartoris* and *The Hamlet*. Further echoes of "Prufrock" can be heard in *Absalom, Absalom!*, where Quentin thinks *"you knew it all already,"* and in *The Town,* where Gavin Stevens, uncomfortably attracted to Linda Snopes, has "space to discard a thousand frantic indecisions" in the time it takes her to walk to the door of his office, after which his afternoon is "filled with a thousand indecisions which each fierce succeeding harassment would revise."

Faulkner seems to take special pleasure in using a couple of phrases which Eliot, in turn, has borrowed from earlier sources. The epigraph to "Portrait of a Lady,"

> Thou has committed—
> Fornication: but that was in another country,
> And besides, the wench is dead,

adapted from Marlowe's *The Jew of Malta,* is paraphrased in *Light in August* when Joe Christmas, remembering the passionate phase of his affair with Joanna Burden, feels that "that was in another time, another life." It appears three times in *A Fable:* once, paraphrased, when General Gragnon, reading *Gil Blas,* cannot believe in the characters "because they were inventions . . . besides being in another country and long ago," and twice, inaccurately quoted, in the memory of the battalion runner.⁵ The phrase "dying fall," quoted by Prufrock from the first scene of *Twelfth Night,* occurs twice in *Sartoris* and once each in *As I Lay Dying, The Unvanquished, The Wild Palms* and *Go Down, Moses.* Faulkner, who read and reread both Marlowe and Shakespeare, undoubtedly encountered these phrases both in their original contexts and in Eliot's poems; and I think we may take it that, whenever he mentions "a dying fall," he is referring to both *Twelfth Night* and "Prufrock"; and that, whenever he suggests that something or someone is "in another country" or another life, he is thinking of *The Jew of Malta,* "Portrait of a Lady," and very likely Hemingway's *The Sun Also Rises* and "In Another Country" as well. I suspect that he wants us to understand that he is using these and other quotations, paraphrases, and references to earlier writings, as Eliot does, in order to bring not only the quoted words but something—and sometimes a great deal—of their original context into his own work, which is thereby expanded and enriched for the reader who is able to enjoy more than one context at a time. This device, as used by Eliot, is more than a supplementary simile or a pleasant recollection. It is a way of packing more meaning into his work, more emotional value, and a richer reverberation of cultural tradition, than a purely contemporary statement would carry. It does the same thing for Faulkner.

The debt Faulkner owes to Keats is unequivocal, and frankly acknowledged. In an interview given in 1956 and published in *The Paris Review,* he illustrated his belief that an artist ought to "rob, borrow, beg, or steal from anybody and everybody to get the work done" by saying, "If a writer has to rob his mother, he will not hesitate; the 'Ode on a Grecian Urn' is worth any number of old ladies."⁶ Keats, and the "Ode on a Grecian Urn" in particular, gave Faulkner many occasions to practice what he preached. One of his earliest published works, a poem called "Naiads' Song," printed in *The Mississippian* for 4 February, 1920,⁷ is an obvious imitation of Keats's octosyllabics:

> Come ye sorrowful and keep
> Tryst with us here in wedded sleep,
> The silent noon lies over us

And shaken ripples cover us,
Our arms are soft as is the stream.
Come keep with us our slumbrous dream

and so on for another forty lines, very much as in Keats's "Fancy." Faulkner's *The Marble Faun* (1924), in the statue which is its principal speaker, embodies the same metaphor as the Grecian urn. In *Sartoris* "Thou still unravished bride of quietness" is quoted twice, and the last sentence ends with the phrase "foster dam of quietude and peace." Linda Snopes is described in three passages of *The Mansion* as "the inviolate bride of silence," "the bride of silence," and "the bride of quietude and silence. . . ."

Darl Bundren in *As I Lay Dying* sees his brother Jewel struggling with Gillespie in the light of the burning barn "like two figures in a Greek frieze, isolated out of all reality by the red glare." In *Light in August* Lena Grove on the road in pursuit of the father of her unborn child appears "like something moving forever and without progress across an urn"; and the image of the urn or vase is used to suggest an ideal of static perfection in two other passages in the same book: Joe Christmas, shocked by his second exposure to the fact of menstruation, has a vision of fair women as "a diminishing row of sauvely shaped urns in moonlight, blanched. And not one was perfect. Each one was cracked and from each crack there issued something liquid, deathcolored, and foul." Gail Hightower has gone to a theological seminary to foster a similarly static ideal, doomed to a comparable disillusionment. "When he believed that he had heard the call it seemed to him that he could see his future, his life, intact and on all sides complete and inviolable, like a classic and serene vase, where the spirit could be born anew sheltered from the harsh glare of living and die so, peacefully. . . ." The same image is used ironically in *Pylon* to describe "the immemorial grapefruit halves" served in a New Valois (New Orleans) restaurant, "age- and timeproofed for intactness and imperviousness like the peasant vases exhumed from Greek and Roman ruins. . . ."

In *The Wild Palms* Keats's sonnet "On First Looking into Chapman's Homer" is echoed when the tall convict, on first seeing the Mississippi River in flood, "stood in quiet and amazed surmise"; and in *A Fable* the flier Levine thinks of the shock of peace to men who have lived in trenches for four years, creeping above ground and "looking about them with dawning incredulous surmise. . . ." In *Go Down, Moses* McCaslin Edmonds explains why his cousin Isaac McCaslin has refrained from shooting the bear, Old Ben, when he could have done so, by reading the "Ode on a Grecian Urn"; and he goes on to remark, paraphrasing Keats's letter to Benjamin Bailey (conjecturally dated

22 November, 1817), that the virtues (or, as Faulkner prefers to call them, the verities) of " *'Courage and honor and pride, and pity and love of injustice and liberty. . . . all touch the heart, and what the heart holds to becomes truth, as far as we know truth.'* " The formula Keats uses is significantly different—"I am certain of nothing but of the holiness of the Heart's affections and the truth of Imagination—What the imagination seizes as Beauty must be truth"—but the similarity of tone and wording makes me think that Faulkner had this letter in mind, perhaps in an imperfectly remembered version.

The Swinburne influence seems to have been more obsessive, as Faulkner's comment suggests, more in control of Faulkner, perhaps, than he was of it. Swinburne's "Sapphics" is practically plagiarized in Faulkner's poem of the same name printed in *The Mississippian* for 26 November, 1919.[8] Two lines of Swinburne's "In the Orchard" are quoted somewhat inaccurately in the prose sketch "The Priest," which Faulkner published in *The Double Dealer* for January-February, 1925. Swinburne's version is

> Hold my hair fast, and kiss me through it so.
> Ah God, ah God, that day should be so soon.

Faulkner's priest thinks, first, "Ah God, ah God, that night should come so soon," and later, " 'hold my hair fast, and kiss me through it—so: Ah, God, ah God, ah God, that day should be soon!' "[9] The first of these lines is paraphrased twice in the silent thoughts of Margaret Powers in *Soldiers' Pay,* as she remembers her first husband, killed in World War I: "Kiss me, kiss me through my hair"; and again, "Kiss me through my hair, Dick, with all your ugly body. . . ." Throughout his works Faulkner uses much of the kind of imagery Swinburne likes, especially that which refers to the fluid feel of experience and the anguish of things passing and lost in the flow of time. But in Faulkner's mature fiction there seems to be little or no direct borrowing from Swinburne.

The total effect of Faulkner's reading of the poets seems to have been bad for his poetry and good for his fiction. His rejection of modern methods and techniques in verse was poor strategy; and if, as seems likely, he remained largely ignorant of the more important and radical experiments, so much the worse. He thereby prevented himself from using his own verse to express his strongest feelings about his most congenial theme, the intense conviction of the concrete sense of life as a dynamic process. Avoidance of the necessity "to create the illusion of force by frenzy and motion" might be all right for Keats, but it would hardly do for Shakespeare, and it did not do at all well for Faulkner. To achieve his best effects, including those of which he was most in control, he needed all the sound and fury he could get. By refraining from violence, he made practically sure that he would be what he later said he was, "a failed poet."[10] On the other hand, his achievement of a sometimes brilliantly poetic quality in his fiction results not merely from the persistence in him of a poetic attitude or temperament but more specifically from his use of poetic methods, devices, and techniques in his prose—if I may speak of prose in this connection not as being opposed to poetry but rather as being a less concentrated medium for it than verse. The devices are various, including rhythm; sound effects such as alliteration, vowel harmony, and onomatopoeia; imagery, much of which is symbolistic; and poetic principles of structure, such as patterns of symbolic images and ordered sequences of feeling and emotion, both of which Faulkner uses more than he uses the logical development of story plots. Our understanding and appreciation of his best work can be considerably enhanced if we keep his background as a writer and reader of poetry firmly and constantly in mind.

The influences of the King James Bible and of Shakespeare on Faulkner are even more obvious and pervasive than that of Keats; mere demonstration of them is not needed here. The story of the Passion Week is so tightly woven into so many of Faulkner's works that we can almost take as a literal statement of his policy and practice the remark he has Dawson Fairchild make in *Mosquitoes:* " 'Genius. . . . is that Passion Week of the heart . . . that passive state of the heart with which the mind, the brain, has nothing to do at all, in which the hackneyed accidents which make up this world—love and life and death and sex and sorrow—brought together by chance in perfect proportions, take on a kind of splendid and timeless beauty." Except that when an author consciously, deliberately uses the structure and feeling of the Christian legend as a forming principle at the heart of his creative activity, as Faulkner repeatedly does, it can hardly be "by chance" if he succeeds in achieving something of that "splendid and timeless beauty" that Fairchild is talking about. The legend of the Fall of Man is almost as ubiquitous, and other Bible matters, such as the story of David and Absalom, are clearly present. Faulkner's use of the Bible is worth a long book by itself, and I have no doubt that some day such a book will appear.

The Shakespeare influence is almost equally substantial, and many critics have discussed it, particularly in connection with the "To-morrow, and to-morrow, and to-morrow" speech in Macbeth, from which the title of *The Sound and the Fury* comes and which is explicitly echoed not only in that book but in many other stories, including *Pylon, Absalom, Absalom!, The Wild Palms, The Hamlet, Go Down, Moses,* the story entitled "Tomorrow" in

Knight's Gambit, Intruder in the Dust, Requiem for a Nun, A Fable, and *The Town.* The "tomorrow and tomorrow" formula strongly expresses Faulkner's feeling for the endless burden of endurance that must be sustained if man, as the Nobel Speech predicts, will ultimately "prevail." Or, as Faulkner put it in the commencement address he delivered at Pine Manor Junior College, in 1953, the world is not finished, and only man can complete it, a labor which "begins at home. . . . Home means not just today, but tomorrow and tomorrow, and then again tomorrow and tomorrow."[11] Imagery associating shadows with players on a stage, derived from the same speech, is often invoked to express the sense of unreality or futility that oppresses men when they try to shoulder their share of the weight of time and change; especially when, like Quentin Compson in *The Sound and the Fury* or Horace Benbow in *Sanctuary,* they feel themselves too weak to carry it, or when, like Joe Christmas in *Light in August,* they suffer from lack of direction or purpose. These feelings are often reinforced by parallels with the situation and some of the speeches of Hamlet, as Sumner C. Powell has pointed out.[12]

These parallels suggest a further possibility, which I think might be worth pursuing in more detail than is possible here; namely that Faulkner not only borrows images and clusters or complexes of imagery from Shakespeare, but that he goes on to adopt what might be called a Shakespearean method of dramatic imagery in his borrowings from other authors and in his own invention of image systems. The example of T. S. Eliot may have helped him to develop such a strategy. Like Shakespeare and like Eliot, Faulkner uses these image systems to constitute a mythical world which then becomes capable of absorbing and assimilating myths already in existence and of relating new and original works to the lengthening body of the cultural tradition at the head of which they bud and grow. He is not merely telling old stories in new ways, but rather telling new stories in such a way as to imply—almost, indeed, to include—the whole history of man, past, present, and future, in the network of structural relations which the imagery creates. This is what Faulkner has said, in the Nobel Speech and other comments, that the writer—unquestionably meaning himself, along with others—has a duty to do. In this sense the imagination of the artist is the creator of history, not merely the recorder, and his work may be regarded, as Faulkner said in the *Paris Review* interview, "as being a kind of keystone in the universe; that, small as that keysteone is, if it were ever taken away the universe itself would collapse."[13]

Most critics have tacitly assumed that the real beginning of Faulkner's literary career was the publication of *Soldiers' Pay* in 1926; and that assumption is not unreasonable, even though he had been writing poetry for ten or twelve years before. Certainly the six months he spent in New Orleans in 1925, during which he contributed his prose sketches to the *Times-Picayune* Sunday supplement and wrote most or all of *Soldiers' Pay,* represents a crucial turning point. In that half year, the most immediate and undoubtedly the strongest influence on him was that of Sherwood Anderson, who quickly became his friend, adviser, and sponsor. He had already conceived a high admiration for Anderson's work, being reported to have told a friend on the way to New Orleans that "he ranked 'I'm a Fool' with Conrad's *Heart of Darkness:* the two finest stories he had ever read."[14] Anderson encouraged Faulkner's conversion to fiction, and, when *Soldiers' Pay* was finished, persuaded his own publisher, Horace Liveright, to bring it out.

This major change of direction in Faulkner's career involved a shift of emphasis in his reading and in his use of influences. Before 1925 he was chiefly concerned with what he could get from the poetry and drama of the English renaissance and the poetry of the nineteenth century in English and French. Anderson was more interested in twentieth-century writing and in an American tradition of fiction. With no more formal education than Faulkner had, and using local and regional material supplied by his own experience, Anderson had achieved a fair amount of popular success and a very high degree of critical acclaim, especially for his impressionistic short stories and for *Winesburg, Ohio.* Faulkner joined the chorus in an article which he published in the Dallas *Morning News* for 26 April, 1925,[15] calling "I'm a Fool" "the best short story in America, to my thinking," and praising the volume it was in, *Horses and Men,* along with the first part of *A Story-Teller's Story,* the novel *Poor White,* and, with particular emphasis, *Winesburg, Ohio.* He admired Anderson's humor, when it was not too self-conscious; the handling in "I'm a Fool" of "a lad's adolescent pride in his profession (horse racing) and his body, of his belief in a world beautiful and passionate created for the chosen to race horses on, of his youthful pagan desire to preen in his lady's eyes that brings him low at last"; and the self-effacing artistry with which the characters are presented and the setting is evoked in *Winesburg, Ohio:* "behind all of them a ground of fecund earth and corn in the green spring and the slow, full hot summer and the rigorous masculine winter that hurts it not, but makes it stronger."

Faulkner learned to do the same things even better. His humor is a basic and vital element in all his best work. He uses horse racing—along with many other activities, such as bear hunting—to articulate a boy's development into manhood; *The Reivers* might almost be read as a developed study of the adolescent reactions to the life of horses and men (and women) which Anderson presents less fully in "I'm a Fool" and "I Want to Know Why." And there is strong reason for the suggestion of William L. Phillips that "The method of Faulkner's Yoknapatawpha novels is an elaboration of the *Winesburg* method. . . . extend Anderson's *Winesburg* almost infinitely in time, space, and depth and one has the massive body of Faulkner's novels."[16]

One of the most important uses Faulkner made of Anderson's example was to help him solve the problem of the relation between regionalism and universality, which had bothered him for some time. In the essay on "American Drama: Eugene O'Neill" which he contributed to *The Mississippian* for 3 February, 1922,[17] Faulkner seems to assume that the cultural environment of the artist in the United States is impossible to work with. He concedes that Shakespeare, Flaubert, and Balzac were deeply rooted in their native localities of time and place, and that perhaps, as he supposes some Frenchman probably said, "art is preeminently provincial. . . ." But the provinces of European writers are steeped in human time and filled with the works of men, whereas "America has no drama or literature worth the name, and hence no tradition." Therefore, Faulkner suggests, we must look to exceptions such as Conrad, who "has overturned all literary tradition in this point," and O'Neill, who writes plays not about the land but about the sea, and who may some day, Faulkner hopes, "make something of the wealth of natural dramatic material in this country, the greatest source being our language."

The immediate practical question for Faulkner was whether he could make the most of himself by staying in Oxford, Mississippi, and using the provincial setting he knew; or whether he should establish himself in some capital—New York or Paris, or perhaps New Orleans—and try to be one of the exceptions. He had already spent some time in New York, and he was saving the money he made as University postmaster to go to Paris by way of New Orleans. But, as we know now, he was really headed for Yoknapatawpha by way of the New Orleans prose sketches and his first two novels. The dedication of his third novel, *Sartoris,* the first in which the land and people of Yoknapatawpha County explicitly appear, shows Faulkner's awareness of the help he received from Anderson along the road: "To Sherwood Anderson through whose kindness I was first published, with the belief that this book will give him no reason to regret that fact."

The problem of the relation between regionalism and universality appears again in *Mosquitoes,* where some of the talk about Dawson Fairchild, who is obviously modeled on Anderson, bears on that point. Some of the other characters suggest that Fairchild is too diffident about his lack of a college degree, that he lets himself be dominated by " 'the ghosts of the Emersons and

Lowells and other exemplifiers of Education with a capital E,' " and that " 'he lacks what they had at command among their shelves of discrete [sic] books and their dearth of heat and vulgarity—a standard of literature that is international.' " The recommended solution is that " 'by getting himself and his own bewilderment and inhibitions out of the way by describing, in a manner that even translation cannot injure (as Balzac did) American life as American life is, it will become eternal and timeless despite him.' " The local can be used to dramatize the universal because " 'Life everywhere is the same, you know. Manners of living it may be different . . . but man's old compulsions, duty and inclination: the axis and the circumference of his squirrel cage, they do not change.' "

How much of the intellectual discussion in *Mosquitoes* can we properly identify with Faulkner's thinking is doubtful, but there can be no question that much of it is addressed to problems that Faulkner had to solve; and one of these was how he could use the material he knew in such a way that he could build on a solid tradition and embody the values of life in all times and places, for all men to appreciate. So stated, the problem required precisely the solution Faulkner arrived at with *Sartoris,* which, he said in the *Paris Review* interview, represents his discovery that "by sublimating the actual into the apocryphal" he could make his "own little postage stamp of native soil" represent all of life, in all of time.[18] The formula, Yoknapatawpha County equals the universe, was in the process of being invented, partly because Anderson had tried, with some success, to make Winesburg, Ohio, equal the same amount.

Another aspect of the Anderson influence leads me to feel that a digression is in order at this point into the question of how much influence Faulkner may have absorbed from impressionist and post-impressionist painting. One of Anderson's chief contributions to the development of American fiction was his firm rejection of the traditional plot as a standard structural device, and his use of an impressionistic method instead. Not that impressionism in prose was entirely his own invention; Poe, Hawthorne, Melville, Henry James, Stephen Crane, and several French and Russian writers had experimented in that direction before him. But Anderson, for all his ostentation of folksy ignorance, his awkwardness of style, and his apparent fumbling of symbolic imagery, regarded himself quite properly as a member in good standing of the "Modern movement" which, he said, "has practically revolutionized painting all over the world" and "has crept into the writing of prose, into the making of song, into sculpture, into architecture."[19] The emphasis on painting is legitimate, for Anderson had many friends among painters, he had seen the 1913 Armory show when it came to Chicago, and he was himself an amateur painter of sufficient note to have had two one-man shows, one in Chicago and the other in New York. Paul Rosenfeld, the avant-garde critic who financed and guided Anderson's tour of Europe in 1921, later wrote that his friend's stories had "a tense form, of Anderson's invention: an impressionistic form curiously akin to that in certain paintings by the young Renoir. Out of blobs of color, scatterings of color-dots and small eddies of events connected by invisible filaments, it composes shapes that grow solid to the distant eye. . . ."[20]

Faulkner had also been a draughtsman and painter in his earlier youth, and he always looked at things with a painter's eye. The narrator of the sketch "Out of Nazareth," printed in the *Times-Picayune* for 12 April, 1925, "remarked to Spratling how no one since Cézanne had really dipped his brush in light. Spratling, whose hand has been shaped to a brush as mine has (alas!) not, here became discursive on the subject of transferring light to canvas. . . ."[21] William Spratling, an instructor in architecture at Tulane, was Faulkner's companion on his trip to Europe later in 1925. Faulkner lived for a time in Paris, at 26 Rue Servandoni, a short street one end of which opens directly opposite the Luxembourg Museum.

At that time the Luxembourg was a central receiving and distributing point for paintings acquired by the French government, and it was full of modern works awaiting placement in various permanent collections. Hemingway once remarked, "I learned to write by looking at paintings in the Luxembourg Museum in Paris," and, more specifically, "I learned how to make a landscape from Mr. Paul Cézanne by walking through the Luxembourg Museum a thousand times with an empty gut, and I am pretty sure that if Mr. Paul was around, he would like the way I make them and be happy that I learned it from him."[22] Faulkner spent a good deal of his time in Paris learning to write in the Luxembourg Gardens, the shortest way to which, from where he lived, led within a few steps of the museum door.

With some of these circumstances in mind, Mr. Kraig Klosson asked Faulkner, at one of the last of the University of Virginia interviews, to comment on the theory of a critic "who is of the opinion that on your first trip to France you became familiar with the works of several of the French impressionists, and especially Cézanne, and who has found a similarity in your use of color in your books and Cézanne's use of color in his paintings." Faulkner said, "I think that criticism probably has a great deal of merit in it. As I was saying before, a writer remembers everything he ever reads or ever sees and then when he needs it, he draws upon his memory and uses it." Mr. Klosson pressed for a more definite statement: "Then, Sir, when you were in Paris you did go to the art galleries and did see and remember the paintings of Cézanne?" Faulkner said, "Yes, that's right."[23]

My guess is that the influence on Faulkner of Cézanne—along with other impressionist and post-impressionist painters—is more than a matter of color, or of how to make a landscape. As in Rosenfeld's suggestion about Anderson and Renoir, it seems to me also a matter of how the artists go about building the structures of the works. Cézanne proceeded by laying on patches of color here and there, filling more and more of his canvas, until the forms emerged —a complex and difficult way to make pictures which are complex and difficult to see. The viewer is forced to do a good share of the labor of composition, to enter into the process of constructing the picture along with the painter, to recapitulate and bring to life the painter's experience of the scene. For those who are not too lazy to do the necessary work, the result is a richly dynamic esthetic experience, which the artist does not present to the viewer so much as he allows and encourages the viewer to share it. Faulkner's method of writing is similar both in the labor it imposes on the reader and in the reward it offers him.

Faulkner and Anderson, in addition to their common interest in impressionist painting, shared an interest in and an indebtedness to the writings of Joseph Conrad, whose "impressionistic" method in fiction was a topic of lively discussion in the 1920's. Faulkner learned much from Conrad; so much indeed that Albert Guerard has called *Absalom, Absalom!* "the culminating triumph of Conradian impressionism. . . ."[24] The use of scrambled chronology, twice and three times removed narrators, and other devices of gradual revelation in Faulkner is easily traceable to Conrad, and there are occasional startling resemblances in style. In the whole of Faulkner's work, the influence of Conrad is the strongest and most pervasive I have found coming from any writer of prose fiction.

It began early: Conrad is mentioned respectfully (as very few others are) in the essay on O'Neill, and again in the review of Joseph Hergesheimer's novels that Faulkner published in *The Mississippian* for 15 December, 1922.[25] On the occasion of Conrad's death in 1924, shortly before Faulkner's advent in New Orleans, Julius Friend published an article in *The Double Dealer* praising Conrad because "He wrote of the eternal verities" and "of the timeless struggle of man" against the forces of nature and against "fear"[26]—as Faulkner, in the Nobel Speech and elsewhere, has said it is the writer's duty to do. The last of the sketches Faulkner contributed to the *Times-Picayune,* "Yo Ho and Two Bottles of Rum," is a badly written imitation of a Conrad sea tale. In two of the University of Virginia interviews Faulkner mentioned, among the titles of works he frequently reread, *The Nigger of the "Narcissus"* (twice), "Falk," "The End of the Tether," "Youth," and *Heart of Darkness.*[27] Internal evidence indicates that *Victory* and *Lord Jim* were also specific influences.

One of the clearest echoes of Conrad in Faulkner's work is from the opening scene of *The Nigger of the "Narcissus"*, where members of the crew appear against the light from the forecastle doors "very black, without relief, like figures cut out of sheet tin." The appearance of Popeye in the opening scene of *Sanctuary*, and Horace Benbow's impressions that "He smells black" and that "he had the vicious depthless quality of stamped tin" come immediately to mind. Approximately the same image appears several times in *Soldiers' Pay*, elsewhere in *Sanctuary*, in *As I Lay Dying*, and as late in Faulkner's career as *A Fable*, where men of the condemned regiment appear "like phantoms or apparitions or perhaps figures cut without depth from tin or cardboard. . . ." One of the more striking examples is in the story "Barn Burning," where the boy, Colonel Sartoris Snopes, sees his father, Ab, "against the stars but without face or depth—a shape black, flat, and bloodless as though cut from tin. . . ." Like Popeye, Ab seems to have "that impervious quality of something cut ruthlessly from tin, depthless, as though, sidewise to the sun, it would cast no shadow." This image, in both Conrad and Faulkner, suggests a more or less mechanistic alienation from humanity, or from life.

The scene of Popeye's meeting with Horace Benbow, beside a spring in the woods near the Old Frenchman place, involves another reverberation which is more complex. The setting that seems to have fascinated Conrad more than any other, except a ship at sea, is a town or settlement or trading post on a river in the midst of a jungle or wilderness. It appears as the town of Sambir on the Pantai River in East Borneo in *Almayer's Folly* and *An Outcast of the Islands*, as Patusan in *Lord Jim*, and as Kurtz's trading post on the Congo River in *Heart of Darkness* and its prototype in "An Outpost of Progress." Similar settings are described in *The Rescue, Victory*, "Karain," "The Lagoon," "The Planter of Malata," and "Because of the Dollars." This setting is regularly associated in Conrad with sexual passion which leads, in obscurely perverse ways, to gestures of ritual impotence. Kurtz has reputedly indulged unspeakable lusts, but Marlow finds him "hollow at the core." Willems in *An Outcast of the Islands* is destroyed by what purports to be an overwhelming sexual desire for Aïssa, who, like the magnificent Negress in *Heart of Darkness*, seems to represent the primitive power of life. In the clinches, however, Willems always finds himself immoblized. The attracting power of sex in this and other Conrad works is not particularly convincing; the fear and horror it inspires are; and so is the fearful and horrible fecundity of life which Aïssa and the jungle setting embody and which is perhaps really what attracts, fascinates, terrifies, and destroys Willems. The somewhat hollow protagonist of *Lord Jim* finds passion in a jungle setting, beside a river, and tries to follow the advice of Stein, " 'In the destructive element immerse,' " only to prove himself unworthy of his woman's trust. Axel Heyst, in *Victory,* involved in life and life's complex responsibilities by his attraction to Lena, also fails her in their time of crisis in the primitive setting of Samburan.[28]

The same general pattern of imagery, in essentially the same combination of setting, theme, and feeling, can be seen not only in *Sanctuary* but repeatedly in Faulkner, whose scenes of passion often occur in conjunction with springs or streams flowing among trees near habitations. The first piece of fiction Faulkner published using a rural Southern setting, the short short story "The Liar" in the *Times-Picayune* for 26 July, 1925,[29] contains such a scene. In *Soldiers' Pay* Gilligan says goodbye to Margaret Powers, who has just refused his offer of marriage, and wanders through woods by a stream and pond before returning to the rector's house. Closest of all to Conrad, in the physical details, is the description of the north shore of Lake Pontchartrian in *Mosquitoes,* where Mrs. Maurier's yacht, like one of Conrad's ships, enters "a sluggish river mouth, broaching a timeless violet twilight between solemn bearded cypresses motionless as bronze. . . . The world was becoming dimensionless, the tall bearded cypresses drew nearer one to another across the wallowing river with the soulless implacability of pagan gods, gazing down upon this mahogany-and-brass intruder with inscrutable unalarm."

Later, when David West and Patricia Robyn run off, they find themselves in the same environment. "Trees heavy and ancient with moss loomed . . . hugely and grayly: the mist might have been a sluggish growth between and among them. No, this mist might have been the first prehistoric morning of time itself; it might have been the very substance in which the seed of the beginning of things fecundated; and these huge and silent trees might have been the first of living things, too recently born to know either fear or astonishment, dragging their sluggish umbilical cords from out the old miasmic womb of a nothingness latent and dreadful." The style in these passages, although the voice is unmistakably Faulkner's, is like that of Conrad in its lush descriptive imagery and in the habit, which Faulkner may have picked up either from Conrad or from his own reading in French, of putting the adjectives after the nouns—"Trees heavy and ancient"—"a nothingness latent and dreadful." David is not corrupted by all this fecundity, as Willems is, perhaps because, unlike Aïssa, Pat is practically devoid of sex, but he is as powerless as Willems or Lord Jim or Heyst to satisfy his woman's needs. The moral implications, as in many Conrad stories, are ambiguous. By one way of looking at it, David's behavior is noble and self-sacrificing: he loves Pat in a spiritual way, respecting her virginity, which is apparently genuine, and her innocence, which is more doubtful. By a slightly different way of looking, David appears to be impotent and possibly, since it seems to be "her flat boy's body" that chiefly attracts him, homosexual as well.

Ike McCaslin, in *Go Down, Moses,* is in some ways a direct descendant of David. Both are isolated, both have associated mostly with men, both experience the fascinating and horrible fecundity of forests and swamps, and both show signs of impotence. These aspects of Ike's character are clear enough in "The Bear," I think, but they are even more obvious in "Delta Autumn," where, after Ike has offered unwanted money and less wanted advice to Roth Edmonds' mulatto mistress, she scornfully inquires, " 'Old man . . . have you lived so long and forgotten so much that you dont remember anything you ever knew or felt or even heard about love?' " And Ike thinks, "This Delta. *This land which man has deswamped and denuded and derivered . . . where cotton is planted and grows man-tall in the very cracks of the sidewalks . . . Chinese and African and Aryan, and Jew, all breed and spawn together until no man has time to say which one is which nor cares. . . .* No wonder the ruined woods I used to know dont cry for retribution! he thought: The people who have destroyed it will accomplish its revenge" (ellipses mine, except the last). Faulkner has plainly declared, in one of the Virginia interviews, that Ike is not one of his most admirable characters: "McCaslin. . . . says, This is bad, and I will withdraw from it. What we need are people who will say, This is bad and I'm going to do something about it, I'm going to change it."[30] The wilderness, the hunting camp on the river, the apparent frigidity of Ike's wife, his failure to make any really constructive use of his inheritance, and his several gestures of impotence toward Roth's mistress all seem to belong to the same pattern that we see in Conrad.

The Faulkner novel which has the most links with the works of Conrad (except, possibly, *Absalom, Absalom!*) is *Light in August,* where the same complex of imagery works in much the same way. Part of the ritual through which Joe Christmas goes before killing Joanna Burden is to sleep in the early morning beside a spring in the woods not far from her house, then shave with the spring as a mirror, eat breakfast, and spend the middle part of the day reading a magazine, sitting by the spring with his back against a tree. The meaning of this behavior is not explained in any way, but some of its associations are clear. Joe has much the same fear and horror of sex that Conrad's men exhibit, and on several occasions his behavior suggests impotence and possibly homosexuality. His experience with the dietician and her lover at the orphanage is remembered, if not understood; and it is reinforced by his revulsion from the Negro girl his companions have seduced and his horror at a friend's account of menstruation, repeated when his prostitute sweetheart, Bobbie Allen, has to explain it to him again. When he first seduces or rapes Joanna Burden, she has for him "A dual personality: the one the woman . . . the other the mantrained muscles and the mantrained habit of thinking. . . . It was as if he struggled physically with another man for an object of no actual value to either. . . ." The next day he thinks, " 'My God . . . it was like I was the woman and she was the man.' " Later Joanna takes the lead and corrupts both herself and him, especially when she meets him outside the house. "She would be wild then, in the close, breathing halfdark without walls, with her wild hair, each strand of which would seem to come alive like octopus tentacles, and her wild hands and her breathing: 'Negro! Negro! Negro!' " He is both fascinated and appalled, sensing, even when he sees her at a distance in the daytime, "beneath the clean, austere garments which she wore that rotten richness ready to flow into putrefaction at a touch, like something growing in a swamp. . . ."

The larger theme of *Light in August,* which the question of Joe's identity serves to focus, is the inescapable involvement of everyone in the actions, the situations, the relationships, and the responsibilities of life. In this theme Faulkner again follows Conrad, who handles it, as Faulkner does, in many ways in many works. There is an especially close affinity between *Light in August* and *Victory,* which also deals with a man's responsibility to another man and to a woman. Heyst, like Byron Bunch and Hightower, has tried to live apart from responsibilities, and like them has discovered that he cannot. He too is trapped into being responsible for a young woman named Lena; and the fact that Heyst's Lena is earlier called Magdalen (as well as Alma) may help to explain the difficult relation between the apparently separate extremes represented in *Light in August* by Lena Grove, the embodiment of social relatedness and of fertility, and Joe Christmas, the isolated and sterile individual who seems at the same time to be some kind of Christ figure.

Many more parallels exist, not only in *Light in August* and *Sanctuary,* but in *The Sound and the Fury* (especially Quentin's section) and in other Faulkner stories. Underlying or accompanying them all is a strong similarity between the two authors in their moral attitudes toward life, or their feelings about morale, so that many passages from Conrad are echoed in the Nobel Speech and other public utterances of Faulkner's later life. For example, in *Typhoon,* when the storm is at its height, and the first mate, Jukes, tells Captain

McWhirr that the boats are being carried away, "again he heard a man's voice —the frail and indomitable sound that can be made to carry an infinity of thought, resolution and purpose, that shall be pronouncing confident words on the last day, when heavens fall, and justice is done—again he heard it, and it was crying to him, as if from very, very far—'All right.' " The same comment is made, more extensively and abstractly, in Conrad's essay on Henry James in *Notes on Life and Letters:* "When the last aqueduct shall have crumbled to pieces, the last airship fallen to the ground, the last blade of grass have died upon a dying earth, man," in the person of some individual gifted with artistic imagination, will still be talking; and, says Conrad, "I am inclined to think that the last utterance will formulate, strange as it may appear, some hope now to us utterly inconceivable. For mankind is delightful in its pride, its assurance, and its indomitable tenacity."

Faulkner, as usual, assimilates his source and goes beyond it. Man is immortal, he says, not merely because his voice will still sound "when the last ding-dong of doom has clanged and faded from the last worthless rock hanging tideless in the last red and dying evening . . . but because he has a soul, a spirit capable of compassion and sacrifice and endurance. . . . The poet's voice need not merely be the record of man, it can be one of the props, the pillars to help him endure and prevail." Conrad, so far as I can recall, with all his magnificent courage, never said "prevail."

Another parallel between the practice of Conrad and that of Faulkner, the use of characters and settings from one story in the telling of one or more others so as to link them together and build a fictional world to which they mutually belong, goes back to Scott, Cooper, and Balzac, and in a sense to Greek epic and tragedy, the Bible, and Shakespeare's history plays. The same device is used, in various degrees and ways, by Mark Twain, Sherwood Anderson, Proust, Joyce, and Mann, all of whom Faulkner admired. In an interview given in 1955, Faulkner indicated his appreciation of this technique by saying, "I like the fact that in Balzac there is an intact world of his own. His people don't just move from page one to page 320 of one book. There is continuity between them all like a blood-stream which flows from page one through to page 20,000 of one book. The same blood, muscle and tissue binds the characters together."[31] Faulkner, using a smaller society and fewer pages but an equal if not greater intensity of imagination, has created another intact world.

His admiration for Balzac, like his feeling for Conrad, began very early and continued strong. In the 1922 essay on O'Neill he remarked that "Balzac is nineteenth century Paris."[32] In *Mosquitoes* the recommendation that Fairchild try to describe American life " 'in a manner that even translation cannot injure (as Balzac did)' " indicates not only what Faulkner may have thought of Anderson, but much more unequivocally what he thought of Balzac. In an interview given in 1953 he said, " 'I was influenced by Flaubert and by Balzac, whose way of writing everything bluntly with the stub of his pen I admire very much.' "[33] In a Virginia interview he remarked more thoughtfully that, whereas Flaubert "was a stylist who was also—had enough talent to write about people too," Balzac "was so busy writing about people that he didn't have much time to bother about style and when he did attain style, he was just as astonished as anybody else."[34] In 1962 he told a group of West Point cadets that he admired "Balzac's people, but not Balzac especially because I think Balzac's writing is bad writing. . . ."[35] If this series of statements represents a change of feeling about Balzac, the change came too late to undermine the importance of Balzac's influence on Faulkner, which was much more a matter of structure than of style anyhow.

In spite of a relative lack of external evidence, I strongly suspect that another influence on Faulkner, bearing in some of the same directions as that of Balzac, is that of Cooper, who was one of Balzac's acknowledged masters. The frontier world of the Leatherstocking Tales is rather similar to that of Yoknapatawpha, and Ike McCaslin is too much like Natty Bumppo for the affinities to be entirely accidental. Faulkner has treated the wilderness theme in much the same way and with something of the same scope as Cooper, most notably in *Go Down, Moses,* and extensively also in a number of separate stories, some of which have been assembled to good effect by Malcolm Cowley in *The Portable Faulkner* and some by Faulkner himself in *Big Woods.*[36]

A more modern reinforcement of Balzac's influence appears to have come from Proust. Faulkner said in 1953, " '. . . I feel very close to Proust. After I had read *A la Recherche du Temps Perdu* I said "This is it!"—and I wished I had written it myself.' "[37] Later he told a questioner in Japan, "When I read Joyce and Proust it is possible that my career as a writer was already fixed, so that there was no chance for it to be influenced other than in the tricks of the trade, you might say. . . ."[38] Here it is possible that Faulkner was being too cautious, in view of the importance that "tricks of the trade" have in most of his best work. There is strong internal evidence indicating that he had read at least part of *Remembrance of Things Past* before he wrote *The Sound and the Fury.* Proust's Marcel remarks at one point that

our dread of a future in which we must forego the sight of faces, the sound of voices that we love, friends from whom we derive to-day our keenest joys, this dread, far from being dissipated, is intensified, if to the grief of such a privation we reflect that there will be added what seems to us now in anticipation an even more cruel grief; not to feel it as a grief at all—to remain indifferent; for if that should occur, our ego would have changed, it would then be not merely the attractiveness of our family, our mistress, our friends that had ceased to environ us, but our affection for them; it would have been so completely eradicated from our heart, in which to-day it is a conspicuous element, that we should be able to enjoy that life apart from them the very thought of which to-day makes us recoil in horror; so that it would be in a real sense the death of ourselves, a death followed, it is true, by resurrection but in a different ego, the life, the love of which are beyond the reach of those elements of the existing ego that are doomed to die.[39]

This bit of typically fine-spun and long-drawn-out speculation is more compactly, and also more cryptically, expressed in the logic of Quentin's determination to commit suicide. Mr. Compson's argument against self-slaughter is Quentin's principal motive for committing it: "you are not lying," Mr. Compson concedes, "but you are still blind to what is in yourself to that part of general truth the sequence of natural events and their causes which shadows every mans brow even benjys you are not thinking of finitude you are contemplating an apotheosis in which a temporary state of mind will become symmetrical above the flesh and aware both of itself and of the flesh it will not quite discard you will not even be dead and i temporary and he you cannot bear to think that someday it will no longer hurt you like this . . . and i temporary and he was the saddest word of all there is nothing else in the world its not despair until time its not even time until it was." But Quentin does prefer death, and hopes for no resurrection: "Until on the Day when He says Rise only the flat-iron would come floating up."

Faulkner's style is very different from that of Proust, if only because Faulkner is less given to discursive analysis; he works, at a much higher ratio of compression, in terms of more nearly naked images. But Proust uses images too, and very skillfully makes them work as *leitmotive* by means of which to hook and tie and lace together the enormous fabric of his masterpiece. The fragrance of the madeleine dipped in tea which evokes Marcel's memory of his childhood at Combray has an effect very similar to that of the odor of honeysuckle which, for Quentin, is "mixed up" with his recollection of Caddy's affairs; the difference, we might say, is that Faulkner's handling embodies about as much more power as it has less finesse. In general, *The Sound and the Fury,* along with most of Faulkner's other outstandingly successful works, has the same obsessive preoccupations with time, with memory, and with change as *Remembrance of Things Past.* Faulkner almost certainly learned something about the techniques he used most handily to deal with these matters from the previous experiments of Proust.

The same appears to be true of Joyce, from whose work, particularly *Ulysses,* Faulkner clearly acquired some of his stream-of-consciousness techniques. His statements about Joyce have been contradictory. He said flatly to Henry Nash Smith in 1932, " 'I have never read "Ulysses." ' " Smith, in his report of the interview, noted the presence of a 1924 edition of the book on Faulkner's desk, and politely accounted for it by supposing that Faulkner had borrowed it "during his recent visit to New York." Faulkner admitted that he " 'had heard of Joyce, of course. . . . Some one told me about what he was doing, and it is possible that I was influenced by what I heard.' "[40] In one of the Japan interviews, asked whether he "read James Joyce's *Ulysses* before you began to write your own?" Faulkner replied, "No, I began to write before I read *Ulysses.* I read *Ulysses* in the middle 20's and I had been scribbling for several years."[41] In the *Paris Review* interview he said, "You should approach Joyce's *Ulysses* as the illiterate Baptist preacher approaches the Old Testament: with faith."[42] Asked in one of the Virginia interviews whether he associated with Anderson and Hemingway in Europe, he said, "I—at that time I didn't think of myself as a writer, I was a tramp then, and I didn't—I wasn't interested in literature nor literary people. They were—I was—there at the same time, I knew Joyce, I knew of Joyce, and I would go to some effort to go to the café that he inhabited to look at him. But that was the only literary man that I remember seeing in Europe in those days."[43] Phil Stone wrote in 1934 that Faulkner was "making use of the new and strange tools which James Joyce has fashioned."[44]

These contradictions are not, I suspect, as difficult to resolve as they may seem at first glance. It is undoubtedly true that Faulkner did not read all of *Ulysses* before the book appeared in 1924—by which time he had been writing for about ten years—and he may not have read every word of it then, or ever. But what I think must have happened, though Faulkner chooses not to mention it, is that he saw some or all of the issues of *The Little Review* from March, 1918, to December, 1920, in which *Ulysses* was serialized, and that he probably read substantial parts of it as it appeared (with some gaps caused by censorship difficulties) in that medium. This exposure would have been sufficiently great and sufficiently early to have provided a formative influence.

Internal evidence strongly supports this probability, especially in *The Sound and the Fury.* Quentin is like Stephen Dedalus in both *Ulysses* and *A Portrait of the Artist as a Young Man;* and Quentin's South is somewhat like Ireland under English rule. Faulkner's approach to his work was like that of

Joyce, too, in that he learned to use himself, his family, and his neighbors in his home town for the construction of his fable. The outcomes are different: unlike Stephen and Joyce, Quentin kills himself, and, unlike Stephen and Joyce again, Faulkner declined the role of the expatriate artist. But the example of Joyce could hardly fail to encourage Faulkner's sublimation of the world of his experience into the world of his art, and to show him in many ways how to go about the job.

An obvious affinity between Joyce and Faulkner is in their handling of time. They both use the juxtaposition of past and present, in running parallels, as Eliot recommended, to constitute and reinforce the structural imagery of their works. For example, in *Ulysses* Stephen thinks, "The [navel] cords of all link back, strandentwining cable of all flesh. That is why mystic monks. Will you be as gods? Gaze in your omphalos. Hello. Kinch [Stephen] here. Put me on to Edenville." This short and somewhat cryptic passage is echoed in at least two places by Faulkner. In *The Sound and the Fury* Quentin speculates, "Like Father said down the long and lonely lightrays you might see Jesus walking, like." And in *Absalom, Absalom!* Quentin thinks, *"Maybe happen is never once but like ripples maybe on water after the pebble sinks, the ripples moving on, spreading, the pool attached by a narrow umbilical watercord to the next pool which the first pool feeds, has fed, did feed. . . ."*

Many other parallels might be pointed out: both authors play on the verb *to be;* they use clocks in similar ways; and Bloom in *Ulysses,* like Quentin in *The Sound and the Fury,* stands on a bridge over a river, sees gulls flying, and thinks, "If I threw myself down?" Later he thinks, ". . . all are washed in the blood of the lamb," a theme which is repeated several times in the Reverend Shegog's Easter sermon. Reference is made three times in *Ulysses* to "the beast with two backs," a phrase that Quentin recalls in connection with Caddy's pregnancy (both are quoting, of course, from *Othello*). Quentin and Stephen are both educated at their siblings' expense. At one point Stephen, like Quentin, gazes into the window of a jeweller's shop. And so on, I suspect, for about as far as any particular reader has strength and interest enough to go.[45]

The same limit, or lack of limit, applies to the pursuit of other European influences, which are certainly numerous and some of which are undoubtedly important. Faulkner had, for example, an extremely high regard for Flaubert, remarking in the *Paris Review* interview that his "standard" was "when the work makes me feel the way I do when I read *La Tentation de Saint Antoine,* or the Old Testament."[46] At Virginia he said that "with the *Bovary* it's as though you know from the very first as soon as you see what he's going to do that he will never disappoint you, that it'll be as absolute as mathematics."[47]

I have not, however, been able to make out that Faulkner used Flaubert directly to any great extent in his own fiction.

Another writer whose work Faulkner read is Dickens, whom he admired for his characters, particularly Mrs. Gamp in *Martin Chuzzlewit.* Faulkner spoke of her in the *Paris Review* interview as "a cruel, ruthless woman, a drunkard, opportunist, unreliable, most of her character was bad, but at least it was character. . . ."[48] In answer to a question asked at Virginia about the Snopeses, Faulkner explained that "They were simply an invention of mine to tell a story. . . . they were simply over-emphasized, burlesqued if you like, which is what Mr. Dickens spent a lot of his time doing, for a valid to him and to me reason, which was to tell a story in an amusing, dramatic, tragic, or comical way."[49] The quality of life, rather than that of realism, is Dickens's strong suit; and undoubtedly Faulkner learned something about the art of lively caricature from the way Dickens handled people like Sarah Gamp. In his fascination with the grotesque, and in a kind of compulsive impressionism wrought by his way of exaggerating, Dickens anticipated some of the better qualities of Mark Twain's work, of Anderson's *Winesburg, Ohio,* and of *The Hamlet, As I Lay Dying, Sanctuary,* and other outrageously funny Faulkner stories.

Further search for European influences undoubtedly should and will go on. Tolstoi and Dostoievski may be important; Gide and Mann are likely prospects; some of the older English prose writers, such as Fielding and Smollett, are probably somewhere in the picture; and individual investigations of many possibilities that I lack the room or the knowledge even to mention will very likely be worth pursuing.

American influences on Faulkner are involved with some rather complex notions of cultural geography which he entertained, with changing emphases, at one time and other. His remark in the 1922 essay on O'Neill "that America has no drama or literature worth the name, and hence no tradition" was supplemented in the companion essay "American Drama: Inhibitions," where, after nominating "the old Mississippi river days, and the romantic growth of railroads" as representative of our "inexhaustible fund of dramatic material," he said, "And yet, when the Mississippi is mentioned, Mark Twain alone comes to mind: a hack writer who would not have been considered fourth rate in Europe, who tricked out a few of the old proven 'sure fire' literary skeletons with sufficient local color to intrigue the superficial and the lazy."[50]

After he met Anderson, Faulkner evidently changed these views, especially as regarded Mark Twain. In later interviews he said that Anderson "was the father of my generation of American writers and the tradition of American writing which our successors will carry on. . . . Dreiser is his older brother and Mark Twain the father of them both."[51] Speaking in Japan, he named these three again and added "Herman Melville . . . Willa Cather . . . Sinclair Lewis . . . Whitman," and "Sandburg" to the list of "indigenous American writers who were produced and nurtured by a culture which was completely American. . . ."[52] In contrast to these he named Hawthorne, Poe, Longfellow, and Henry James,[53] and in *Mosquitoes* by implication Emerson and Lowell, as being essentially European. He expressed a particular dislike for James, whom he called "a prig, except *The Turn of the Screw*, which was very fine *tour de force*. . . ."[54] It is not at all clear, however, that he was influenced only by the "indigenous" tradition; I suspect that he may have owed more to Poe, Hawthorne, and perhaps even James than he cared to admit.

    Absalom, Absalom! for example might have been entitled, without gross impropriety, *The Fall of the House of Sutpen;* and Sutpen's mansion, like the House of Usher, has an air of sentience. As Quentin and Miss Rosa approach it on a hot night, we are told that "the dead furnace-breath of air in which they moved seemed to reek in slow and protracted violence with a smell of desolation and decay as if the wood of which it was built were flesh." In both Poe's story and Faulkner's there are strong suggestions of incestuous feeling between brother and sister. Poe's narrator learns that Roderick and Madeline Usher "had been twins, and that sympathies of a scarcely intelligible nature had always existed between them." In *Absalom, Absalom!* Mr. Compson, referring to Henry and Judith Sutpen, speaks of " 'that rapport not like the conventional delusion of that between twins but rather such as might exist between two people who, regardless of sex or age or heritage of race or tongue, had been marooned at birth on a desert island,' " and " 'that curious and unusual relationship which existed between them. . . .' " The apparent reference, and the repetition of the phrase "existed between them," suggest that Faulkner may have read or reread "The Fall of the House of Usher" while he was working on *Absalom, Absalom!*

    Hawthorne also uses many houses, with many family associations, notably the House of the Seven Gables, which is said to be "like a great human heart, with a life of its own, and full of rich and sombre reminiscences." Specific and general parallels between Hawthorne and Faulkner have been pointed out by several critics,[55] and two of them, Harold Douglas and Robert Daniel, have convincingly argued that "The substructure of Faulkner's early masterpiece, *As I Lay Dying*, resembles *The Scarlet Letter* in ways that virtually establish a direct influence."[56]

    When William Van O'Connor inquired whether the title *The Marble*

Faun, which was used for Faulkner's first published volume, indicated an influence, he was told by Phil Stone that " 'Bill read some Hawthorne, but I don't think he read a great deal. . . . the title had nothing to do with Hawthorne at all. I know because I am the man that put this title on it.' "[57] I take this statement to mean that Faulkner was not the one who borrowed the title *The Marble Faun;* I cannot, however, accept the apparent inference that Faulkner was not influenced by Hawthorne's handling of the faun image. There is too much circumstantial evidence pointing the other way. Faulkner's marble faun, like Hawthorne's, embodies a contrasting juxtaposition of the primitive Arcadian life to the life of a modern civilization; and other fauns in Faulkner serve the same time-jumping function. The echo from Hawthorne seems especially clear when Mrs. Maurier in *Mosquitoes* thinks that the countenance of Gordon, the sculptor, seen by moonlight, is "like a silver faun's face"; Hawthorne's Donatello is closely associated with the sculptor Kenyon, and his own name is that of an Italian sculptor of the fifteenth century.

The primitive innocence of the faun, his ignorance of both good and evil, parallel to that of Adam in Eden, is used by Faulkner much as it is by Hawthorne. Faulkner's idiots exemplify this innocence, and one of them, Ike Snopes in *The Hamlet,* has "pointed faun's ears. . . ." Some other characters are almost as invincibly ignorant or naive as the idiots; and these too are sometimes explicitly faunlike. Another example from *The Hamlet* is Labove, the school master, described as having "legs haired-over like those of a faun." Donald Mahon, the wounded and traumatized flyer of *Soldiers' Pay,* is presented several times in terms of the faun image.

This parallel in imagery coincides with a broader parallel between Hawthorne and Faulkner in their handling of the theme of individual development, which is basic and pervasive in the work of both. Innocence, in the sense of ignorance of good and evil, is one of the most serious shortcomings a character can have. The point of their best fiction generally turns on the protagonist's development into maturity. The outcome of the typical crisis depends on the ability of the central character, who usually begins as a young or at any rate immature man, to accept, assimilate, and exercise the responsibilities of a father of a family and a grown-up citizen in a community. If, like Robin in Hawthorne's "My Kinsman, Major Molineux" or Chick Mallison in Faulkner's *Intruder in the Dust,* he can overcome his fear of evil and his reluctance to face the issues it raises and deal with them constructively, he may emerge successfully from his trials, which constitute a kind of initiation ceremony, and be accepted into adult society. If, on the other hand, like Hawthorne's young Goodman Brown or Faulkner's Horace Benbow (especially as he appears in

Sanctuary), the immature man insists on remaining immature or fails to stand up under the burden of responsibility to himself, his family, and the community, he is lost.

The most impressive works of both Hawthorne and Faulkner are generally those in which the struggle is most intense and the outcome least clear, as *The Scarlet Letter* looked at from Dimmesdale's point of view, *The Sound and the Fury* or *Absalom, Absalom!* looked at from Quentin's point of view, *Sanctuary* [sic] looked at from Joe Christmas's point of view. In the work of both authors, the greatest possible tension between the dynamic energy of potential growth and the static inertness of the social and psychological obstacles that tend to frustrate growth makes for the most telling effect; and the protagonists who suffer the most agonizing failures often generate the greatest tension.

The suspicion of a direct influence from Hawthorne on Faulkner is reinforced by many close and specific parallels of detail, their similar handling of such odd items as jails, family curses, ancestral crimes, mirrors and portraits, mazes and circles, and the character and equipages of the two country peddlers, Hawthorne's Dominicus Pike in "Mr. Higginbotham's Catastrophe" and Faulkner's Ratliff in *The Hamlet*. An amusing example, and one which has the advantage of indicating an early influence, is the presence in each author's work of a small cluster of sketches in which ambitious young men set out to conquer the world, fail, and point an "Acres of Diamonds" moral. The unsuccessful author who is Hawthrone's narrator and protagonist in "Fragments from the Journal of a Solitary Man" writes that " 'The truly wise, after all their speculations, will be led into the common path, and, in homage to the human nature that pervades them, will gather gold, and till the earth, and set out trees, and build a house.' " More succinctly, and somewhat more colloquially, Faulkner's disillusioned policeman in "The Cop," one of the *Double Dealer* sketches, thinks to himself, "Certainly man does not ever get exactly what he wants in this world, and who can say that a wife and a home and a position in the world are not, after all, the end of every man's desire."[58] The close coincidence of these passages might conceivably be, but I think it is not, accidental.

The influence of Melville on Faulkner, which has been less noted than that of Hawthorne, is at least as easy to establish, partly because *Moby Dick* was one of Faulkner's favorite books. In a Virginia interview, asked what he thought was "the single greatest book in American literature," Faulkner said, "Probably *Moby Dick*." He thought that *Huckleberry Finn* (numerous critics to the contrary notwithstanding) was "a complete controlled effort and *Moby*

Dick was still an attempt that didn't quite come off, it was bigger than one human being could do."[59]

Melville was apparently not among the very early influences Faulkner submitted to, probably because the Melville revival did not begin until the middle 1920's; but in Faulkner's mature work it is strong and pervasive. If *Absalom, Absalom!* for example derives in part from "The Fall of the House of Usher" and *The House of the Seven Gables,* it has even more in common with *Moby Dick.* Sutpen, like Ahab, is a monomaniac, isolated by pride and suffering, "wounded" and seeking revenge by means of a ruthless exploitation of nature and other men; and like Ahab, he finally destroys himself and many of those around him because he tries to use and dominate, instead of participating in, the creative forces of love and fertility. As Ahab is symbolically and almost literally castrated, so, in his battle with the West Indian slaves, Sutpen has acquired " 'scars, one of which, Grandfather said, came pretty near leaving him that virgin for the rest of his life too.' " Ahab "looked like a man cut away from the stake, when the fire has overrunningly wasted all the limbs without consuming them. . . ." Sutpen "looked. . . . like a man who had been through some solitary furnace experience," leaving him with "a face whose flesh had the appearance of pottery. . . ." Like Ahab, who is heard "lowly humming to himself, producing a sound so strangely muffled and inarticulate that it seemed the mechanical humming of the wheels of his vitality in him," Sutpen, for three years after building the shell of his house, "had remained completely static, as if he were run by electricity and someone had come along and removed, dismantled the wiring of the dynamo." Another echo seems to combine the monkey rope and the mat-making scenes of *Moby Dick* when Judith Sutpen is quoted as saying, " ' "You get born and you try this and you dont know why only you keep on trying it and you are born at the same time with a lot of other people, all mixed up with them, like trying to, having to, move your arms and legs with strings only the same strings are hitched to all the other arms and legs and the others all trying and they dont know why either except that the strings are all in one another's way like five or six people all trying to make a rug on the same loom only each one wants to weave his own pattern into the rug. . . ." ' "

Ocean and water imagery resembling that in *Moby Dick* crops up in several Faulkner stories. In *The Wild Palms* the short convict's choice of the Mississippi penal farm rather than the federal prison in Atlanta is called "another manifestation of the closeguarded and solitary enigma of his character, as something recognisable roils momentarily into view from beneath stagnant and opaque water, then sinks again." In the other part of the book,

Charlotte Rittenmeyer seems to be recalling "The Lee Shore" when she says that love is " 'like the ocean: if you're no good, if you begin to make a bad smell in it, it just spews you up somewhere to die. You die anyway, but I had rather drown in the ocean than be urped up onto a strip of dead beach and be dried away by the sun into a little foul smear with no name to it, just *This Was* for an epitaph.' " Ike Snopes, the faun-eared idiot in *The Hamlet,* is characterized by the same image as Pip in *Moby Dick.* Pip is said to have been "carried down alive to wondrous depths, where strange shapes of the unwarped primal world glided to and fro before his passive eyes. . . . He saw God's foot upon the treadle of the loom, and spoke it; and therefore his shipmates called him mad." When Ratliff meets Ike Snopes, he finds himself looking into "the eyes which at some instant, some second once, had opened upon, been vouchsafed a glimpse of, the Gorgon-face of that primal injustice which man was not intended to look at face to face and had been blasted empty and clean forever of any thought. . . ."

The strongest and broadest resemblances are perhaps between *Moby Dick* and "The Bear," where Isaac McCaslin undergoes an initiation like that of Ishmael, helped by Sam Fathers somewhat as Ishmael is by Queequeg; and Old Ben in the wilderness is like Moby Dick in the ocean. As Ishmael, in "Loom-ings," has an imaginative foresight of whaling and especially of "one grand hooded phantom, like a snow hill in the air," Ike imagines the bear: "It loomed and towered in his dreams before he even saw the unaxed woods where it left its crooked print . . . not even a mortal beast but an anachronism indomitable and invincible out of an old dead time, a phantom, epitome and apotheosis of the old wild life. . . ." Like Moby Dick, "Old Ben was an extra bear (the head bear, General Compson called him) and so had earned a name such as a human man could have worn and not been sorry." In each of the stories the final chase of the hunted animal is handled with tremendous verve and momentum, which is made possible by painstaking accounts given earlier of the people involved, the setting, the history and traditions of the hunt, and the techniques and tools used, as well as the power and character of the quarry. As in his use of other influences, Faulkner gives us Melville with a difference, most obviously when the bear, unlike the immortal whale, is killed by one of the least worthy of his hunters; Faulkner, it seems, was more apprehensive than Melville that men might succeed one day in dominating, mechanizing, and completely destroying the universal principle of life which is symbolized by the hunted animals.

The most important of all the American influences on Faulkner, as on Hemingway, is evidently that of Mark Twain. With his usual small regard for rigid consistency, Faulkner said in Japan that "Mark Twain was the first truly

American writer. . . . It was only with Twain, Walt Whitman, there became a true indigenous American culture. . . . Of course, Whitman was in chronology the first, but Whitman was an experimenter with the notion there might be an American literature. Twain was the first that grew up in the belief that there is an American literature and he found himself producing it. So I call him the father of American literature, though he is not the first one."[60] Mark Twain epitomized the indigenous tradition in American literature in which Faulkner wanted to place himself. "Of course," he said, speaking of his whole generation of novelists, "Mark Twain is all of our grandfather."[61]

The influence of *Huckleberry Finn,* at any rate, is pervasive in Faulkner's work, and the parallels are often explicit. Financial operations of the old Negro coachman, Simon Strother, in *Sartoris* are described in much the same terms as those of Jim as he tries to explain them to Huck, except that Simon demands a different kind of collateral. The girl Quentin in *The Sound and the Fury* says, as Huck does in another context, " 'I don't care . . . I'm bad and I'm going to hell, and I dont care. I'd rather be in hell than anywhere where you are.' " Jason's narrative voice might almost be Huck's, if Huck had gone sour; but his character is more like that of the King and Duke, in that he suffers repeatedly from his failure to apply his own principle that "a man that can live as long as I have and not know when to quit is a fool." His loss of his own money along with Miss Quentin's is closely parallel to the unhappy experience of the King and Duke in the chapter "Over-reaching Don't Pay."

In *As I Lay Dying* the minister, Whitfield, decides to confess his adultery with Addie Bundren; and, like Huck after deciding to turn Jim in, he is greatly relieved: "It was already as though it were done. My soul felt freer, quieter than it had in years; already I seemed to dwell in abiding peace again as I rode on." In *The Unvanquished* the room in the Sartoris house that Granny calls "the library" contains a small collection of books like those in the Grangerford house and "The House Beautiful" in *Life on the Mississippi,* and in addition "a complete Walter Scott, a complete Fenimore Cooper," and "a paper-bound Dumas" which are not owned by the Grangerfords but many of which have evidently been studied by Tom Sawyer. In *Absalom, Absalom!* Miss Rosa Coldfield, in the manner of Emmeline Grangerford, has "established herself as the town's and the county's poetess laureate by issuing to the stern and meager subscription list of the county newspaper poems, ode, eulogy and epitaph. . . ." Various characters, such as Sutpen in *Absalom, Absalom!* and the tall convict in *The Wild Palms,* try to act on formulas found in the books they read, as Tom Sawyer does in liberating Jim. In *The Mansion* one of Huck's most telling comments is echoed when we learn that Gavin Stevens hates horses more than dogs because, "though both were parasites, the dog at least had the grace to be a sycophat too; it at least fawned on you and so kept you healthily ashamed of the human race."

R. W. B. Lewis has shown the close thematic resemblance between *Huckleberry Finn* and "The Bear" "in their common sense of the kinship between white and black, in their common identification of slavery as a kind of original sin, in their common reversal of the conventional morality that legitimizes social injustice."[62] The resemblance extends further to a common handling of the relation between slavery and the plantation aristocracy of the old South in *Pudd'nhead Wilson* as well as in *Huckleberry Finn* and in *Sartoris, The Unvanquished, Light in August, Absalom, Absalom!* and *Go Down, Moses,* among others. The closest parallel, perhaps, is between Huck's experience and that of Chick Mallison in *Intruder in the Dust.* Both boys develop mature feelings of responsibility in the process of freeing Negroes; both are forced to choose between social formulas and human feelings; and both reject the prejudices of society in favor of immediate personal commitments. Both are made, in much the same way, to recognize the unalienable rights and the unassailable dignity of the individual human being beneath the social stereotype of the "nigger."

Concreteness of feeling is extremely important in Faulkner, as it is in Mark Twain; and Faulkner often uses naive points of view, like Huck's, from which to look at various rigidities and inconsistencies of social behavior. Such witnesses as Benjy Compson, Vardaman Bundren, and Ike Snopes, because they have no awareness of the theories that govern civilized life, testify most vividly, without discursive comment, to the ironies which the author wishes to plant in the reader's mind. They also help Faulkner, as Huck helped Mark Twain, to discipline his style, to unify his structure, and to define his esthetic distance from his material.

The Mark Twain influence is strongly reinforced by Faulkner's knowledge of other writers belonging to the literary tradition of Southwest frontier humor, and perhaps equally by the survival in north Mississippi of a vigorous oral tradition in the same genre. Both writers, in fact, have something of the same skill in combining oral and literary techniques to produce a style distinguished by its rhythms, by the force of its rhetoric, and by the neatness with which it is capable, on occasion, of turning a phrase. Both tend to emphasize a feeling for energetic and often violent movement, which they share with nineteenth-century humorists for whom the frontier was still a violent, moving reality. It is likely that, as various critics have suggested, "The Bear" owes something to T. B. Thorpe's "The Big Bear of Arkansas"; that some of

Faulkner's horse-trading episodes are based on A. B. Longstreet's *Georgia Scenes;* that the vivid descriptions of the founding and early history of Jefferson are informed by J. G. Baldwin's *The Flush Times of Alabama and Mississippi;* and that some of Faulkner's most outrageously violent funny stories are inspired in part by G. W. Harris's Sut Lovingood yarns.[63]

Faulkner has also read a great deal of history, philosophy, and popular science, as many references in his work and in the interviews indicate. I cannot attempt anything like a thorough survey of these materials, but I will very briefly indicate some uses he seems to have made of two sources which are not, strictly speaking, within the realm of purely imaginative literature.

The influence of Sir James Frazer's *The Golden Bough* on *As I Lay Dying* has been convincingly argued by Carvel Collins and Barbara Cross, and its possible relation to *Sanctuary, Light in August, The Hamlet,* and "The Bear" has been suggested by Robert M. Slabey.[64] I think it extremely probable that Faulkner, prompted perhaps by T. S. Eliot's reference to Frazer in the notes to *The Waste Land,* read at least the one-volume edition of *The Golden Bough* which was published in 1922 and a copy of which was owned by Phil Stone. A number of parallels may be seen in *The Sound and the Fury,* where the emphasis on fire recalls Frazer's discussion of Easter fires, where Benjy's castration and Quentin's half-formed wish to castrate himself are like the castration and self-castration which Frazer describes in connection with a number of fertility cults, and where the emphasis on incest in Quentin's section recalls several superstitions mentioned in *The Golden Bough.*[65]

There seems to be a specific borrowing in Quentin's association of Caddy's seducer Dalton Ames, who *"could lift her to his shoulder and run with her running Running,"* with *"the swine of Euboeleus running";* Frazer recounts a legend according to which a swineherd named Eubuleus was tending his herd near the place where Pluto seized and carried off Persephone, and the swine were engulfed along with the god and his ravished bride. A broader parallel is the resemblance between Caddy and the Arician Diana, in whose grove at Nemi the Golden Bough was found, and who was so closely associated with trees as almost to be identified with them. She was also associated with the water nymph Egeria, who inhabited a spring in the grove. Both were fertility figures who helped women to conceive and bear children. Caddy, who smells like trees and who immerses herself in the "branch" that flows among trees in the Compson pasture, who is worshipped by the castrated Benjy, who gives herself to *"too many"* men, and who conceives and bears a child, is a fairly thorough embodiment of the goddess. Faulkner, like Eliot, has used this imagery, along with a good deal of Christian imagery, to show the sterility of modern society, which has no use for either the goddess or the God of love. This combination of images pervades the whole body of the Yoknapatawpha chronicle, throughout which Christ after Christ is crucified, and time after time the principle of fertility, as represented in Caddy, Dewey Dell Bundren, Ruby Goodwin, Lena Grove, Eula Varner, and others, is outcast, dishonored, betrayed, distorted, or suppressed.

Henri Bergson provided a different kind of influence, which Faulkner used in a different way. In an interview which Loïc Bouvard, Faulkner remarked that his conception of God was " 'very close to Bergson's.' " He went on to say, " 'I agree pretty much with Bergson's theory of the fluidity of time. There is only the present moment, in which I include both the past and the future, and that is eternity. In my opinion time can be shaped quite a bit by the artist; after all, man is never time's slave.' " He also took occasion, perhaps partly because his interviewer was French, to say that he had been influenced by Flaubert, Balzac, " 'And by Bergson, obviously. And I feel very close to Proust.' "[66] Balzac, Bergson, and Proust were among Faulkner's predecessors in the use of time in unorthodox ways to show the immediate, concrete qualities of life. Several critics have noted parallels between Faulkner's practice and Bergson's theory, not only with regard to time, but in their relation of abstract ideas to actual experience, in their feeling about the dynamic quality of the subjective personality, and in their common emphasis on the difficulty of communicating anything about their intuitive feeling for the flow of reality by means of signs or symbols which are relatively static.[67] None of the published criticism has strongly suggested, as yet, that Faulkner read Bergson; my own opinion, however, is that he probably read *Creative Evolution* and *Laughter,* which were translated in 1911, and very possibly also *Introduction to Metaphysics,* translated in 1912. A few examples, sketchily presented, will have to suffice for my demonstration here.

Bergson's ideas about God and time are suggested by his remarks on the relation of organic evolution to the second law of thermodynamics: "There are no things, there are only actions. More particularly, if I consider the world in which we live, I find that the automatic and strictly determined evolution of this well-knit whole is action which is unmaking itself, and that the unforeseen forms which life cuts out in it, forms capable of being themselves prolonged into unforeseen movements, represent the action that is making itself. . . . Now, if the same kind of action is going on everywhere, whether it is that which is unmaking itself or whether it is that which is striving to remake itself, I simply express this probable similitude when I speak of a centre from which worlds shoot out like rockets in a fire-works display—provided, however, that I do not present this centre as a *thing,* but as a continuity of shooting out. God thus defined, has nothing of the already made; He is unceasing life, action, freedom."[68] Faulkner seems to have felt these thoughts, or something like them, from the beginning of his career; finding them intelligibly stated (not that Bergson's statements are always entirely clear) certainly would have been helpful to him in learning to communicate his own sense of life as motion, of motion as change, and of change as growth, development, or evolution.

Bergson's theory of humor proposes the idea that we laugh at people when they operate rigidly and mechanically instead of moving with the sinuosity of life. Faulkner uses this idea frequently, as in the macabre humor with which he treats the doll-like figure of Popeye, and the only slightly less mechanical figure of Temple Drake, in *Sanctuary.* Perhaps with Popeye he goes too far. Bergson cautions that "the general appearance of the person, whose every limb has been made rigid as a machine, must continue to give us the impression of a living being."[69] Popeye, with his arms like sticks and his eyes like rubber knobs, seems mechanical enough; whether he is human enough to be laughed at may be questioned. Elsewhere, especially in *The Hamlet,* the same device is used in such a way that laughter is spontaneous, hearty, and sometimes even good-natured. "I just never went far enough," Ratliff thinks, after having underestimated Flem Snopes. "I went as far as one Snopes will set fire to another Snopeses barn and both Snopeses know it, and that was all right. But I stopped there. I never went on to where that first Snopes will turn around and stomp the fire out so he can sue that second Snopes for the reward and both Snopeses know that too." This observation is expanded in the tall tale invented by Ratliff later, according to which Flem Snopes beats the devil out of hell by getting the best of the bargain Doctor Faustus gets the worst of in Marlowe's play.

Faulkner's way of working is strongly suggested by some of Bergson's theories of art and literature, as these are stated both in *Laughter* and in *Introduction to Metaphysics,* where, after making his usual observation on the impossibility of communicating the inner truth of experience directly by means of either concepts or images, Bergson goes on to say, "the image has at least this advantage, that it keeps us in the concrete. No image can replace the intuition of duration, but many diverse images, borrowed from very different orders of things, may, by the convergence of their action, direct consciousness to the precise point where there is a certain intuition to be seized. . . . But, then, consciousness must at least consent to make the effort. For it will have been shown nothing: it will simply have been placed in the attitude it must take up in order to make the desired effort, and so come by itself to the intuition."[70]

A truer description could hardly be found of the situation in which Faulkner and his readers more or less cooperatively attack the difficulties of communication. Faulkner, as Bergson recommends, gathers wildly incompatible images and flings them at us in a stunning and apparently random profusion. Perhaps we are put in the right position—at least we are driven out of most of the wrong positions—to generate an intuition of dynamic movement; but we have to work like demons, along with Faulkner and his demon, to get the desired result. It seems to me reasonably certain that Faulkner learned to do his share of the work partly by studying Bergson's theories.

Faulkner's literary background is too large and too various to be described by any simple statement. Neither is Faulkner merely eclectic; this enormous amount and variety of material is not picked up at random or used haphazardly, but is sorted by strong prejudices, thoroughly assimilated to Faulkner's unique purposes and patterns, and made into the fabric of works which, the more they make use of precedents, the more they seem stamped with Faulkner's inimitable marks of creation and ownership. I suppose it is because of his complete possession of the assets he has inherited from others that hitherto little effort has been made to trace them back to their former owners. The masters by whom he has consented to be influenced have, in proportion as he has profited by their teaching, become his willing and effective servants, just as he has declared himself willing and eager to be the servant of anyone strong enough to use him.

The scope of this paper does not permit detailed discussion of Faulkner's method, but I have a feeling that it was formatively influenced by the critical theories of T. S. Eliot, to which Faulkner must have been liberally exposed when he was reading modern poetry in the little magazines. I think it is practically certain that he read several of Eliot's essays, including "Tradition and the Individual Talent" in *The Egoist* in 1919 and "Ulysses, Order, and Myth" in *The Dial* in 1924. It seems to me that, like F. Scott Fitzgerald in *The Great Gatsby* and Hemingway in *The Sun Also Rises*, Faulkner consciously and systematically used what Eliot called "the mythical method" of rendering chaotic contemporary experience usable in works of art by "manipulating a continuous parallel between contemporaneity and antiquity," making a traditional myth, or a combination of several myths, supply a structure and a system of imagery by means of which a modern story could be invested with meaning, unity, and value. In my judgment, Faulkner's most successful major works, *The Sound and the Fury, As I Lay Dying, Sanctuary, Light in August, Absalom, Absalom!, The Hamlet,* and *Go Down, Moses,* are the ones in which he uses this method most cogently and well.

I conclude that Falkner adds his individual talent to the tradition of nineteenth and early twentieth century fiction by using Biblical legend, especially the Passion Week story, and classical mythology, chiefly from *The Golden Bough,* reinforced with references to Shakespeare and other writers, mostly poets, of the English renaissance, and to Keats and other poets, both English and French, of the nineteenth and early twentieth centuries. The result is the marvelous realm of Yoknapatawpha, in which the chaos of concrete reality around us here and now is filled with an epic resonance of organized and effectively disciplined feeling, in which the universal values of human life are embodied on Faulkner's "own little postage stamp of native soil," that backward province which his genius has raised into universal significance and value.

1. Reprinted in *William Faulkner: Early Prose and Poetry,* ed. Carvel Collins (Boston, 1962), pp. 114–118; hereafter referred to as *Early Prose and Poetry.*

2. *Early Prose and Poetry,* pp. 74–76.

3. F. L. Gwynn, "Faulkner's Prufrock—and Other Observations," *JEGP,* LII (Jan., 1953), 63–70.

4. Reprinted in *William Faulkner: New Orleans Sketches,* ed. Carvel Collins (New Brunswick, N. J., 1958), pp. 73–74; hereafter referred to as *New Orleans Sketches.*

5. This borrowing, along with similar uses of the same quotation by Hemingway and other writers, is discussed in Phyllis Bartlett, "Other Countries, Other Wenches," *MFS,* III (Winter, 1957-58), 345–349.

6. Reprinted in *Writers at Work: The Paris Review Interviews,* ed. Malcolm Cowley (New York: Compass Books, 1959), pp. 123–124; hereafter referred to as *Writers at Work.*

7. *Early Prose and Poetry,* pp. 55–56.

8. *Early Prose and Poetry,* pp. 51–52.

9. *New Orleans Sketches,* p. 39.

10. *Writers at Work,* p. 123.

11. "Faith or Fear," *Atlantic Monthly,* CXCII (Aug., 1953), 54.

12. S. C. Powell, "William Faulkner Celebrates Easter, 1928," *Perspective,* II (Summer, 1949), 208–209. Powell emphasizes the close association between Biblical and Shakespearean influences in *The Sound and the Fury,* an association which, I would suggest, is frequently present in Faulkner's other works as well.

13. *Writers at Work,* p. 141.

14. Carvel Collins, Introduction to *New Orleans Sketches,* p. 18.

15. Reprinted in *PULC,* XVIII (Spring, 1957), 89–94.

16. W. L. Phillips, "Sherwood Anderson's Two Prize Pupils," *U of Chi Mag,* XLVII (Jan., 1955), 12.

17. *Early Prose and Poetry,* pp. 86–89.

18. *Writers at Work,* p. 141.

19. Sherwood Anderson, *The Modern Writer* (San Francisco, 1925), pp. 4–5.

20. Paul Rosenfeld, Introduction to *The Sherwood Anderson Reader* (Boston, 1947), p. ix (ellipsis in Rosenfeld's text).

21. *New Orleans Sketches,* pp. 101–102.

22. Lillian Ross, "Profiles: How Do You Like It Now, Gentlemen?" *New Yorker,* XVI (13 May, 1950), 57, 59–60.

23. Letter from Kraig Klosson, 4 May, 1962. So far as I know, this interview was not taped. Mr. Klosson's report is as nearly verbatim as he could make it without a recording.

24. A. J. Guerard, *Conrad the Novelist* (Cambridge, Mass., 1958), p. 127.

25. *Early Prose and Poetry,* p. 102.

26. J. W. Friend, "Joseph Conrad: An Appreciation," *Double Dealer,* VII (Oct., 1924), 3, 4.

27. *Faulkner in the University,* ed. F. L. Gwynn and J. L. Blotner (Charlottesville, Va., 1959), pp. 144, 150.

28. For a thorough discussion of this complex in Conrad, see Guerard, pp. 78–84 et passim.

29. *New Orleans Sketches,* pp. 171–184.

30. *Faulkner in the University,* p. 246.

31. Cynthia Grenier, "The Art of Fiction: An Interview with William Faulkner—September, 1955," *Accent,* XVI (Summer, 1956), 168.

32. *Early Prose and Poetry,* p. 86.

33. Loïc Bouvard, "Conversation with William Faulkner," *MFS,* V (Winter, 1959–1960), 363. This interview was not recorded, and the version I use is a translation by Henry Dan Piper back into English from Bouvard's French. How accurately it reports Faulkner's exact words is therefore doubtful; however, it certainly sounds like the Faulkner we hear in the recorded interviews.

34. *Faulkner in the University,* p. 56.

35. "Faulkner," *Vogue,* CXL (July, 1962), 114.

36. Cooper's relation to Faulkner has been well discussed in Ursula Brumm, "Wilderness and Civilization: A Note on William Faulkner," *PR,* XXII (Summer, 1955), 341–342; and Otis Wheeler, "Faulkner's Wilderness," *AL,* XXXI (May, 1959), 127–136.

37. Bouvard, p. 364.

38. *Faulkner at Nagano,* ed. R. A. Jelliffe (Tokyo, 1956), p. 44.

39. Marcel Proust, *Within a Budding Grove, Remembrance of Things Past* (New York, 1934), I, 509–510. Only the first four of the seven novels comprising *Remembrance of Things Past* were published in the United States before 1929: *Swann's Way* in 1922, *Within a Budding Grove* in 1924, *The Guermantes Way* in 1925, and *Cities of the Plain* in 1927.

40. Henry Nash Smith, "Writing Right Smart Fun, Says Faulkner," Dallas *Morning News,* 14 Feb., 1932 Sec. IV, p. 2.

41. *Faulkner at Nagano,* p. 203.

42. *Writers at Work,* p. 135.

43. *Faulkner in the University,* p. 58.

44. Phil Stone, "William Faulkner, the Man and His Work," *Oxford Magazine,* Copy 1 (1 April, 1934), p. 14.

45. Carvel Collins, in "The Interior Monologues of *The Sound and the Fury,*" *English Institute Essays: 1952* (New York, 1954), p. 31, has noted some of these parallels, along with some others which are equally plausible.

46. *Writers at Work,* p. 129.

47. *Faulkner in the University,* p. 56.

48. *Writers at Work,* p. 137.

49. *Faulkner in the University,* p. 282.

50. *Early Prose and Poetry,* p. 94.

51. *Writers at Work,* p. 135.

52. *Faulkner at Nagano,* p. 140.

53. *Faulkner at Nagano,* pp. 15, 26, 140.

54. *Faulkner in the University,* p. 16.

55. See for example Malcolm Cowley, Introduction to *The Portable Faulkner* (New York, 1946), p. 22; and Randall Stewart, "Hawthorne and Faulkner," *CE,* XVII (Feb., 1956), 258–262.

56. H. J. Douglas and R. Daniel, "Faulkner and the Puritanism of the South," *Tenn Stud in Lit,* II (1957), 6. The comparison between the two writers is developed on pp. 5–9.

57. W. V. O'Connor, "Hawthorne and Faulkner: Some Common Ground," *VQR,* XXXIII (Winter, 1957), 121–122.

58. *New Orleans Sketches,* p. 46.

59. *Faulkner in the University,* p. 15.

60. *Faulkner at Nagano,* p. 88.

61. *Faulkner in the University,* p. 281.

62. R. W. B. Lewis, "The Hero in the New World: William Faulkner's *The Bear,*" *KR,* XIII (Aug., 1951), 653.

63. See especially W. L. Miner, *The World of William Faulkner* (Durham, N. C., 1952), pp. 122–123; and W. V. O'Connor, *The Tangled Fire of William Faulkner* (Minneapolis, 1954), pp. 116–17, 123, 129–130.

64. Carvel Collins, "The Pairing of *The Sound and the Fury* and *As I Lay Dying,*" *PULC,* XVIII (Spring, 1957), 119–122; Barbara Cross, "Apocalypse and Comedy in *As I Lay Dying,*" *Tex Stud in Lit and Lang,* III (Summer, 1961), 252–255; R. M. Slabey, "Myth and Ritual in *Light in August,*" *Tex Stud in Lit and Lang,,* II (Autumn, 1960), 329–347.

65. These parallels were pointed out by Mrs. Randi Kahn in a Tulane seminar paper, spring, 1962.

66. Bouvard, pp. 362, 364.

67. See A. L. Scott, "The Myriad Perspectives of *Absalom, Absalom!*"*AQ,* VI (Fall, 1954), 219; Peter Swiggart, "Time in Faulkner's Novels," *MFS,* I (May, 1955), 27–29; Darrell Abel, "Frozen Movement in *Light in August,*" *Boston Univ Stud in Engl,* III (Spring, 1957), 32–34; Donald Tritschler, "The Unity of Faulkner's Shaping Vision," *MFS,* V (Winter, 1959), 343; and W. J. Slatoff, *Quest for Failure* (Ithaca, N. Y., 1960), pp. 242–248. The most complete discussion I have seen is Shirley Callen, *Bergsonian Dynamism in the Writings of William Faulkner* (unpubl. dissertation, Tulane University, 1962).

68. Henri Bergson, *Creative Evolution,* tr. Arthur Mitchell (New York, 1911), p. 248.

69. Bergson, *Laughter,* tr. Cloudesley Brereton and Fred Rothwell (New York, 1911), pp. 30–31.

70. Bergson, *Introducing to Metaphysics,* tr. T. E. Hulme (New York and London, 1912), pp. 16, 17.

AN EXAMINATION OF THE POETRY OF WILLIAM FAULKNER

BY GEORGE P. GARRETT, JR.

IN ADDITION TO the extensive body of his prose fiction William Faulkner is the author of two volumes of verse, *The Marble Faun* (1924) and *A Green*

Reprinted with permission from *Princeton University Library Chronicle,* XVIII (Spring 1957), 124–135.

Bough (1933), and twenty-five other poems which appeared in print from 1919 to 1933.[1] Faulkner's verse has been largely ignored by the critics even though he began by writing poems and thought well enough of his efforts to publish *A Green Bough* when he had already produced seven novels and almost thirty short stories. This is significant, for we know how rigorously he honored the inner gift which had created *The Sound and the Fury* and *As I Lay Dying:* he was willing, during a time of hardship, to pay for the privilege of rewriting *Sanctuary* in order to do justice to those books.[2] *A Green Bough* appeared later and one can assume that he felt no need to be ashamed of that work. Other than reviews the only notice which Faulkner's poetry has received is Harry Runyan's "Faulkner's Poetry," *Faulkner Studies,* III, Nos. 2–3 (Summer-Autumn, 1954), 23–29. Mr. Runyan's article is chiefly useful in demonstrating the kind of judgment which has permitted critics to shy away from Faulkner's verse. He stresses the derivative nature of the poetry and concludes that the effect of the poems is "one of immature romanticism."[3]

It would be difficult to argue that Faulkner's reputation as poet would be great if he were known as a writer of verse alone.[4] However, this is a hypothetical situation, and the fact that he is a great novelist gives his verse importance. It is objected that the poems of William Faulkner are youthful exercises. In answer one may reply that the poems of the young are asked only to reflect the vision of the young; they cannot be wholly "mature" and they are apt to be imitative. If, however, they are true to youth's vision and imitate with taste, discretion and vitality, they deserve to be heard by those who profess to take pleasure in poetry. If the poems happen to be the work of a man who has achieved great literary stature, they deserve to be treated as valuable documents.

The Marble Faun is a highly complex literary exercise. The poems are, as Phil Stone says in his preface, "the poems of youth," but they are promising in more ways than it was possible to see then. The book fails, but the principal cause of failure is in the almost impossible task which the young poet set for himself. *The Marble Faun* is a cycle of nineteen poems, including a prologue and an epilogue, in the pastoral mode. The writing of serious pastoral poetry in our time has been restricted by the lack of an adequate pastoral idiom. This has always been the problem for poets writing pastoral forms in English, but it has been intensified by the decay of the literary language and the requisite quest for a new idiom, fitting for our time and place. Faulkner's attempt was unusual. He challenged directly, avoiding the alternative, the way of irony and the juxtaposition of past and present. He tried to make a mythological poem, composed in a language of echoes and innuendoes and arranged in a kind of musical order. This was fixed in the formal context of traditional conventions of the English eclogue, using the cycle of the four seasons and the hours of the day to establish a relationship between separate poems. The effect gained by joining the evocative method of symbolist poetry with the highly developed patterns of the English pastoral is a unique conjunction. It could scarcely have been attempted by an unlettered, accidental poet. The structure of the book, separate poems joined together by common subject and both external and internal devices, indicates an early awareness of the problems of creating structural unity. Concern with form has marked Faulkner's work from the beginning and throughout a career noted for variety and subtlety of structural experiment.

The mood of the nineteen pieces is elegiac, though it is not death but a personal sense of loss that the poet laments. He speaks in the person of the marble faun, sometimes "marble-bound" physically in the space of "this gray old garden," more often the prisoner of interior powers which isolate him from the quick unthinking vitality of the idealized pastoral scene. His separation comes from knowledge, a sense of the identity and loss, the memory of the dreamy past and a sense of the recurrence and repetition of all things, good and evil. The burden of his separation is awareness; its anguish is increased by the contrast between the impotence of knowledge and the thoughtless vigor of natural life, everywhere personified, or, more exactly, made animal, everywhere swaying and moving to a dance he cannot share. But he can hear the tune and be moved by it. The music and the gestures of Pan, model and original poet-shepherd of the pastoral scene as well as the Greek original of Faunus, echo through the cycle at once a torment and solace to the marble faun. The myth of Narcissus is repeatedly evoked. Time and again objects are seen in mirror image. All things, including Pan and the speaker, come to self-awareness in this way. The speaker, though, plagued by the knowledge of change, decay, mutability, and the rigors of rebirth, remains sad for "things I know, yet cannot know." The inner dialectic of the poem is stressed by the struggle of opposing images, fire and ice, dancing and immobility, silence and music, youth and age, spring and winter, night and day. It is unresolved, ending as it began, the full circle implied by the device of the first two rhymes of the prologue matching the last two rhymes of the epilogue, "fro-go," "go-snow." Concealed in the guise of this pastoral cycle is one of the dominant themes of our literature, the struggle to identity, in this case defined in symbolic terms.

The achievement of a pastoral myth of such austere purity required a finished idiom, and it would have been a small miracle if the poet had possessed that gift at the start. The failure of *The Marble Faun* lies in the language and syntax. It is not entirely the result of the frequent archaisms, inversions, and old-fashioned poeticisms. These are tools and Faulkner used them to give the poem a timeless quality. He used the same devices skillfully in *A Green Bough,* and this kind of stylization, for a somewhat different purpose, was to become a characteristic of the highly regarded "fugitive" verse, particularly in some of the poems of John Crowe Ransom. Neither is the failure of the poem the result of the apparently rigid stanzaic pattern. Except for the song of Pan, six quatrains in the sixth poem of the cycle (pp. 22–23), the poem is made up of stanzas of varying length, in lines of iambic tetrameter, rhyming in couplets. However, within this form there is considerable variation. The basic stanza is a unit of either twelve or fourteen lines, but there are fourteen different stanza units, ranging from six lines to twenty-six. Rhythm is varied by half-lines, run-on lines, and lines with shifted or added stress. Similarly, there is some variation in rhyme. The dominant music is of pure masculine end rhyme, but there are occasional feminine rhymes, some internal rhymes, and a few un-rhymed lines. Faulkner was looking for a form rigid enough to confirm the abstraction of his theme, yet flexible enough to overcome the risk of monotony. It is not surprising that he had not mastered by labor the tools of language to accomplish this. It is remarkable that he was possessed so early by the idea of what he must try to do.

Ultimately the success or failure of the cycle depended on verbal texture, the conveyed sensuous values and relations of the sounds of words. In this poem the immediate sensuous affective experience is crucial. The verbal texture, however, is weakened by lack of sophistication: not, as has been supposed, by literary naïveté, but by the absence of the precision that comes only from the craft of making poems. The language Faulkner commanded would not stand the strain and he was forced to depend upon conventional "poetic" language. It is this weakness that has given some critics cause to dismiss the book as derivative in a pejorative sense. With the undeniable advantage of hindsight, we can see the importance of the fact that Faulkner's first great literary problem was texture. Like Joyce, he developed in his prose a dazzling variety and distinction in the use of verbal texture. Still, even in *The Marble Faun* there are moments when there appears, as Phil Stone suggested, "a hint of coming muscularity of wrist and eye." Faulkner had already achieved something of the French symbolists' ability to suggest correspondences by analogy, to describe the experience of one of the senses in the terms of another, a familiar device in his later fiction. And there are a few examples of the striking similes that were to become characteristic of his prose: the flight of blackbirds in a twilight sky "like shutters swinging to and fro," or again, like "burned scraps of paper"; silence is "like a hood"; lilacs are "faint as cries"; mist is "as soft and thick as hair."

Between the date of composition of *The Marble Faun,* "April, May, June, 1919," and its publication, Faulkner continued to write verse as well as prose. The verse published during this time indicates a consolidation of the interests evident in *The Marble Faun.* Of thirteen poems printed in *The Mississippian* during 1919–1920, four are "from Verlaine," and they show his continuing interest in the abstract lyricism of symbolist verse. At this time Faulkner was studying French formally at the University, and we know that he did very well.[5] He was developing an increasing stylization of diction and syntax and a dependence on the controlling factors of formal verse patterns. It was not all apprentice work. Faulkner's first published work, "L'Apres-Midi d'un Faune," appeared in *The New Republic,* August 6, 1919. Affiliations with Mallarmé's poem of the same title are vague, but the poem is of some interest as an intense condensation of the mood and argument of *The Marble Faun.*

During the years between *The Marble Faun* and *A Green Bough,* while Faulkner was busy with prose, he found some time for his poetry, and fourteen of his poems appeared in periodicals. Moreover he made use of his verse in his first two novels. The epigraph of *Soldiers' Pay* was to reappear in *A Green Bough,* XXX, and verse quoted in *Mosquitoes,* pp. 246–247, 249, and 252, was also used, revised, in *A Green Bough.* In general this verse shows a refinement and development with some variation in kinds, a new hardness, some irony, and, in a few cases, satire. It is not surprising, though, that Faulkner's verse generally strives for a level of high seriousness. In "Verse Old and Nascent: A Pilgrimage,"[6] Faulkner's most explicit extended statement on the aims of poetry, he came out in favor of a formal and traditional poetry, one which he felt was under the obligation to convey "spiritual beauty." He described his progress through a series of early admirations which concluded at the point when he discovered the permanent virtues of Shelley and Keats. Contrasting these with what he saw as the main direction of modern poetry, he praised their "beautiful awareness, so sure of its own power that it is not necessary to create the illusion of force by frenzy and motion. Take the odes to a Nightingale, to a Grecian urn, 'Music to hear,' etc.; here is the spiritual beauty which the moderns strive vainly for with trickery, and yet beneath it one knows are entrails; masculinity." These are important implications in Faulkner's position. Poetry is the communication of spiritual beauty; its virtues are restraint, formality, and power in disguise, not dramatized. A poetry complementing this point of view would tend to avoid the light, the occasional, and, to a degree, the colloquial; it would tend to be exclusive. Faulkner's concept of the use of poetry is a lofty one, and, in a sense, an inhibiting one for the poet. For the full sweep and play of imagination and, perhaps most important, for the free introduction of humor, Faulkner would necessarily, if regretfully, depend on prose.[7]

Many of the poems in *A Green Bough* were written early, but, on the evidence of the poems which appeared in periodicals, Faulkner continued to polish his work. The question of Faulkner's revisions has been obscured by misinterpretation and casual scholarship. An excellent example of misinterpretation accepted as fact begins with Faulkner's remark about the composition of *As I Lay Dying* in the introduction to the Modern Library edition of *Sanctuary.* There Faulkner said: "I wrote *As I Lay Dying* in six weeks, without changing a word." Interpretation of this to mean that Faulkner did not at any stage revise the work was passed along until even so usually astute a critic as Olga Vickery confidently wrote that *As I Lay Dying* was "published without a single line of revision."[8] In *The Paris Review,* IV, No. 12 (Spring, 1956) [32–33], there is a reproduction of the last manuscript page of *As I Lay Dying.* There are a number of revisions on this page and a comparison with the published version of the novel will reveal still other differences not evident on this manuscript sheet. Similarly, study of the short stories indicates many cases of revision occurring between the time that a story appeared in periodical form and the appearance of the same story in book form.

A number of the poems in *A Green Bough* further exemplify Faulkner's concern with revision. Of particular interest are the revisions of poems which had appeared in the Faulkner issue of *Contempo,* I, No. 17 (Feb. 1, 1932). It is likely that the verse dates from an earlier period, but there was revision between February, 1932 and the publication of *A Green Bough* the following year. The poem "Spring" in *Contempo,* XXXVI in *A Green Bough,* shows how he worked over a finished poem in minor details to sharpen its over-all effect.

Spring

Gusty trees windily lean on green
Eviscerated skies, the surging wind
Against the sun's gold collar stamps, to lean
His weight. And once the furrowed day behind,
The golden steed browses the field he breaks
And full of flashing teeth, where he has been,
Trees, the waiting mare his neighing shakes,
Hold his heaving shape a moment seen.

Upon the hills, clashing the stars together,
Stripping the tree of heaven of its blaze,

Stabled, richly grained with golden weather . . .
Within the trees that he has reft and raped
His fierce embrace by riven boughs is shaped,
While in the lonely hills he stamps and neighs.

A Green Bough, XXXVI

Gusty trees windily lean on green
eviscerated skies, the stallion, Wind,
against the sun's gold collar stamps, to lean
his weight. And once the furrowed day behind,
the golden steed browses the field he breaks
and full of flashing teeth where he has been
trees, the waiting mare his neighing shakes,
hold his heaving shape a moment seen.

Upon the hills, clashing the stars together,
stripping the tree of heaven of its blaze,
stabled, richly grained with golden weather—

within the trees that he has reft and raped
his fierce embrace by riven boughs in shaped,
while on the shaggy hills he stamps and neighs.

The most obvious difference between the two versions is that in revision
capitals are dropped as the insignia of individual lines. This is not accidental;
of all the poems in *A Green Bough,* only six do not use capitals at the beginning
of each line. Two, XXXVI and XVI, use capitals to mark the grammatical
beginning of individual sentences. There is a distinct effect gained by this
change: an increased run-on quality in the lines, making the individual stanza
the unit in the sonnet, rather than the line. And movement, the movement and
violence of the wind and the coming of spring suggested in rhythm, texture
and imagery, is enhanced. The breakup of the last stanza into two units tends
to stress the coherence of the first octave, its development of a single complex
figure. That figure Faulkner clarified and emphasized by replacing "surging"
with "stallion," and by capitalizing the metaphorical subject of development,
Wind, separating it by commas. Similarly he eliminated two commas in line
six which impede the forward movement.[9] The purpose of this kind of slight
revision was to sharpen the original intention of the poem. Most of the other
revisions are similar in purpose, the most drastic being the removal of an entire
four-line stanza from the sonnet "Knew I Love Once" to form, with minor
changes, the ten-line poem XXXIII of *A Green Bough.* Even slight changes
are of some significance. For example, in revising "The Lilacs," *The Double*

Dealer, VII, No. 44 (June, 1925), 185–187, to make I of *A Green Bough*, Faulkner made a number of small changes, the most important being the elimination, as much as possible, of the poet speaker as singular, replacing him with a collective pronoun, thus increasing the dramatic conflict in the poem without the danger of the poet's being explicitly identified as more than a spectator.

A Green Bough appeared at a time when there was little sympathy in critical circles for an abstract lyric poetry chiefly concerned with the communication of "spiritual beauty." Most of the objections to the book are contained in a review by Morris U. Schappes, "Faulkner as Poet," *Poetry*, XLIII, No. 1 (Oct., 1933), 48–52. Mr. Schappes was bothered by the absence of pressing social issues in Faulkner's poetry and noted that in no poem had Faulkner come to grips with the problem of "the proletariat" in Mississippi. He was disturbed by the deliberate artifice of the poems and he criticized Faulkner for obscurity. There was another criticism, one based on the notion of art as a vaguely therapeutic gesture. "Inevitably," Schappes wrote, "there is driven home the impression that these poems are not the lyric definition of the relation of an integrated personality with the world about him but mere emotional poses." It was not enough that the poet write poems; he must also offer for inspection "an integrated personality." William Rose Benét, in "Faulkner as Poet," *The Saturday Review of Literature*, IX, No. 41 (Apr. 29, 1933), 565, found the same fault and added to it the defect of incompletely assimilated "influences." Only a magician could assimilate all the forces Benét found at work in Faulkner's poems. Among the principals were Eliot, Housman, Cummings, Hart Crane, Rossetti, and Swinburne. "Mr. Faulkner is an apt pupil in his poetry," Benét wrote, "choosing the most approved modern influences, but he can scarcely be said to have absorbed them." Peter Monro Jack's review, *The New York Times Book Review*, May 14, 1933, p. 2, stressed "lack of originality" and added H. D. to Benét's diverse gallery of influences. Only Eda Lou Walton's review in *New York Herald Tribune Books*, April 30, 1933, p. 2, praised the book, treating the verse in terms of its own demands. A subtle kinship between the disciplines of his verse and prose fiction was suggested and a comparison made of his methods with those of Joyce.

Although his poetry has by no means the absolute artistry of Joyce's "Chamber Music," one is reminded in reading him of the difference between Joyce, the novelist, and Joyce, the lyric singer. Faulkner, the novelist, is not Faulkner, the poet. But the two have one thing in common. Both have learned an art from conscientious study of various other artists' styles. Both have come through this discipline with something their own.

It is difficult to talk with certainty or assurance about movements in contemporary literature, and perhaps not really useful under any circumstances; but anyone who has followed the "trends" in little magazines and volumes of new verse is aware that the situation has changed enough during the last twenty years so that it is now possible to examine a book of verse like *A Green Bough* without being necessarily perturbed by deliberate artifice or the absence of current political and social issues.[10] We are not even so disturbed by "influences" any more. One of the things a half century of scholarship has taught us is that a wholly original poetic style is rare indeed. Now we are apt to think more of models than influences, and even the once honored term *imitation* is regaining some of its prestige. In superficial aspects certain poems in *A Green Bough* are distinctly imitative, but in a deeper sense there is much that belongs singularly to Faulkner. In a casual way the first poem of the volume has suggestions of Eliot. It begins with a tea party and moves into mythology. There is some dialogue and, on occasion, an echo of the rhythmic patterns of the early Eliot. The second has with less justice been compared to Eliot's "Portrait of a Lady."[11] Similarly XXVII, in quatrains and treating the myth of Philomel, calls to mind "Sweeney among the Nightingales," but the differences are important. Faulkner's poem begins where Eliot's ended and has no satirical comment on present reality by means of the myth. It is a pure lyric. Poem XV suggests Housman, it is true, with its repetition of "bonny," and four poems suggest the manner of Cummings in the absence of capitals at least. These eight poems, which make no attempt to disguise allusions to the work of other poets, represent the main evidence for those who have complained that Faulkner's verse is unduly derivative.

The poems of *A Green Bough* show a considerable variety of form and subject matter. They range from the lyric for song to the most intense and compressed imagery. The second stanza of XIX, describing a swimmer in sun-filled water, shows the more traditional music he was capable of.

> Within these slow cathedralled corridors
> Where ribs of sunlight drown
> He joins in green caressing wars
> With seamaids red and brown. . . .

The concluding stanza of XIV indicates the economy and clarity in Faulkner's suggestion of the world of the folk song and ballad. In this poem a young man has been hanged.

> Being dead he will forgive you
> And all that you have done,
> But he'll curse you if you leave him
> Grinning at the sun.

This can be set in contrast to the complexity of the second stanza of XXXIV, the image of Mary at twilight.

> Her soft doveslippered eyes strayed in the dusk
> Creaming backward from the fallen day,
> And a haughty star broke yellow musk
> Where dead kings slept the long cold years away.

There are echoes of *A Marble Faun* in the images of any number of the individual poems, enough to give the careful reader a sense of continuity in Faulkner's entire poetic work, and the dominant mood of the whole book is pastoral.[12] The cycle of the seasons in a classical landscape merges with the figure of a plowman at sunset in X and evokes an image that haunts Faulkner's prose as well as his verse.

> Nymph and faun in this dusk might riot
> Beyond all oceaned Time's cold greenish bar
> To shrilling pipes, to cymbals' hissing
> Beneath a single icy star
>
> Where he, to his own compulsion
> —A terrific figure on an urn—
> Is caught between his two horizons,
> Forgetting that he cant return.

If there is continuity in Faulkner's verse there is, as in his prose, a restless experimentation, and an attempt to achieve, within the limitations which he demanded for verse, new variations on the oldest themes. The final effect is not one of "immature romanticism." It is rather one of strenuous effort to create a poetry which, had it been continued, might have been a sophisticated lyric strain in contemporary verse. The final poem of *A Green Bough,* XLIV, which had been previously published as "My Epitaph" and *This Earth,* significantly closes Faulkner's career as poet on a note of subdued tranquillity and a return to roots in the earth he has chosen not only to celebrate, but as his home. *A Green Bough* shows a poet, not always successful or equally skillful, who knows the value of words, rhythm, image, texture, and, above all, structure; and it shows us a writer who, contrary to popular myth, was a meticulous craftsman, aware of the tradition of letters and the best contemporary work.

Faulkner never achieved all that he asked of himself in poetry, but he could at least have the sense of satisfaction he put into the words of the natural poet in the sketch "Out of Nazareth": "You see, I wrote this, and I liked it. Of course it ain't as good as I wisht it was. But you are welcome to it."[13]

1. Of the thirty-one poems published during this period by Faulkner, six were to appear in *A Green Bough*. I include the unsigned poem "Nocturne," *Ole Miss*, XXV (1921), 214–215.

2. Introduction to the Modern Library edition of *Sanctuary*, 1932.

3. Mr. Runyan also prints a check list of Faulkner's poetry which adds nothing to the list compiled by Robert W. Daniel, *A Catalogue of the Writings of William Faulkner*, New Haven, Yale University Library,1942.

4. Still, this has been done. Eda Lou Walton, reviewing *A Green Bough* for *New York Herald Tribune Books*, Apr. 30, 1933, p. 2, wrote: "If William Faulkner had not been interested in becoming an important novelist and short story writer, it seems most probable that he would hold rank as one of the better of the minor poets of this period." Similarly, *The Marble Faun* received a perceptive review which saw the poems of that book as promising real achievement: John McClure, "Literature and Less," the New Orleans *Times-Picayune*, Sunday magazine section, Jan. 25, 1925, p. 6.

5. A. Wigfall Green, "William Faulkner at Home," *Sewanee Review*, XL, No. 3 (July-Sept., 1932), 300. Reprinted in Frederick J. Hoffman and Olga W. Vickery eds., *William Faulkner: Two Decades of Criticism* [East Lansing], 1951, p. 40. Faulkner's study of the French symbolists is confirmed by Phil Stone in a letter to James B. Meriwether, February 19, 1957: "As to the French symbolist poets, Bill and I think they had some influence upon his own verse."

6. *The Double Dealer*, VII, No. 43 (Apr., 1925), 129–131.

7. Answering a question about Eliot and Poe, Faulkner made his distinction between the aims of poetry and the aims of prose quite clear: "Well, with Eliot there is this difference—Poe dealt in prose, while the poet deals with something which is so pure and so esoteric that you cannot say he is English or Japanese—he deals in something that is universal. That's the distinction I make between the prose writer and the poet, the novelist and the poet—that the poet deals in something universal, while the novelist deals in his own traditions." *Faulkner at Nagano*, edited by Robert A. Jelliffe, Tokyo [1956], p. 16.

8. *William Faulkner: Two Decades of Criticism*, p. 189

9. In line thirteen, "his fierce embrace by riven boughs in shaped," "in" is obviously a misprint in the original text. This is corrected by R. N. Raimbault in his bilingual edition, *Le Rameau Vert*, Paris [1955], p. 182.

10. An excellent discussion of the trend toward "mythological" subjects as against "occasional" subjects in W. H. Auden's "Foreword" to W. S. Merwin's book of poems *A Mask for Janus*, New Haven, 1952.

11. Frederick L. Gwynn, "Faulkner's Prufrock—and Other Observations," *The Journal of English and Germanic Philology*, LII, No. 1 (Jan., 1953), 63–70. Mr. Gwynn's article actually deals with the influence of Eliot on the early novels but he finds (p. 63) that the first two poems of *A Green Bough* "owe their situation and tone and many of their phrases to Eliot's 'Portrait of a Lady,' while No. XXVII is almost a parody of 'Sweeney among the Nightingales.'"

12. Something remains to be said of the continuity between Faulkner's verse and his prose. The pastoral feeling of *The Hamlet* echoes many images in *The Marble Faun* and *A Green Bough*.

13. *New Orleans Sketches by William Faulkner*, edited by Ichiro Nishizaki [Tokyo, 1955], p. 79.

ONE CONTINUOUS FORCE: NOTES ON FAULKNER'S EXTRA-LITERARY READING

M. GIDLEY

SOME CRITICS ARE now beginning to plumb the profundities of Faulkner's art and (to a lesser extent, insofar as it is a separable element) his thought; but it is still quite commonly believed that he was an untutored genius of the sort the Romantics are said to have popularised. Admittedly, he himself sometimes tended to add weight to this opinion by seeming proud of the comparative brevity of his time at school and speaking of himself (usually when not at home in Mississippi) as a farmer rather than, to use his expression, "a literary man." Of course, if pressed he would elevate himself to the position of "a writer"— but a writer unable to "refer to philosophy," an "untrained thinker."[1] As a measure of Faulkner's *ability* comments like these have quite rightly been thought deceptively simple and shrugged off; yet as offering an indication of his actual reading and interests many critics have taken them at face value. For instance, Frederick J. Hoffman, while acknowledging Faulkner's undoubted intelligence, has remarked, rather curtly, that Faulkner's views were all "strictly homespun."[2] William Van O'Connor, in his influential book, *The Tangled Fire of William Faulkner,* says that though Faulkner's friend, Phil Stone, lent the young novelist books on "aesthetics and pure philosophy" they were always returned "with the margins as clean and untouched as when Stone handed [them] to him."[3] O'Connor's assertion—undocumented—has in fact been flatly contradicted by Stone himself in his statement that Faulkner was greatly influenced by *The Creative Will* (1916), a book on aesthetics by Willard Huntington Wright.[4] In any case, if works on "aesthetics and pure philosophy" were returned unmarked this in itself would not constitute proof that Faulkner had not read them; Joseph Blotner, in his Introduction to *William Faulkner's Library—A Catalogue,* observes that Faulkner *never* marked his books.[5]

Of course Faulkner's primary interests were literary. To insist otherwise

Reprinted with permission from *Mississippi Quarterly,* XXIII, No. 3 (Summer 1970), 299–314.

of the author of a score of novels, an author who claimed he read *Don Quixote* "every year," *Moby Dick* "every four or five years," the Old Testament "once every ten . . . or fifteen years"—and so on through Flaubert, Dostoevsky, Dickens and Conrad (pp. 110–111)—would be ludicrous. However, by emphasizing the novelist's non- or extra-literary reading our picture of his development may be brought closer to completion; this essay attempts but a preliminary sketch towards such a rounding out, so to speak, of Faulkner's figure.

That Faulkner was indeed acquainted with some aesthetics and pure philosophy is borne out by his own works and comments. I will give but two examples. In an essay on O'Neill (1922) in *Early Prose and Poetry* he says, "Someone has said—a Frenchman, probably; they have said everything—that art is pre-eminently provincial: i.e., it comes directly from a certain age and a certain locality. This is a very profound statement; for Lear and Hamlet . . . could never have been written anywhere save in England during Elizabeth's reign . . . nor could Madame Bovary have been written in any place other than the Rhone Valley in the nineteenth century [etc.]"[6] The Frenchman's formulation that Faulkner most likely had in mind here is Hippolyte Taine's famous *"race, milieu, et moment."* We cannot be certain that Faulkner actually read Taine's *History of English Literature* (1864), but the above quotation shows he was definitely aware of the kind of determinism originated by Taine.[7]

Faulkner's wry homage to the French intellect, his respect generally for French writers—since handsomely "repaid" by some of the greatest critical minds in France, Sartre, Camus and Malraux—is apparent also in my example from his published comments. He told Loic Bouvard that he believed in " 'a deity very close to Bergson's,' " not a " 'personified or a mechanical God, but a God who is the most complete expression of mankind, a God who rests both in eternity and in the now,' " and that his concept of time also resembled Bergson's: " 'There isn't any time. . . . I agree pretty much with Bergson's theory of the fluidity of time. There is only the present moment, in which I include both the past and the future, and that is eternity. In my opinion time can be shaped quite a bit by the artist; after all, man is never time's slave' " (p.70). Richard P. Adams has pointed to several Bergsonian ideas in Faulkner's fiction[8] and Shirley P. Callen has gone even further by demonstrating both that Bergsonian dynamism was a formative and crucial force in the composition of the fiction and that it can serve as a useful tool in its analysis.[9]

Consequently it seems worthwhile to examine the Appendix to *William Faulkner's Library.* This was compiled by James B. Meriwether from Phil Stone's files and lists some of the works Stone ordered in the 'twenties from the Brick Row Bookshop in New Haven with Faulkner "in mind."[10] We know from Faulkner's *Early Prose and Poetry* that he certainly read some of the writers included there—Conrad Aiken (pp. 74–76), Joseph Hergesheimer (pp. 101–103) and O'Neill (pp. 86–89) to name the most obvious. And a case could be made out to show that he was aware of H. L. Mencken's listed classic *The American Language* (first published 1919, ordered 1922). In the chapter "The Future of the Language, English or American"—which predicts (it now appears rightly) the comparative eclipse of English by American—Mencken exhorts American authors to write in American in just the manner that Synge and others had written in Irish.[11] Faulkner was not merely one of the most talented writers to respond—in his fiction—to Mencken's challenge; but also publicly declared the same view. At the close of his early comments on O'Neill —in which he refers to *Playboy of the Western World*—Faulkner writes, "Nowhere today, saving in parts of Ireland, is the English language spoken with the same earthy strength as it is in the United States" (p. 89). A little later, in a general article on drama (1922), he repeats the point: "One rainbow we have on our dramatic horizon: language as it is spoken in America. In comparison with it British is a Sunday night affair of bread and milk—melodious but slightly tiresome nightingales in a formal clipped hedge" (p.95).

Mencken is not the only author appearing in the Appendix who is likely to have influenced the maturing Faulkner; elsewhere I have attempted to demonstrate Faulkner's affinities with Louis Berman and Havelock Ellis,[12] and with Aldous Huxley.[13] As the introduction of the more extra-literary names here—Berman was a physiologist and Ellis a psychologist—might remind us, the real importance of the Appendix for our purpose is that we can assume we will find there, if anywhere, some of the works on extra- or non-literary subjects—even on "aesthetics and pure philosophy"—that William Van O'-Connor would have us believe Stone lent to Faulkner to no avail. And certainly, as we see at first glance, it contains some "aesthetics" in the form of Percy Lubbock's *The Craft of Fiction* (1921) and, in a collection of Plato's dialogues, some "pure philosophy." Moreover, Faulkner does appear to have had some knowledge of these volumes, both of which, like all the books we are considering from the Appendix, were ordered in 1922. For instance, Lubbock's remarks on Balzac would have engaged the young novelist's attention: he asks, "Who has ever known so much about his own creations as Balzac? —and who has ever felt that Balzac's people had the freedom of a bigger world than that very solid and definite habitation he made for them?"[14] Stone's wife puts it this way: "Together they [Phil and Bill] read [all of Balzac] joyously outraged as Balzac consistently outwitted them with his superior insights into the human heart, into his characters who never did quite what the boys had expected."[15] Yet, on the other hand, Lubbock's carefully phrased criticism of Balzac's repeated use of the same characters (pp. 208–210) would, to Faulkner, have been anathema. The same could be said of the book's anti-Tolstoyan strain, especially its reservations on the creation of Anna Karenina (p.246), for she represented for Faulkner one of the peaks of characterization (*Lion*, p. 128). Also, through Faulkner's repeated insistence that the story should determine the form of the novel, we can see that he was seemingly too anarchic to have had much sympathy with the particularly Jamesian aims Lubbock propagated. But, at the same time, Faulkner did believe in form; of Twain he has this to say: "People will read *Huck Finn* for a long time. Twain has never really written a novel, however. His work is too loose. We'll assume that a novel has set rules. His work is just a mess of stuff—just a series of events."[16] What Faulkner wanted—and achieved—was a fluid form, but one which was recognisable *as* form.

Faulkner believed that "the verities have been the same ever since Socrates"[17]—and we know that Keats's neo-Platonism, embodied in the "Odes," appealed to him.[18] Also, I do not consider it quite frivolous to posit a connection between Plato's "Apology," "Crito," and "Phaedo"—all of which relate to the trial and death of Socrates and are in the collection ordered by Stone —and Faulkner's dialogue-novel, *Requiem for a Nun* (1951). The old philosopher's friends go to him to seek enlightenment on his actions and beliefs; Gavin Stevens escorts Temple Drake Stevens to the prison to behold Nancy Mannigoe for the same purpose. As Socrates, by questioning, by probing, acts like a "midwife" in bringing forth knowledge, so Gavin (who has in fact been characterised by Olga Vickery in Socratic terms[19]) behaves towards Temple— though in *Requiem* the knowledge comes ultimately from Nancy, and it is not rational. To be sure, the relevant items in the Appendix demand and deserve study.

However, before proceeding with such an examination, I think it should be stressed that there is no justification for believing that the Appendix of Stone's orders represents his taste to the exclusion of Faulkner's own—for thinking, in other words, that Faulkner only read extra-literary works because Stone lent them to him. The Appendix in fact reads—and this must be taken for granted by those unacquainted with Blotner's *Catalogue*—rather like a miniature version of the library holdings; several of the authors mentioned above—Melville, O'Neill, Aiken—appear in both lists, as if Stone's purchases were intended to augment Faulkner's own collection of books. In general terms this is certainly true; we discover in the Appendix representatives of many of the categories we might isolate in the *Catalogue* itself: classics (Appian, Defoe,

Catullus, Sophocles); works later to become classics (Cather and Fitzgerald, Gissing and Joyce, Lawrence and Ransom); what now seem only bafflingly popular novels (Edna Ferber's *The Girls,* recently tarnished Masefields, Ann Douglas Sedgwick's *Adrienne Toner*); representative poets of all descriptions —the minor (Bodenheim), the new (William Carlos Williams), the bad (Florence K. Mixter), and the superseded (Swinburne). Again, as in the library itself, the Appendix reveals a wide range of non-fiction books, from a travel journal by the ornithologist and explorer William Beebe, through the historical and political records of T.E. Lawrence and Walter Lippman, to the essays of Lytton Strachey and Chauncey Brewster Tinker's biography of Boswell.

Faulkner's independent reading of "aesthetics and pure philosophy" is further corroborated by the library *Catalogue* itself. We learn that after Stone's mentorship had waned Faulkner continued, by whatever means, to obtain such works—indeed, after the publication of *Go Down, Moses* in 1942, after the end, that is, of what Melvin Backman has rightly dubbed Faulkner's "major years," when Faulkner himself admitted he was writing less and obviously had more time for reading and reflection, there seems to be a renewal of interest in this kind of literature. Amongst others, the following additions to the library testify to such a renewal: a 1947 translation of Sartre's *Age of Reason;* an edition of Thomas Aquinas published in 1948; a 1953 French edition of Van Gogh's letters to his brother Theo—in which the painter exposed his aesthetic intentions in fascinating detail; a selection made in 1954 from the philosophical works of Spinoza; and books on Picasso from both 1946 and 1955. Naturally, while there is the possibility that Faulkner read works which came into his possession after the end of his formative years partly on the understanding that they would mirror aspects of his own thought (or for the pleasure of discovering that they did), it would be preposterous to imply that they could have *influenced* his major work. But this is not necessarily the case with writers he came across earlier, such as the ones we are able to look at from the Appendix, or those which, equally importantly, came into the library independently of Stone: Voltaire's *A Philosophical Dictionary* (1764) and Ludwig Lewisohn's compilation, *A Modern Book of Criticisms* (1919).

The *Dictionary* belongs to a 1910 American edition of Voltaire[20] and had probably been in the Falkners' possession since William's childhood. It takes little ingenuity to notice that, in the most sophisticated of veins, it proffers just that kind of world-weary fatalism which Faulkner's readers meet in some of his memorable characters—Mr. Compson *et al. A Modern Book,* containing Hamilton Basso's autograph, was also in the library itself and, since Basso was a contributor to *The Double Dealer* and a resident of New Orleans during

Faulkner's sojourn there,[21] it appears likely that the book left his hands due to some voluntary act on Faulkner's part—he "borrowed" it, bought it, or accepted it as a gift. *A Modern Book's* possible influence is much more difficult to assess—and as I have elsewhere discussed in some detail its relevance to *Mosquitoes* (1927) as a "novel of ideas" (see n. 13 above), it must suffice here to draw several more general or, at least, diverse conclusions.

Through it Faulkner had the opportunity to come in contact with some of the most persuasive and significant thinkers of his time—Remy de Gourmont, Shaw, Randolph Bourne, Van Wyck Brooks and James Huneker—as well as some engaging and/or profound theories. Anatole France—one of whose works also appears in the Appendix—contributes what really amounts to a philosophical essay on the constitution of reality; "reality and appearance," he concludes, "are all one. To love and to suffer in this world, images suffice; it is not necessary that their objectivity be demonstrated."[22] Wilhelm Dilthey discusses the "creative imagination," and one of his central observations concerns the importance of memory to the imagination; like Bergson and Proust, he declares that the respective functions of the memory and the imagination are similar (pp. 45–51). Richard Moritz Meyer details the development of the poet from primitive ages to the present (pp. 57–65) while Hugo Von Hofmannsthal puts forward the somewhat startling notion that when modern man reads newspapers, scientific textbooks, and like material, he is really still seeking poetry (pp. 66–73). Alfred Kerr, in meaning if not manner akin to Oscar Wilde, writes on the critic as creator (pp. 85–88). Arthur Symons discusses Balzac, offering a judgement to be echoed by Faulkner many years later: Balzac was a great novelist but not a great writer of prose.[23] Arnold Bennett (who later said "Faulkner writes like an angel"[24]) tries in his essay to revive enthusiasm for Swinburne (pp. 122–125), a poet who for Faulkner had not been superseded.[25] Lastly (though I could continue) Joel Elias Spingarn demonstrates convincingly and with sharp skill many common fallacies of criticism—or, rather, he inventories many common fallacious critical methods (pp. 157–167), the tenor of his essay suggesting that he would have appreciated Lubbock.

Two further observations on Lewisohn's collection seem in order. First, *A Modern Book* constitutes, through its many references to Taine (e.g., pp. 21–22, 30, 107–111, 125 and 126), one of the most likely sources for Faulkner's knowledge of that figure. Second, it should be pointed out that H. L. Mencken was a contributor to the volume: he takes Paul Elmer More and other "new humanists" to task for proving themselves incapable of recognising true originals—like Dreiser—and praising only the "orthodox," a state of affairs he attributes to the Puritan heritage in America (pp. 168–172). He himself became increasingly powerful during Faulkner's young manhood—as both a caustic cultural arbiter and an editor. It was he who declared that *The Double Dealer* was delivering the South from a state he had earlier satirized as "the Sahara of the Bozart;"[26] perhaps it was in the pages of that journal that he first came across Faulkner's work. In any case, as editor of the *American Mercury,* despite his initial dislike (described by Charles Angoff), he was ultimately responsible for publishing several of Faulkner's short stories.[27] Though Faulkner in his turn later pronounced Mencken "mad,"[28] I suspect that a thorough investigation of their interaction might yield greater affinities.

I wish now to resume our consideration of items of an extra-literary nature in the Stone-Meriwether Appendix to Blotner's *William Faulkner's Library—A Catalogue.* One of these is tantamount to aesthetics—Elie Faure's *History of Art*—and the other may at least be described as "impure" philosophy, James Harvey Robinson's *The Mind in the Making.*

Faure was an influential figure during the 'twenties. As an art historian, an author of short stories and as an autobiographer, his work was translated into English, appeared in magazines like the *Dial,* and was praised by Havelock Ellis.[29] (Faure, like Mencken, contributed a tribute in his turn to a memorial volume for Ellis.)[30] His *History* consists of four volumes translated between 1921 and 1924 and a more theoretical volume, called *The Spirit of the Forms,* which was published in 1929. It is virtually certain that Faulkner knew at least the four volumes of the *History;* not only did Stone order it, but Faulkner particularly mentions it in "Elmer," an unpublished manuscript written in 1925. As Michael Millgate's commentary on "Elmer" shows, the reference to Faure is not incidental; it has a function in that Elmer, perhaps like Faulkner himself (as a young man he loved to draw), is also studying Clive Bell and other authorities on modern painting.[31]

If Faulkner did read it he would have discovered much that he has shown elsewhere was at least temporarily congenial to him. Walter Pack, in his Translator's Preface, points out that Faure refers "contantly to the philosophy, social life, and ideals of the people under examination, and not to their art alone" (p. xl). In this sense—that he treats art as the product of certain men at a defined epoch in a particular place—Faure follows Taine; indeed he mentions him (p. xix). However, the core of the study is better evoked by the title of the fifth volume, *The Spirit of the Forms;* that is, it seems brimming with notions of dynamism. Faure was probably assisted towards this vision by Bergson, to whom he refers (p. xxvii), and certainly his style, though less vivid, recalls that of Bergson:

All aspects of life interpenetrate one another, general energy is in flux and reflux, it flowers at every moment, to wither and reflower in endless metamorphoses; the symphony of the colors and the symphony of the murmurs are but little else than the perfume of the inner symphony which issues from the circulation of forces in the continuity of forms. (p. xxxii)

We must try, especially, to restore [to man's gestures, particularly in art] their dynamic character, that unbroken germination of nascent forces engendered by the ceaseless play of the forces of the past on the forces of the present. Every man, every act, every work, is a musician or an instrument in an orchestra. (p. xxxix)

At the end of the fourth volume of the *History* there is a particularly suggestive paragraph:

I have finished the History of Art, which is the history of man; I have listened with gratitude to all the voices which, for ten thousand years, man has used in order to speak to me. . . . I shall die. Men live. I believe in them. Their adventure will come to an end only with the adventure of the earth, and, when the earth is dead, it will perhaps continue elsewhere. It is only a moment of it I have recounted in this book. But every living moment contains the whole of life. Whoever participates with confidence in the adventure of man has his portion of immortality. (IV, p. 496)

This one passage is shot through with a multiplicity of ideas that possess affinities with ones professed by Faulkner. Faulkner frequently insisted on art as the history, the record, of man, the sign, as he puts it, that "Kilroy was here" (e.g. *Lion,* pp. 106 and 202). In the Nobel Prize Acceptance Speech he echoes Faure when he evokes man's "puny inexhaustible voice" as a token of his endurance[32]—though, it must be admitted, he considered it a lesser entity than man's "soul," which is the sign of his capacity "to prevail." Faulkner believed passionately in mankind's immortality, as the Nobel Prize Speech and other later utterances testify. Faure says that "every living moment contains the whole of life." This deceptively simple assertion would have commanded Faulkner's agreement. In saying this I do not intend to imply that in sum Faulkner's concepts of time lack complexities; indeed, on the contrary, they are pregnant with them, but in an essay of the present sort it is, I trust, sufficient to remember what he told Bouvard: " 'I agree pretty much with Bergson's theory. . . . There is only the present moment, in which I include both the past and the future, and that is eternity.' " Finally, it is evident from *Lion in the Garden* that Faulkner believed that the man "who writes the books and composes the music and paints the pictures" has his "proof," his portion, of immortality (p. 103). (Some of these conceptions of the artist and of mankind are also prominently displayed in *A Modern Book of Criticisms;* for example, just as Faulkner proclaimed at Stockholm that art is one of the "pillars" of mankind, Friedrich Hebbel has an aphorism which reads, "Art is the conscience of mankind" [p.42].)

Robinson's *The Mind in the Making* (1921) is first and foremost a polemical book advocating a radical empiricism, even scepticism. It urges that we examine very minutely the ideas we inherit in order to see if there exists some better, more rational approach to the dilemmas which face us. Thus it is fitting that H. G. Wells (two of whose books, one being *The Outline of History,* were on Faulkner's shelves) should contribute an Introduction to the British edition. Robinson traces the development of the mind from so-called primitive man onwards to show how man has acquired—and acquires—the ideas, many of them fallacious, which he takes to his heart. A by-product of this analysis forms the other main theme of the book: man's intellectual history. In a sense, it is a popular history of ideas from the earliest times to the first quarter of the twentieth century.

Amongst the numerous ideas thus ransacked there are several that exhibit a kinship with ones propounded by Faulkner. For example, Robinson quotes from G. Stanley Hall a notion of time we have already observed endorsed by Faulkner: "True greatness," says Hall, "consists solely in seeing everything, past, future or afar, in terms of Here and Now, or in the power of 'presentification.' "[33] In other words, Robinson refers to many thinkers, both ancient and modern, that Faulkner almost certainly knew. He commends Bergson's views on the memory (p.50), discusses Freud's work on "the 'free association of ideas' " (p. 53), quotes Walter Lippman on modern man's "responsibility" (p. 227), summarizes the ideas of Plato (pp. 129–133), and mentions such figures as H. G. Wells, James Branch Cabell, and Ellis.

Moreover, it is conceivable that *The Mind in the Making* introduced Faulkner to certain minds; it definitely possesses the capacity to have done so, for Robinson offers—I give but few examples—the following: a précis each of St. Anselm's and Descartes' ideas of God (pp. 125–126); a discussion of the cosmology and metaphysics of Democritus (pp. 127–129); a resumé of Aristotle's most prominent theories (pp. 133–137); and he mentions briefly the work of Hobbes, of Keynes, of Tawney and G. D. H. Cole, and of Dewey, Russell and Hegel.

In sum, to oversimplify, what Lewisohn's anthology does for criticism and aesthetics, Robinson's book does for philosophy and social thought; in effect, both books could be viewed, I suppose, as products of the American

Progressive movement. By this I am not at all suggesting that Faulkner himself was a Progressive, adhering to a monolithic structure of ideas (not that the movement was monolithic); I mean, rather, to show that he was abreast of at least one of the main currents of intellectual opinion running through the time of his youth and early manhood. Also, in Faulkner's own and in the age's intellectual ferment few ideas remained static and affixed to any particular point of origin or appropriation. In Faulkner's case they were matured, refined, and ultimately often transmuted into fiction: a process, albeit of major importance, for the most part regrettably beyond the scope of this paper. And if we look at the age we find other figures who both contributed to and garnered from its stock of ideas. One of these was the elderly Henry Adams of *The Education*, a patrician anti-slaver who with wit and urbanity had always made himself more or less at ease near, though not in, the seats of political, even business, power. *The Education of Henry Adams* (privately printed 1907, pub. 1918), the final Stone purchase to be considered here, is both fascinating in its own right because, amongst innumerable other reasons, we witness in it a sensitive man's conscious reflections on his intellectual debts, and because in relating it to Faulkner we can observe the further flight, occasionally undeviated, of ideas with which we are familiar.

To posit any affinity between Faulkner—Southern, almost obsessively private, subject to accusations of vulgarity—and Adams may at first seem strange. But it might well be the case that Adams' autobiography, precisely *due* to the disparities between the two men, could have assumed a special revelatory character for a youngster from Mississippi, and thus have furnished him with material for his fiction. For example, he could have learnt how Harvard College, which is featured in *The Sound and the Fury* (1929), might impinge on the consciousness of one of its Southern students;[34] and is not something like the following embodied in and dramatised by Joanna Burden of *Light in August* (1932), that scion of a Northern, Puritan and abolitionist family: "The Puritan thought his thought higher and his moral standards better . . . he inherited dogma and *a priori* thought from the beginning of time; and he scarcely needed a violent reaction like anti-slavery politics to sweep him back into Puritanism with a violence as great as that of a religious war" (p. 26).

From other standpoints the two authors draw nearer to one another. Faulkner was fond of Swinburne's poetry; Adams had enjoyed the cascade of the poet's talk and verse during Swinburne's prime (pp. 140–142). And they both worried ambiguously over Progress, technological progress. Faulkner, in real life as well as within his fiction, had a great admiration for the early motor car and the aeroplane. Yet, at the same time, he mourned the passing of the wilderness before the onslaught of technology *(Go Down, Moses)* and the dehumanizing power of 'planes over the people who flew them *(Pylon,* 1935). His last book *The Reivers* (1962), can actually be interpreted, simultaneously, as an elegy for lost courtliness in the days of innocence and slow gracious living and as a eulogy to the new automobile (the car's movements are what propel the rambling plot; and remember how lovingly Faulkner described it[35]) which in time, as Faulkner realized, would destroy that gracious living. Adams, born "with better cards" than almost anyone of his generation for life's "game of chance" (p. 4), became increasingly restive and alienated, and "failed" to adjust to the changing world, his *Education* intended to serve as a record of that failure. Yet, in venture after diverse venture, instead of condemning or standing apart from the wholesale change he regarded, Adams exercised his marked conceptual gifts in an effort to understand it and adjust to it, for paradoxically, he positively revered change. At one point he says of himself "what he valued most was Motion, and . . . what attracted his mind was Change" (p. 231).

In this attraction Adams was followed by Faulkner. In *The Town* (1957) he gives Gavin Stevens great faith in (capitalized) Motion: "Nothing cannot remain anywhere . . . Nothing steadily and perennially full of perennially now and perennially renewed anguishes for me to measure my stature against whenever I need reassurance that I also am Motion."[36] And Gavin needs this reassurance because to Faulkner, as he insisted publicly, *life* is Motion. "Since people exist only in life, they must devote their time simply to being alive. Life is motion and is concerned with what makes man move."[37] Clearly, we have arrived once again at a notion of dynamism, and for Adams this took the form of constructing a "Dynamic Theory of History."

It is probable that Faulkner, in Adams' phrase, obtained "much of education" from the older man's researches. Adams was greatly—and suitably— moved by the unadorned force of the dynamos at the Great Exposition of 1900. In seeking for some other force with which that of the dynamo could be conpared he hit upon or, rather, fell back before, the Virgin. What seemed true of them both was that they are "supersensual"; the results of their operation can be seen in industry (the dynamo) or in the windows of Chartres (the Virgin), but the actual force they radiate is mysterious, unseen, invisible, and must be inferred (pp. 381–383). When Adams began to investigate the nature of the Virgin's power he found that it derived to some extent from that of Venus, who "was reproduction—the greatest and most mysterious of all energies; all she needed was to be fecund" (p. 384). We have only to think of Dewey

Dell in *As I Lay Dying* (1930) to know that Faulkner too was drawn to this force. Or perhaps Lena Grove of *Light in August* is more significant; for Lena's story forms a quite deliberate counterpoint to that of Joe Christmas. Though ultimately a victim, Joe to some degree is a paragon of the modern world as he thrusts down the same "corridor" for fifteen years, an alien, his fingers perpetually over "frictionsmooth" lunch counters. He can practically be said to symbolize modern force and, as such, he lies at a far pole from Lena. Lena, she simply needs to be fecund, she simply *is* and, as Hightower envisions, her offspring will people the good earth. . . .

Plunging further, Adams' quest for the secret of the Virgin grew more theological. He learnt from Aquinas (p. 428) and embraced the unconscious pantheism of the schools—"God as actual; continuous movement, universal cause, and interchangeable force" (p. 429)—but still yearned for a "Unity" more modern than pantheism. For him it seemed at first that the kinetic theory of gases provided such a Unity; but, after closer examination, this hypothesis —which states that all things can be reduced to millions of atoms—does not, Adams insists, speak of Unity at all, but of Multiplicity. Unity and Multiplicity, "the two things were the same, all forms of being shifting phases of motion" (p. 431), a truly Faure-like, Bergsonian judgement.

Adams, thrown in again on himself, turned to philosophy and then to psychology—for which, as he says, Harvard was a focus (p. 432). Lost in his own labryinth, Quentin Compson, at Harvard in 1910, has only one course of study picked out for him by Faulkner: psychology[38]—perhaps because, along with any influence Adams might have had, Faulkner knew that version of dynamism—epitomised by the "stream of consciousness'—propagated by William James, who also died in 1910. This last is pure speculation, perhaps demonstrating the possible pitfalls lying in this paper's approach. But I think Faulkner would have agreed with Adams' ultimate conclusion: thought itself, he says, is "one continuous force" (p. 434). Faulkner was not a backwoodsman somehow stumbling, unsurely, onto "eternal verities." To totally dismiss this view and substitute for it a more realistic portrait, Faulkner's critics, in order to feel the force, at the risk of a few falls, must seek the links in the continuity.

1. *Lion in the Garden: Interviews with William Faulkner 1926–1962,* ed. James B. Meriwether and Michael Millgate (New York: Random House, 1968), pp. 8, 59, 64, 134 and many others. All subsequent page references given for Faulkner's public comments are to this book unless otherwise indicated.

2. Letter to the present writer, 1 December 1966.

3. Minneapolis: University of Minnesota Press, 1954, p. 18.

4. See Stone's letter to Louis Cochran in James B. Meriwether, "Early Notices of Faulkner by Phil Stone and Louis Cochran," *Mississippi Quarterly,* XVII (Summer 1964), 141.

5. Charlottesville: University of Virginia Press, 1964, p. 7. Another instance of how this kind of question is bedeviled by confused thinking is however provided by Blotner himself. He insists that books Faulkner signed were amongst his favourites, a facile assumption.

6. Ed. Carvel Collins (Boston: Atlantic-Little, Brown, 1962), p. 86. Subsequent page references to the early writings are to this edition.

7. First English-language version published in Edinburgh in 1871. Edition commonly used in the 'twenties was translated in four volumes by H. Van Laun (London: Chatto and Windus, 1920).

8. "William Faulkner's Apprenticeship," *Tulane Studies in English,* XII (1962), 113–156.

9. Unpublished dissertation, "Bergsonian Dynamism in the Writings of William Faulkner" (Tulane, 1962).

10. A *Catalogue,* p. 6. All the books referred to in this paper as being in the *Catalogue* are listed either alphabetically by author in the Appendix or alphabetically by author under the relevant national literature in the Catalogue itself.

11. New York: Knopf, 1919. Van Wyck Brooks makes much the same point in "America's Coming-of-age" (1915), reprinted in *Three Essays on America* (New York: Dutton, 1934) pp. 22–24.

12. See my essay, "Another Psychologist, a Physiologist and William Faulkner," to be published in a forthcoming issue of *Ariel: A Review of International English Literature.*

13. See my essay "Some Notes on Faulkner's Reading," in the British *Journal of American Studies,* IV (July 1970), 100–105.

14. London: Cape, 1921, p. 48. All subsequent page references are to this edition.

15. Emily Whitehurst Stone, "How a Writer Finds His Material," *Harper's Magazine,* CCXXXI (November 1965), 58.

16. *Lion in the Garden,* p. 56. Cf. his remarks on "scientific aesthetics" in *Early Prose and Poetry,* p. 74.

17. *Faulkner at West Point,* ed. Joseph L. Fant and Robert Ashley (New York: Random House, 1964), p. 76.

18. See John W. Hunt, *William Faulkner: Art in Theological Tension* (Syracuse: Syracuse University Press, 1965), pp. 151–155. For a good general study of Plato's appeal to Southern writers see Frank Baldanza, "Plato in Dixie," *Georgia Review,* XII (1958), 151–167.

19. *The Novels of William Faulkner: A Critical Interpretation* (Baton Rouge: Louisiana State University Press, 1964), p. 123.

20. Volume IV of *The Works of Voltaire: A Contemporary Version,* trans. William H. Fleming (Akron: The Saint Hubert Guild, 1910).

21. See Basso, "William Faulkner: Man and Writer," *Saturday Review,* XLV (July 28, 1962), 11–14. Also, Michael Millgate, *The Achievement of William Faulkner* (London: Constable, 1966), p. 13.

22. *A Modern Book of Criticisms* (New York: Modern Library, 1919), p. 7. All page references are to this edition.

23. *A Modern Book,* pp. 104–105; cf. *Faulkner at West Point,* p. 54.

24. See Richard Hughes, "Faulkner and Bennett," *Encounter,* XXI (1963), 59–61.

25. See, for example, *Early Prose,* pp. 114–116.

26. "Sahara of the Bozart," *Prejudices: Second Series* (New York: Knopf, 1920), pp. 136–154; cf. *"The South Rebels Again,"* Chicago *Sunday Tribune,* 7 December 1924; reprinted in *The Bathtub Hoax and Other Blasts and Bravos. . . . ,* ed. Robert McHugh (New York: Knopf, 1958), pp. 249–254.

27. See the Appendix—the short story schedule—to James B. Meriwether's *The Literary Career of William Faulkner: A Bibliographical Study* (Princeton: Princeton University Library, 1961).

For Angoff's remarks see his *H. L. Mencken: A Portrait from Memory* (New York: Thomas Yoseloff, 1956), pp. 107–109.

28. *Faulkner in the University,* ed. Frederick L. Gwynn and Joseph L. Blotner (New York: Vintage, 1965), p. 55.

29. Faure, *History of Art,* I (London: John Lane, New York: Harper, 1921), ix. Page references in the text are to this volume unless otherwise indicated.

30. *Havelock Ellis: In appreciation by E. Faure et al,* ed. J. Ishill (Berkeley Heights, N. J., 1929).

31. See *The Achievement,* pp. 4 and 20.

32. *Essays, Speeches and Public Letters,* ed. James B. Meriwether (New York: Random House, 1965), p. 120.

33. London: Cape, 1926, p. 14. Note that the author's name *is* James Harvey Robinson, *not* (as the Appendix has it) James Henry Robinson. All other page references are to this edition.

34. *The Education* (New York; Modern Library, 1931), pp. 57–59. (All further page references are to this edition). See Robert M. Slabey, "The 'Romanticism' of *The Sound and the Fury,*" *Mississippi Quarterly,* XVI (Summer 1963), 146–159; Slabey draws a convincing connection between Quentin, the Southerner as Romantic, and Adams' portrait of Robert E. Lee's son.

35. London: Chatto and Windus, 1962, p. 30 especially.

36. *The Town* (London. Chatto and Windus, 1965), p. 121.

37. *Lion in the Garden,* p. 253; see also p. 131.

38. *The Sound and the Fury* (New York: Modern Library, 1951), p. 120.

SOME USES OF FOLK HUMOR
BY FAULKNER

OTIS B. WHEELER

IN 1926, EARLY in his career, Faulkner wrote: "We have one priceless universal trait, we Americans. That trait is our humor.[1] What a pity it is that it is not more prevalent in our art. This characteristic alone, being national and indigenous, could by concentrating our emotional forces inward upon themselves, do for us what English insularity did for English art during the reign of Elizabeth."[2]

This judgment may or may not be true, but true or false, it shows Faulkner's early concern with incorporating in his art that humor which a great many people besides himself have recognized as national and indigenous. How he goes about it is a question best approached through a brief review of the sources and qualities of this native American humor.

Reprinted with permission from *Mississippi Quarterly,* XVII (Spring 1964), 107–122.

The two most important strains are the "Down East" type, identified generally with New England, and the "Frontier" type, identified generally with the Old Southwest—Georgia, Alabama, Tennessee, Arkansas, Missouri, Mississippi, Louisiana, and East Texas. The Down East type is a good deal more civilized than the Frontier type. It is usually couched in the form of stories by or about a sharp trader or a sharp observer of humanity. In the case of Sam Slick the itinerant clockpeddler the central character is both sharp trader and sharp observer—his success as trader grows out of his clear-eyed, even cynical view of humanity. He can sell a clock to anybody, whether he needs it or not, and it is all done, in Sam's words, by a knowledge of "soft sawder" and human nature. The soft sawder is fulsome flattery which gets him welcomed into a house. Then on pretext of needing some place to store a clock until he can pick it up on his way back through the country, he leaves it with the farmer and his wife, all set up and ticking away on the mantlepiece; he walks out secure in the knowledge that the clock is as good as sold for forty dollars—a clock that cost him six dollars and fifty cents. This is where the knowledge of human nature comes in; for, says Sam, "We can do without any article of luxury we never had, but when once obtained, it is not in human nature to surrender it voluntarily." He knows, because he and his partners have sold twelve thousand clocks that way and had to take back only ten.[3]

Another quality of Down East humor, not so consistent in Sam Slick as in some of the other characters, like Lowell's Hosea Biglow, of the *Biglow Papers,* is the use of dialect. The writers are very careful to transcribe from life the actual speech patterns of the class to which the characters belong. We find here too a very careful attention to descriptive detail that gives a further air of reality through the setting.

These traits are to be found as well in Frontier humor, which, if less civilized than Down East, is far more vital and exuberant. To begin with, the society of the Southwest was far more heterogeneous than that of New England, affording material for some wonderfully ludicrous contrasts. One writer described life on the frontier this way:

There is one little town in them diggins which is all sorts of a stirring place. In one day, they recently had two street fights, hung a man, rode three men out of town on a rail, got up a quarter race, a turkey shooting, a gander pulling, a match dog fight, had preaching by a circus rider, who afterwards ran a footrace for apple jack all around, and, as if this was not enough, the judge of the court, after losing his year's salary at single-handed poker, and licking a person who said he didn't understand the game, went out and helped to lynch his grandfather for hog-stealing.[4]

Admittedly this is a bit of a caricature, but one could draw the material for a gusty humor from times far less stirring than these.

In frontier humor certain character types and themes recur. There is the sharp trader, much like the Yankee peddler, but usually even less scrupulous, sometimes just a thief and swindler. The archetypal horse-trader, metamorphosed in our time into the used car salesman of the joke books and cartoons, is an example. An even better example is found in Captain Simon Suggs of Alabama, the leader of a militia company called the Tallapoosa Volunteers, sometimes known as the forty thieves, an outrageous misnomer according to the captain because there were only thirty-nine on the roll. Simon's motto is "It's best to be shifty in a new country," and he illustrates it well as he moves about the frontier, cheating at cards, posing as a land agent, as a rich relative, or as a repentant sinner at a camp meeting, this for the purpose of stealing a collection made to set him up in the preaching business. Appropriately, the Captain sometimes evaluates his experiences in his natural idiom of card sharping: "I come in on nary a pair and won a pile. . . . If them fellers ain't done to a cracklin I'll never bet on two pair agin!"[5] Some of Mark Twain's swindlers, though better known, are in the same vein: Jim Smiley, the man who poured the famous jumping frog full of buckshot; or the King and the Duke in *Huckleberry Finn.* The King even uses Simon's trick of absconding with the camp-meeting collection.

Davy Crockett is famous as a character in frontier humor mostly for the tall stories that cluster about his name. This special type of folk humor uses extreme exaggeration told in a straight-faced, laconic style—for example, the story of Davy's coon-hunt.[6] In this yarn, when Davy identifies himself, in response to a question from the coon high up in the tree, the coon says that he will come down and die without being shot, for he considers himself as good as dead if he is in Davy Crockett's sights.

Another recurrent pattern is the brutal practical joke, always violent, sometimes fatal, and often bawdy and scatalogical. The antics of Sut Lovingood, the "natural born durn fool," best exemplify these qualities. In "Mrs. Yardley's Quilting"[7] Sut recounts with some zest how a terrified horse running through a house broke up a quilting party and led to the death of a woman. The sketch opens with his callous and off-hand remark that he has been helping bury old Mrs. Yardley. Then follows his account of the party, with strong emphasis on the elemental pleasures of the "he's and she's." "Everybody war thar," he notes, "scept the constibil and the suckit-rider, two damn easily-spared pussons." His eulogy of quiltings clearly defines the tone of the gathering: "Quiltings, managed in a moril and sensible way, truly am good things—good fur free drinkin, good fur free eatin, good fur free huggin, good fur free dancin, good fur free fitin, and goodest ov oll fur poperlatin a country fast." When Sut, in jealous pique at being outshone by some of the "town fellers," ties a clothesline of quilts to the saddle horn of one of the tethered horses and then shatters a fence-paling over his croup, the terrified horse joins the party, and Mrs. Yardley is mortally injured.

The story is told by means of the classic framework device, the use of an educated, sophisticated narrator to introduce the low-brow character who then proceeds to tell the story. Like Chaucer, in *The Canterbury Tales,* the author, by saying, or implying, "I'm only writing down what was said" protects himself to some degree from squeamish readers who might object to his frankness.

The framework device also implies that the form of the story has its basis in oral narrative. The men who wrote this humor were men of affairs—lawyers, steamboatmen, journalists, doctors, politicians. Johnson J. Hooper, the author of the Simon Suggs stories, was lawyer, politician, journalist; George Washington Harris, creator of Sut Lovingood, was a steamboat captain, politician, journalist, postmaster, hunter, and inventor. The writing was done in the midst of a busy life and the stories were based on the lie-swapping that went on in barrooms, around rural post-offices, on steamboats, and in any other place where men gathered to drink, whittle, and talk.

So the stories are essentially oral, and when they were introduced into the written tradition, the natural rhythm, the racy diction, the vulgar syntax, supplied a transfusion of new blood that was badly needed at the time in American literature. Mark Twain was, of course, the writer largely responsible for this transfusion. In *Huckleberry Finn,* by removing the traditional framework and by injecting new moral and social perspectives, he brought the oral tale into the serious literary tradition. If, as Hemingway has said, all modern American fiction grows out of *Huckleberry Finn,* then the connection between Faulkner and folk humor is going to be strong. I believe Hemingway was not entirely right, but if he was only partly right, we can expect to find some line of development from frontier humor, through Mark Twain's work, into Faulkner's work.

The influence is less in Faulkner's early work than in the later. It would seem in a general way that as he matured as an artist he came to rely more heavily on the materials and techniques of that humor he wrote of in 1926. Looking at his first novel, *Soldiers' Pay,* one would hardly suspect that Faulkner was capable of the robust humor that appears in the later works. In subject, it is a translation of *The Sun Also Rises* to a small town in Georgia:

the wounded soldier, the frustrated woman, the sterility of lust, the failure of all traditional values. It is Faulkner's attempt to deal with the wasteland theme of the twenties. It lacks the impact of the later books partly because the setting lacks specification—it is a kind of generalized Southern village—and partly because the characters lack the sense of belonging to their native scene, as do the inhabitants of Yoknapatawpha County. Indirectly, this is to say that the sense of the folk, the sense of close-knit community, of lives close to the soil and inextricably knit together, though not always happily, is missing. When this sense is achieved, as it is in most of the Yoknapatawpha stories, it comes in no small part from the expert handling of folk humor.

It would be too neat, as well as inaccurate, to say that Faulkner's talent matured in direct proportion to his reliance on folk humor. Some of the books of the great productive period of 1929–32 show very little specific influence of it: *Sartoris,* or *The Sound and the Fury,* for instance. In *Light in August* it is so general and tenuous as to be almost impossible to demonstrate simply— mostly in the diction and tone of the sections told from the point of view of Byron Bunch. It is slightly evident in *Sanctuary* in the story of Uncle Bud and the three madams or in the activities of Clarence Snopes or in the story of the naive country boys looking for a cheap hotel in Memphis and innocently living in a brothel for two weeks: But all these are narrated by a sophisticated writer, not by a folk character.

A clearer debt to folk materials is found in the main narrative pattern of *As I Lay Dying,* a kind of a tall story—the grotesque, almost unbelievable adventures of the Bundren family in taking the body of Addie, the wife and mother, to Jefferson for burial. Her last wish is to be buried in Jefferson, and in spite of flood, fire, upset, and the hastening corruption of the body they doggedly make their way to the town, finally accompanied by a spiral of buzzards. The husband shares some of the qualities of the "natural born durn fool," on the pattern of Sut Lovingood. None of the catastrophes touch him noticeably, any more than the death of his wife has, and at the end of the book he returns to the wagon leading a "duck-shaped" woman from whom he has borrowed a shovel to dig his wife's grave, and says to the children, "Meet Miz Bundren." Dewey Dell's adventures with the drug store clerk also smack of Southwestern humor. However, the dominant and remarkable qualities of the book—that is, the emotional and psychological insights achieved through interior monologue and shifting point of view—may very well obscure the folk humor elements.

Another novel following the tall story pattern is *Old Man,*[8] about a convict from Parchman prison farm in the great flood of 1927. Two convicts are ordered to take a skiff up a flooded bayou and rescue a woman on a cypress snag and a man on the roof of a cotton house. When the two are thrown from the skiff by the current, only one is rescued; the other is presumed drowned and is accordingly marked off the prison books. But actually he has regained the skiff and rescued the woman before the current has carried him out into the main channel of the river. With the woman, he rides the flood to New Orleans, fighting moccasins and alligators, and delivering her baby on the way. When the flood recedes, he doggedly works his way back up the river, still with the skiff and woman and baby, and seven weeks from the time he stepped into the boat, he pulls it up to the levee where he started, surrenders to a deputy sheriff, and says laconically, "Yonder's your boat, and here's the woman. But I never did find that bastard on the cotton house."[9] As a reward he has ten years added to his sentence on a charge of attempted escape.

That Faulkner was experimenting with folk humor techniques is evident from a short story of the mid-thirties called "Black Music"; it is a curious adaption of these techniques for the purpose of psychological portraiture. In it we find a one-time New Yorker, formerly an employee of an architectural firm, talking somewhat like a character in a Sut Lovingood yarn. The ex-architect, who is introduced by means of the framework device, is a beach-comber on a Caribbean island; twenty-five years earlier he had been engaged by a rich woman to remodel a Virginia farm into a country estate, a job which he found distasteful. On the train taking him from New York down to the farm he fell and bumped his head, was given some whiskey as a tonic, and suddenly believed himself transmuted into a faun. He got more whiskey, bought himself a tin whistle in imitation of the pipes of Pan, took off his clothes, and proceeded on his mission which now was to discourage the rich woman from desecrating the natural beauty of the farm. Carrying his portfolio, his whiskey, and his whistle, he let a mad bull out of its pen and chased the woman into the bull's pasture. Here is his version of what followed:

"She kicked off her slippers (I nigh broke my neck over one of them) so she could run better, and I could hear her going whump whump whump inside, like a dray horse, and when she would begin to slow up a little I would let out another toot on the whistle and off she would go again.

"I couldn't keep up with her carrying that portfolio and trying to blow on that whistle too; seemed like I never would get the hang of it somehow. But maybe that was because I had to start trying so quick, before I had time to kind of practice up, and running all the time too. So I threw the portfolio away and then I caught up with her where she was standing with her back against the tree, and that bull running around and around the tree, not bothering her, just running around the tree, making a right smart of fuss, and her leaning there whispering [her husband's name] 'Carleton' 'Carleton' like she was afraid she'd wake him up."[10]

This clearly has the flavor of the oral tale of frontier humor: the situation of the brutal joke, the framework device to introduce the narrator, the speech rhythm, syntax, and idiom. Curiously, the speech rhythm, syntax, and idiom are not those of a Manhattanite or even a Caribbean beachcomber, but of a southern hillbilly. It is almost Sut Lovingood in the twentieth century, except for the use of classical mythology as a source of allusion and symbolism.

When these techniques of the oral tale are brought back to Mississippi in a story called "Was" we find frontier humor in an almost pure form. It is a story of the back-country planter aristocracy which ought to give the *coup de grace* to the moonlight and magnolias myth of antebellum Southern life. It concerns the hunt for a slave, the half-brother of his master, who is always running away to see his girl on the neighboring plantation, where the old-maid mistress lies in wait to trap the runaway's master into matrimony when he comes after his property. The story, though narrated in the third person is told from the point of view of a nine-year-old boy who goes with his uncle to bring home the runaway. Here is the beginning.

When Cass Edmonds and Uncle Buck ran back to the house from discovering that Tomey's Turl had run again, they heard Uncle Buddy cursing and bellowing in the kitchen, then the fox and the dogs came out of the kitchen and crossed the hall into the dogs' room, then they saw them cross the hall again into Uncle Buddy's room and heard them run through Uncle Buddy's room into the kitchen again and this time it sounded like the whole kitchen chimney had come down and Uncle Buddy bellowing like a steamboat blowing, and this time the fox and the dogs and five or six sticks of firewood all came out of the kitchen together with Uncle Buddy in the middle of them hitting at everything in sight with another stick. It was a good race.

When Cass and Uncle Buck ran into their room to get Uncle Buck's necktie the fox had treed behind the clock on the mantel. Uncle Buck got the necktie from the drawer and kicked the dogs off and lifted the fox down by the scruff of the neck and shoved it back into the crate under the bed and they went into the kitchen where Uncle Buddy was picking the breakfast up out of the ashes and wiping it off with his apron.[11]

After breakfast they make their way to the neighboring plantation and are put off in one way or another by Mister Hubert, the old maid's brother, who is eager to give his sister every chance. After several toddies, dinner, and a nap, there follows an abortive hunt for the runaway, in which Uncle Buck is run over by the Negro and falls on the whiskey bottle in his hip pocket. Naturally this ends the hunt for the night. Uncle and nephew go back to the house, now dark, to sleep. Uncle Buck chooses a room as far as possible from the one where he believes Miss Sophonsiba to be sleeping, only to realize too late that he has been outfoxed. As he pulls off his trousers and rolls into bed, Miss Sophonsiba sits up on the other side and starts to scream. When things have quieted somewhat her brother reads the verdict:

"Well, Filus, She's got you at last. . . . You come into bear-country of your own free will and accord. All right; You were a grown man and you knew it was bearcountry and you knew the way back out like you knew the way in and you had your chance to take it. But no. You had to crawl into the den and lay down by the bear. And whether you did or didn't know the bear was in it don't make any difference. So if you got back out of that den without even a claw-mark on you, I would not only be unreasonable, I'd be a damned fool. After all, I'd like a little peace and quiet and freedom myself, now I got a chance for it. Yes. sir. She's got you, Filus, and you know it. You run a hard race and you run a good one, but you skun the henhouse one time too many."[12]

The situation is finally resolved by a poker game between Uncle Buddy and Mister Hubert, in which the loser has to take Miss Sophonsiba. Hubert loses, and the brothers return to a scene almost exactly like the one with which the story opened.

This story is probably the nearest thing to pure frontier humor that Faulkner has written, although he has slightly modified the traditional form precisely as Mark Twain did in *Huckleberry Finn*—has eliminated the framework device and used a boy as the point of view from which the reader sees the action. Though it is told in the third person rather than in the first, like *Huckleberry Finn,* still the style is that of a boy rather than of a mature and sophisticated person. In terms of material it is largely high jinks, more for the fun of it than for social criticism. But it shows his mastery of the method which served him well when he came to chronicle the Snopes family, a chronicle of many subtle perspectives and clear social vision.

The saga of the Snopeses began with isolated stories about Flem Snopes and his kin in the little crossroads settlement of Frenchman's Bend. The Snopeses are like cockroaches; no one knows where they come from but every month or so a new one turns up. They are ignorant, vicious, rapacious, running the gamut from preternatural shrewdness to idiocy. Wherever they go, they defile, degrade, and take over.

By 1940 the doings of the Snopeses in Frenchman's Bend had become a novel, *The Hamlet,* fusing a number of the original stories into a coherent narrative covering the time from the arrival of the first Snopes until they are ready, having devoured the village, to move on the town of Jefferson. *The Town,* 1957, also utilizes earlier stories and deals with Flem Snopes' quest for wealth and respectability. *The Mansion,* 1959, chronicles Flem's empty triumph and his death at the hands of another Snopes whom he has betrayed.

The dedicatory note of *The Town* reads, "To Phil Stone: he did half the laughing for thirty years." The importance of this note is not in the sentiment for a friend, but in the attitude toward the material. He could dedicate to Stone because Stone shared his feelings that however frightful the antics of the Snopeses, there was also a humorous dimension to them.

Actually the Snopes stories are the chief repository of frontier humor in Faulkner's work. The earliest one is a classic horse-trading story, in which Ab Snopes, the father of the clan, gets shaved by Pat Stamper, the greatest horse-trader those parts have ever seen. It is narrated by V. K. Ratliff, the witty, shrewd, itinerant sewing machine agent, and it follows the pattern of the swindler swindled. Ab starts out with a fair mule, a gaunt, broken-down horse, and twenty-four dollars. He sets a bent fish-hook under the skin of the horse's withers to make it act lively when he slaps the reins. He trades this team to Pat for a team of mules which Pat has doped just enough so that Ab gets to town with them before they collapse. When Ab finally gets them back to Pat's place and asks for his original team, Pat says he has sold the horse, but brings out Ab's mule with a fat black horse and offers him this team for the twenty-four dollars. Ab has to take it in order to get his wagon back home; but it rains on the way, the paint washes off the black horse, Ab discovers a bicycle tire valve set in the horse's hide, and when he lets the air out of him, it is the same gaunt bay that he left home with.

Flem Snopes is a better horse trader than his father, for in a story called "Spotted Horses," without admitting to ownership of them he sells a string of wild Texas ponies to his neighbors. When the story first appeared in *Scribner's Magazine* in 1931 the editors noted its kinship with frontier humor. The humorous climax, when one of the new owners enters the barn-lot to try to catch his horse, sounds very much like Sut Lovingood's account of Mrs. Yardley's quilting. Ratliff, again, is the narrator.

I was in my room in my underclothes, with one sock on and one sock in my hand leaning out the window when the commotion busted out, when I heard something run into the melodeon in the hall; it sounded like a railroad engine. Then the door to my room come sailing in like when you throw a tin bucket top into the wind and I looked over my shoulder and see something that looked like a fourteen-foot pinwheel a-blaring its eyes at me. It had to blare them fast, because I was already done jumped out the window.

I reckon it was anxious, too. I reckon it hadn't never seen barbed wire or shelled corn before, but I know it hadn't ever seen underclothes before, or maybe it was a sewing machine agent it hadn't never seen. Anyway, it whirled and turned to run back up the hall and outen the house, when it met Eck Snopes and that boy just coming in, carrying a rope. It swirled again and run down the hall and out the back door just in time to meet Mrs. Littlejohn. She had just gathered up the clothes she had washed, and she was coming onto the back porch with a armful of washing in one hand and a scrubbingboard in the other, when the horse skidded up to her, trying to stop and swirl again. It never taken Mrs. Littlejohn no time atall.

"Git outen here you son," she says. She hit it across the face with the scrubbing board; that ere scrubbing board split as neat as ere a axe could have done it, and when the horse swirled to run back up the hall, she hit it again with what was left of the scrubbing board not on the head this time. "And stay out," she says.

Eck and that boy was half-way down the hall by this time. I reckon that horse looked like a pinwheel to Eck too. "Get to hell outen here, Ad," Eck says. Only there wasn't time. Eck dropped flat on his face, but the boy never moved. . . . That horse swoared over his head without touching a hair. I saw that, because I was just coming back up the front steps, still carrying that ere sock and still in my underclothes, when the horse come onto the porch again. It taken one look at me and swirled again and run to the end of the porch and jumped the bannisters and the lot-fence like a hen-hawk and lit in the lot running and went out the gate again and jumped eight or ten upsidedown wagons and went on down the road. It was a full moon then. Mrs Armstid was still setting in the wagon like she had done been carved outen wood and left there and forgot.[13]

With wagons, houses, and barns wrecked, and two men nearly dead, nobody but the reader holds it against Flem. In fact, there seems to be a grudging admiration on the part of the victims for anyone who can skin them in a trade. As I. O. Snopes says to the assembled loafers in the front of the store the next day, "You boys might just as well quit trying. You can't get ahead of Flem. You can't touch him. Ain't he a sight now?" And Ratliff adds, "I be dog if he ain't. If I had brung a herd of wild cattymounts into town and sold them to my neighbors and kin folks, they would have lynched me. Yes. sir."[14]

Even Ratliff, who has not bought a horse, ultimately finds himself over-matched when he tries to swindle Flem out of some property where Ratliff and two friends have discovered a small amount of buried money—because he believes there is more buried there. They catch on after they have bought the otherwise worthless property that Flem has buried the money there for them to find.

Davy Crockett and Mike Fink were the subjects of tall stories of superhuman accomplishments because they were folk heroes. A rascal of Flem's dimensions may be offensive to the cultivated mind but to the folk he is a kind of hero. And, sure enough, Flem Snopes becomes the subject of a tall story in which he goes to Hell and beats Satan at a trade. This again is told by Ratliff, but in a curious revery sequence in *The Hamlet*. This bargaining with the Devil suggests a kinship both to the Faust legend, and to Benet's *The Devil and Daniel Webster,* both of which grow out of folklore.

In the Snopes chronicles there are many other specific stories that grow out of folk humor: "Mule in the Yard," in which a crazy mule, a flock of chickens, and two half-crazy old women are all mixed up in a chase which results in the house being burned down; or "Centaur in Brass," which is in part a cuckoldry story involving another hilarious chase; or the story of Montgomery Ward Snopes running a brothel in the back room of a YMCA canteen. But to go into these would only delay getting to another question which is probably more important, namely, how does Faulkner modify and adapt his borrowings from the folk humor tradition for more serious purposes within the formal literary tradition?

First, let us clarify certain of Faulkner's attitudes. He despised Snopesism; he saw it as the force of greed and rapacity which destroys morality and decency wherever it comes in contact with them. In general it is more of a threat to the 'haves' than to the 'have-nots' because the Snopeses are after the possessions and the status of the 'haves.' But whatever its objects, Snopesism could not destroy if its antagonists were not decadent or weak or foolish. For weakness Faulkner has great compassion, but for decadence and foolishness he has the lash of humor. This is the first and most obvious way that folk humor is used to comment on the human comedy. Often there is a certain justice in Flem's fleecing those sheep who stand waiting for it or in swindling those who have larceny in their own hearts.

But though individual episodes may have this aspect of justification by humor, Flem's total career is pretty frightening—an idea pointed up by Ratliff's curious revery about Flem's besting Satan and taking over Hell. Flem is hero of a tall story, but he is demonic rather than benign. To this frightening element, the other humorous qualities of the Snopes stories stand in bright contrast; they set it off in sharp relief. This is a second way in which Faulkner is using folk humor.

A third way is easy to illustrate but not so easy to name. The excerpt above from "Spotted Horses" was taken from the original magazine version. When he incorporated the story into *The Hamlet* Faulkner adopted a third-person omniscient point of view and expanded it to roughly three times the original length. It will be instructive, I believe, to compare the corresponding portion of *The Hamlet* with the excerpt from the magazine story. Here is the later version:

They saw the horse the Texan had given them whirl and dash back and rush through the gate into Mrs. Littlejohn's yard and run back up the front steps and crash once on the wooden veranda and vanish through the front door. Eck and the boy ran up onto the veranda. A lamp sat on a table just inside the door. In its mellow light they saw the horse fill the long hallway like a pinwheel, gaudy, furious and thunderous. A little further down the hall there was a varnished yellow melodeon. The horse crashed into it; it produced a single note, almost a chord, in bass, resonant and grave, of deep and sober astonishment; the horse with its monstrous and antic shadow whirled again and vanished through another door. It was a bedroom; Ratliff, in his under-clothes and one sock and with the other sock in his hand and his back to the door, was leaning out the open window facing the lane, the lot. He looked back over his shoulder. For an instant he and the horse glared at one another. Then he sprang through the window as the horse backed out of the room and into the hall again and whirled and saw Eck and the little boy just entering the front door, Eck still carrying his rope. It whirled again and rushed on down the hall and onto the back porch just as Mrs. Littlejohn, carrying an armful of clothes from the line and the washboard, mounted the steps.

"Get out of here you son of a bitch," she said. She struck with the washboard; it divided neatly on the long mad face and the horse whirled and rushed back up the hall, where Eck and the boy stood.

"Get the hell out of here, Wall!" Eck roared. He dropped to the floor, covering his head with his arms. The boy did not move, and for the third time the horse soared above the unwinking eyes and the unbowed and untouched head and onto the front veranda again just as Ratliff, still carrying the sock, ran around the corner of the house and up the steps. The horse whirled without breaking or pausing. It galloped to the end of the veranda and took the railing and soared outward, hobgoblin and floating, in the moon. It landed in the lot still running and crossed the lot and galloped through the wrecked gate and among the overturned wagons and the still intact one in which Henry's wife still sat, and on down the lane and into the road.[15]

Though the revision is certainly not written in the baroque style of *Absalom, Absalom!* its style is clearly more elevated, more poetic than that of the original. A certain fundamental tension exists between the sonorous gravity of the style and the violent slapstick tone of the material. In the original version the horse crashing into the melodeon sounded like a railroad engine. The revision says that the melodeon, when the horse crashed into it, "produced a single note, almost a chord, in bass, resonant and grave, of deep and sober astonishment." The first version describes the horse's final escape thus: "It run to the end of the porch and jumped the bannisters and the lot-fence like a hen-hawk and lit in the lot running. . . ." The revision says, "It galloped to the end of the veranda and took the railing and soared outward, hobgoblin and floating, in the moon. It landed still running. . . ." These changes in style involve changes in metaphor which in turn produce a certain unreal and dream-like quality in the episode. Where a vital, violent, and low-brow humor is the dominant quality of the first version, the bizarre and grotesque are more the qualities of the second, deriving largely from the tension between style and material. What Faulkner has done here then, and I believe it could be demonstrated by numerous other excerpts, is to take his materials from the folk humor tradition but to treat them in a sophisticated style, thus simultaneously suggesting two perspectives on the action and producing this quality that I have called, perhaps not very satisfactorily, the grotesque.

A fourth use of folk humor by Faulkner is found in his manipulation of the point of view. This is not as well and consciously done in *The Hamlet* or *The Mansion* as it is in *The Town*. The latter book is ostensibly narrated by three persons: Chick Mallison, Gavin Stevens, and V. K. Ratliff. Through more or less regular alternation of narrators the events of the novel are set out, some events being recounted by two or even all three of the narrators. This allows Faulkner to present three different attitudes and perspectives on the material he is dealing with. By means of this device, developed in the great novels such as *The Sound and the Fury, Absalom, Absalom!* and *Light in August,* he simultaneously establishes and compensates for the fact that no single vision of human experience can be objective and complete. In *The Town* it is significant that two of the three point of view characters have close relations to folk humor. The third, in contrast, is almost over-sophisticated.

At the beginning I spoke of the itinerant clock peddler, Sam Slick, as the example in Down East folk humor of the sharp trader and sharp observer of humanity. Ratliff is also an itinerant peddler who makes a sharp trade whenever he can and who functions in the book as the sharp observer of humanity. I think it is more than coincidence that this stereotyped figure of folk humor is so nearly duplicated in Ratliff, for by using such a figure, Faulkner can get the tolerant, amused, disengaged, but penetrating perspective that belongs to such a person. It is Ratliff who understands first and best the real driving force in Flem Snopes—the desire for the appearance of respectability—but he is content to watch the play being played out, waiting for the other characters to understand, all the while commenting for the reader. Thus the character nearest to a folk humor type is at once the most knowing, least anguished, and most informative of the three point of view characters. His view is that life is a rough and grotesque joke, but one at which you might as well laugh.

Chick Mallison, the boy, is a slightly more civilized version of Huckleberry Finn, that nice balance between knowing and naivete that an intelligent twelve-year-old can sometimes maintain. One comment, I think, will show how much like Huck Finn he is. The sheriff has warned the boys in town that if they don't stop stealing watermelons from Ab Snopes' melon patch, the old man will burst a blood vessel and die. The boys refrain, but learn that Snopes' grandsons, Vardaman and Bilbo, give false alarms about the melons just to watch their grandfather get riled up. All the boys in town, says Chick, "would go out and hide behind the fence and watch. We never had seen anybody bust a blood vessel and die and we wanted to be there when it happened to see what it would look like."[16] Chick's knowing naivete provides another view of events complementary to Ratliff's slightly sardonic humor.

Gavin Stevens provides the sophisticated view. Graduate of Harvard, a Heidelburg Ph. D., County Attorney, he nevertheless is unable to observe Snopesism without anguish and indecision and a sense of helplessness. He represents the established class which Snopesism is undermining; he is frantically aware of it and frantically unable to do anything about it. It is not accidental that Faulkner's handling of Stevens' situation often echoes Prufrock: "now only the afternoon remained: the interminable time until a few minutes after half past three, filled with a thousand indecisions which each fierce succeeding harassment would revise."[17] Stevens' vision of Snopesism is primarily horrific—when he has a laugh it is usually at the invitation of Ratliff, and then he laughs only with the bottom part of his face. Snopesism is a horrid creeping fungus with which he is fated to fight, but to which he is doomed to lose.

These three visions, taken together, complete Faulkner's ambivalent picture of the town at once laughable and frightful. As Malcolm Cowley said a good many years ago, "The truth is that Faulkner unites in his work two of the dominant trends in American literature from the beginning: that of the psychological horror story as developed by Hawthorne, Poe, and Stephen Crane, among others; and that of realistic frontier humor, with Mark Twain as its best example. If you imagine Huckleberry Finn living in the House of Usher and telling uproarious stories while the walls crumble about him, that will give you the double quality of Faulkner's work at its best."[18]

1. The matter of humor is a topic of perennial interest to students of Faulkner, having been dealt with in some degree by most of the book-length studies and explored in three separate articles: Cecil D. Eby, "Faulkner and the Southwestern Humorists," *Shenandoah,* XI (Autumn 1959), 13–21; Frank M. Hoadley, "Folk Humor in the Novels of William Faulkner." *Tennessee Folklore Society Bulletin,* XXIII (1957), 75–82; and Thomas M. Inge, "William Faulkner and George Washington Harris: In the Tradition of Southwestern Humor," *Tennessee Studies in Literature,* VII (1962), 47–59.

2. John Arthos, "Ritual and Humor in the Writing of William Faulkner," *Accent,* IX (August 1948), 21.

3. Walter Blair, ed., *Native American Humor* (New York, 1937), pp. 229–32.

4. *Ibid.,* p. 69.

5. *Ibid.,* pp. 323–5.

6. Walter Blair, Theodore Hornberger, and Randall Stewart, eds., *The Literature of the United States,* rev. ed., 2 vols. (New York, 1953), II, 273.

7. *Ibid.,* pp. 285 ff.

8. Not all readers will want to regard *Old Man* as a separate novel. I do so, without going into the merits of the cause, because Faulkner himself sanctioned an edition which extricates *Old Man* from *The Wild Palms* (New York, 1954).

9. *Ibid.,* p. 228.

10. *Doctor Martino and Other Stories* (New York, 1934), p. 284.

11. *The Portable Faulkner,* p. 105.

12. *Ibid.,* p. 122.

13. *Scribners Magazine,* LXXXIX (June 1931), 591–2.

14. *Ibid.,* p. 597.

15. *The Portable Faulkner,* pp. 405–6.

16. *The Town* (New York, 1957), p. 131.

17. *Ibid.,* p. 206.

18. Malcolm Cowley, "William Faulkner's Human Comedy," *New York Times Book Review* (October 29, 1944), p. 4.

I. The Work: Studies of the Work as a Whole

FAULKNER'S MYTHOLOGY

GEORGE MARION O'DONNELL

1

WILLIAM FAULKNER IS really a traditional moralist, in the best sense. One principle holds together his thirteen books of prose—including his new novel, *The Wild Palms*—giving his work unity and giving it, at times, the significance that belongs to great myth. That principle is the Southern social-economic-ethical tradition which Mr. Faulkner possesses naturally, as a part of his sensibility.

However, Mr. Faulkner is a traditional man in a modern South. All around him the antitraditional forces are at work; and he lives among evidences of their past activity. He could not fail to be aware of them. It is not strange, then, that his novels are, primarily, a series of related myths (or aspects of a single myth) built around the conflict between traditionalism and the antitraditional modern world in which it is immersed.

In a rearrangement of the novels, say for a collected edition, *The Unvanquished* might well stand first; for the action occurs earlier, historically, than in any other of the books, and it objectifies, in the essential terms of Mr. Faulkner's mythology, the central dramatic tension of his work. On one side of the conflict there are the Sartorises, recognizable human beings who act traditionally. Against them the invading Northern armies, and their diversified allies in the reconstruction era, wage open war, aiming to make the traditional actions of the Sartorises impossible.

The invaders are unable to cope with the Sartorises; but their invasion provides another antagonist with an occasion within which his special anti-Sartoris talent makes him singularly powerful. This antagonist is the landless poor-white horse trader, Ab Snopes; his special talent is his low cunning as an *entrepreneur*. He acts without regard for the legitimacy of his means; he has

Reprinted with permission from *The Kenyon Review,* Summer, 1939, pp. 285–99.

no ethical code. In the crisis brought about by the war, he is enabled to use a member of the Sartoris family for his own advantage because, for the first time, he can be useful to the Sartorises. Moreover, he is enabled to make this Sartoris (Mrs. Rosa Millard) betray herself into an act of self-interest such as his, and to cause her death while using her as his tool.

The characters and the conflict are particular and credible. But they are also mythological. In Mr. Faulkner's mythology there are two kinds of characters; they are Sartorises or Snopeses, whatever the family names may be. And in the spiritual geography of Mr. Faulkner's work there are two worlds: the Sartoris world and the Snopes world. In all of his successful books, he is exploring the two worlds in detail, dramatizing the inevitable conflict between them.

It is a universal conflict. The Sartorises act traditionally; that is to say, they act always with an ethically responsible will. They represent vital morality, humanism. Being antitraditional, the Snopeses are immoral from the Sartoris point of view. But the Snopeses do not recognize this point of view; acting only for self-interest, they acknowledge no ethical duty. Really, then, they are amoral; they represent naturalism or animalism. And the Sartoris-Snopes conflict is fundamentally a struggle between humanism and naturalism.

As a universal conflict, it is important only philosophically. But it is important artistically, in this instance, because Mr. Faulkner has dramatized it convincingly in the terms of particular history and of actual life in his own part of the South—in the terms of his own tradition.

In *Sartoris,* which was published before *The Unvanquished* but which follows it in historical sequence, the conflict is between young Bayard Sartoris (the grandson of the Bayard Sartoris who was a youth in *The Unvanquished*) and the Snopes world of the 1920's. "General Johnston or General Forrest wouldn't have took a Snopes into his army at all," one of the characters says; but, significantly enough, one Flem Snopes has come, by way of local political usefulness, to be vice-president of old Bayard Sartoris' bank. Young Bayard's brother, John, has been killed in a war; but it is clear that it was a Snopes war and not a Sartoris war. Bayard himself is extremely conscious of his family's doom; he feels cheated because he did not die violently, in the tradition, like his brother; finally, he kills himself, taking up an aeroplane that he knows will crash.

The Snopes world has done more than oppose the Sartorises. It has weakened them internally (as it weakened Rosa Millard) in using them for its advantage; it has made them self-conscious, queer, psychologically tortured. Bayard Sartoris has something of the traditional instinct for noble and disinterested action, under a vital ethical code. But the strength is so warped internally by the psychological effects of the Snopes world upon it, and it is so alien to the habitual actions of that world, that it can only manifest itself in meaningless violence, ending in self-destruction.

The same pattern recurs, varied somewhat and handled in miniature, in the short story about the Sartorises—"There Was a Queen." Here the real conflict centers in Narcissa Benbow, the widow of young Bayard Sartoris, who has given herself to a detective in order to recover from his possession a collection of obscene letters that one of the Snopeses had written to her anonymously and afterwards stolen. The consciousness of Narcissa's deed kills the embodiment of the virile tradition, old Miss Jenny Sartoris (Mrs. DuPré). Narcissa's yielding to the detective is the result of the *formalization* of one aspect of her traditional morality—her pride—through the constant opposition of the Snopes world to it; this formalization allows the Snopes world to betray her into antitraditionalism by creating a situation in which she must make a formalized response. It is a highly significant tactic. For the moment a tradition begins to be formalized into a code, it commences to lose vitality; when it is entirely formalized, it is dead—it becomes pseudo-tradition.

As early as *Soldiers' Pay* (1926) the same theme is the basis for Mr. Faulkner's organization of experience; and it is the best possible indication of the urgency of the theme with him that it should be central in his first novel. Mahon, the old Episcopal clergyman, conscious of sin, tolerant of human weakness, is still unaware of the vital opponent to his formalized, and so impotent, tradition—the amorality with which history has surrounded him. Donald Mahon, his son, is brought home from the World War, dying; in him, the minister's code has faced antitraditional history. Because Donald is not dead, the conflict must continue; locally, it is between the preacher and Cecily Saunders (Donald's fiancée before he went to war) with her family and associates who are typical of the new Jazz Era. Obviously, Cecily's world of jazz and flappers and sleek-haired jelly-beans represents the same antitraditional historical movement that brought Flem Snopes into Bayard Sartoris' bank. The names and the settings are different; that is all.

In *The Sound and the Fury,* Quentin Compson represents all that is left of the Sartoris tradition. The rest of his family have either succumbed entirely to the Snopes world, like Jason Compson, or else have drugs to isolate them from it—Mr. Compson his fragments of philosophy, Uncle Maury his liquor, Mrs. Compson her religion and her invalidism, Benjy his idiocy. But Quentin's very body is "an empty hall echoing with sonorous defeated names."[1] His world is peopled with "baffled, outraged ghosts"; and although Quentin himself is "still too young to deserve yet to be a ghost," he is one of them. However, it is evident that Quentin's traditionalism is far gone in the direction of formalization, with its concomitant lack of vitality; he is psychologically kin to Bayard Sartoris and to Narcissa Benbow. When he discovers that his sister Candace has been giving herself to the town boys of Jefferson, Mississippi, and is pregnant, he attempts to change her situation by telling their father that he has committed incest with her. It is a key incident. Quentin is attempting to transform Candace's yielding to the amorality of the Snopes world into a sin, within the Sartoris morality; but the means he employs are more nearly pseudo-traditional and romantic than traditional; and he fails.

Quentin tells his father: "It was to isolate her out of the loud world so that it would have to flee us of necessity." Precisely. The loud world is the Snopes world, with which the Compson house has become thoroughly infected and to which it is subject. Quentin is really *striving toward the condition of tragedy* for his family; he is trying to transform meaningless degeneracy into significant doom. But because his moral code is no longer vital, he fails and ends in a kind of escapism, breaking his watch to put himself beyond time, finally killing himself to escape consciousness. Only he is aware of the real meaning of his struggle, which sets up the dramatic tension in *The Sound and the Fury*.

In a way, Quentin's struggle is Mr. Faulkner's own struggle as an artist. In *Sartoris,* Mr. Faulkner wrote of the name: "There is death in the sound of it, and a glamorous fatality." Sartoris—all that the name implies—is the tragic hero of his work; it is doomed, like any tragic hero. But the doom toward which the Sartoris world moves should be a noble one. In *Absalom, Absalom!,* although apparently with great difficulty, as if he were wrestling with the Snopes world all the while, Mr. Faulkner finally achieves the presentation of a kind of "glamorous fatality" for the Sartoris world—embodied in Thomas Sutpen and his house.

The book is really a summary of the whole career of the tradition—its rise, its fatal defects, its opponents, its decline, and its destruction. The action is of heroic proportions. The figures are larger than life; but, as Mr. T. S. Eliot has suggested of Tourneur's characters, they are all distorted to scale, so that the whole action has a self-subsistent reality. And the book ends with a ritualistic purgation of the doomed house, by fire, which is as nearly a genuine tragic scene as anything in modern fiction.

For the first time, Mr. Faulkner makes explicit here the contrast between traditional (Sartoris) man and modern (Snopes) man, dissociated into a se-

quence of animal functions, lacking in unity under essential morality. One of
the characters says of traditional men:

People too as we are, and victims too as we are, but victims of a different
circumstance, simpler and therefore, integer for integer, larger, more heroic
and the figures therefore more heroic too, not dwarfed and involved but
distinct, uncomplex who had the gift of living once or dying once instead of
being diffused and scattered creatures drawn blindly from a grab bag and
assembled.

It was the world of these "diffused and scattered creatures" in which
Quentin Compson lived; and it was the effort not to be "diffused and scattered"
—to transform his own family's doom into the proportions of the world of
Sutpen and Sartoris—that led to his death. But it is significant that it should
be Quentin through whose gradual understanding the story of Sutpen is told,
and that it should be Quentin who watches the final destruction of Sutpen's
house. For Sutpen's tradition was defective, but it was not formalized as
Quentin's was; and his story approaches tragedy.

As I Lay Dying stands a little apart from the rest of Mr. Faulkner's novels,
but it is based upon the philosophical essence of his Sartoris-Snopes theme—
the struggle between humanism and naturalism. The naïf hill folk who appear
in the book are poor and ungraceful, certainly; they are of low mentality;
sexually, they are almost animalistic. But when Anse Bundren promises his
dying wife that he will bury her in Jefferson, he sets up for himself an ethical
duty which he recognizes as such—though not in these terms. It is the fulfillment of this obligation, in spite of constant temptation to abandon it, and in
spite of multiplied difficulties put in his way by nature itself, that makes up
the action of the novel.

Fundamentally, *As I Lay Dying* is a legend; and the procession of ragged,
depraved hillmen, carrying Addie Bundren's body through water and through
fire to the cemetery in Jefferson, while people flee from the smell and buzzards
circle overhead—this progress is not unlike that of the medieval soul toward
redemption. The allegories of Alanus de Insulis and the visions of Sister
Hildegard of Bingen would yield a good many parallels. On a less esoteric
plane, however, the legend is more instructive for us. Because they are simpler
in mind and live more remotely from the Snopes world than the younger
Sartorises and Compsons, the Bundrens are able to carry a genuine act of
traditional morality through to its end. They are infected with amorality; but
it is the amorality of physical nature, not the artificial, self-interested amorality

of the Snopeses. More heroism is possible among them than among the inhabitants of Jefferson.

2

So far I have been concerned mainly with exegesis, aiming to show how fundamental the Sartoris-Snopes conflict is in Mr. Faulkner's novels. To provide such exegesis of the six books that I have discussed, it is necessary to do violence to the fictions themselves, by abstraction. This is the significant point, for criticism; because the necessity for abstraction is evidence that, in these six books, the theme is really informed in the fictions or myths.

The Sartorises and the Sutpens and the Compsons do not represent the tradition in its various degrees of vitality, as *x, y,* and *z* may represent a sequence of numbers in mathematics. They are people, in a certain way of life, at a particular time, confronted with real circumstances and with items of history. And their humanity (or their illusion of humanity, on a larger-than-life scale) is not limited, ultimately, by their archetypal significance. Moreover, in each book there is a dramatically credible fiction which remains particular and (sometimes with difficulty) coherent as action, even though the pattern is true, in a larger sense, as myth. In short, Mr. Faulkner's successful work has the same kind, though certainly not the same degree, of general meaning that is to be found in Dante's *Divina Commedia* or in the *Electra* of Sophocles. The only close parallel in American literature is the better work of Nathaniel Hawthorne, whom Mr. Faulkner resembles in a great many ways.

However, as I have suggested already, a literary and personal tension arises, for William Faulkner the artist, out of the same conflict that is central in his work. This tension sets up his crucial problem as an artist, and his failures result from it. In so far as he can sustain his inherent tradition, he is enabled to project the central conflict in the valid terms of myth. However, as a Sartoris artist in a Snopes world, he is constantly subject to opposition that tends to force him into the same kind of reactionary formalization of tradition that betrayed Narcissa Benbow as a character. When, because of the opposition and his reaction to it, Mr. Faulkner writes as *formal* traditionalist rather than as *vital* traditionalist, he writes allegory. Allegory might be defined, indeed, as formalized—and therefore dead—myth.

Sanctuary, which is unfortunately the most widely known and misunderstood of Mr. Faulkner's novels, is a failure of this kind. In simple terms, the pattern of the allegory is something like this: Southern Womanhood Corrupted but Undefiled (Temple Drake), in the company of the Corrupted Tradition (Gowan Stevens, a professional Virginian), falls into the clutches of amoral

Modernism (Popeye), which is itself impotent, but which with the aid of its strong ally Natural Lust ("Red") rapes Southern Womanhood unnaturally and then seduces her so satisfactorily that her corruption is total, and she becomes the tacit ally of Modernism. Meanwhile Pore White Trash (Godwin) has been accused of the crime which he, with the aid of the Naïf Faithful (Tawmmy), actually tried to prevent. The Formalized Tradition (Horace Benbow), perceiving the true state of affairs, tries vainly to defend Pore White Trash. However, Southern Womanhood is so hopelessly corrupted that she willfully sees Pore White Trash convicted and lynched; she is then carried off by Wealth (Judge Drake) to meaningless escape in European luxury. Modernism, carrying in it from birth its own impotence and doom, submits with masochistic pleasure to its own destruction for the one crime that it has not yet committed—Revolutionary Destruction of Order (the murder of the Alabama policeman, for which the innocent Popeye is executed).

Here Mr. Faulkner's theme is forced into allegory, not projected as myth. In this sense, the book is a "cheap idea"—as Mr. Faulkner himself calls it in his preface to the Modern Library edition. Its defects are those of allegory in general. The characters are distorted, being more nearly grotesques than human beings; and they are not distorted to scale (Temple is only a type; Benbow is a recognizably human character, and so is Miss Reba, the keeper of the bawdy house); accordingly, the book lacks the "self-subsistent reality" which may be found in a work like *Absalom, Absalom!* It is powerful; and it contains some passages of bawdy folk humor that are of a high order of excellence; but is is fundamentally a caricature.

When *Light in August* appeared in England, an anonymous reviewer for *The Illustrated London News* suggested that it might be a parable of the struggle between good and evil. The notion is not entirely fanciful. But, more specifically, the book might be considered as an allegory based upon Mr. Faulkner's usual theme, with the clergyman, Hightower, standing for the Formalized Tradition. The simple-hearted Byron Bunch corresponds with the naïf traditionalist, Anse Bundren; Christmas, the mulatto, is a Snopes character, as is his partner, Lucas Burch, the seducer of Lena Grove. And the pregnant Lena might represent, vaguely, life itself, which Byron and Hightower are futilely attempting to protect from Lucas Burch and Christmas and their kind.

But the book is not so transparently allegorical as *Sanctuary;* indeed, it is a confused allegory in which realism is present as well. It fails, partly, because of this confusion, which never permits the two sides of the conflict really to join the issue. But it fails, even more clearly, because of the disproportionate emphasis upon Christmas—who ought to be the antagonist but who becomes, like Milton's Satan, the real protagonist in the novel.

This defines the second general type of failure in Mr. Faulkner's work: Mr. Faulkner is unable to sustain his traditionalism at all, and the forces of antitraditionalism become the protagonists.

The discussion reaches a dangerous point here. Since the time of Flaubert, at least, it has been customary to hold the view that one mark of a novelist's craft is his skill in creating all of his characters in the round and in maintaining an equal sympathy for all of them. However, it is not necessary to repudiate this view to suggest that there is a difference in kind between Flaubert's studies of human character in the behavior of the French bourgeois world and Mr. Faulkner's books, which are essentially myths, built around the conflict of two different worlds, to one of which Mr. Faulkner belongs as an artist, though he is of physical necessity a citizen of the other.

When one possesses traditional values of conduct, he has naturally a kind of hierarchy of sympathy, dependent upon the values, which makes him more or less sympathetic to characters in proportion as they are or are not traditional. Mr. Faulkner appears to maintain such a hierarchy in the greater part of his work; although he projects the characters of the Snopes world as clearly as he projects those of the Sartoris world, in his better books he is always seeing them and determining their proportionate stature from the Sartoris point of view.

But in *Light in August* the proportionate dramatic content of the characters is the reverse of the norm set up by the others; and there is a corollary confusion of the whole scheme of traditional values. The Sartoris characters, like Hightower, are vague or typical; Christmas, the Snopes character, dominates sympathy, and his tortured amorality determines the ethical tone of the book. In proportion as Christmas becomes the protagonist, the Snopes world, with its total lack of values, seems to have supplanted the Sartoris values *within the artist himself,* although against his will. And the confused, malproportioned fiction, wavering between realism and allegory, seems to be the artistic issue of Mr. Faulkner's violent—but, in this case, unavailing—effort to maintain the Sartoris point of view in his work.

Mr. Faulkner never gives his whole consent to such a confusion of values. That he is not content to remain within the characters of his protagonists when they are antitraditional, but must go outside them for "purple passages," seems to be evidence of this fact. *Pylon* is a case in point. It is a study of the effect of machinery upon human beings; the aviators who people it are timeless and placeless; they stay drunk most of the time to aggravate their insensitiveness; they have oil in their veins instead of blood; flying is their obsession, and when they are not in the air they do not live at all. In short, they are artifacts of the Snopes world. Against the background of an airport opening and a Mardi-Gras carnival in a Southern city, they move like characters in an animated cartoon, performing incredible antics but never being alive. Unable to speak through them, Mr. Faulkner speaks about them, in an androgynous prose-poetry that is not to be found anywhere else in his work. *Pylon* is his most conspicuous failure; and his imperfect sympathy with, and his inability to control, the protagonists, who should be the antagonists, seem to account for the failure.

Mosquitoes fails for similar reasons. Here, however, the imperfect sympathy issues in satire—of the Snopes-world Bohemia that existed in the Vieux Carré section of New Orleans during the 1920's. Since this is Mr. Faulkner's second novel, and since it was written just after he had lived in the Vieux Carré himself, while he was still under thirty, it offers another clear indication of the centrality of his traditionalism. It shows how great is the distance separating him from many of his contemporaries, such as, let us say, Mr. Ernest Hemingway. For *Mosquitoes* makes it very plain that if Mr. Faulkner is of the "lost generation," it is only of the lost generation of Sartorises. But it shows, too, that Mr. Faulkner is not an Aldous Huxley and should not try to be one. He is primarily a mythmaker; and there can be no such thing as a satiric myth.

3

William Faulkner's latest novel, *The Wild Palms,* tells two entirely different stories, in alternating sections; but the stories are complementary in that they both derive from the conflict between humanism and naturalism.

For Harry, the young doctor, and Charlotte, his mistress, all humanistic morality is equated with the Snopes code of mere "respectability," into which all morality has degenerated. Of that code, one of the characters says: "If Jesus returned today we would have to crucify him quick in our own defense, to justify and preserve the civilization we have worked and suffered and died . . . for two thousand years to create and perfect in man's own image." Charlotte and Harry are attempting to escape from the code into pure naturalism. Charlotte is natural, or amoral, Woman; with her, Harry becomes natural, amoral Man. They are constantly insisting upon the entirely physical nature of their love—and in no evasive terms. Their fear of any code amounts to an obsession: when they begin to feel as if they were married, living and working together in Chicago, they run off to a remote mining settlement in order to escape respectability. But Harry is conscious of doom: "So I am afraid. Because They [the forces of the code] are smart, shrewd, They will have to be; if They were to let us beat Them, it would be like unchecked murder and robbery. Of course we can't beat Them; we are doomed, of course. . . ." The fear is justified; for they are defeated by the very naturalism to which they have fled: Charlotte dies from the effects of an abortion that Harry attempts to perform on her.

The other story concerns a nameless convict, adrift in a small boat on the Mississippi River during the flood of 1927. Like Harry and Charlotte, the convict exists in a realm of unchecked natural forces; but unlike them, he has been put there against his will. With him in the skiff is a pregnant woman whom he has been sent to rescue. Like Anse Bundren, the convict is capable of genuine moral action; and his struggle with naturalism is based upon the ethical urge to return to his prison and to carry back the woman he has saved. When he is finally captured, he says: "Yonder's your boat and here's the woman"; with simple-minded tenacity, he has fulfilled his ethical obligation.

Technically, the book fails; only the complementary themes connect the two parts, and the connection is not strong enough for any sort of fictional unity. Indeed, it is a pity that the two parts are printed together; for the story of Charlotte and Harry is one of Mr. Faulkner's failures, whereas the story of the convict is one of his successes.

Charlotte and Harry, fleeing the Snopes world but fleeing all codes, too, are products of the antitraditional overbalancing in Mr. Faulkner which yielded *Pylon.* And the failure of their story derives, like the failure of that book, from the fact that in them the natural protagonist-antagonist schematism of Mr. Faulkner's myth is reversed. Sympathy must be given to them reluctantly; for though they are, as a matter of fact, running away from the Snopes world, they are running away from the Sartoris world, too; and, as Harry says, if they were to succeed, it would be like unchecked robbery and murder. In defense of one's own humanism, one must not yield entire sympathy to human beings who enter the realm of pure animalism.

But the story of the nameless convict is an heroic legend, similar to *As I Lay Dying;* it must be counted as one of Mr. Faulkner's definite achievements. Moreover, it has a quality of gusty humor (a sense of the outrageously grotesque heroic, related to the humor of the "tall tales" in folk literature) which is rarer in Mr. Faulkner's work but which is always impressive when it appears. It is to be found in some of the scenes of *Sanctuary,* notably in the gangster funeral and in the drunken "afternoon tea" of the middle-aged harlots at Miss Reba's house. It shows up in some of the short stories—"Spotted Horses," for example. And it appears in the scenes of the convicts' alligator hunting in *The Wild Palms.* However, this quality does not destroy, but serves rather to strengthen, the heroic legend as a whole.

4

William Faulkner's myth finds expression in work that is definitely romantic; when he comes near to tragedy, it is the tragedy of Webster. His art, like Webster's, is tortured. In form, each of his novels resembles a late-Elizabethan blank verse line, where the meter is strained, threatens to break, sometimes breaks, but is always exciting. He is an original craftsman, making his own solutions to his problems of form, often blundering, but occasionally striking upon an effect that no amount of studious craftsmanship could achieve. Consequently, like Dostoevsky, or like Miss Djuna Barnes in our own time, he is very special; and his work cannot be imitated except futilely, for he works within no general tradition of craft and hands on no tradition to his successors.

But Mr. Faulkner's difficulties of form derive, in part, from the struggle that he has to make to inform his material. The struggle is manifest, even in the prose itself. Discounting the results of plain carelessness in all of the books, the correlation between the fictions and the quality of the prose in Mr. Faulkner's books is instructive. It appears significant that *The Unvanquished* contains his least tortured and *Pylon* his most tortured prose.

He has worked to project in fiction the conflict between his inherent traditional values and the modern world; and the conflict has affected his fictional projection, so that all of his work is really a *striving toward* the condition of tragedy. He is the Quentin Compson or the Bayard Sartoris of modern fiction. He does not always fail; but when he does, his failure is like theirs—he ends in confused or meaningless violence. And for the same reasons: his heritage is theirs, and it is subject to the same opposition to which they are subject as characters. When he is partially successful, the result is tortured but major romantic art.

Now, in 1939, Mr. Faulkner's work may seem melodramatic. Melodrama differs from tragedy only in the amount of meaning that is subsistent in the pattern of events; and in our time the values of Mr. Faulkner's tradition are available to most men only historically, in the same way that, let us say, medieval values are available. The significance of the work as myth depends, then, upon the willingness of the reader to recover the meaning of the tradition —even historically.

---

1. The quotations are from *Absalom, Absalom!*, the other novel in which Quentin appears; but they are necessary for an understanding of his function in *The Sound and the Fury.*

WILLIAM FAULKNER

ROBERT PENN WARREN

AT THE AGE of fifty-three, William Faulkner has written nineteen books which for range of effect, philosophical weight, originality of style, variety of characterization, humor, and tragic intensity are without equal in our time and country. Let us grant, even so, that there are grave defects in Faulkner's work. Sometimes the tragic intensity becomes mere sensationalism, the technical virtuosity mere complication, the philosophical weight mere confusion of mind. Let us grant that much, for Faulkner is a very uneven writer. The unevenness is, in a way, an index to his vitality, his willingness to take risks, to try for new effects, to make new explorations of material and method. And it is, sometimes at least, an index to a very important fact about Faulkner's work. The fact is that he writes of two Souths: he reports one South and he creates another. On one hand he is a perfectly straight realistic writer, and on the other he is a symbolist.

Let us speak first of that realistic South, the South which we can recognize by its physical appearance and its people. In this realistic way we can recognize that county which Faulkner calls Yoknapatawpha County, the county in which most of his stories occur and most of his people live. Jefferson, the county seat of Yoknapatawpha County, is already the most famous county seat in the nation, and is as solidly recognizable as anybody's home town. There is Miss Emily's house, the big squarish frame house, once white, decorated with cupolas and spires and scrolled balconies, in the heavily lightsome style of the seventies, once on the most select street but now surrounded by garages and cotton gins, lifting its stubborn and coquettish decay above the cotton wagons and gasoline pumps. There is Uncle Gavin's law office. There is the cedar-bemused cemetery. There is the jail where a hundred years ago, or near, the jailer's daughter, a young girl, scratched her name with a diamond on a windowpane. There are the neat small new one-story houses designed in

Reprinted with permission from Robert Penn Warren, *Selected Essays* (New York: Random House, 1958), 59–79.

Florida and California, set with matching garages in their neat plots of clipped grass and tedious flower beds. Then beyond that town where we recognize every item, the country stretches away, the plantation houses, the cotton fields the back country of Frenchman's Bend, where Snopeses and Varners live, the Beat Four section, where the Gowrie clan holds the land and brawls and makes whiskey in the brush.

We know everything about Yoknapatawpha County. Its 2,400 square miles lie between the hills of north Mississippi and the rich black bottom lands. No land in all fiction lives more vividly in its physical presence than this county of Faulkner's imagination—the pine-winey afternoons, the nights with a thin sickle of moon like the heel print of a boot in wet sand, the tremendous reach of the big river in flood, yellow and sleepy in the afternoon, and the little piddling creeks, that run backward one day and forward the next and come busting down on a man full of dead mules and hen houses, the ruined plantation which was Popeye's hangout, the swamps and fields and dusty roads, the last remnants of the great original forests, "green with gloom" in summer, "if anything actually dimmer than they had been in November's gray dissolution, where even at noon the sun fell only in windless dappling upon earth which never completely dried." A little later I shall speak of what the physical world means to Faulkner, but for the moment I wish only to insist on its vividness, its recognizability.

This county has a population of 15,611 persons, who spill in and out of Faulkner's books with the startling casualness of life, not explaining themselves or asking to be explained, offering their being with no apology, as though we, the readers, were the intruders on their domain. They compose a society with characters as various as the Bundrens of *As I Lay Dying;* the Snopeses of *The Hamlet* and several stories; the Gowries of *Intruder in the Dust;* Ike McCaslin of "The Bear" and "Delta Autumn"; Percy Grimm, the gun-mad Nazi prototype of *Light in August;* Temple Drake, the dubious little heroine of *Sanctuary;* the Compsons, the ruined great family; Christmas, the tortured and self-torturing mulatto of *Light in August;* Dilsey, the old Negro woman, heroic and enduring, who stands at the center of *The Sound and the Fury;* Wash, the no-good poor-white; and Sutpen, the violent bearer of the great design which the Civil War had brought to nothing, in *Absalom, Absalom;* and the tall convict of *The Wild Palms.* No land in all fiction is more painstakingly analyzed from the sociological point of view. The descendants of the old families, the descendants of bushwhackers and carpetbaggers, the swamp rats, the Negro cooks and farm hands, the bootleggers and gangsters, tenant farmers, college boys, county-seat lawyers, country storekeepers, peddlers—all are here in their fullness of life and their complicated interrelations. The marks of class, occupation, and history are fully rendered, and we know completely their speech, food, dress, houses, manners, and attitudes.

Faulkner not only gives us the land and the people as we can see them today; he gives us glimpses of their history. His stories go back to the time when the Indians occupied Yoknapatawpha County and held slaves, and the first Compson came with a small, light-waisted, strong-hocked mare that could do two furlongs in under a half-minute, and won all the races from Ikkemotubbe's young braves until Ikkemotubbe swapped him a square mile of that land for the little mare. We know how Sartorises, the aristocrats, and Sutpens, nameless, driven, rancorous, ambitious men, seized the land, created a society, fought a war to defend that society, lost the war, and watched their world change and the Snopeses arise. The past is dramatized in situation after situation, in its full complication. It is a recognizable past, not a romanticized past, though we find many characters in Faulkner who are themselves romantics about that past, Quentin of *The Sound and the Fury* or Hightower of *Light in August.*

The land, the people, and their history—they come to us at a realistic level, at the level of recognition. This realistic, recognizable world is one of the two Souths about which Faulkner writes. As a realist he knows this world; it is the world he lives in and carries on his daily business in. To represent this world with full fidelity is in itself a great achievement, and I would not underrate it. But this achievement is not Faulkner's claim to our particular attention. That claim is the world he creates out of the materials of the world he presents. Yoknapatawpha County, its people and its history, is also a parable—as Malcolm Cowley has called it, a legend.

We can approach the significance of this legend by thinking of the land and its history as a fate or doom—words that are often on Faulkner's page. From the land itself, from its rich soil yearning to produce, and from history, from an error or sin committed long ago and compounded a thousand times over, the doom comes. That is, the present is to be understood, and fully felt, only in terms of the past.

The men who seized the land from the Indians were determined to found an enduring and stable order. They brought to this project imagination and rectitude and strength and integrity and cunning and endurance, but their project—or their great "design," to use Sutpen's word from *Absalom, Absalom*—was doomed from the first. It was "accurst"—to use one of Faulkner's favorite words—by chattel slavery. There is a paradox here. The fact of slavery itself was not a single, willed act. It was a natural historical growth. But it was an evil, and all its human and humane mitigations and all its historical necessity could not quiet the bad conscience it engendered. The Civil War began the fulfillment of the doom. The war was fought with courage and fortitude and strength but with divided conscience. Not that the enemy was the bearer of light—the enemy was little better than a blind instrument of doom or fate. After the Civil War the attempt to rebuild according to the old plan and for the old values was defeated by a combination of forces: the carpetbaggers, the carriers of Yankee exploitation—or better, a symbol of it, for the real exploiters never left their offices fifteen hundred miles away—and the Snopeses, a new exploiting indigenous class descended from the bushwhackers and landless whites.

Meanwhile, most of the descendants of the old order are in various ways incompetent. For one thing, in so far as they carry over into the new world the code of behavior prescribed by the old world, some sense of honor and honesty, they are at a disadvantage in dealing with the Snopeses, who have no code, who are pure pragmatists. But often the descendant of the old order clings to the letter of his tradition and forgets the spirit. George Marion O'Donnell, in one of the first perceptive essays ever published on Faulkner, pointed out the story "There was a Queen" as an example of this. The heroine, in order to get possession of certain obscene and insulting letters written her by a Snopes, gives herself to a detective who has blackmailed her. That is, to protect her reputation, she is willing to perform the act which will render the reputation of a mere sham.

We find something of the same situation with the whining Mrs. Compson, the mother in *The Sound and the Fury*, who with her self-pity and insistence on her "tradition" surrenders all the decency which the tradition would have prescribed, the honor and courage. Or the exponents of the tradition may lose all contact with reality and escape into a dream world of alcohol or rhetoric or madness or sexual dissipation. Or they fall in love with defeat and death, like Quentin Compson, who commits suicide at Harvard. Or they lose nerve and become cowardly drifters. Or, worst of all, they try to come to terms with reality by adopting Snopesism, like the last Jason of *The Sound and the Fury*, whose portrait is one of the most terrifying in all literature—the paranoidal self-deceiver, who plays the cotton market and when he loses, screams about those "kikes" in New York who rob him, who himself robs the daughter of his sister Caddy over the years and in the end makes her into the desperate and doomed creature she becomes, who under the guise of responsibility for his family—the ailing mother, the idiot brother, the wild niece—tortures them all with an unflagging sadistic pleasure.

The point to insist on here is that you do not characteristically have noble examples of antique virtue beset by little and corrupt men. There are a few such examples of the antique virtue—ole Ike McCaslin, for example, whom we shall come to later—but the ordinary situation is to find the descendant of the old order contributing, actively or passively, to his own ruin and degradation. He is not merely a victim, and he frequently misunderstands his own tradition.

Over against these people there stand, as we have said, the forces of "modernism," embodied in various forms. There are, of course, the Snopeses, the pure exploiters, descendants of barn-burners and bushwhackers, of people outside of society, belonging to no side, living in a kind of limbo, not even having the privilege of damnation, reaching their apotheosis in Flem Snopes, who becomes a bank president in Jefferson. But there is also Popeye, the gangster of *Sanctuary,* with eyes like "rubber knobs," a creature with "that vicious depthless quality of stamped tin," the man who "made money and had nothing he could do with it, spend it for, since he knew that alcohol would kill him like poison, who had no friends and had never known a woman." Popeye is a kind of dehumanized robot, a mere mechanism, an abstraction, and as such he is a symbol for what Faulkner thinks of as modernism, for the society of finance capitalism.

It is sometimes said that Faulkner's theme is the disintegration of the Southern traditional life. For instance, Malcolm Cowley, in his fine introduction to the *Portable Faulkner,* says that the violence of Faulkner's work is "an example of the Freudian method turned backward, being full of sexual nightmares that are in reality social symbols. It is somehow connected in the author's mind with what he regards as the rape and corruption of the South." And Maxwell Geismar, whose lack of comprehension of Faulkner strikes me as monumental, interprets Faulkner's work as merely Southern apologetics, as "the extreme hallucinations" of a "cultural psychosis."

It is true that Faulkner deals almost exclusively with the Southern scene, it is true that the conflict between past and present is a constant concern for him, it is true that the Civil War is always behind his work as a kind of backdrop, and it is true, or at least I think it is true, that in Faulkner's work there is the implication that Northern arms were the cutting edge of modernism. But granting all this, I should put the emphasis not in terms of South and North, but in terms of issues common to our modern world.

The Faulkner legend is not merely a legend of the South but of a general plight and problem. The modern world is in moral confusion. It does suffer from a lack of discipline, of sanction, of community of values, of a sense of mission. We don't have to go to Faulkner to find that out—or to find that it is a world in which self-interest, workableness, success provide the standards of conduct. It was a Yankee who first referred to the bitch goddess Success. It is a world in which the individual has lost his relation to society, the world of the power state in which man is a cipher. It is a world in which man is the victim of abstraction and mechanism, or at least, at moments, feels himself to be. It can look back nostalgically upon various worlds of the past, Dante's world of the Catholic synthesis, Shakespeare's world of Renaissance energy, or the world of our grandfathers who lived before Shiloh and Gettysburg, and feel loss of traditional values and despair in its own aimlessness and fragmentation. Any of those older worlds, so it seems now, was a world in which, as one of Faulkner's characters puts it, men "had the gift of living once or dying once instead of being diffused and scattered creatures drawn blindly from a grab bag and assembled"—a world in which men were, "integer for integer," more simple and complete.

At this point we must pause to consider an objection. Someone will say, and quite properly, that there never was a golden age in which man was simple and complete. Let us grant that. But we must grant that even with that realistic reservation man's conception of his own role and position has changed from time to time. It is unhistorical to reduce history to some dead level, and the mere fact that man in the modern world is worried about his role and position is in itself significant.

Again, it may be objected, and quite properly, that any old order that had satisfied human needs would have survived; that it is sentimental to hold that an old order is killed from the outside by certain wicked people or forces. But when this objection is applied to Faulkner it is based on a misreading of his work. The old order, he clearly indicates did *not* satisfy human needs, did *not* afford justice, and therefore was "accurst" and held the seeds of its own ruin. But the point is this: the old order, even with its bad conscience and confusion of mind, even as it failed to live up to its ideal, cherished the concept of justice. Even in terms of the curse, the old order as opposed to the new order (in so far as the new order is equated with Snopesism) allowed the traditional man to define himself as human by setting up codes, ideas of virtue, however mistaken; by affirming obligations, however arbitrary; by accepting the risks of humanity. But Snopesism has abolished the concept, the very possibility of entertaining the idea of virtue. It is not a question of one idea and interpretation. It is simply that no idea of virtue is conceivable in the world in which practical success is the criterion.

Within the traditional world there had been a notion of truth, even if man in the flow of things could not readily define or realize his truth. Take, for instance, a passage from "The Bear."

'All right,' he said, 'Listen,' and read again, but only one stanza this time and closed the book and laid it on the table. 'She cannot fade, though thou has not thy bliss,' McCaslin said: 'Forever wilt thou love, and she be fair.'

'He's talking about a girl,' he said.

'He had to talk about something,' McCaslin said. Then he said, 'He was talking about truth. Truth is one. It doesn't change. It covers all things which touch the heart—honor and pride and pity and justice and courage and love. Do you see now?'

The important thing, then, is the presence of the concept of truth—that covers all things which touch the heart and define the effort of man to rise above the mechanical process of life.

When it is said, as it is sometimes said, that Faulkner is "backward-looking," the answer lies, I think, in the notion expressed above. The "truth" is neither of the past nor of the future. Or rather, it is of both. The constant ethical center of Faulkner's work is to be found in the glorification of human effort and human endurance, which are not confined to any one time. It is true that Faulkner's work contains a savage attack on modernity, but the values he admires *are* found in our time. The point is that they are found most often in people who are outside the stream of the dominant world, the "loud world," as it is called in *The Sound and the Fury.* Faulkner's world is full of "good" people—Byron Bunch, Lucas Beauchamp, Dilsey, Ike McCaslin, Uncle Gavin, Benbow, the justice of the peace in *The Hamlet,* Ratliff of the same book, Hightower of *Light in August*—we could make an impressive list, probably a longer list from Faulkner than from any other modern writer. "There are good men everywhere, at all times," Ike McCaslin says in "Delta Autumn."

It is not ultimately important whether the traditional order (Southern or other) as depicted by Faulkner fits exactly the picture which critical historical method provides. Let it be granted that Faulkner does simplify the matter. What remains important is that his picture of the traditional order has a symbolic function in contrast to the modern world which he gives us. It is a way of embodying his values—his "truth."

In speaking of the relation of the past to the present, I have mentioned the curse laid upon the present, the Southern present at least, by slavery. But also, as I have said, Faulkner is not concerned ultimately with the South, but with a general philosophical view. Slavery merely happens to be the particular

Southern curse. To arrive at his broader philosophical view, we can best start with his notions of Nature.

For one thing, one of the most impressive features of Faulkner's work is the vivid realization of the natural background. It is accurately observed, as accurately as in Thoreau, but observation provides only the stuff from which Faulkner's characteristic effects are gained. It is the atmosphere that counts, the infusion of feeling, the symbolic weight. Nature provides a backdrop—of lyric beauty, as in the cow episode of *The Hamlet;* of homely charm, as in the trial scene after the spotted horses episode of the same book; of sinister, brooding force, as in the river episodes from *The Wild Palms*—a backdrop for the human action and passion.

Nature is, however, more than a backdrop. There is an interrelation between man and nature, something not too unlike the Wordsworthian communion. At least, at moments, there is the communion, the interrelation. The industructible beauty is there, beyond man's frailty. "God created man," Ike McCaslin says in "Delta Autumn," "and He created the world for him to live in and I reckon He created the kind of world He would have wanted to live in if He had been a man."

Ideally, if man were like God, as Ike McCaslin puts it, man's attitude toward nature would be one of pure contemplation, pure participation in nature's great forms and appearances, pure communion. The appropriate attitude for this communion is love, for with Ike McCaslin, who is as much Faulkner's spokesman as any other character, the moment of love is equated with godhood. But since man "wasn't quite God himself," since he lives in the world of flesh, he must be a hunter, user, and violator. To return to McCaslin's words: God "put them both here: man and the game he would follow and kill, foreknowing it. I believe He said, 'So be it.' I reckon He even foreknew the end. But He said, 'I will give him his chance. I will give him warning and foreknowledge too, along with the desire to follow and the power to slay. The woods and the fields he ravages and the game he devastates will be the consequence and signature of his crime and guilt, and his punishment.' "

There is, then, a contamination implicit in the human condition—a kind of Original Sin, as it were—the sin of use, exploitation, violation. So slavery is but one of the many and constant forms of that Original Sin. But it is possible —and necessary if man is to strive to be human—to achieve some measure of redemption through love. For instance, in "The Bear," the great legendary beast which is pursued from year to year to the death is also an object of love and veneration, and the symbol of virtue; and the deer hunt of "Delta Autumn" is for old Ike McCaslin a ritual of renewal. Those who have learned the right relationship to nature—"the pride and humility" which Ike as a boy learns from the half-Negro, half-Indian Sam Fathers (he learns it appropriately from an outcast)—are set over against those who do not have it. In "The Bear," General Compson speaks up to Cass McCaslin to defend the wish of the boy Ike McCaslin to stay an extra week in the woods:

"You've got one foot straddled into a farm and the other foot straddled into a bank; you aint even got a good hand-hold where this boy was already an old man long before you damned Sartorises and Edmondses invented farms and banks to keep yourselves from having to find out what this boy was born knowing and fearing too maybe but without being afraid, that could go ten miles on a compass because he wanted to look at a bear none of us had ever got near enough to put a bullet in and looked at the bear and came the ten miles back on the compass in the dark; maybe by God that's the why and the wherefore of farms and banks."

The Sartorises and Edmondses, according to General Compson, have in their farms and banks something of the contamination, they have cut themselves off from the fundamental truth which young Ike already senses. But the real contamination is that of the pure exploiters, the apostles of abstractionism, those who have the wrong attitude toward nature and therefore toward other men.

We have a nice fable of this in the opening of *Sanctuary,* in the contrast between Benbow, the traditional man, and Popeye, the symbol of modernism. While the threat of Popeye keeps Benbow crouching by the spring, he hears a Carolina wren sing, and even under these circumstances tries to recall the local name for it. And he says to Popeye: "And of course you dont know the name of it. I dont suppose you'd know a bird at all, without it was singing in a cage in a hotel lounge, or cost four dollars on a plate." Popeye, as we may remember, spits in the spring (he hates nature and must foul it), is afraid to go through the woods ("Through all them trees?" he demands when Benbow points out the short cut), and when an owl whisks past them in the twilight, he claws at Benbow's coat with almost hysterical fear. "It's just an owl," Benbow explains. "It's nothing but an owl."

The pure exploiters are, however, caught in a paradox. Though they may gain ownership and use of a thing, they never really have it. Like Popeye, they are impotent. For instance, Flem Snopes, the central character and villain of *The Hamlet,* who brings the exploiter's mentality to the quiet country of Frenchman's Bend, finally marries Eula Varner, a kind of fertility goddess or earth goddess; but his ownership is meaningless, for she never refers to him as anything but "that man"—she does not even have a name for him—and he had got her only after she had given herself willingly to one of the hot-blooded boys of the neighborhood. In fact, nothing can, in one sense, be "owned." Ike McCaslin, in "The Bear," says of the land which had come down to him:

'It was never Father's and Uncle Buddy's to bequeath to me to repudiate because it was never Grandfather's to bequeath them to bequeath me to repudiate because it was never old Ikkemotubbe's to sell to Grandfather for bequeathment and repudiation. Because it was never Ikkemotubbe's fathers' fathers' to bequeath Ikkemotubbe to sell to Grandfather or any man because on the instant when Ikkemotubbe discovered, realized, that he could sell it for money, on that instant it ceased ever to have been his forever, father to father to father, and the man who bought it bought nothing.'

In other words, reality cannot be bought. It can only be had by love.

The right attitude toward nature and man is love. And love is the opposite of the lust for power over nature or over other men, for God gave the earth to man, we read in "The Bear," not "to hold for himself and his descendants inviolable title forever, generation after generation, to the oblongs and squares of the earth, but to hold the earth mutual and intact in the communal anonymity of brotherhood, and all the fee He [God] asked was pity and humility and sufferance and endurance and the sweat of his face for bread." It is the failure of this pity that curses the earth and brings on the doom. For the rape of nature and the rape of man are always avenged. Mere exploitation without love is always avenged because the attitude which commits the crime in itself leads to its own punishment, so that man finally punishes himself. It is along this line of reasoning that we can read the last page of "Delta Autumn":

This land which man has deswamped and denuded and derivered in two generations so that white men can own plantations and commute every night to Memphis and black men own plantations and ride in jim crow cars to Chicago to live in millionaires' mansions on Lakeshore Drive, where white men rent farms and live like niggers and niggers crop on shares and live like animals, where cotton is planted and grows man-tall in the very cracks of the sidewalks, and usury and mortgage and bankruptcy and measureless wealth, Chinese and African and Aryan and Jew, all breed and spawn together until no man has time to say which one is which nor cares. . . . No wonder the ruined woods I used to know dont cry for retribution! he thought: The people who have destroyed it will accomplish its revenge.

Despite the emphasis on the right relation to nature, and the communion with nature, the attitude toward nature in Faulkner's work does not involve a sinking into nature. In Faulkner's mythology man has "suzerainty over the earth," he is not of the earth, and it is the human virtues that count—"pity and humility and endurance." If we take even the extreme case of the idiot Snopes and his fixation on the cow in *The Hamlet* (a scene whose function in the total order of the book is to show that even the idiot pervert is superior to Flem), a scene in which the human being appears as close as possible to the "natural" level, we find that the scene is the most lyrical in Faulkner's work: even the idiot is human and not animal, for only human desires, not animal desires, must clothe themselves in poetry. I think that George Marion O'Donnell is right in pointing to the humanism-naturalism opposition in Faulkner's work, and over and over again we find that the point of some story or novel has to do with the human effort to break out of the mechanical round of experience at the merely "natural" level—"not just to eat and evacuate and sleep warm," as Charlotte Rittenmeyer says in *The Wild Palms,* "so we can get up and eat and evacuate in order to sleep warm again," or not just to raise cotton to buy niggers to raise cotton to buy niggers, as it is put in another place. Even when a character seems to be caught in the iron ring of some compulsion, of some mechanical process, the effort may be discernible. And in Quentin's attempt in *The Sound and the Fury* to persuade his sister Caddy, who is pregnant by one of the town boys of Jefferson, to confess that she has committed incest with him, we find among other things the idea that "the horror" of the crime and the "clean flame" of guilt would be preferable to the meaninglessness of the "loud world." More is at stake in Quentin's attitude than the snobbery of a Compson, which would prefer incest to the notion that his sister has had to do with one of the underbred town boys.

And that leads us to the question of class and race. There is a current misconception on this point, the notion that Faulkner's Snopesism is a piece of snobbery. It is true that the Snopeses are poor whites, descendants of bushwhackers (those who had no side in the Civil War but tried to make a good thing out of it), but any careful reader should realize that a Snopes is not to be equated with a poor white. For instance, the book most fully about the poor white, *As I Lay Dying,* is charged with sympathy and poetry. There are a hundred touches like that in Cash's soliloquy about the phonograph: I reckon it's a good thing we ain't got ere a one of them. I reckon I wouldn't never get no work done a-tall for listening to it. I don't know if a little music ain't about the nicest thing a fellow can have. Seems like when he comes in tired of a night, it ain't nothing could rest him like having a little music played and him resting.

Or like the long section devoted to Addie Bundren, a section full of eloquence like that of this paragraph:

And then he died. He did not know he was dead. I would lie by him in the dark, hearing the dark land talking of God's love and His beauty and His sin; hearing the dark voicelessness in which the words are the deeds, and the other words that are not deeds, that are just the gaps in peoples' lacks, coming down like the cries of geese out of the wild darkness in the old terrible nights, fumbling at the deeds like orphans to whom are pointed out in a crowd two faces and told, That is your father, your mother.

The whole of *As I Lay Dying* is based on the heroic effort of the Bundren family to fulfill the promise to the dead mother to take her body to Jefferson; and the fact that Anse Bundren, after the effort is completed, immediately gets him a new wife, "the duck-shaped woman," does not negate the heroism of the effort or the poetry in which it is clothed. We are told by one critic that "what should have been the drama of the Bundrens thus becomes in the end a sort of brutal farce," and that we are "unable to feel the tragedy because the author has refused to accept the Bundrens, as he did accept the Compsons, as tragic." Rather, I should say, the Bundrens come off a little better than the latter-day Compsons, the whining, selfdeluding mother, the promiscuous Caddy, the ineffectual Quentin, and the rest, including the vile Jason. The Bundrens at least are capable of the heroic effort. What the conclusion indicates is that even such a fellow as Anse Bundren, in the grip of an idea, in terms of promise or code, can rise above his ordinary level; Anse falls back at the end, but only after the prop of the obligation has been removed. And we can recall that Wash Jones has been capable of some kind of obscure dream, as his attachment to Sutpen indicates, and that in the end, in his murder of Sutpen, he achieves dignity and manhood.

The final evidence that the Snopeses are not to be equated with "poor white" comes in *The Hamlet*. The point of the book is the assault made by the Snopes family on a community of plain, hard-working small farmers. And if the corruption of Snopesism does penetrate into the community, there is no one here, not even Flem Snopes, who can be compared to Jason of *The Sound and the Fury*, the Compson who has embraced Snopesism.

As for the poor white, there has been a grave misconception in some quarters concerning the Negro in Faulkner's work. In one of Faulkner's books it is said that every white child is born crucified on a black cross, and remarks like this have led to the notion that Faulkner "hates" Negroes—or at least all Negroes except the favored black servitors. For instance, we find Maxwell Geismar exclaiming what a "strange inversion" it is to take the Negro, who is the "tragic consequence," and to exhibit him as the "evil cause" of the failure of the old order in the South. But all this is to misread the text. It is slavery, not the Negro, which is defined quite flatly as the curse, and the Negro is the black cross in so far as he is the embodiment of the curse, the reminder of the guilt, the incarnation of the problem. The black cross is, then, the weight of the white man's guilt, the white man who now sells slaves and potions to "bleach the pigment and straighten the hair of Negroes that they might resemble the very race which for two hundred years had held them in bondage and from which for another hundred years not even a bloody civil war would have set them completely free." The curse is still operative, as the crime is still compounded.

The actual role of the Negro in Faulkner's fiction is consistently one of pathos or heroism. There is Dilsey, under whose name in the Compson genealogy Faulkner writes, "They endured," and whose role in *The Sound and the Fury* is to be the very ethical center of the book, the vessel of virtue and compassion. Then there is the Negro in "Red Leaves," the slave held by Indians who is hunted down to be killed at the funeral of the chief. When he is overtaken, one of the Indians says to him, "You ran well. Do not be ashamed," and when he walks among the Indians, he is "the tallest there, his high, close, mud-caked head looming above them all." And old Sam Fathers is the fountain of the wisdom which Ike McCaslin, Faulkner's philosopher, finally gains, and the repository of the virtues central for Faulkner—"an old man, son of a Negro slave and an Indian king, inheritor on the one hand of the long chronicle of a people who had learned humility through suffering and learned pride through the endurance which survived the suffering, and on the other side the chronicle of a people even longer in the land than the first, yet who now existed there only in the solitary brotherhood of an old and childless Negro's alien blood and the wild and invincible spirit of an old bear." Even Christmas in *Light in August* is a mixture of pathos and heroism. With his mixed blood, he is the lost, suffering, enduring creature, and even the murder he commits at the end is a fumbling attempt to define his manhood, an attempt to break out of the iron ring of mechanism, for the woman whom he kills has become a figure of the horror of the human which has surrendered human attributes.

Or for a general statement let us take a passage from "The Bear":

'Because they will endure. They are better than we are. Stronger than we are. Their vices are vices aped from white men or that white men and bondage have taught them: improvidence and intemperance and evasion—not laziness: evasion: of what white men had set them to, not for their aggrandisement or even comfort but his own—' and McCaslin

'All right. Go on: Promiscuity. Violence. Instability and lack of control. Inability to distinguish between mine and thine—' and he

'How distinguish, when for two hundred years mine did not even exist for them?' and McCaslin

'All right. Go on. And their virtues—' and he

'Yes. Their own. Endurance—' and McCaslin

'So have mules:' and he

'—and pity and tolerance and forbearance and fidelity and love of children—' and McCaslin

'So have dogs:' and he

'—whether their own or not or black or not. And more: what they got not only from white people but not even despite white people because they had it already from the old free fathers a longer time free than us because we have never been free—'

It is in *Intruder in the Dust,* however, that his views of the Negro are most explicit and best dramatized. Lucas Beauchamp, the stiff-necked and high-nosed old Negro man, is accused on good evidence of having shot a white man in the back, and is lodged in the Jefferson jail with a threat of lynching. The lyching is averted and Lucas's innocence established by a boy and an old lady. But what is important about the book is two-fold: First, there is the role of Lucas as hero, the focus of dignity and integrity. Second, there is the quite explicit and full body of statement, which comes to us through the lips of Gavin, the lawyer-uncle of the boy who saves Lucas. To quote Gavin:

' . . . the postulate that Sambo is a human being living in a free country and hence must be free. That's what we are really defending [against the North]: the privilege of setting him free ourselves: which we will have to do for the reason that nobody else can since going on a century ago now the North tried it and have been admitting for seventy-five years now that they failed. So it will have to be us. Soon now this sort of thing [the lynching] wont even threaten anymore. It shouldn't now. It should never have. Yet it did last Saturday and it probably will again, perhaps once more, perhaps twice more. But then no more, it will be finished; the shame will still be there of course but then the whole chronicle of man's immortality is in the suffering he has endured, his struggle toward the stars in the stepping-stones of his expiations. Someday Lucas Beauchamp can shoot a white man in the back with the same impunity to lynchrope or gasoline as a white man; in time he will vote anywhen and anywhere a white man can and send his children to the same school anywhere the white man's children go and travel anywhere the white man travels as the white man does it. But it won't be next Tuesday. . . . '

This is not the whole passage, or even the burden of the whole passage, but it merits our lingering. The motive behind the notion of "defending" against the North is not merely resentment at easy Phariseeism. It is something else, two other things in fact. First, the realization that legislation in itself never solves a really fundamental question. Legislation can only reflect a solution already arrived at. Second, the problem is finally one of understanding and, in a sense, conversion: conversion and, as the passage puts it, expiation. That is, the real problem is a spiritual and moral one. The story of *Intruder in the Dust* is, in a sense, the education of the boy, and the thing he learns is a lesson in humanity. This can be brought to focus on two parallel episodes. He sees Lucas on the street one day, and Lucas walks past him without recognition. Later he realizes that Lucas had been grieving for his dead wife. Again, in the cemetery where the body of a Gowrie had been exhumed, he sees old Stub Gowrie, the father of the man Lucas had presumably killed, and realizes that this head of the brawling, mean, lawless Gowrie clan is grieving, too. The recognition of grief, the common human bond, that is his education.

That is the central fact in Faulkner's work, the recognition of the common human bond, a profound respect for the human. There are, in one way, no villains in his work, except those who deny the human bond. Even some of the Snopes family are, after all, human: the son of the barn-burner in the story "Barn-Burning," or Mink in *The Hamlet.* The point about the Gowries in *Intruder in the Dust* is the same: the Gowries seem to be the enemy, the pure villains, but in the end there is the pure grief on old Stub's face, and he is human, after all.

If respect for the human is the central fact of Faulkner's work, what makes that fact significant is that he realizes and dramatizes the difficulty of respecting the human. Everything is against it, the savage egotism, the blank appetite, stupidity and arrogance, even virtues sometimes, the misreading of our history and tradition, our education, our twisted loyalties. That is the great drama, however, the constant story. His hatred of "modernism"—and we must quote the word to give it his special meaning—arises because he sees it as the enemy of the human, as abstraction, as mechanism, as irresponsible power, as the cipher on the ledger or the curve on a graph.

And the reference to modernism brings us back to the question of the past and the present. But what of the future? Does Faulkner come to a dead end, setting up traditional virtues against the blank present, and let the matter stand there? No, he does not. But he holds out no easy solutions for man's "struggle toward the stars in the stepping-stones of his expiations." He does, however, give a sense of the future, though as a future of struggle in working out that truth referred to in "The Bear." We can remember that old Ike McCaslin, at the end of "Delta Autumn" gives General Compson's hunting horn to the mulatto girl who has been deserted by his young kinsman, saying, "We will have to wait." And *The Sound and the Fury,* which is Faulkner's *Waste Land,* ends with Easter and the promise of resurrection.

WILLIAM FAULKNER: THE IMPORTANCE OF LOVE

LAWRENCE EDWARD BOWLING

SINCE WILLIAM FAULKNER has been generally considered the greatest American novelist of the twentieth century and since love has always been the most universal subject in literature, we may very appropriately ask: what contribution did Faulkner make to the most universal of literary subjects?

If asked to name Faulkner's greatest love story, most readers would probably think first of *The Wild Palms.* As originally published, this book contains two separate stories. The story of Charlotte Rittenmeyer and Harry Wilbourne may be said to deal more with sex than with love, and the story of the tall convict ends with the hero's refusing to accept any responsibility for either love or sex.

Do these facts imply that Faulkner chose to ignore or to flout the most universal of literary subjects? Faulkner's own explicit answer to this question is contained in "The Stockholm Address," delivered on the occasion of his accepting the Nobel Prize in literature for 1950. The writer today, Faulkner stated, must leave "no room in his workshop for anything but the old verities and truths of the heart, the old universal truths lacking which any story is ephemeral and doomed—love and honor and pity and pride and compassion and sacrifice." Not only is love here listed first among the universal truths; it is repeated and amplified in three of the other five terms, "pity" and "compassion" and "sacrifice", which are merely different aspects of love.

Many commentators have asserted that the statement of principles contained in "The Stockholm Address" bears no resemblance to the author's literary practice. If we examine Faulkner's writings in the light of these univer-

Reprinted with permission from *Dalhousie Review,* XLIII (Winter 1963), 474–482.

sal truths, however, we find that love really is the central subject of all his greatest work. We may go even further and say that all of Faulkner's significant writings constitute merely a series of variations on a single idea: *the importance of love.*

This fact has generally been overlooked, for two reasons. First, because of the romantic tradition in literature, most readers tend to identify love with romantic courtships and illicit sexual activity, whereas Faulkner conceives of love in terms of pity and compassion and sacrifice and faith and patience and endurance. To him, the greatest love is based not upon sensation but upon the spiritual affinity between man and nature, between man and his fellow man, and among the members of a family. Another reason why readers overlook the significance of love in Faulkner's writing is that its importance is often emphasized indirectly through its absence or perversion. The need for love is the central issue in the most un-lovely of Faulkner's books—such as *The Sound and the Fury, Absalom, Absalom!* and *Sanctuary*—in which we behold the depravity and desperation and horror of human actions divorced from pity and compassion and sacrifice.

The importance of love in the family is well acknowledged by Faulkner in the most complimentary and also most significant dedication he ever wrote to any of his books, the dedication of *Go Down, Moses:*

To Mammy
CAROLINE BARR
Mississippi
[1840–1940]
Who was born in slavery and who gave to my family a fidelity
without stint or calculation of recompense and to my childhood an immeasurable devotion and love

Faulkner's great lovers are not Harry Wilbourne and Charlotte Rittenmeyer in *The Wild Palms,* but people such as young Isaac McCaslin in "The Bear," Charles Mallison, Jr. in *Intruder in the Dust,* Lena Grove in *Light in August,* the wife of Goodwin in *Sanctuary,* the old Negro Dilsey in *The Sound and the Fury,* and eleven-year-old Lucius Priest in *The Reivers.* These are not glamorous but very modest people who (like Caroline Barr) give their full measure of fidelity and devotion and love, without selfish consideration and without pay. As the Negro Ned McCaslin remarks to Lucius Priest in the concluding chapter of *The Reivers,* they "never done it for money." This is the same point made by Faulkner in the opening remark of "The Stockholm Address", in which he stated that his life's work had been pursued not for glory "and least of all for profit."

With Faulkner, the basic unit of society—and also the area of human activity in which love is most essential—is the family. Faulkner says very little about romantic lovers, but he says a great deal about the importance—the absolute necessity—of love within the family group, the love which binds the family together in a strong unit and gives each member happiness and a sense of security, the kind of love which makes a home and causes each individual to feel at home in the home. Whereas most novelists and short story writers deal with individual people, Faulkner commonly writes of whole families—the Sutpens, the Snopeses, the Sartorises, the Compsons, and the McCaslins. Usually he depicts these families in a process of decay (or a state of incoherence) caused by the absence of love. This disintegration not only destroys individuals and families but often overflows the family circle and involves the community.

Absalom, Absalom! is the story of the family of Thomas Sutpen, a man who spends the whole of his adult life trying to spell the word *love* with the wrong letters, trying to build a home with the wrong ingredients. He never does discover the right answer, for he never fully understands what he is trying to do.

It is significant that the story of Thomas Sutpen begins with the disintegration of his family, immediately following the death of his mother, when Tom is ten years old. Thereafter, the Sutpen family (lacking the vitalizing and cohering force of a mother and a mother's love) deteriorates into a state of "sloven and inert coherence like a useless collection of flotsam on a flooded river." This process continues until Tom is fourteen, when he suddenly realizes that his home is not a home, that his family is not truly a family but merely a group of relatives living under a common roof, and that he and his sisters and their father are living in a state of "brutehood." Within a few hours of this discovery, the boy makes a triple vow which dominates all his actions during the remainder of his life: he determines to build a fine home, found a respectable family, and live on the level of a human being. To accomplish this threefold objective, "he believed that all that was necessary was courage and shrewdness and the one he knew he had and the other he believed he could learn." The great truth which Thomas Sutpen did not know as a boy and which he never did learn, though he lived to be an old man, was that his objectives were not achievable through courage and shrewdness alone.

Subsequent events proved unquestionably that Thomas Sutpen had or acquired both courage and shrewdness in great measure. He succeeded in marrying two wives, begetting two sons and three daughters, building the finest house on the largest plantation in northern Mississippi, and amassing two fortunes. But the wives and the children do not constitute families, the house he builds is not a home, and the fortunes he makes do not enable him or his children to live above the level of brutehood. In the end, the children have destroyed themselves and burned the house, Sutpen himself has died like an animal, and his only surviving descendant is a part-Negro idiot howling in the wilderness.

Sutpen never does discover that his error is fundamental and moral and not just "a minor tactical mistake." In his attempt to build a home, found a family, and live humanly, Sutpen has completely ignored the one ingredient most essential in these endeavors. Although he has thought and acted very strictly in terms of courage and shrewdness and even justice, he has never once considered the one element, love, without which all his efforts are doomed to failure. He acquires a wife and children, not because he loves them for themselves but because he considers them merely "adjunctive" to the forwarding of his "design." All his actions are selfish and therefore brutish.

The story of the Sutpen family in *Absalom, Absalom!* is closely related to the story of the Compson family in *The Sound and the Fury.* The only person to whom Thomas Sutpen ever confided his family history was old General Compson, who passed the story on to his grandson Quentin Compson, the narrator of the major part of *Absalom, Absalom!* and the same Quentin Compson who, in *The Sound and the Fury,* commits suicide at the end of his freshman year at Harvard. Quentin's narration of the Sutpen story to his Harvard roommate, Shreve McCannon, comes chronologically in the middle of *The Sound and the Fury,* five months before Quentin's death. Although there is no continuity of plot from one novel to the other, their themes are essentially the same. It is the close thematic parallel between the two stories which causes Quentin to be obsessed with the Sutpen story to the extent of narrating it, in the desperate hope that he may eventually understand it. But Quentin, like Sutpen, is never able to discover exactly what Sutpen's mistake had been. If he could have grasped the universal significance of Sutpen's story, Quentin would have been able also to understand and resolve his own personal problem, and he would not then have felt compelled to commit suicide.

Like Sutpen, Quentin has a "design." As one of Sutpen's ambitions had been to found a family free from the taint of Negro blood, so Quentin has from childhood cherished the idea of his sister's purity and has determined to protect her from any moral taint. Both Quentin's and Sutpen's designs, although formulated ostensibly for unselfish motives, are pursued without love or pity or compassion or sacrifice. As Thomas Sutpen had loved neither his wives nor his children but only the *idea* that these wives and children must be of pure white stock, so Quentin Compson is "incapable of love, accepting the fact that he must value not [his sister] but the virginity of which she was custodian." Quentin's major concern, therefore, is not love but merely "some concept of Compson honor."

The central issue in *The Sound and the Fury,* however, is much deeper and more complex than a brother's egocentric obsession with the idea of his sister's virginity. This novel is concerned not merely with the relationship between Quentin and Caddy but with the lack of love in the whole Compson family. From this novel and from other of Faulkner's writings, one may deduce the idea that the centre of the family is the mother and that she is the primary source of family love. Mrs. Compson, however, is the exact reverse of everything a mother should be. Instead of taking care of her children and giving them the love and understanding which children normally need, Mrs. Compton is constantly whining in order to attract attention to herself. She is so far from what a mother should be that she has developed self-pity and selfishness into a disease. Throughout the thirty years covered by the novel, she is both physically and psychologically an invalid. She not only spends most of her time in bed but uses her self-inflicted illness as a means of gaining attention from others and as an excuse for upbraiding and annoying all the members of her household.

As a result of this lack of love at its centre, the Compson family disintegrates. Quentin attempts to be a substitute mother to Caddy, but his feeling toward her is not spiritual love but a perverted and thinly disguised selfishness. Jason, instead of loving his sister as a brother should, is constantly blackmailing her for his personal gain. Caddy, thus deprived of family affection, seeks a substitute in the animal urges of the local town boys. When her actions result in the birth of an illegitimate daughter, Caddy does not attempt to perform as best she can the duties of a mother but abandons her child to the same household which had been the cause of her own ruin, while she herself makes a profession of being a free-lance mistress to the various men interested in her physical attractions. Quentin commits suicide. Mr. Compson drinks himself into an early grave. The illegitimate daughter runs away with a "pitchman who was already under sentence for bigamy." When Mrs. Compson dies, Jason commits his idiot brother to that loveless and marriageless institution, an insane asylum, cuts up the family house into apartments, and sells it for use as a boarding house, another loveless and marriageless institution. Having now "freed" himself from "the rotting family" and the "rotting house", Jason does not marry and start a family and a home of his own. Instead, he moves into "a pair of offices up a flight of stairs above the supply store containing his cotton ledgers and samples" and procures not a wife but a semi-private prostitute on a part-time basis. In Jason's life, there will be no marriage, no children, no home, and no love. In short, there will be nothing to distinguish Jason's life from that of animals. Thus, the Compson family, like the Sutpen family, ends in a state of brutehood.

In *Light in August*, Faulkner portrays the fragments of several broken families which have disintegrated or failed to cohere because of lack of love. Lena Grove is an orphan who, because she felt unwanted in the household of her sister and her brother-in-law, sought love in an illicit affair with a boy who later fled when he learned of her pregnancy. Joe Christmas is an illegitimate child whose grandfather left him on the steps of a foundling home; later Joe is adopted by a harsh Presbyterian Scotsman who can have no children and who knows nothing about love but is obsessed with the idea of justice. Miss Burden is an old maid who lives alone, the last survivor of a family whose male members have been motivated by hatred and selfishness which they have deceived themselves into believing is love and self-sacrifice. The Reverend Gail Hightower, whose mother died when he was eight years old, is a childless widower and ousted minister who has never loved either his wife or the church but has used both marriage and the ministry as a selfish means of living in the town which he has romantically associated with his grandfather. His selfishness causes the destruction of his family, the death of his wife, and his own rejection by both the congregation of his church and the members of the community in which he lives. Only in the last few hours of his life does Hightower make the sacrifice of performing unselfish acts because of love for other people.

In the trilogy composed of *The Hamlet, The Town,* and *The Mansion,* Faulkner portrays the Snopes family. Although there are several variations and a few exceptions within the type, the distinguishing characteristics of the Snopeses are their greed for money and their complete lack of love for each other or for anybody else. They will suffer almost any insult or ignominy to achieve material gain. Ab Snopes, instead of being loyal to either side during the Civil War, steals and sells horses indiscriminately. I. O. Snopes causes his mules to be killed on the railroad in order to collect damages. For a price (part of which is the Old Frenchman's Place), Flem Snopes marries his employer's pregnant daughter and accepts her illegitimate child as his own. At the end of *The Hamlet,* Flem has tricked V. K. Ratliff and Henry Armstid into buying from him the Old Frenchman's Place, in the belief that the land contains buried treasure, and Armstid goes insane while furiously digging in the soil for the money which exists only in his deranged imagination.

Flem has now squeezed all the material gain he can get out of the little "hamlet" of Frenchman's Bend and is now ready to move on to bigger gains in the nearby "town" of Jefferson. As he and Eula and her daughter depart, they have the appearance of a family. But they do not constitute a family, for Flem is not only not the father of the illegitimate daughter: he is incapable of being either a father or a husband. The oft-repeated implication is that Flem is incapacitated by both sterility and impotence, two physical handicaps which, according to Faulkner, often accompany spiritual deficiency and the inability to love.

In *The Town,* Flem rises to economic prominence and power by capitalizing upon the illicit love affair between his wife and a local politician. It is through this trafficking upon his wife's affections that Flem acquires the largest house in Jefferson. As is true in the Sutpen story, however, a large house does not constitute a home. At the end of *The Town,* Eula kills herself because of lack of love. When Ratliff remarks, "Maybe she was bored", Gavin Stevens, one of the men who had failed Eula in love, replies: "Yes, she was bored. She loved, had a capacity to love, for love, to give and accept love. Only she tried twice and failed twice to find somebody not just strong enough to deserve, earn it, match it, but even brave enough to accept. Yes, of course she was bored."

In *The Mansion,* Flem continues living in the great house, sometimes accompanied by his wife's illegitimate daughter, who cares as little for him as he does for her. There, in the evenings, she sits alone in one room while he sits alone in another room, doing nothing but going through the mechanical motion of chewing. He no longer chews tobacco or even gum; he merely chews on "a little ball of air." There he is sitting, staring vacantly into space and chewing on nothing, when his cousin Mink Snopes returns, after thirty-eight years in the state prison, to kill him. When Mink enters the room, carrying in his hand a cheap revolver, Flem does not even bother to defend himself or try to escape. He merely turns around in his chair, momentarily stops chewing, and watches indifferently while Mink cocks the revolver, snaps it without firing, and laboriously cocks it again for another try. Before the hammer falls the second time, Flem has again begun the ineffectual motion of chewing nothing.

To describe Flem's condition when he is killed at the conclusion of *The Mansion,* one can do no better than repeat Gavin Stevens' remark following Eula's suicide at the end of *The Town:* "Bored. Of course [he] was bored." And his boredom, like hers, had resulted from the lack of love. But Flem's predicament had been, in at least one respect, even worse than Eula's. Although she had not found anybody strong enough to deserve or return or even accept her love, she had had a capacity to give and to accept love. But Flem had been spiritually, as well as physically, impotent: he had been incapable either of giving or of receiving love.

The family which the reviewers and the scholars often consider the diametrical opposite of the Snopeses is that of the Sartorises. They are commonly thought to embody Faulkner's personal sentiments and ideals because Colonel John Sartoris is modeled on Faulkner's grandfather and his grandson Bayard is modeled to some extent on William Faulkner and/or his brother John. Most of the Sartoris men, however, are guilty of the same crime as the Snopeses—selfishness. The difference is that the Sartoris selfishness has a bent for bravado rather than materialism. Through their extreme daring and exhibitionism, they endeavor to achieve a reputation for being heroic. However, since the two most fundamental elements of heroism are discretion and the willingness to sacrifice selfish interests, the Sartoris men generally are not truly heroic: they are merely foolhardy individuals intoxicated with their own egotism. Through their foolish pursuit of self-interest, the Sartorises (like the Snopeses) bring destruction to themselves, misery to their families, and misfortune to all others with whom they are associated.

Faulkner's nearest approach to a personification of complete depravity and absolute lovelessness is the characterization of Popeye in *Sanctuary*. As a piece of mechanism, Popeye is nearly perfect, but he is completely incapable not only of love, but even of sex. He violates Temple Drake with a corncob, kills the harmless idiot who is trying to protect her, has an innocent man convicted for these crimes, abducts Temple into a house of prostitution and debauches her, procures for her a lover in order to watch them perform the sexual act, and later kills the lover. When finally sentenced to die—not for any of these crimes but for another crime which he did not commit—Popeye is so disgusted and bored with his loveless existence that, like Flem Snopes, he goes to his death without making any defence.

When this life of crime is nearing its end, we learn the cause of Popeye's depravity: there was no love at his begetting. His father was a man completely devoid of principle or scruple. A professional strike-breaker, he would "ride with one as soon as another", and he would also "just as soon be married to one as another, the same way." Popeye's mother was the daughter of the keeper of a boarding house, a recurrent Faulknerian symbol of lovelessness. Popeye was conceived out of wedlock, and the father deserted the mother before the child was born. By the time Popeye was five, he was "already a kind of day pupil at an institution." When a wealthy lady attempted to show him some affection by buying him a new suit and giving a children's party for him, Popeye repaid her kindness by killing her two pet birds. They were "love-birds", and he cut them up alive with a pair of scissors. Three months later, he cut up a kitten in the same manner and was sent to a home for incorrigible children. Thus began the paltry, puny life of Popeye, who, because of lack of love, could "never be a man, properly speaking."

If there is one idea which Faulkner may be said to adhere to consistently above all others, it is this: without love, no one can ever be a human being, properly speaking. With Faulkner, the opposite of love is not hate: it is *doom*, a key-word which appears frequently throughout his writings. In the remark already quoted from "The Stockholm Address", he says that any story lacking the old universal truths—love and honor and pity and pride and compassion and sacrifice—is ephemeral and *doomed*. He even uses "Doom" as a nickname for Ikkemotubbe, the Chickasaw Indian who, through murder and cunning, became chief of his tribe, seized the tribal lands as his personal property, and then sold, bartered, gambled away, and otherwise "dispossessed" himself of the tribal "birthright" (the *home*land), knowing that he did not personally own it but being "ruthless enough to pretend that it had been his to convey." Foreseeing the destructive consequences of his actions, Ikkemotubbe, "himself a man of wit and imagination as well as a shrewd judge of character, including his own", nicknamed himself Doom. For doom, Faulkner implies, is the certain fate of any man who, ignoring love, pursues selfish ends. In Faulkner's writings, the lovers are never losers, and the non-lovers are always losers—even when they win.

At the conclusion of *Absalom, Absalom!* Shreve McCannon makes to Quentin Compson the following prophecy concerning Thomas Sutpen's only surviving heir, the part-Negro Jim Bond, who had taken refuge in the wilderness and could be heard howling there at night like an animal:

Do you want to know what I think? . . . I think that in time the Jim Bonds are going to conquer the western hemisphere. Of course it won't quite be in our time and of course as they spread toward the poles they will bleach out again like the rabbits and the birds do, so they won't show up so sharp against the snow. But it will still be Jim Bond.

In this prophecy, Shreve may appear to be stating only the idea that the Negroes and the whites will eventually fuse into one race. But through and behind Shreve's words, Faulkner is suggesting a much more profound thought and a far less pleasing prospect. Faulkner is prophesying that Western man—if he does not re-learn the old verities (especially love and pity and compassion and sacrifice)—is doomed to return ultimately to the state of brutehood. Whether the survivors are black or white or mixed will really make no significant difference: that which they call Jim Bond, by any other name, will howl the same.

WILLIAM FAULKNER
VISION OF GOOD AND EVIL

CLEANTH BROOKS

PROFESSOR RANDALL STEWART, in his very stimulating little book *American Literature and Christian Doctrine,* asserts that "Faulkner embodies and dramatizes the basic Christian concepts so effectively that he can with justice

Reprinted with permission from Cleanth Brooks, *The Hidden God,* (Yale U. Press, 1963), 22–43.

be regarded as one of the most profoundly Christian writers in our time. There is everywhere in his writings the basic premise of Original Sin: everywhere the conflict between the flesh and the spirit. One finds also the necessity of discipline, of trial by fire in the furnace of affliction, of sacrifice and the sacrificial death, of redemption through sacrifice. Man in Faulkner is a heroic, tragic figure." This is a view with which I am in basic sympathy. I agree heartily with Professor Stewart on the matter of Faulkner's concern with what he calls "original sin," and with Faulkner's emphasis upon discipline, sacrifice, and redemption. But to call Faulkner "one of the most profoundly Christian writers in our time" seems somewhat incautious. Perhaps it would be safe to say that Faulkner is a profoundly religious writer; that his characters come out of a Christian environment, and represent, whatever their shortcomings and whatever their theological heresies, Christian concerns; and that they are finally to be understood only by reference to Christian premises.

Probably the best place to start is with the term "original sin." The point of reference might very well be T. E. Hulme, one of the profoundly seminal influences on our time, though a critic and philosopher whom Faulkner probably never read. In "Humanism and the Religious Attitude" Hulme argued for a return to orthodox doctrine. His concern with religion, however, had nothing to do with recapturing what he called "the sentiment of Fra Angelico." Rather, "What is important," he asserted, "is what nobody seems to realize —the dogmas like that of Original Sin, which are the closest expression of the categories of the religious attitude. That man is in no sense perfect, but a wretched creature, who can apprehend perfection. It is not, then, that I put up with the dogma for the sake of the sentiment, but that I may possibly swallow the sentiment for the sake of the dogma."

Hulme's position as stated here would seem to smack of scholastic Calvinism rather than of the tradition of Catholic Christianity. His emphasis at least suggests that nature is radically evil and not merely gone wrong somehow— corrupted by a fall. But if Hulme's passage is so tinged, that very fact may make it the more relevant to Faulkner, who shows, in some aspects, the influence of Southern Puritanism.

Be that as it may, Hulme's is not a didactic theory of literature, which stresses some direct preachment to be made. On the contrary, his "classicism" derives from a clear distinction between religious doctrine and poetic structure. It is romantic poetry which blurs that distinction, competing with religion by trying to drag in the infinite. With romanticism we enter the area of "split religion," and romantic "damp and fugginess." For Hulme, the classic attitude involves a recognition of man's limitations—his finitude. Since the classical view of man recognizes his limitations and does not presume upon them, the classical attitude, Hulme argues, is a religious attitude. For Hulme is quite convinced that man, though capable of recognizing goodness, is not naturally good. It is only by discipline that he can achieve something of value.

The whole point is an important one, for Faulkner's positive beliefs are often identified with some kind of romantic primitivism. Thus his concern with idiots and children and uneducated rural people, both white and Negro, is sometimes interpreted to mean that man is made evil only by his environment with its corrupting restrictions and inhibitions, and that if man could only realize his deeper impulses, he would be good.[1]

Allied to this misconception is another, namely that Faulkner's characters have no power of choice, being merely the creatures of their drives and needs, and that they are determined by their environment and are helplessly adrift upon the tides of circumstance. It is true that many of his characters are obsessed creatures or badly warped by traumatic experiences, or that they are presented by Faulkner as acting under some kind of compulsion. But his characters are not mere products of an environment. They have the power of choice, they make decisions, and they win their goodness through effort and discipline.

If Faulkner does not believe that man is naturally good and needs only to realize his natural impulses, and if he does believe that man has free will and must act responsibly and discipline himself, then these beliefs are indeed worth stressing, for they are calculated to separate him sharply from writers of a more naturalistic and secularistic temper. But I grant that to attribute to Faulkner a belief in original sin or in man's need for discipline would not necessarily prove him a Christian. The concept of grace, for example, is either lacking or at least not clearly evident in Faulkner's work.

Let us begin, then, by examining Faulkner's criticism of secularism and rationalism. A very important theme in his earlier work is the discovery of evil, which is part of man's initiation into the nature of reality. That brilliant and horrifying early novel *Sanctuary* is, it seems to me, to be understood primarily in terms of such an initiation. Horace Benbow is the sentimental idealist, the man of academic temper, who finds out that the world is not a place of moral tidiness or even of justice. He discovers with increasing horror that evil is rooted in the very nature of things. As an intellectual, he likes to ponder meanings and events, he has a great capacity for belief in ideas, and a great confidence in the efficacy of reason. What he comes to discover is the horrifying presence of evil, its insidiousness, and its penetration of every kind of rational or civilized order. There is in this story, to be sure, the unnatural rape of the seventeen-year-old girl by the gangster Popeye, and the story of Popeye's wanton murder of Tommy, but Horace Benbow might conceivably accept both of these things as the kinds of cruel accidents to which human life is subject. What crumples him up is the moral corruption of the girl, which follows on her rape: she actually accepts her life in the brothel and testifies at the trial in favor of the man who had abducted her. What Horace also discovers is that the forces of law and order are also corruptible. His opponent in the trial, the district attorney, plays fast and loose with the evidence and actually ensures that the innocent man will not only be convicted but burned to death by a mob. And what perhaps Horace himself does not discover (but it is made plainly evident to the reader) is that Horace's betrayal at the trial is finally a bosom betrayal: Horace's own sister gives the district attorney the tip-off that will allow him to defeat her brother and make a mockery of justice. Indeed, Horace's sister, the calm and serene Narcissa, is, next to Popeye, the most terrifying person in the novel. She simply does not want her brother associated with people like the accused man, Lee Goodwin, the bootlegger, and his common-law wife. She exclaims to her brother, "I don't see that it makes any difference who [committed the murder]. The question is, are you going to stay mixed up with it?" And she sees to it with quiet and efficient ruthlessness that the trial ends at the first possible date, even though this costs an innocent man's life.

Sanctuary is clearly Faulkner's bitterest novel. It is a novel in which the initiation which every male must undergo is experienced in its most shattering and disillusioning form. Horace not only discovers the existence of evil: he experiences it, not as an abstract idea but as an integral portion of reality. After he has had his interview with Temple Drake in the brothel, he thinks: "Perhaps it is upon the instant that we realize, admit, that there is a logical pattern to evil, that we die," and he thinks of the expression he had once seen in the eyes of a dead child and in the eyes of the other dead: "the cooling indignation, the shocked despair fading, leaving two empty globes in which the motionless world lurked profoundly in miniature."

One of the most important connections has already been touched upon in what I have said earlier. Horace Benbow's initiation into the nature of reality and the nature of evil is intimately associated with his discovery of the true nature of woman. His discovery is quite typical of Faulkner's male characters. In the Faulknerian notion of things, men have to lose their innocence, confront the hard choice, and through a process of initiation discover reality. The women are already in possession of this knowledge, naturally and instinctively. That is why in moments of bitterness Faulkner's male characters—Mr.

Compson in *The Sound and the Fury*, for example—assert that women are not innocent. Mr. Compson tells his son Quentin: "Women are like that [;] they don't acquire knowledge of people[. Men] are for that[. Women] are just born with a practical fertility of suspicion. . . . they have an affinity for evil[—]for supplying whatever the evil lacks in itself[—]drawing it about them instinctively as you do bed clothing in slumber. . . ." Again, "Women only use other people's codes of honour."

I suppose that we need not take these Schopenhauerian profundities of the bourbon-soaked Mr. Compson too seriously. It might on the whole be more accurate to say that Faulkner's women lack the callow idealism of the men, have fewer illusions about human nature, and are less trammeled by legalistic distinctions and niceties of any code of conduct.

Faulkner's view of women, then, is radically old-fashioned—even medieval. Woman is the source and sustainer of virtue and also a prime source of evil. She can be either, because she is, as man is not, always a little beyond good and evil. With her powerful natural drives and her instinct for the concrete and personal, she does not need to agonize over her decisions. There is no code for her to master—no initiation for her to undergo. For this reason she has access to a wisdom which is veiled from man; and man's codes, good or bad, are always, in their formal abstraction, a little absurd in her eyes. Women are close to nature; the feminine principle is closely related to the instinctive and natural: woman typically manifests pathos rather than ethos.

A little later I shall have something more to say about Faulkner's characters in confrontation with nature. At this point, however, I want to go back and refer to another aspect of *Sanctuary*. The worst villains in Faulkner are cut off from nature. They have in some profound way denied their nature, like Flem Snopes in *The Hamlet,* who has no natural vices, only the unnatural vice of a pure lust for power and money. In *Sanctuary* Popeye is depicted as a sort of *ludus naturae*. Everybody has noticed the way in which he is described, as if he were a kind of automaton, with eyes like "two knobs of soft black rubber." As Horace watches him across the spring, Popeye's "face had a queer, bloodless color, as though seen by electric light; against the sunny silence, in his slanted straw hat and his slightly akimbo arms, he had that vicious depthless quality of stamped tin." Faulkner's two figures of speech are brilliantly used here. They serve to rob Popeye of substance and to turn him into a sinister black silhouette against the spring landscape. The phrase "as though seen by electric light" justifies the description of his queer, bloodless color, but it does more than this. Juxtaposed as it is to the phrase "against the sunny silence," it stresses the sense of the contrived, the artificial, as though Popeye constituted a kind of monstrous affront to the natural scene. These suggestions of a shadowy lack of substance are confirmed at the end of the sentence with the closing phrase: "depthless quality of stamped tin." Faulkner relentlessly forces this notion of the unnatural: Popeye deliberately spits into the spring, he cringes in terror from the low swooping owl, he is afraid of the dark.

Popeye has no natural vices either. He cannot drink. Since he is impotent, he is forced to use unnatural means in his rape of Temple. As a consequence, some readers take Popeye to be a kind of allegorical figure, a representation of the inhumanly mechanistic forces of our society. We may say that Popeye is quite literally a monster, remembering that the Latin *monstrum* signifies something that lies outside the ordinary course of nature.

Though Popeye represents an extreme case, in this matter he is typical of all of Faulkner's villains. For example, Thomas Sutpen, in *Absalom, Absalom!*, is a man of great courage and heroic stature, who challenges the role of a tragic protagonist. Yet he has about him this same rigid and mechanical quality. Sutpen, as an acquaintance observes, believes "that the ingredients of morality were like the ingredients of pie or cake and once you had measured them and balanced them and mixed them and put them into the oven it was all finished and nothing but pie or cake could come out."

Sutpen has a great plan in mind, his "design," he calls it—which involves his building a great plantation house and setting up a dynasty. As he tells General Compson, "I had a design. To accomplish it I should require money, a house, and a plantation, slaves, a family—incidentally, of course, a wife." But when he finds later that his wife has a trace of Negro blood, he puts her aside, and he does it with an air of honest grievance. He says "[Her parents] deliberately withheld from me the one fact which I have reason to know they were aware would have caused me to decline the entire matter, otherwise they would not have withheld it from me—a fact which I did not learn until after my son was born. And even then I did not act hastily. I could have reminded them of these wasted years, these years which would now leave me behind with my schedule. . . ." (The last term is significant: Sutpen, modern man that he is, works in accordance with a timetable.) He tells General Compson that when he put aside his wife and child, "his conscience had bothered him somewhat at first but that he had argued calmly and logically with his conscience until it was settled." General Compson is aghast at this revelation of moral myopia. He calls it "innocence," and by the term he means a blindless to the nature of reality. And since the writer is Faulkner, the blindness involves a blindness to the nature of woman. For Sutpen has actually believed that by providing a more than just property settlement he could reconcile his wife to his abandoning her. General Compson had thrown up his hands and exclaimed: "Good God, man . . . what kind of conscience [did you have] to trade with which would have warranted you in the belief that you could have bought immunity from her for no other coin but justice?—"

Evil for Faulkner, then, involves a violation of nature and runs counter to the natural appetites and affections. And yet, as we have seen, the converse is not true; Faulkner does not consider the natural and instinctive and impulsive as automatically and necessarily good. Here I think rests the best warrant for maintaining that Faulkner holds an orthodox view of man and reality. For his men, at least, cannot be content merely with being natural. They cannot live merely by their instincts and natural appetites. They must confront the fact of evil. They are constrained to moral choices. They have to undergo a test of their courage, in making and abiding by the choice. They achieve goodness by discipline and effort. This proposition is perhaps most fully and brilliantly illustrated in Faulkner's story "The Bear." Isaac McCaslin, when he comes of age, decides to repudiate his inheritance. He refuses to accept his father's plantation and chooses to earn his living as a carpenter and to live in a rented room. There are two powerful motives that shape this decision: the sacramental view of nature which he has been taught by the old hunter, Sam Fathers, and the discovery of his grandfather's guilt in his treatment of one of his slaves: the grandfather had incestuously begotten a child upon his own half-Negro daughter.

"The Bear" is thus a story of penance and expiation, as also of a difficult moral decision made and maintained, but since it is so well known and has received so much commentary, I want to illustrate Faulkner's characteristic drama of moral choice from a less familiar story, "An Odor of Verbena," which is the concluding section of Faulkner's too little appreciated but brilliant novel *The Unvanquished.* As this episode opens, word has come to Bayard Sartoris, a young man of twenty-four off at law school, that his father has been assassinated by a political enemy. Ringo, the young Negro man of his own age and his boyhood companion, has ridden to the little town where Bayard is at law school to bring the news. Bayard knows what is expected of him—the date is 1874, the tradition of the code of honor still lingers, the devastating Civil War and the Reconstruction have contorted the land with violence, and Bayard knows that the community expects him to call his father's assassin to account. Even the quiet and gentle Judge Wilkins with whom he is studying law expects him to do so, and though he speaks to the boy with pity ("Bayard, my son, my dear son"), he offers him not only his horse but his pistol as well. Certainly also Bayard's father's Civil War troop expect him to avenge his father. Bayard's young stepmother, eight years older than he, expects it. Speaking in a "silvery ecstatic voice" like the priestess of a rite wrought up to a point of hysteria, she offers Bayard the pistols when he returns to the family home. Even Ringo expects it.

Some years before, when Bayard and Ringo were sixteen, at the very end of the Civil War, when the region had become a no-man's land terrorized by bushwhackers, Bayard's grandmother had been killed by a ruffian named Grumby, and Bayard and Ringo had followed him for weeks until finally they had run him down and killed him. Bayard had loved his grandmother, and was resolved that her murderer should be punished. But there was no law and order in this troubled time to which he could appeal; the two sixteen-year-old boys had to undertake the punishment themselves.

Now as the two young men ride back to Jefferson, Ringo says to Bayard, "We could bushwhack him. . . . Like we done Grumby that day. But I reckon that wouldn't suit that white skin you walks around in." Bayard in fact has resolved that he will not kill again.

The motive for this decision is complex. For one thing, he realizes that his father had become a proud and abstracted and ruthless man. Bayard had loved his father but is well aware that his father had pressed his opponent, Redmond, far too hard. George Wyatt, the countryman who had served under his father, earlier had in fact come to Bayard to ask him to restrain his father: " 'Right or wrong,' he said, 'us boys and most of the other folks in this county know John's right. But he ought to let Redmond alone. I know what's wrong: he's had to kill too many folks, and that's bad for a man. We all know Colonel's brave as a lion, but Redmond ain't no coward either and they ain't any use in making a brave man that made one mistake eat crow all the time. Can't you talk to him?' "

Another powerful motive is evidently the psychic wound that Bayard has suffered in the killing of Grumby. He has executed vegeance once, and in that instance there were extenuating circumstances to justify his taking the law into his own hands. But this case is different, and as he says to himself before he begins his journey home, "If there [is] anything at all in the Book, anything of hope and peace for [God's] blind and bewildered spawn," the command " ' *Thou Shalt not kill*' must be it." Finally, and not least, there is the example of his own father. Even his father had decided that there had been too much killing. Two months before, he had told Bayard: "Now I shall do a little moral house cleaning. I am tired of killing men, no matter what the necessity or the end." Thus Bayard, in resolving not to avenge his father, may be said to be following his father's own resolve.

But Bayard, as a member of a tightly knit community, does not want to be branded as a coward; he respects his community's opinion, and he feels compelled to live up to what the community expects of him. And so he resolves, though the reader does not learn of it until late in the story, to face Redmond, but to face him unarmed.

There is one person who understands his dilemma and can support him in his decision. It is his Aunt Jenny, who tells him when he arrives home that night: " 'Yes. All right. Don't let it be Drusilla, poor hysterical young woman. And don't let it be [your father], Bayard, because he's dead now. And don't let it be George Wyatt and those others who will be waiting for you tomorrow morning. I know you are not afraid.' 'But what good will that do?' I said. 'What good will that do?' . . . 'I must live with myself, you see.' 'Then it's not just Drusilla? Not just him? Not just George Wyatt and Jefferson?' 'No,' I said."

It is indeed not just Drusilla and George Wyatt and the other outsiders that are forcing Bayard to take his proposed course of action. As he tells his aunt, it is not enough that *she* knows that he is not afraid. He must prove it to himself. "I must live with myself," he says. This is the situation of many a Faulkner character. He must live with himself. He must prove to himself that he possesses the requisite courage.

Bayard is fortunate. The man that he goes to meet is also brave, also decent. He has decided that, having killed the father, he will not kill the young son. Thus, when Bayard walks up the stairs past the small faded sign *"B. J. Redmond. Atty at Law"* and opens the door, he sees Redmond sitting "behind the desk, not much taller than Father, but thicker as a man gets that spends most of his time sitting and listening to people, freshly shaven and with fresh linen; a lawyer yet it was not a lawyer's face—a face much thinner than the body would indicate, strained (and yes, tragic; I know that now) and exhausted beneath the neat recent steady strokes of the razor, holding a pistol flat on the desk before him, loose beneath his hand and aimed at nothing." Redmond fires twice but Bayard can see that the gun was not aimed at him and that the misses are deliberate. Then Redmond gets up from his desk, blunders down the stairs and walks on out past George Wyatt and the six other members of Colonel Sartoris' old troop. He "walked through the middle of them with his hat on and his head up (they told me how someone shouted at him: 'Have you killed that boy too?' saying no word, staring straight ahead and with his back to them, on to the station where the south-bound train was just in and got on it with no baggage, nothing, and went away from Jefferson and from Mississippi and never came back."

George Wyatt rushes up to Bayard, mistakenly thinking that he had taken Redmond's pistol away from him and then missed him, missed him twice. "Then he answered himself . . . 'No; wait. You walked in here without even a pocket knife and let him miss you twice. My God in heaven.' " But he adds, " 'You ain't done anything to be ashamed of. I wouldn't have done it that way, myself. I'd a shot at him once, anyway. But that's your way or you wouldn't have done it." And even Drusilla, the wrought-up priestess of violence, before she leaves the house forever to go back to her kinsfolk in Alabama, leaves on Bayard's pillow a sprig of verbena because it is the odor of courage, "that odor which she said you could smell alone above the smell of horses," as a token that she too has accepted his act as brave and honorable.

One further observation: as I have already marked, it is the men who have to be initiated into the meaning of reality, who have to observe a code of conduct, who have to prove themselves worthy. Aunt Jenny, as a woman, is outside the code. Indeed she sees the code as absurd and quixotic, thought she knows that Bayard as a man will have to observe it. And what shall we say of Drusilla, who is a woman, and yet is the very high priestess of the code? Drusilla is the masculinized woman, who as a type occurs more than once in Faulkner. Drusilla's story is that she has lost her fiancé early in the war and finally in her boredom and despair has actually ridden with the Confederate cavalry. She is brave and Faulkner gives her her due, but he is not celebrating her as a kind of Confederate Joan of Arc. Her action exacts its penalty and she ends a warped and twisted woman, truly a victim of the war.

I realize that I am risking oversimplification in pressing some of these issues so hard—for example, the contrast between man and woman, in their relation to nature and to their characteristic roles as active and passive. One may be disposed to doubt that even a traditional writer writing about a traditional society would stylize these relationships as much as I have suggested Faulkner has. Yet I am very anxious to sketch in, even at the risk of overbold strokes, the general nature of Faulkner's conception of good and evil, and so I mean to stand by this summary: Faulkner sees the role of man as active; man makes choices and lives up to the choices. Faulkner sees the role of woman as characteristically fostering and sustaining. She undergirds society, upholding the family and community mores, sending her men out into battle, including the ethical battle. This generalization I believe, is, if oversimplified, basically true. And I should like to relate it to Faulkner's "Calvinistic" Protestantism. In so far as his Calvinism represents a violent repression and constriction of natural impulse, a denial of nature itself, Faulkner tends to regard it as a terrible and evil thing. And the natural foil to characters who have so hardened their hearts in accordance with their notion of a harsh and vindictive God is the feminine principle as exemplified by a person like Lena Grove, the heroine of *Light in August.* Lena has a childlike confidence in herself and in mankind. She is a creature of warm natural sympathies and a deep instinctive commitment to her natural function.

But Faulkner has still another relation to Calvinistic Protestantism. Insofar as the tradition insists that man must be brought up to the urgency of decision, must be set tests of courage and endurance, must have his sinews strung tight for some moral leap or his back braced so as to stand firm against the push of circumstance, Faulkner evidently derives from this tradition. From it may be derived the very necessity that compels his male characters to undergo an initiation. The required initiation may be analogous to the crisis of conversion and the character's successful entrance into knowledge of himself, analogous to the sinner's experiencing salvation.

On the conscious level, Faulkner is obviously a Protestant anticleric, fascinated, but also infuriated, by some of the more violently repressive features of the religion that dominates his country. This matter is easily illustrated. One of his masterpieces, *Light in August,* provides a stinging criticism of the harsher aspects of Protestantism. Indeed a basic theme in *Light in August* is man's strained attempt to hold himself up in a rigid aloofness above the relaxed female world. The struggle to do so is, as Faulkner portrays it in his novel, at once monstrous, comic, and heroic, as the various characters take up their special postures.

In a character like old Doc Hines, there is a definite distortion and perversion. His fury at "bitchery and abomination" is the fury of a crazed man. In her conversation with Bunch and Hightower, Mrs. Hines states quite precisely what has happened to her husband: he began "then to take God's name in vain and in pride to justify and excuse the devil that was in him." His attribution of his furies to God is quite literally a taking of God's name in vain, blasphemy. The tendency to call one's own hates the vengeance of a just God is a sin to which Protestantism has always been prone. But not merely Southern Protestantism and, of course, not merely Protestantism as such.

Calvin Burden represents another instance of the militant Protestant, but this man's heartiness and boisterous energy have something of the quality of comedy. He is the son of a Unitarian minister; but when he runs away to the West, he becomes a Roman Catholic and lives for a year in a monastery. Then, on his marriage, he repudiates the Catholic Church, choosing for the scene of his formal repudiation "a saloon, insisting that every one present listen to him and state their objections." Then, though he cannot read the English Bible—

he had learned from the priests in California to read Spanish—he begins to instruct his child in the true religion, interspersing his readings to the child in Spanish with "extemporised dissertations composéd half of the bleak and bloodless logic which he remembered from his father on interminable New England Sundays and half of immediate hellfire and tangible brimstone." Perhaps he differs from the bulk of doctrinaire hellfire and brimstone Protestants in not being a "proselyter" or a "missionary." But everything else marks him as truly of the breed; his intensity, his stern authoritarianism, and his violence. He has killed a man in an argument over slavery and he threatens to "frail the tar" out of his children if they do not learn to hate what he hates —hell and slaveholders.

The case of the Rev. Gail Hightower is one of the most interesting of all. He is the only one of these Protestants who has had formal theological training. Because of that fact one might expect him to be the most doctrinaire. He is not. He seems at the beginning of the book the most tolerant and pitying of all the characters, the one who recoils in horror at man's capacity for evil and man's propensity to crucify his fellows: he is a man whose only defense against violence is nonresistance. One may be inclined to say that Hightower had rebelled against his Calvinist training and repudiated the jealous and repressive God. Certainly, there is truth in this notion. Hightower is a disillusioned man and a man who has learned something from his sufferings. But there is a sense in which he has never broken out of the mold: he still stresses a God of justice rather than of mercy, for his sincerest belief is that he has somehow "bought immunity." He exclaims: "I have paid. I have paid"—in confidence that God is an honest merchant who has receipted his bill and will honor his title to the precious merchandise he has purchased at such cost.

Lastly there is the case of Joe Christmas, the violent rebel against hellfire Protestantism. His detachment from any kind of human community is shocking. Here is a man who has no family ties, no continuity with the past, no place in any community whatsoever. He is a man who has literally tried to kick the earth out from under his feet. Yet his very alienation and his insistence upon his own individual integrity are touched with the tragically heroic. As a child he is conscious that he is being hounded by old Doc Hines; he resists stubbornly the discipline imposed by his foster father McEachern, whom he finally brains with a chair; and when his paramour, Joanna Burden, threatens him with hell and insists that he kneel with her and pray for forgiveness, he decapitates her. Yet there is a most important sense in which Joe Christmas is the sternest and most doctrinaire Calvinist in the book.

He imbibes more from the training of his foster father than he realizes. For all that he strains in fierce resistance against him, he "could depend" on "the hard, just, ruthless man." It is the "soft kindness" of the woman, his foster mother that he abominates. If one mark of the Calvinists in this novel is their fear and distrust of women and their hatred of the female principle, then Joe Christmas is eminently qualified to take a place among them. He even has affinities with his old childhood ogre, Doc Hines, and Hines' fury at the bitchery of women and the abomination of Negro blood. Joe, hearing the "fecundmellow" voices of Negro women, feels that he and "all other man-shaped life about him" had been returned to the "lightless hot wet primogenitive Female" and runs from the scene in a kind of panic.

Christmas too wants not mercy but justice, is afraid of the claims of love and its obligations, and yearns only for a vindication of his identity and integrity—a vindication made the more difficult by his not really knowing precisely what he would vindicate. When he puts aside the temptation to marry Joanna and win ease and security, he does it by saying: "If I give in now, I will deny all the thirty years that I have lived to make me what I chose to be." Finally, Joe is something of a fatalist, and his fatalism is a kind of perversion of Calvinist determinism. On his way to murder Joanna, "he believed with calm paradox that he was the volitionless servant of the fatality in which he believed that he did not believe." But so "fated" is his act of murder that he keeps saying to himself "I had to do it"—using the past tense, as if the act had already been performed.

Lena (along with Eula of *The Hamlet*) has sometimes been called an earth goddess. The description does have a certain aptness when applied to Eula, especially in some of the more rhapsodic passages of *The Hamlet*. But it is a little highfalutin' for Lena. It is more accurate to say that Lena is one of Faulkner's several embodiments of the female principle—indeed one of the purest and least complicated of his embodiments. Her rapport with nature is close. She is never baffled as to what course of action to take. She is never torn by doubts and indecisions. There is no painful introspection. This serene composure has frequently been put down to sheer mindlessness, and Lena, to be sure, is a very simple young woman. But Faulkner himself undoubtedly attributes most of Lena's quiet force to her female nature. In this novel the principal male characters suffer alienation. They are separated from the community, are in rebellion against it—and against nature. But Lena moves serenely into the community, and it gathers itself about her with protective gestures. Its response to her, of course, is rooted in a deep and sound instinct: Lena embodies the principle upon which any human community is founded.

She is the carrier of life and she has to be protected and nurtured if there is to be any human community at all.

I have said that *Light in August* depicts man's strained attempt to hold himself up in rigid aloofness above the relaxed female world. In terms of the plot, Lena is the direct means by which Byron Bunch and the indirect means by which Hightower are redeemed from their pallid half lives and brought back into the community. This coming back into the community is an essential part of the redemption. Unless the controlling purposes of the individuals are related to those that other men share, and in which the individual can participate, he is indeed isolated, and is forced to fall back upon his personal values, with all the risk of fanaticism and distortion to which such isolation is liable.

The community is at once the field for man's action and the norm by which his action is judged and regulated. It sometimes seems that the sense of an organic community has all but disappeared from modern fiction, and the disappearance accounts for the terrifying self-consciousness and subjectivity of a great deal of modern writing. That Faulkner has some sense of an organic community still behind him is among his most important resources as a writer.

In *Light in August* Faulkner uses Lena to confirm an ideal of integrity and wholeness in the light of which the alienated characters are judged; and this is essentially the function of Dilsey, the Negro servant in *The Sound and the Fury*, regarded by many people as Faulkner's masterpiece. Dilsey's role, to be sure, is more positive than Lena's. She has affinities not with the pagan goddess but with the Christian saint. She is not the young woman and young mother that Lena is. She is an older woman and an older mother, and she is the sustaining force—the only possible sustaining force of a broken and corrupted family.

Yet Dilsey's primary role is generally similar to Lena's: she affirms the ideal of wholeness in a family which shows in every other member splintering and disintegration. *The Sound and the Fury* can be regarded as a study in the fragmentation of modern man. There is Benjy, the idiot brother who represents the life of the instincts and the unreflective emotions; there is Quentin, the intellectual and artistic brother, who is conscious of his own weakness and failure and yet so hagridden by impossible ideals that he finally turns away from life altogether and commits suicide; and there is Jason, the brother who represents an aggressive and destructive rationalism that dissolves all family and community loyalties and attachments. There has been a somewhat strained attempt to portray the brothers in Freudian terms: Benjy as the *id,*

Quentin as the tortured *ego,* and Jason as the tyrannical and cruel *super-ego.* Faulkner's own way of regarding the three brothers (as implied in the appendix he supplied for the Modern Library edition) is interesting. Benjy is an idiot, of course; Quentin, in his obsession, is obviously half-mad; and Jason is perfectly sane, the first "sane" Compson for generations. Faulker's mocking choice of the term "sane" to characterize Jason's coldly monstrous self-serving (all of Faulkner's villains, let me repeat, are characterized by this devouring and destructive rationalism) is highly significant. It is as if Faulkner argued that mere sanity were not enough—indeed that pure sanity was inhuman. The good of man has to transcend his mere intellect with some overflow of generosity and love.

But we ought not to confine outselves to the three brothers, for Dilsey is being contrasted not merely with them but with the whole of the family. There is Mr. Compson, who has been defeated by life and has sunk into whisky and fatalism. There is Mrs. Compson, the mother, whom Faulkner calls a "cold, weak" person. She is the whining, self-centered hypochondriac who has poisoned the whole family relationship. She is evidently the primary cause of her husband's cynicism; she has spoiled and corrupted her favorite son, Jason; and she has withheld her love from the other children. Quentin, on the day of his suicide, can say to himself bitterly, "If I only had a mother." Mrs. Compson is all that Dilsey is not. It is the mother role that she has abandoned that Dilsey is compelled to assume. There is lastly the daughter of the family, Candace, who in her own way also represents the dissolution of the family. Candace has become a wanton. Sex is her particular escape from an unsatisfactory home, and she is subject to her own kind of specialization, the semiprofessionalism of a sexual adventuress.

In contrast with this splintered family, Dilsey maintains a wholeness. Indeed, Dilsey's wholeness constitutes her holiness. (It is well to remember that *whole* and *holy* are related and come from the same root.) In Dilsey the life of the instincts, including the sex drive, the life of the emotions, and the life of ideal values and of rationality are related meaningfully to one another. To say this is to say, of course, that Dilsey is a profoundly religious person. Her life with its round of daily tasks and responsibilities is related to the larger life of eternity and eternal values. Dilsey does not have to strain to make meaningful some particular desire or dream or need. Her world is a solid and meaningful world. It is filled with pain, toil, and difficulty, but it is not wrenched by agonizing doubts and perplexities.

I said a moment ago that Dilsey was sometimes compared to the saint and in what I am going to say I do not mean to deprive her of her properly deserved halo. But we must not allow the term to sentimentalize her. If she treats with compassion the idiot Benjy, saying "You's de Lawd's chile, anyway," she is quite capable of dealing summarily with her own child, Luster, when he needs a rebuke: "Lemme tell you somethin, nigger boy, you got jes es much Compson devilment in you es any of em. Is yo right sho you never broke dat window?" Dilsey's earthiness and her human exasperations are very much in evidence in this novel. Because they are, Dilsey's "saintliness" is altogether credible and convincing.

One may say in general of Faulkner's Negroes that they remain close to a concrete world of values—less perverted by abstraction—more honest in recognizing what is essential and elemental than are most of the white people. Faulkner certainly does not assume any inherent virtue in the Negro race. But he does find among his Negro characters less false pride, less false idealism, more seasoned discipline in the elemental human relationships. The Negro virtues which Faulkner praises in "The Bear" are endurance, patience, honesty, courage, and the love of children—white or black. Dilsey, then, is not a primitive figure who through some mystique of race or healthiness of natural impulses is good. Dilsey is unsophisticated and warm-hearted, but she is no noble savage. Her role is in its general dimensions comparable to that of her white sisters such as the matriarchs Aunt Jenny and Mrs. Rosa Millard, fostering and sustaining forces. If she goes beyond them in exemplifying the feminine principle at its best, still hers is no mere goodness by and of nature, if one means by this a goodness that justifies a faith in man as man. Dilsey does not believe in man; she believes in God.

To try for a summary of a very difficult and complicated topic: Evil for Faulkner involves the violation of the natural and the denial of the human. As Isaac's older kinsman says in "The Bear," "Courage and honor and pride, and pity and love of justice and of liberty. They all touch the heart, and what the heart holds to becomes truth, as far as we know truth." A meanness of spirit and coldness of calculation which would deny the virtues that touch the heart is by that very fact proven false. Yet Faulkner is no disciple of Jean-Jacque Rousseau. He has no illusions that man is naturally good or that he can safely trust to his instincts and emotions. Man is capable of evil, and this means that goodness has to be achieved by struggle and discipline and effort. Like T. S. Eliot, Faulkner has small faith in social arrangements so perfectly organized that nobody has to take the trouble to be good. Finally Faulkner's noblest characters are willing to face the fact that most men can learn the deepest truths about themselves and about reality only through suffering. Hurt and pain and loss are not mere accidents to which the human being is subject; nor

are they mere punishments incurred by human error; they can be the means
to the deeper knowledge and to the more abundant life.

1. Faulkner, a few years ago, in defining his notion of Christianity, called it a "code of behavior
by means of which (man) makes himself a better human being than his nature wants to be, if he
follows his nature only" (*Paris Review*, Spring 1956, p. 42).

III. The Work:

Studies of Method and Language

WILLIAM FAULKNER: THE NOVEL AS FORM

CONRAD AIKEN

THE FAMOUS REMARK made to Macaulay—"Young man, the more I consider the less can I conceive where you picked up that style"—might with advantage have been saved for Mr. William Faulkner. For if one thing is more outstanding than another about Mr. Faulkner—some readers find it so outstanding, indeed, that they never get beyond it—it is the uncompromising and almost hypnotic zeal with which he insists upon having a style, and, especially of late, the very peculiar style which he insists upon having. Perhaps to that one should add that he insists *when he remembers*—he can write straightforwardly enough when he wants to; he does so often in the best of his short stories (and they are brilliant), often enough, too, in the novels. But that *style* is what he really wants to get back to; and get back to it he invariably does.

And what a style it is, to be sure! The exuberant and tropical luxuriance of sound which Jim Europe's jazz band used to exhale, like a jungle of rank creepers and ferocious blooms taking shape before one's eyes,— magnificently and endlessly intervolved, glisteningly and ophidianly in motion, coil sliding over coil, and leaf and flower forever magically interchanging,—was scarcely more bewildering, in its sheer inexhaustible fecundity, than Mr. Faulkner's style. Small wonder if even the most passionate of Mr. Faulkner's admirers—among whom the present writer honors himself by enlisting—must find, with each new novel, that the first fifty pages are always the hardest, that each time one must learn all over again

Reprinted with permission from *The Atlantic Monthly*, November, 1939, pp. 650–54.

how to read this strangely fluid and slippery and heavily mannered prose, and that one is even, like a kind of Laocoön, sometimes tempted to give it up.

Wrestle, for example, with two very short (for Mr. Faulkner!) sentences, taken from an early page of *Absalom, Absalom!*

Meanwhile, as though in inverse ratio to the vanishing voice, the invoked ghost of the man whom she could neither forgive nor revenge herself upon began to assume a quality almost of solidity, permanence. Itself circumambient and enclosed by its effluvium of hell, its aura of unregeneration, it mused (mused, thought, seemed to possess sentience as if, though dispossessed of the peace —who was impervious anyhow to fatigue—which she declined to give it, it was still irrevocably outside the scope of her hurt or harm) with that quality peaceful and now harmless and not even very attentive—the ogreshape which, as Miss Coldfield's voice went on, resolved out of itself before Quentin's eyes the two half-ogre children, the three of them forming a shadowy background for the fourth one.

Well, it may be reasonably questioned whether, on page thirteen of a novel, that little cordite bolus of suppressed reference isn't a thumping aesthetic mistake. Returned to, when one has finished the book, it may be as simple as daylight; but encountered for the first time, and no matter how often reread, it guards its enigma with the stony impassivity of the Sphinx.

Or take again from the very first page of *The Wild Palms*—Mr. Faulkner's latest novel, and certainly one of his finest—this little specimen of "exposition": "Because he had been born here, on this coast though not in this house but in the other, the residence in town, and had lived here all his life, including the four years at the State University's medical school and the two years as an intern in New Orleans where (a thick man even when young, with thick soft woman's hands, who should never have been a doctor at all, who even after the six more or less metropolitan years looked out from a provincial and insulated amazement at his classmates and fellows: the lean young men swaggering in the drill jackets on which—to him—they wore the myriad anonymous faces of the probationer nurses with a ruthless and assured braggadocio like decorations, like flower trophies) he had sickened for it." What is one to say of that—or of a sentence only a little lower on the same page which runs for thirty-three lines? Is this, somehow perverted, the influence of the later Henry James—James the Old Pretender?

In short, Mr. Faulkner's style, though often brilliant and always interesting, is all too frequently downright bad; and it has inevitably offered an all-too-easy mark for the sharpshooting of such alert critics as Mr. Wyndham

Lewis. But if it is easy enough to make fun of Mr. Faulkner's obsessions for particular words, or his indifference and violence to them, or the parrotlike mechanical mytacism (for it is really like a stammer) with which he will go on endlessly repeating such favorites as "myriad, sourceless, impalpable, outrageous, risible, profound," there is nevertheless something more to be said for his passion for overelaborate sentence structure.

Overelaborate they certainly are, baroque and involuted in the extreme, these sentences: trailing clauses, one after another, shadowily in apposition, or perhaps not even with so much connection as that; parenthesis after parenthesis, the parenthesis itself often containing one or more parentheses—they remind one of those brightly colored Chinese eggs of one's childhood, which when opened disclosed egg after egg, each smaller and subtler than the last. It is as if Mr. Faulkner, in a sort of hurried despair, had decided to try to tell us everything, absolutely everything, every last origin or source or quality or qualification, and every possible future or permutation as well, in one terrifically concentrated effort: each sentence to be, as it were, a microcosm. And it must be admitted that the practice is annoying and distracting.

It is annoying, at the end of a sentence, to find that one does not know in the least what was the subject of the verb that dangles *in vacuo*—it is distracting to have to go back and sort out the meaning, track down the structure from clause to clause, then only to find that after all it doesn't much matter, and that the obscurity was perhaps neither subtle nor important. And to the extent that one *is* annoyed and distracted, and *does* thus go back and work it out, it may be at once added that Mr. Faulkner has defeated his own ends. One has had, of course, to emerge from the stream, and to step away from it, in order properly to see it; and as Mr. Faulkner works precisely by a process of *immersion,* of hypnotizing his reader into *remaining immersed* in his stream, this occasional blunder produces irritation and failure.

Nevertheless, despite the blunders, and despite the bad habits and the willful bad writing (and willful it obviously is), the style as a whole is extraordinarily effective; the reader *does* remain immersed, *wants* to remain immersed and it is interesting to look into the reasons for this. And at once, if one considers these queer sentences not simply by themselves, as monsters of grammar or awkwardness, but in their relation to the book as a whole, one sees a functional reason and necessity for their being as they are. They parallel in a curious and perhaps inevitable way, and not without aesthetic justification, the whole elaborate method of *deliberately withheld meaning,* of progressive and partial and delayed disclosure, which so often gives the characteristic shape to the novels themselves. It is a persistent offering of obstacles, a cal-

culated system of screens and obtrusions, of confusions and ambiguous inter-
polations and delays, with one express purpose; and that purpose is simply to
keep the form—and the idea—fluid and unfinished, still in motion, as it were,
and unknown, until the dropping into place of the very last syllable.

What Mr. Faulkner is after, in a sense, is a *continuum.* He wants a
medium without stops or pauses, a medium which is always *of the moment,*
and of which the passage from moment to moment is as fluid and undetectable
as in the life itself which he is purporting to give. It is all inside and underneath,
or as seen from within and below; the reader must therefore be steadily *drawn
in;* he must be powerfully and unremittingly hypnotized inward and down-
ward to that image-stream; and this suggests, perhaps, a reason not only for
the length and elaborateness of the sentence structure, but for the repetitiveness as well. The repetitiveness, and the steady iterative emphasis—like a kind
of chanting or invocation—on certain relatively abstract words ("sonorous,
latin, *vaguely* eloquent"), have the effect at last of producing, for Mr. Faulkner,
a special language, a conglomerate of his own, which he uses with an astonishing virtuosity, and which, although in detailed analysis it may look shoddy,
is actually for his purpose a life stream of almost miraculous adaptability. At
the one extreme it is abstract, cerebral, time-and-space-obsessed, tortured and
twisted, but nevertheless always with a living *pulse* in it; and at the other it
can be as overwhelming in its simple vividness, its richness in the actual, as
the flood scenes in *The Wild Palms.*

Obviously, such a style, especially when allied with such a *concern* for
method, must make difficulties for the reader; and it must be admitted that Mr.
Faulkner does little or nothing as a rule to make his highly complex "situation" easily available or perceptible. The reader must simply make up his mind
to go to work, and in a sense to cooperate; his reward being that there *is* a
situation to be given shape, a meaning to be extracted, and that half the fun
is precisely in watching the queer, difficult, and often so laborious evolution
of Mr. Faulkner's idea. And not so much idea, either, as form. For, like the
great predecessor whom at least in this regard he so oddly resembles, Mr.
Faulkner could say with Henry James that it is practically impossible to make
any real distinction between theme and form. What immoderately delights
him, alike in *Sanctuary, The Sound and the Fury, As I Lay Dying, Light in
August, Pylon, Absalom, Absalom!* and now again in *The Wild Palms,* and
what sets him above—shall we say it firmly—all his American contemporaries,
is his continuous preoccupation with the novel *as form,* his passionate concern
with it, and a degree of success with it which would clearly have commanded
the interest and respect of Henry James himself. The novel as revelation, the

novel as slice-of-life, the novel as mere story, do not interest him: these he would say, like James again, "are the circumstances of the interest," but not the interest itself. The interest itself will be the use to which these circumstances are put, the degree to which they can be organized.

From this point of view, he is not in the least to be considered as a mere "Southern" writer: the "Southernness" of his scenes and characters is of little concern to him, just as little as the question whether they are pleasant or unpleasant, true or untrue. Verisimilitude—or, at any rate, *degree* of verisimilitude—he will cheerfully abandon, where necessary, if the compensating advantages of plan or tone are a sufficient inducement. The famous scene in *Sanctuary* of Miss Reba and Uncle Bud in which a "madam" and her cronies hold a wake for a dead gangster, while the small boy gets drunk, is quite false, taken out of its context; it is not endowed with the same *kind* of actuality which permeates the great part of the book at all. Mr. Faulkner was cunning enough to see that a two-dimensional cartoon-like statement, at this juncture, would supply him with the effect of a chorus, and without in the least being perceived as a change in the temperature of truthfulness.

That particular kind of dilution, or adulteration, of verisimilitude was both practised and praised by James: as when he blandly admitted of *In the Cage* that his central character was "too ardent a focus of divination" to be quite credible. It was defensible simply because it made possible the coherence of the whole, and was itself absorbed back into the luminous texture. It was for him a device for organization, just as the careful cherishing of "viewpoint" was a device, whether simply or in counterpoint. Of Mr. Faulkner's devices, of this sort, aimed at the achievement of complex "form," the two most constant are the manipulation of viewpoint and the use of the flashback, or sudden shift of time-scene, forward or backward.

In *Sanctuary,* where the alternation of viewpoint is a little lawless, the complexity is given, perhaps a shade disingenuously, by violent shifts in time; a deliberate disarrangement of an otherwise straightforward story. Technically, there is no doubt that the novel, despite its fame, rattles a little; and Mr. Faulkner himself takes pains to disclaim it. But, even done with the left hand, it betrays a genius for form, quite apart from its wonderful virtuosity in other respects. *Light in August,* published a year after *Sanctuary,* repeats the same technique, that of a dislocation of time, and more elaborately; the time-shifts alternate with shifts in the viewpoint; and if the book is a failure it is perhaps because Mr. Faulkner's tendency to what is almost a hypertrophy of form is not here, as well as in the other novels, matched with the characters and the theme. Neither the person nor the story of Joe Christmas is seen fiercely enough—by its creator—to carry off that immense machinery or narrative; it would have needed another Popeye, or another Jiggs and Shumann, another Temple Drake, and for once Mr. Faulkner's inexhaustible inventiveness seems to have been at fault. Consequently what we see is an extraordinary power for form functioning relatively *in vacuo,* and existing only to sustain itself.

In the best of the novels, however,—and it is difficult to choose between *The Sound and the Fury* and *The Wild Palms,* with *Absalom, Absalom!* a very close third,—this tendency to hypertrophy of form has been sufficiently curbed; and it is interesting, too, to notice that in all these three (and in that remarkable *tour de force, As I Lay Dying,* as well), while there is still a considerable reliance on time-shift, the effect of richness and complexity is chiefly obtained by a very skillful fugue-like alternation of viewpoint. Fugue-like in *The Wild Palms*— and fugue-like especially, of course, in *As I Lay Dying,* where the shift is kaleidoscopically rapid, and where, despite an astonishing violence to plausibility (in the reflections, and *language* of reflection, of the characters) an effect of the utmost reality and immediateness is nevertheless produced. Fugue-like, again, in *Absalom, Absalom!* where indeed one may say the form is really circular—there is no beginning and no ending properly speaking, and therefore no *logical* point of entrance: we must just submit, and follow the circling of the author's interest, which turns a light inward towards the center, but every moment from a new angle, a new point of view. The story unfolds, therefore, now in one color of light, now in another, with references backward and forward: those that refer forward being necessarily, for the moment, blind. What is complete in Mr. Faulkner's pattern, *a priori,* must nevertheless remain incomplete for us until the very last stone is in place; what is "real," therefore, at one stage of the unfolding, or from one point of view, turns out to be "unreal" from another,' and we find that one among other things with which we are engaged is the fascinating sport of trying to separate truth from legend, watching the growth of legend from truth, and finally reaching the conclusion that the distinction is itself false.

Something of the same sort is true also of *The Sound and the Fury*—and this, with its massive four-part symphonic structure, is perhaps the most beautifully *wrought* of the whole series, and an indubitable masterpiece of what James loved to call the "fictive art." The joinery is flawless in its intricacy; it is a novelist's novel—a whole textbook on the craft of fiction in itself, comparable in its way to *What Maisie Knew* or *The Golden Bowl.*

But if it is important, for the moment, to emphasize Mr. Faulkner's genius for form, and his continued exploration of its possibilities, as against the usual concern with the violence and dreadfulness of his themes—though we might pause to remind carpers on this score of the fact that the best of Henry James is precisely that group of last novels which so completely concerned themselves with moral depravity—it is also well to keep in mind his genius for invention, whether of character or episode. The inventiveness is of the richest possible sort—a headlong and tumultuous abundance, an exuberant generosity and vitality, which makes most other contemporary fiction look very pale and chaste indeed. It is an unforgettable gallery of portraits, whether character or caricature, and all of them endowed with a violent and immediate vitality.

"He is at once"—to quote once more from James—"one of the most corrupt of writers and one of the most naïf, the most mechanical and pedantic, and the fullest on *bonhomie* and natural impulse. He is one of the finest of artists and one of the coarsest. Viewed in one way, his novels are ponderous, shapeless, overloaded; his touch is graceless, violent, barbarous. Viewed in another, his tales have more color, more composition, more grasp of the reader's attention than any others. [His] style would demand a chapter apart. It is the least simple style, probably, that was ever written; it bristles, it cracks, it swells and swaggers; but it is a perfect expression of the man's genius. Like his genius, it contains a certain quantity of everything, from immaculate gold to flagrant dross. He was a very bad writer, and yet unquestionably he was a very great writer. We may say briefly, that in so far as his method was an instinct it was successful, and that in so far as it was a theory it was a failure. But both in instinct and in theory he had the aid of an immense force of conviction. His imagination warmed to its work so intensely that there was nothing his volition could not impose upon it. Hallucination settled upon him, and he believed anything that was necessary in the circumstances."

That passage, from Henry James's essay on Balzac, is almost word for word, with scarcely a reservation, applicable to Mr. Faulkner. All that is lacking is Balzac's greater *range* of understanding and tenderness, his great freedom from special preoccupations. For this, one would hazard the guess that Mr. Faulkner has the gifts—and time is still before him.

WILLIAM FAULKNER'S STYLE

WARREN BECK

NO OTHER CONTEMPORARY American novelist of comparable stature has been as frequently or as severely criticized for his style as has William Faulkner. Yet he is a brilliantly original and versatile stylist. The condemnations of his way of writing have been in part just; all but the most idolatrous of Faulkner's admirers must have wished he had blotted a thousand infelicities. However, an enumeration of his faults in style would leave still unsaid the most important things about his style. There is need here for a reapportionment of negative and positive criticism.

It is true that the preponderant excellences of Faulkner's prose, when recognized, make his faults all the more conspicuous and irritating. And under criticism Faulkner has not only remained guilty of occasional carelessness, especially in sentence construction, but seems to have persisted in mannerisms. On the other hand, his progress as a stylist has been steady and rapid; his third novel, *Sartoris*, while still experimenting toward a technique, was a notable advance over his first two in style as well as in theme and narrative structure, and in his fourth novel, *The Sound and the Fury*, style is what it has continued to be in all his subsequent work, a significant factor, masterfully controlled. This growth has been made largely without the aid of appreciative criticism, and in the face of some misunderstanding and abuse of the most dynamic qualities in his writing. It is quite possible that Faulkner would have paid more attention to the critics' valid objections if these had not been so frequently interlarded with misconceptions of his stylistic method, or indeed complete insensitivity to it.

Repetition of words, for instance, has often seemed an obvious fault. At times, however, Faulkner's repetitions may be a not unjustifiable by-product of his thematic composition. Some of his favorites in *Absalom, Absalom!*—not just Miss Rosa's "demon," which may be charged off to her own mania, nor "indolent" applied to Bon, but such recurrent terms as *effluvium, outrage,*

Reprinted with permission from *American Prefaces* (Spring 1941), 195–211.

grim, indomitable, ruthless, fury, fatality—seem to intend adumbration of the tale's whole significance and tone. Nor is the reiteration as frequent or as obvious here as in earlier books; perhaps Faulkner has been making an experiment over which he is increasingly gaining control.

Faulkner often piles up words in a way that brings the charge of prolixity. He has Wilbourne say of his life with Charlotte in Chicago,

"it was the mausoleum of love, it was the stinking catafalque of the dead corpse borne between the olfactoryless walking shapes of the immortal unsentient demanding ancient meat."

However, these word-series, while conspicuous at times, may have a place in a style as minutely analytical as Faulkner's. In their typical form they are not redundant, however elaborate, and sometimes their cumulative effect is undeniable—for example, the "long still hot weary dead September afternoon" when Quentin listens to Miss Rosa's story. Colonel Feinman, the wealthy exploiter of impecunious aviators, had as secretary "a young man, sleek, in horn rim glasses," who spoke "with a kind of silken insolence, like the pampered intelligent hateridden eunuchmountebank of an eastern despot," and here the amplification redounds to the significance of the whole scene. Quite often too these series of words, while seemingly extravagant, are a remarkably compressed rendering, as in the phrase "passionate tragic ephemeral loves of adolescence."

In fairness it must be noted too that Faulkner's later work never drops to the level of fantastic verbosity found in the thematic paragraph introducing his second novel, *Mosquitoes.* Nor does he any longer break the continuum of his narrative with rhapsodies like the notable description of the mule in *Sartoris,* a sort of cadenza obviously done out of exuberance. In the later books profuseness of language is always knit into the thematic structure. Thus the elaborate lyrical descriptions of the sunrise and of a spring rain in book three of *The Hamlet* furnish by their imagery and mood a sharp, artistically serviceable contrast to the perversion of the idiot Ike Snopes, and as such they deepen the melancholy perspective from which this episode is observed.

Faulkner's studied use of a full style and his sense of its place in the architectonics of an extended and affecting narrative is well displayed in the last chapters of *Light in August,* chapter nineteen closing with the first climax, of Joe Christmas' death, poetically expressed; chapter twenty closing similarly in the second and more comprehensive climax of Hightower's final vision; and then chapter twenty-one, which completes the book, furnishing a modulation to detached calm through the simply prosaic, somewhat humorous account, by a new and neutral spokesman, of the exodus of Lena and Byron into Tennessee. Indeed, one of the best indexes to the degree of Faulkner's control of eloquence is in a comparison of the novels' conclusions—some of them in a full descriptive style, as in *Soldiers' Pay, Sartoris, Sanctuary,* and to a degree in *The Sound and the Fury* and *The Unvanquished;* more of the novels closing with a meaningful but plainly stated utterance or gesture of a character, as in *Mosquitoes, As I lay Dying, Pylon, Absalom, Absalom!, The Wild Palms,* and *The Hamlet*—(the last that wonderful "Snopes turned his head and spat over the wagon wheel. He jerked the reins slightly. 'Come up,' he said.") This ratio suggests that while Faulkner does not avoid elaboration, neither is he its slave.

Faulkner's diction, charged and proliferate though it may be, usually displays a nice precision, and this is especially evident in its direct imagery. An example is in the glimpse of Cash, after he has worked all night in the rain, finishing his mother's coffin:

In the lantern light his face calm, musing; slowly he strokes his hands on his raincoated thighs in a gesture deliberate, final and composed.

Frequently, however, Faulkner proceeds in descriptive style beyond epithet and abstract definition to figurative language. Having written,

It is just dawn, daylight: that gray and lonely suspension filled with the peaceful and tentative waking of birds.

he goes on in the next sentence to a simile:

The air, inbreathed, is like spring water.

The novels abound in examples of his talent for imaginative comparisons; for instance, the hard-boiled flier Shumann, dressed up:

He wore a new gray homburg hat, not raked like in the department store cuts but set square on the back of his head so that (not tall, with blue eyes in a square thin profoundly sober face) he looked out not from beneath it but from within it with open and fatal humorlessness, like an early Briton who has been assured that the Roman governor will not receive him unless he wear the borrowed centurion's helmet.

There is nothing unique, however, in Faulkner's use of direct and forceful diction or fine figurative image. What is most individual in his style is its persistent lyrical embroidery and coloring, in extended passages, of the narrative theme. In this sense Faulkner is one of the most subjective of writers, his brooding temperament constantly probing and interpreting his subject matter.

Thus his full style is comprehensive in its intention. He may often be unfashionably rhapsodic, but he seldom falls into the preciosity that lingers over a passage for its own sweet sake. Definition of his story as a whole and the enhancement of its immediate appeals to the imagination are his constant aims.

The latest of Faulkner's novels demonstrates the grasp he has developed upon all the devices of his style. *The Hamlet* is a sort of prose fantasia; the various episodes employ colloquial tall stories, poetic description, folk humor, deliberate reflective narration, swift cryptic drama, and even a grotesque allegory, of Snopes in hell. Differing in tone from the elegaic brooding of *Light in August,* or the exasperated volubility of *Pylon,* the modulant intricacy and fusion of *Absalom, Absalom!,* the tender directness of *The Unvanquished,* or the eloquent turbulence of *The Wild Palms, The Hamlet* seems an extravaganza improvised more freely in a more detached mood, the author apparently delighting in the realizations of varied subject-matters through the flexibilities of his multiform style.

A number of passages in *The Hamlet* give precise indications of Faulkner's purpose as a stylist, inasmuch as they are reworkings of material released as short stories in magazines from four to nine years before the novel's publication. "Spotted Horses," which appeared in *Scribner's* for June, 1931, contains in germ Flem Snopes' whole career in *The Hamlet.* The story is in first person; Ratliff is the reciter, but he is not quite the shrewd and benevolent spectator he becomes under the touches of Faulkner's own descriptions in the third-person narrative of the novel. The short story moves faster, of course, sketching the drama more broadly and making no pause for brooding lyrical interpretation. Faulkner's omniscient narration of the episode is almost twice as long as Ratliff's simple monologue, and rises to an altogether different plane of conception and diction. The contrast is almost like that between a ballad and a tone-poem.

This difference, which certainly must indicate Faulkner's free and considered choice and his fundamental aesthetic inclination, can be defined by a comparison of parallel passages from the horse-auction scene, when the Texan tries to hold one of the animals and continue his salestalk. The Scribner short story read as follows:

'Look it over,' he says, with his heels dug too and that white pistol sticking outen his pocket and his neck swole up like a spreading adder's until you could just tell what he was saying, cussing the horse and talking to us all at once: 'Look him over, the fiddle-headed son of fourteen fathers. Try him, buy him, you will get the best—' Then it was all dust again, and we couldn't see nothing but spotted hide and mane, and that ere Texas man's boot-heels like a couple of walnuts on two strings, and after a while that two-gallon hat come sailing out like a fat old hen crossing a fence. When the dust settled again, he was just getting outen the far fence corner, brushing himself off. He come and got his hat and brushed it off and come and clumb onto the gate post again.

In the novel the parallel passage has been recast thus:

'Look him over, boys,' the Texan panted, turning his own suffused face and the protuberant glare of his eyes toward the fence. 'Look him over quick. Them shoulders and—' He had relaxed for an instant apparently. The animal exploded again; again for an instant the Texan was free of the earth, though he was still talking:'—and legs you whoa I'll tear your face right look him over quick boys worth fifteen dollars of let me get a holt of who'll make me a bid whoa you blare-eyed jack rabbit, whoa! They were moving now—a kaleidoscope of inextricable and incredible violence on the periphery of which the metal clasps of the Texan's suspenders sun-glinted in ceaseless orbit, with terrific slowness across the lot. Then the broad clay-colored hat soared deliberately outward; an instant later the Texan followed it, though still on his feet, and the pony shot free in mad, stag-like bounds. The Texan picked up the hat and struck the dust from it against his leg, and returned to the fence and mounted the post again.

Obviously the difference is not only quantitative but qualitative. Instead of Ratliff's "that old two-gallon hat come sailing out like a fat old hen crossing a fence" there is Faulkner's "the broad clay-colored hat soared deliberately outward"; Ratliff sees "that ere Texas man's bootheels like a couple of walnuts on two strings," but Faulkner shows a "kaleidoscope of inextricable and incredible violence on the periphery of which the metal clasps of the Texan's suspenders sun-glinted in ceaseless orbit with terrific slowness across the lot." This latter represents the style Faulkner has chosen to develop; he can do the simpler and more objective narration, but when given such an opportunity as in the amalgamating of these magazine stories into a novel, he insists on transmuting the factual-objective into the descriptive-definitive colored by his imagination and elaborated by his resourcefulness in language.

In its typical exercise this style gives image only incidentally and exists primarily to enhance and sustain mood. Thus Wilbourne's first approach to the house where his meeting with Charlotte is to begin their passionate and disastrous love story is set in this key:

. . . they entered: a court paved with the same soft, quietly rotting brick. There was a stagnant pool with a terra-cotta figure, a mass of lantana, the single palm the thick rich leaves and the heavy white stars of the jasmine bush where light fell upon it through open French doors, the court balcony—overhung too on three sides, the walls of that same annealing brick lifting a rampart broken and nowhere level against the glare of the city on the low eternally overcast sky, and over all, brittle, dissonant and ephemeral, the spurious sophistication of the piano like symbols scrawled by adolescent boys upon an ancient decayed rodent-scavengered tomb.

The reporter's mood of anxious inquiry and the frustration which is thematic in *Pylon* are both represented as he telephones:

Now he too heard only dead wirehum, as if the other end of it extended beyond atmosphere, into cold space; as though he listened now to the profound sound of infinity, of void itself filled with the cold unceasing murmur of aeonweary and unflagging stars.

This organic quality of Faulkner's style, sustaining through essentially poetic devices an orchestration of meaning, makes it impossible to judge him adequately by brief quotation. In the description of Temple's first hours in Madame Reba's brothel, for instance, the thematic recurrence from page to page of subjectively interpreted imagery builds up in a time continuum the mood of the girl's trance-like state of shock and also the larger fact of her isolation in the sordid. First,

The drawn shades, cracked into a myriad pattern like old skin, blew faintly on the bright air, breathing into the room on waning surges the sound of Sabbath traffic, festive, steady, evanescent . . .

and then, three pages further,

The shades blew steadily in the windows, with faint rasping sounds. Temple began to hear a clock. It sat on the mantel above a grate filled with fluted green paper. The clock was of flowered china, supported by four china nymphs. It had only one hand, scrolled and gilded, halfway between ten and eleven, lending to the otherwise blank face a quality of unequivocal assertion, as though it had nothing whatever to do with time . . .

and then, two pages further,

In the window the cracked shade, yawning now and then with a faint rasp against the frame, let twilight into the room in fainting surges. From beneath the shade the smoke-colored twilight emerged in slow puffs like signal smoke from a blanket, thickening in the room. The china figures which supported the clock gleamed in hushed smooth flexions: knee, elbow, flank, arm, and breast in attitudes of voluptuous lassitude. The glass face, become mirror-like, appeared to hold all reluctant light, holding in its tranquil depths a quiet gesture of moribund time, one-armed like a veteran from the wars. Half past ten oclock. Temple lay in the bed, looking at the clock, thinking about half-past-ten-oclock.

Yet side by side with this richly interpretative style there exists in almost all of Faulkner's work a realistic colloquialism, expressing lively dialogue that any playwright might envy, and even carrying over into sustained first-person narrative the flavor of regionalism and the idiosyncrasies of character. In the colloquial vein Faulkner's brilliance is unsurpassed in contemporary American fiction. He has fully mastered the central difficulty, to retain verisimilitude while subjecting the prolix and monotonous raw material of most natural speech to an artistic pruning and pointing up. *Sanctuary,* for an example, is full of excellent dialogue, sharply individualized. And Faulkner's latest book not only contains some of his most poetic writing but has one of his best talkers, Ratliff, both in extended anecdote in monologue and in dramatic conversations. Ratliff's reflective, humorous, humane, but skeptical nature, a triumph in characterization, is silhouetted largely out of his talk about the hamlet's affairs.

Faulkner also can weave colloquial bits into the matrix of a more literary passage, with the enlarging effect of a controlled dissonance. Thus Quentin imagines Henry Sutpen and Charles Bon, at the end of the war, Charles determined to marry Judith, Henry forbidding; and then into Quentin's elaboration of the scene breaks the voice of his father, continuing the story, giving its denouement in the words vulgarly uttered by Wash Jones:

(It seemed to Quentin that he could actually see them . . . They faced one another on the two gaunt horses, two men, young, not yet in the world, not yet breathed over long enough, to be old but with old eyes, with unkempt hair and faces gaunt and weathered as if cast by some spartan and even niggard hand from bronze, in worn and patched gray weathered now to the color of dead leaves, the one with the tarnished braid of an officer, the other plain of cuff, the pistol lying yet across the saddle bow unaimed, the two faces calm, the voices not even raised: *Don't you pass the shadow of this post, this branch, Charles;* and *I am going to pass it, Henry)*—and then Wash Jones sitting that saddleless mule before Miss Rosa's gate, shouting her name into the sunny and peaceful quiet of the street, saying, 'Air you Rosie Coldfield? Then you better come on out yon. Henry has done shot that durn French feller. Kilt him dead as a beef.'

Master of colloquialism in dramatic scene though he is, Faulkner sometimes lays aside this power in order to put into a character's mouth the fullest
expression of the narrative's meaning. The mature Bayard Sartoris, looking
back to Civil War times, telling the story of his boyhood and youth in *The
Unvanquished,* opens what is Faulkner's most straightforward narrative, and
his only novel related throughout by one character in first person, in this strain:

Behind the smokehouse that summer, Ringo and I had a living map. Although
Vicksburg was just a handful of chips from the woodpile and the River a trench
scraped into the packed earth with the point of a hoe, it (river, city, and terrain)
lived, possessing even in miniature that ponderable though passive recalcitrane
of topography which outweighs artillery, against which the most brilliant of
victories and the most tragic of defeats are but the loud noises of a moment.

At times it seems as though the author, after having created an unsophisticated
character, is elbowing him off the stage, as when the rustic Darl Bundren sees
"the square squat shape of the coffin on the sawhorses like a cubistic bug," or
as when in the short story, "All The Dead Pilots," the World War flier John
Sartoris is characterized as having a vocabulary of "perhaps two hundred
words" and then is made to say,

. . . I knew that if I busted in and dragged him out and bashed his head off,
I'd not only be cashiered, I'd be clinked for life for having infringed the articles
of alliance by invading foreign property without warrant or something.

For the most part, however, the transcending of colloquial verisimilitude in the
novels is a fairly controlled and consistent technique, the characters Faulkner
most often endows with penetration and eloquence being his philosophical
spectators. Undoubtedly his chief concern, though, is with a lyric encompass-
ment of his narrative's whole meaning rather than with the reticences of
objective dramatic representation.

Thus many of his characters speak with the tongues of themselves and of
William Faulkner. As Quentin and his Harvard roommate Shreve evolve the
reconstruction of Thomas Sutpen's story which constitutes the second half of
Absalom, Absalom!, Quentin thinks when Shreve talks, "He sounds just like
father," and later, when Quentin has the floor, Shreve interrupts with "Don't
say it's just me that sounds like your old man," which certainly shows that
Faulkner realizes what he is doing. Actually he does make some differences
among these voices: Miss Rosa rambles and ejaculates with erratic spinsterish
emotion, Mr. Compson is elaborately and sometimes parenthetically ironic,
Quentin is most sensitively imaginative and melancholy, Shreve most detached

and humorous. What they have in common is the scope and pitch of an almost lyrical style which Faulkner has arbitrarily fixed upon for an artistic instrument. The justification of all such practices is empirical; imaginative writing must not be judged by its minute correspondence to fact but by its total effect; and to object against Faulkner's style that men and women don't really talk in such long sentences, with so full a vocabulary so fancifully employed, is as narrowly dogmatic as was Sinclair Lewis, in *Main Street,* insisting that Sir Launcelot didn't actually speak in "honeyed pentameters."

Typical instances of Faulkner's endowing his characters with precise diction and fluency may show that on the whole it is not an unacceptable convention. Thus Wilbourne's full and finished sentence:

"We lived in an apartment that wasn't bohemian, it wasn't even a tabloid love-nest, it wasn't even in that part of town but in a neighborhood dedicated by both city ordinance and architecture to the second year of wedlock among the five-thousand-a-year bracket . . ."

though it is not stylistically rooted in his manner as characterized up to this point, is not inconsistent with his personality and sensibilities, and it does get on with the story. Equally acceptable is Ratliff's remark about the platitudinous family-fleeing I.O. Snopes,

"What's his name? that quick-fatherer, the Moses with his mouth full of mottoes and his coat-tail full of them already half-grown retroactive sons?"

Its keen diction and nice rhythm are not essentially false to Ratliff, but only an idealization in language of the percipient humorous sewing-machine salesman the reader already knows. The same is true of those tumbling floods of phrases, too prolonged for human breath to utter, with which the reporter in *Pylon* assaults the sympathies of editor Hagood; they are not so much a part of dialogue as an intense symbol of the pace of racing aviation and the reporter's frantic concern for his proteges among the fliers.

It is interesting to note that Faulkner's full style somewhat resembles older literary uses, such as the dramatic chorus, the prologue and epilogue, and the *dramatis personae* themselves in soliloquy and extended speech. The aim of any such device is not objective realism but revelation of theme, a revelation raised by the unstinted resourcefulness and power of its language to the highest ranges of imaginative outlook. No wonder that with such a purpose Faulkner often comes closer than is common in these times to Shakespeare's imperial and opulent use of words. If unfortunately his ambition has sometimes led Faulkner to perpetrate some rather clotted prose, perhaps these lapses may be judged charitably in the light of the great endeavor they but infrequently flaw.

More particularly Faulkner's full sentence structure springs from the elaborateness of his fancies ramifying in descriptive imagery. Thus editor Hagood, perpetually beset by small annoyances and chronically irritated by them, drops himself wearily into his roadster's low seat,

. . . whereupon without sound or warning the golfbag struck him across the head and shoulder with an apparently calculated and lurking viciousness, emitting a series of dry clicks as though produced by the jaws of a beast domesticated though not tamed, half in fun and half in deadly seriousness, like a pet shark.

Another typical source of fullness in Faulkner's sentences is a tendency to musing speculation, sometimes proceeding to the statement of alternative suggestions. Thus Miss Rosa speaks of wearing garments left behind by the eloping aunt in "kindness or haste or oversight," that doing its bit in a sentence well over three hundred words long. Such characteristic theorizing may run to the length of this postscript of a description of Flem Snopes:

. . . a thick squat soft man of no establishable age between twenty and thirty, with a broad still face containing a tight seam of mouth stained slightly at the corners with tobacco, and eyes the color of stagnant water, and projecting from among the other features in startling and sudden paradox, a tiny predatory nose like the beak of a small hawk. It was as though the original nose had been left off by the original designer or craftsman and the unfinished job taken over by someone of a radically different school or perhaps by some viciously maniacal humorist or perhaps by one who had only time to clap into the center of the face a frantic and desperate warning.

Even the most elaborate and esoteric of these speculations are not limited to third-person narrative; Faulkner's pervasive subjectivity injects such abstractions too, as well as extended imagery, into the reflections and speech of many of his characters, again most typically those who contemplate and interpret the action of the stories, who act as chorus or soliloquize. Here too the device proves itself in practice. When such characters brood over the events, painstakingly rehearsing details, piling one hypothesis upon another, their very tentativeness creates for the reader the clouded enigmatic perspective of reality itself. Thus Miss Rosa's account, with reinterpretation imposed upon memory, of Sutpen's driving in to church with his family:

It was as though the sister whom I had never laid eyes on, who before I was born had vanished into the stronghold of an ogre or a djinn, was now to return through a dispensation of one day only, to the world which she had quitted, and I a child of three, waked early for the occasion, dressed and curled as if for Christmas, for an occasion more serious than Christmas even, since now and at last this ogre or djinn had agreed for the sake of the wife and the children to come to church, to permit them at least to approach the vicinity of salvation, to at least give Ellen one chance to struggle with him for those children's souls on a battleground where she could be supported not only by Heaven but by her own family and people of her own kind; yes, even for the moment submitting himself to redemption, or lacking that, at least chivalrous for the instant even though still unregenerate.

The foregoing examples, however, do not illustrate Faulkner's style at its most involved, as in this passage from Quentin's consciousness, while he listens to Miss Rosa's reconstruction of the Sutpen family history:

It should have been later than it was; it should have been late, yet the yellow slashes of mote-palpitant sunlight were latticed no higher up the impalpable wall of gloom which separated them; the sun seemed hardly to have moved. It (the talking, the telling) seemed (to him, to Quentin) to partake of that logic-and reason-flouting quality of a dream which the sleeper knows must have occurred, still-born and complete, in a second, yet the very quality upon which it must depend to move the dreamer (verisimilitude) to credulity—horror or pleasure or amazement—depends as completely upon a formal recognition of and acceptance of elapsed and yet-elapsing time as music or a printed tale.

By its parentheses and involution and fullness this last sentence illustrates that occasionally extreme eccentricity most often and most rightfully objected to in its author's style. At the same time this sentence may give a key to Faulkner's entire method and typify its artistic purposefulness—to create "that logic- and reason-flouting quality of a dream," yet to depend upon the recognized verisimilitude of "elapsed and yet-elapsing time." Such a product is not necessarily mere nightmare; it is often a real quality of experience at its greatest intensity and acuteness. In his most characteristic writing Faulkner is trying to render the transcendent life of the mind, the crowded composite of associative and analytical consciousness which expands the vibrant moment into the reaches of all time, simultaneously observing, remembering, interpreting, and modifying the object of its awareness. To this end the sentence as a rhetorical unit (however strained) is made to hold diverse yet related elements in a sort of saturated solution, which is perhaps the nearest that language as the instrument of fiction can come to the instantaneous complexities of consciousness itself. Faulkner really seems to be trying to give narrative prose another dimension.

 To speak of Faulkner's fiction as dream-like (using Quentin's notion as a key) does not imply that his style is phantasmagoric, deranged, or incoherent. Dreams are not always delirium; and association, sometimes the supplanter of pattern, can also be its agent. The dreaming mind, while envisaging experience strangely, may find in that strangeness a fresh revelation, all the more profound in that the conventional and adventitious are pierced through. Similarly inhibitions and apathies must be transcended in any really imaginative inquiry, and thus do Faulkner's speculative characters ponder over the whole story, and project into cumulative drama its underlying significations. Behind all of them, of course, is their master-dreamer; Faulkner's own dominating temperament, constantly interpreting, is in the air of all these narratives, reverberant. Hence no matter how psychological the story's material, Faulkner never falls into the mere enumeration which in much stream-of-consciousness writing dissolves all drama and reduces the narrative to a case history without the shaping framework of analysis, or even to an unmapped anachronistic chaos of raw consciousness. Faulkner is always a dynamic story-teller, never just a reporter of unorganized phenomena. His most drastic, most dream-like use of stream-of-consciousness, for instance, in *The Sound and the Fury,* is not only limited to the first two sections of the book, but it sketches a plot which in the lucid sections that follow gradually emerges clear-cut.

As clear-cut, at least, as Faulkner's stories can be. Here again is illustrated the close relation of his style to his whole point of view. If Faulkner's sentences sometimes soar and circle involved and prolonged, if his scenes become halls of mirrors repeating tableaux in a progressive magnification, if echoes multiply into the dissonance of infinite overtones, it is because the meanings his stories unfold are complex, mysterious, obscure, and incomplete. There is no absolute, no eternal pure white radiance in such presentations, but rather the stain of many colors, refracted and shifting in kaleidoscopic suspension, about the center of man's enigmatic behavior and fate, within the drastic orbit of mortality. Such being Faulkner's view of life, such is his style.

To this view the very rhythm of Faulkner's prose is nicely adjusted. It is not emphatic; rather it is a slow prolonged movement, nothing dashing, even at its fullest flood, but surging with an irresistible momentum. His effects insofar as they depend on prose rhythms are never staccato, they are cumulative rather than abrupt. Such a prose rhythm supplements the contributions of full vocabulary and lengthy sentence toward suspension rather than impact, and consequently toward deep realization rather than quick surprise. And the prolonged even murmur of Faulkner's voice throughout his pages is an almost

July 4

hypnotic induction into those detailed and darkly-colored visions of life which drift across the horizons of his imagination like clouds—great yet vaporous, changing yet enduring, unearthly yet of common substance. It might be supposed that his occasionally crowded and circumlocutory style would destroy narrative pace and consequence. Actually this hovering of active imagination, while employing the sustained lyricism and solid abstraction which differentiate Faulkner from the objective realist, furnishes the epitome of drama. The whole aim is at perspective, through the multiple dimensions of experience, upon a subject in that suspension which allows reflection. The accomplishment is the gradual, sustained, and enriched revelation of meaning; in Faulkner's novels drama is of that highest form which awaits the unfolding of composite action, characterization, mood, and idea, through the medium of style.

Faulkner himself probably would admit the relative inadequacy of instrument to purpose, would agree with Mr. Compson in calling language "that meager and fragile thread by which the little surface corners and edges of men's secret and solitary lives may be joined for an instant." Faulkner perhaps has no greater faith in the word than have his contemporaries who have partially repudiated it, but instead of joining that somewhat paradoxical literary trend, he seems determined to exploit an imperfect device to the uttermost within the limits of artistic illusion. Thus although in certain passages he has demonstrated his command of a simplified objective method, he has not made it his invariable device, nor does he allow its contemporary vogue to prevent his using words in the old-fashioned way for whatever they are worth descriptively and definitively.

Faulkner's whole narrative method, as described, may seem to be a retrogression in technique. Two main tendencies in modern fiction have been toward a more and more material dramatic presentation, depending simply upon the naming of objects and acts and the reporting of speech, and on the other hand, toward an ostensibly complete and unbroken reproduction of the free flow of consciousness. These methods have produced books as radically different as *The Sun Also Rises* and *Ulysses,* yet they have elements in common. In both types the author attempts to conceal himself completely behind his materials, to give them the quality of integral phenomena, and in line with this purpose the style aims at pure reproduction, never allowing definition and interpretation from any detached point of view. These have been honest attempts, a great deal of fine craftsmanship has gone into them, and some of the products have been excellent in their kind. Yet at their most extreme these have been movements in the one direction toward bareness, impoverishment, and in the other toward incoherence. Confronted by the imperfections and confusions of the present scene, and made hyper-skeptical by deference to scientific method, the writers who have attempted absolute objectivity (whether dramatic or psychological, whether in overt event or stream of association) have sometimes produced what looks like an anti-intellectual aesthetic of futility and inconsequence. So in another sense Faulkner's narrative technique, particularly as implemented by his full style, instead of being a retrogression may represent one kind of progression through the danger of impasse created by too great submission to vogues of photographic or psychographic reproduction.

Yet Faulkner's is not altogether a return to an older expressiveness, not a complete departure from the modern schools of Hemingway and Joyce. In his colloquial passages he is quite as objectively dramatic as the one, in his rehearsal of the fantasies of acute consciousness he follows the other—and it should be remembered that he is superlatively skillful at both, so that it cannot be said that he puts these objective methods aside because he cannot use them. Furthermore, Faulkner is fond of employing in extended passages one of the favorite modern means of objectivity in fiction, the first-person narrator, using the device toward its most honored modern purpose, the attainment of detached perspective and the creation of realistic illusion concerning large vistas of the story. In short, there is no method in modern fiction which Faulkner does not comprehend and use on occasion. Fundamentally Faulkner's only heterodoxy by present standards of style is his fullness, especially as it takes the form of descriptive eloquence or abstraction and definitiveness. What is stylistically most remarkable in his work is the synthesis he has effected between the subtleties of modern narrative techniques and the resources of language employed in the traditionally poetic or interpretative vein. That such a synthesis is feasible is demonstrated in the dynamic forms of his novels, and it may be prelude to significant new developments in the methods of fiction.

THE EDGE OF ORDER: THE PATTERN
OF FAULKNER'S RHETORIC

WALTER J. SLATOFF

IN WILLIAM FAULKNER'S short story "Delta Autumn," Ike McCaslin says that "the heart dont always have time to bother with thinking up words that fit together."[1] In *Absalom, Absalom!,* when Charles Bon leaves for college, Faulkner describes him as "almost touching the answer, aware of the jig-saw puzzle picture integers of it waiting, almost lurking, just beyond his reach, inextricable, jumbled, and unrecognizable yet on the point of falling into pattern which would reveal to him at once, like a flash of light, the meaning of his whole life" (313). The integers never do fall into place for Charles Bon. Much the same can be said about Benjy and Quentin Compson, Darl Bundren, Gail Hightower, Thomas Sutpen and numerous other characters in Faulkner's novels.

Every Faulkner novel in some way provides the reader with the problem of fitting pieces together, and many readers of Faulkner feel with respect to the meanings of the novels much as Charles Bon did about the meaning of his life. Much Faulkner criticism has been devoted to explaining, both in particular novels and in his works in general, how the pieces do fit together, the patterns of meaning they do form. A good many such patterns have been discovered and offered as the essential meanings of the novels and of Faulkner's vision as a whole.

In this paper I wish to suggest that in many ways and on many levels Faulkner seems very anxious to keep pieces from fitting together, and that this is a crucial aspect of his work. It has been generally recognized that the purpose of some of Faulkner's structural complexities is to keep his material in a state of flux or suspension. But it has also generally been thought and argued or assumed that these suspensions are finally resolved, that by the ends of the novels the jig-saw picture puzzle integers do fall into place. There is much evidence, I think, that Faulkner is willing and even anxious to leave most

Reprinted with permission from *Twentieth Century Literature,* October, 1957, pp. 107–27.

of them in a high degree of suspension, or at least a suspension that cannot be resolved in logical or rational terms. Nor has it been recognized how very much his moment to moment presentation of experience involves a juxtaposition of elements which do not seem to fit together and which to some degree resist synthesis or resolution.

1

A remarkably frequent and persistent phenomenon in Faulkner's writing is his presentation of opposed or contradictory suggestions. In some instances the contradictions are more apparent than real; in others they seem quite real. I shall not try to distinguish between them. My purpose here is simply to suggest something of the number and variety of things which are presented in conflicting terms. Again and again, for example, Faulkner describes objects and events in terms which at once suggest motion and immobility. A large number of wagons, buggies, and engines are described as moving "without progress" or with an effect of "nomotion." The carcasses of hogs hang "immobilized by the heels in attitudes of frantic running" (*ID,* 4). Rosa Coldfield and Clytie face one another: "I motionless in the attitude and action of running, she rigid in that furious immobility" (*AA,* 140). Psychological conditions are often similarly rendered. When the schoolbell rings, Quentin Compson's "insides would move, sitting still. *Moving sitting still*" (*SF,* 107). "Though Joe had not moved since he entered, he was still running" (*LIA,* 187). Frequently the contradictory suggestions are compressed into phrases like "poised and swooping immobility," "terrific immobility," or "dynamic immobility."

Sound and silence, also, are frequently presented as existing simultaneously. Silence often seems not so much the absence of sound as a container for it, a presence even while the sounds are occurring. We read of a "silence filled with the puny sounds of men" (*LIA,* 259) and "a sound . . . which silence itself, seemed to find strange and hard to digest" (*MCS,* 19–20). Very frequently, just as he gives maximum simultaneity and compression to motion and immobility in images like "dynamic immobility," Faulkner compresses the suggestions of sound and silence to the condition of oxymoron. Thus, again and again we find phrases like "crashing silently," "exploded soundlessly," "soundless yelling," and "quiet thunderclap." On at least three occasions Faulkner sets up, in effect, double oxymorons of sound and silence, the most compact being "soundless words in the pattering silence" (*CS,* 899).

Perhaps the most common physical and psychological conditions presented by Faulkner are ones which simultaneously contain elements of quiescence and turbulence. A flood is likely to exhibit a calm, still surface above its raging currents or to suggest "fury in itself quiet with stagnation" (*AILD*, 458). Fights commonly occur in silence or in tranquil surroundings. Characters, even the most violent and tormented, are most apt to possess quiet or calm exteriors, to exhibit furious immobility or quiet rage, or to behave with quiet fury or calm violence. When their tension or torment has become unbearable they may, like a farmer in *The Hamlet*, become "calm and contained and rigidly boiling" (222), or they may like the dietitian in *Light in August* and Wilbourne in *The Wild Palms*, be described as going calmly and quietly mad.

Opposed suggestions are not at all confined to these areas. In every Faulkner novel an astonishing number and variety of characters and events are described in oxymoronic or near oxymoronic terms. Here is a small sampling from two of Faulkner's novels which may give some idea of the pervasiveness of the phenomenon and of the variety of contexts in which it occurs.

In *Light in August*, Doc Hines is "paradoxically rapt and alert at the same time" (323) and has the ability "to flux instantaneously between complete attention that does not seem to hear, and that comalike bemusement in which the stare of his apparently inverted eye is as uncomfortable as though he held them [his companions] with his hand" (334). His wife's face is at the same time "peaceful and terrible" and her attitude is "at once like a rock and like a crouching beast" (348). The face of Hightower, with whom the Hineses are talking, is "at once gaunt and flabby" (77). The Sunday morning service in the church in which he once preached has a "stern and formal fury" (321). He hears singing from the church: "a sound at once austere and rich, abject and proud" (65). When he resigns his pulpit "the town was sorry with being glad" (60). Joe Christmas' feet are capable of moving at "deliberate random" (291). He can "hear without hearing them wails of terror and distress quieter than sighs all about him" (293). Lena Grove gives Armstid, Winterbottom, and Armstid's wagon a glance which is at once "innocent and profound" (7). Later she and the wagon come slowly together "without any semblance of progress" (10). She passes fields and woods "at once static and fluid" (24).

In *The Hamlet* Will Varner is "at once active and lazy" (6). His son Jody wears a costume which is "at once ceremonial and negligee" (11). Tull has a "gentle, almost sad face until you unravelled what were actually two separate expressions—a temporary one of static peace and quiet overlaying a constant one of definite even though faint harriedness" (10). Armstid's eyes are "at once vague and intense" (331). After his illness Ratliff emanates "a sort of delicate robustness" (78). Ab Snopes' homestead is a "cluttered desolation" (54). Eula Varner seems to exist in a "teeming vacuum" (107). At the age of eleven, sitting on the schoolhouse steps eating a cold potato, she "postulated that ungirdled quality of the very goddesses in . . . Homer and Thucydides: of being at once corrupt and immaculate, at once virgins and the mothers of warriors and of grown men" (128). She is "at once supremely unchaste and inviolable" (131). Her admirers depart "seething and decorous" and ride in "furious wordless amity" (150). Houston and the girl he is to marry are "chained irrevocably . . . not by love but by impacable constancy and invincible repudiation" (237). Up to a point their struggle, "for all its deadly seriousness . . . had retained something of childhood, something both illogical and consistent, both reasonable and bizarre" (239).

Some of Faulkner's oxymorons are brilliant and completely justified by their context; others seem mechanical or excessive. I am not here concerned with discriminating between them. What I wish to emphasize is their remarkable frequency and variety, remarkable even in our contemporary literary environment which prizes paradox and linguistic shock. More than anything else, I believe, that baffling figure can help to illuminate Faulkner's work. Not only does its abundance indicate a good deal about Faulkner's general intentions and effects, but the figure, itself, in miniature and extreme form contains or suggests many of the most important qualities of his art and vision.

Like Faulkner's writing in general, the oxymoron involves sharp polarity, extreme tension, a high degree of conceptual and stylistic antithesis, and the simultaneous suggestion of disparate or opposed elements. Moreover, the figure tends to hold these elements in suspension rather than to fuse them. Both terms of an oxymoron are in a sense true. One's recognition that the contradiction is apparent rather than real does not eliminate the tension between the terms for the conflicting elements remain. Neither negates the other. The oxymoron, on the one hand, achieves a kind of order, definiteness, and coherence by virtue of the clear and sharp antithesis it involves. On the other, it moves toward disorder and incoherence by virtue of its qualities of irresolution and self-contradiction. Its validity is usually intuitive and emotional rather than logical or intellectual. It does not so much explore or analyze a condition as render it forcefully. Traditionally it has often been used to reflect desperately divided states of mind.

2

Any oxymoron to some degree defies our customary intellectual desire for logical resolution, for even when we see beyond the contradiction, it still leaves us with the conflicting assertions. But many of Faulkner's oxymorons (e.g., "vague and intense") leave us with especially insoluble suspensions. They involve so complete or balanced a contradiction that they not only oppose our desire for resolution, but remain in opposition to it; no amount of thought and analysis can move us beyond the suspension of opposed elements. In the traditional oxymoron such as "cruel kindness" or "living death" at least a partial resolution is usually possible because one of the opposing elements is given subordinate emphasis either by context or by logical or grammatical subordination. Faulkner, on the other hand, seems especially fond of juxtaposing contradictory terms of equal rank and emphasis, and often further blocks resolution by the prefatory phrase "at once" (e.g., "at once corrupt and immaculate"). That he may be indifferent to the effects even when his oxymorons do involve logical or grammatical subordination is suggested by his apparently synonymous use of "implacable weariness" and "weary implacability" (*H*, 254–255). The essential purpose and effect of most of Faulkner's oxymorons, I believe, is not to force the reader to grasp a reality or unity beneath an apparent contradiction but to leave him with the tension of the contradiction itself. We are to feel and to continue to feel, for example, that the struggle between Houston and his wife had in it "something both illogical and consistent, both reasonable and bizarre."

I have stressed this as much as I have because I wish to show as conclusively as I can that Faulkner frequently seems willing and even anxious to leave his reader with suspensions which are not resolvable in rational terms. This is not to say that he always does so nor does it prove that his novels as wholes are similarly unresolvable, but it does suggest that his novels may be more ambiguous and more resistant to rational analysis than has often been supposed. This possibility is strenghtened by the many other aspects of his presentation which resist rational analysis and leave us with an unresolved suspension of varied or opposed suggestions.

A large number of Faulkner's extended metaphors, for example, have these qualities. This partial description of the sermon of the visiting preacher in *The Sound and the Fury* is characteristic.

He tramped steadily back and forth . . . hunched, his hands clasped behind him. He was like a worn small rock whelmed by the successive waves of his voice. With his body he seemed to feed the voice that, succubus like, had fleshed its teeth in him. And the congregation seemed to watch with its own eyes while the voice consumed him, until he was nothing and they were nothing and there was not even a voice but instead their hearts were speaking to one another in chanting measures beyond the need for words, so that when he came to rest against the reading desk, his monkey face lifted and his whole attitude that of a serene, tortured crucifix that transcended its shabbiness and insignificance and made it of no moment, a long moaning expulsion of breath rose from them, and a woman's single soprano: "Yes, Jesus!" (310).

In context the passage has considerable emotional force and conveys a sense of the minister's power and effect on the congregation. On the other hand, it is full of opposed and varied suggestions which resist rational integration. We shift from naturalistic description to a simile in which the preacher is likened to a rock and his voice to waves. The voice then acquires teeth, and "succubus like" (i.e., like an *evil* spirit!) consumes him. Is the ugliness of the image intentional, we wonder. Does Faulkner perhaps add teeth because they are in antithesis to the "suck" suggestion of "succubus"? The minister and the congregation become "nothing" but still have hearts. There is no voice but the hearts "speak" to one another, although without words. We are then reminded of the naturalistic monkey face immediately before the preacher's figure (which was a "rock," fleshly food, "nothing," and a speaking "heart") becomes suggestive of a crucifix, at once "serene" and "tortured," "that transcended its [the attitude's? the crucifix's?] shabbiness and insignificance." Upon close examination even the general nature of the experience of the congregation is perplexing, because there is the implication of a peaceful speaking of hearts and then of release of tension. Faulkner's mixed metaphors of this sort are not simply occasional accidents, for in general he makes no effort to keep them consistent and often makes use of the most "mixed" for his most important communications. And as in the oxymoron, the irresolvable elements are not accidental but seem an integral part of structure. Comparable to these mixed metaphors in effect are Faulkner's frequent synesthetic images which may be considered psychological oxymorons. Typical examples are "dark cool breeze" (*SF,* 149), "visibility roaring soundless down about him" (*H,* 195), and "walked out of their talking" (*LIA,* 9).

Less obvious, perhaps, but equally common are the conflicting suggestions which often occur in Faulkner's extended presentations of characters and events. A relatively compact illustration is the episode in *Light in August* in which McEachern attacks Joe Christmas in the dancehall.

Before this episode, what has been emphasized, above all, about McEachern is his absolute sense of self-righteousness, and the calm, heavy, methodical quality of all of his actions, even his violent ones. When he realizes that Joe has climbed out of his room and gone off to what he is sure is lechery, he saddles "his big, old, strong white horse" and goes down the road at a "slow and ponderous gallop" (176). So far he is still very much in character. Faulkner then inserts a suggestion of speed by means of metaphor: ". . . the two of them, man and beast, leaning a little stiffly forward as though in some juggernautish simulation of terrific speed though the actual speed itself was absent, as if in that cold and implacable and undeviating conviction of both omnipotence and clairvoyance of which they both partook known destination and speed were not necessary" (176–177). When McEachern reaches the dancehall, however, Faulkner has him move with actual speed. He dismounts "almost before the horse had stopped. He did not even tether it. He got down, and in the carpet slippers and the dangling braces and his round head and his short, blunt, outraged beard ran toward the open door" (177). In the next paragraph Faulkner goes on to describe him as thrusting through the dancers, and running toward Joe and the waitress, and then thundering "Away, Jezebel! . . . Away, harlot!" (178)

McEachern's disarray and uncontrolled running and thunderous shouting provide an emotional climax of strong impact and intensity; but they may come as rather a shock to the understanding of the reader in view of Faulkner's earlier characterizations of the man as utterly deliberate and controlled (124–34). The next paragraph reads:

Perhaps it did not seem to him that he had been moving fast nor that his voice was loud. Very likely he seemed to himself to be standing just and rocklike and with neither haste nor anger while on all sides the sluttishness of weak human men seethed in a long sigh of terror about the actual representative of the wrathful and retributive Throne. Perhaps they were not even his hands which struck at the face of the youth whom he had nurtured and sheltered and clothed from a child, and perhaps when the face ducked the blow and came up again it was not the face of that child. But he could not have been surprised at that, since it was not that child's face which he was concerned with: it was the face of Satan, which he knew as well. And when, staring at the face, he walked steadily toward it with his hand still raised, very likely he walked toward it in the furious and dreamlike exaltation of a martyr who has already been absolved, into the descending chair which Joe swung at his head, and into nothingness. (178)

We begin with what appears not to be the real version of what happened but the way it appeared to McEachern. But the passage slips gradually toward what is presumably a statement of what did happen, and the final picture we have is of the McEachern we knew earlier, who, staring at Joe-Satan, walks "steadily" toward the raised chair "in the furious and dreamlike exaltation of a martyr." In a generally emotive way we are satisfied by the suggestiveness and general movement of the passage. If we stop to reflect, however, we wonder how the event did happen, which image of McEachern to accept: the one of a ponderous and deliberate man whose conviction is such that speed is not necessary; the one suggested by the hanging braces, carpet slippers, the running and thundering rage; or the one of a convinced and peaceful and yet somehow furious martyr? We wonder what McEachern is like. We wonder, also, whether McEachern has been killed. The final description of him offers no resolution: "He looked quite peaceful now. He appeared to sleep: blunt-headed, indomitable even in repose, even the blood on his forehead peaceful and quiet" (178). This final statement is typical of many of Faulkner's endings to situations and even to whole works. It is effective emotionally and dramatically but does not resolve questions which the earlier presentation has raised for the understanding. There is a suggestion of resolution, in this case supplied by the emphasis upon peace and quiescence. At the same time, however, there remain tensions and opposing suggestions, here provided by the unquiet words "bluntheaded," "indomitable," and "blood."

One of the most striking and widely commented upon aspects of Faulkner's writing is his use of marathon sentences whose structure and syntax are often perplexing or obscure. Here is a fragment of a sentence from *Go Down, Moses,* a sentence which runs for over a page and a half. Among sentences and fragments of this type, it is one of the least complex. Contextually, the sentence and fragment would seem to be important, for they presumably communicate a significant part of Ike McCaslin's education and experience.

. . . a boy who wished to learn humility and pride in order to become skillful and worthy in the woods but found himself becoming so skillful so fast that he feared he would never become worthy because he had not learned humility and pride though he had tried, until one day an old man who could not have defined either led him as though by the hand to where an old bear and a little mongrel dog showed him that, by possessing one thing other, he would possess them both; and a little dog, nameless and mongrel and many-fathered, grown yet weighing less than six pounds, who couldn't be dangerous because there was nothing anywhere much smaller, not fierce because that would have been called just noise, not humble because it was already too near the ground to genuflect, and not proud because it would not have been close enough for anyone to discern what was casting that shadow and which didn't even know it was not going to heaven since they had already decided it had no immortal soul, so that all it could be was brave even though they would probably call that too just noise. (295–296)

We may note first, that all but one of the clauses beginning "because," "since," or "so that," are deliberate non-sequiturs. Moreover, the final statement about the dog's bravery is not consistent with the statement about his fierceness. In one instance the existence of a quality depends upon what people call it; in the other it does not. At the same time, in opposition to the illogicality, there is a promise of clarity, order, and logicality, a frequent characteristic of Faulkner's writing. The description of the dog pretends to be a definition (presumably of "the one thing other") arrived at through careful exclusion and negation. Further promise of clarity and simplicity is made by the cause and effect terminology, antithesis, persistent parallelism, and general division of things into simple pairs. There is also the promise communicated by the suggestion that the mongrel dog showed Ike that *"one* thing" (italics mine) would solve his problem of gaining humility and pride.

The passage quoted is characteristic of many of Faulkner's other structures, also, in its shifts in tone. The context of the description of the dog is serious. Presumably our understanding of the nature of the dog is essential to our understanding of the nature of pride and humility, and to our understanding of Ike. The surrounding passages are serious. The description of the dog's qualities, however, is largely playful.

As in many other passages close scrutiny leads only to further difficulties. There is first the hurdle of the oxymoron "humility and pride." We are then told that the possession of one thing "other" would enable Ike to possess both qualities. If the one thing other is "bravery" (we cannot be sure), we may wonder why Faulkner communicates it so ambiguously, and may wonder about the relationship between bravery, humility, and pride. Our understanding of that relationship is not aided by the fact that the dog, who has the bravery, is described specifically as neither humble nor proud. When we read further we are led to Keats' "Ode on a Grecian Urn" and to the statement that *"Truth is one. It doesn't change. It covers all things which touch the heart— honor and pride and pity and justice and courage and love"* (297), a statement which McCaslin indicates ought to clarify things for Ike. Even if one is not troubled by the meanings of the words "covers" and "touch" and does not wonder whether such qualities as hatred and greed "touch" the heart, one must certainly wonder why humility is missing from the list. A few lines later Faulkner drops this subject and moves to a "discussion" of the curse on the land.

Again Faulkner's presentation has left us with tensions and questions we cannot resolve. I have dwelt upon the difficulties structures of this sort pose for the understanding, and have emphasized their resistance to analysis, because I wish to make clear that they may be organized not merely so as to make intellectual resolution difficult but so as to discourage it and make it impossible, just as synesthetic images make precise sense localization impossible and many of Faulkner's oxymorons make logical resolution impossible. The difficulties in the way of understanding are often not resolvable nor meant to be.

The preceding illustrations show some of the ways by which Faulkner keeps his reader from fitting things together. Instead of moving toward synthesis and resolution, his presentation often provides a suspension of varied or opposed suggestions. Two specific devices which further contribute to this suggestive suspension warrant mention.

The first is the frequent use of "perhaps" and "maybe," and other inconclusive or conjectural terms or phrases in describing motivations, thoughts, and events. The second is that which Warren Beck has labelled "the statement of alternative suggestions"[2] "The woman had never seen him but once, but perhaps she remembered him, or perhaps his appearance now was enough."[3] Sometimes the juxtaposed alternatives are so important and so divergent that a choice would be of immense philosophic and practical significance, as in *Go Down, Moses* where McCaslin says that the Bible was written to be read "by the heart, not by the wise of the earth because *maybe they dont need it or maybe the wise no longer have any heart*" (260, italics mine). On occasion the alternatives are diametrically opposed:

It was as if only half of her had been born, that mentality and body had somehow become either completely separated or hopelessly involved; that either only one of them had ever emerged, or that one had emerged, itself not accompanied by, but rather pregnant with, the other. (*H,* 109)

Note the complete position of the alternatives "completely separated" and "hopelessly involved." If we substitute "at once . . . and" where Faulkner has used "either . . . or," the result is an oxymoron. Even as worded in the text, however, the passage is, in effect, an oxymoron, because no real choice is offered. As is true for almost all of Faulkner's "alternative" suggestions, we are to keep in mind both alternatives; no choice or resolution is possible.

3

Faulkner's novels, of course, are far more complex than the structures we have been looking at, and I certainly do not wish to suggest that the kinds of qualities I have been illustrating fully explain or describe them. I do contend, however, that they resemble these structures more closely than has generally been recognized. They have certain kinds of unity and resolution, of course, but in many ways they remain insoluble. Obviously, a thorough or conclusive study of the novels is impossible here. I can do little more than suggest something of the extent to which they are suspensions of the sort I have indicated. Apart from the evidence we have already seen which suggests this possibility, and apart from internal evidence I shall consider later, there is also some external evidence that Faulkner might regard too much coherence as a kind of failure.

In a recent interview Faulkner is quoted as saying:

I was asked the question who were the five best contemporary writers and how did I rate them. And I said Wolfe, Hemingway, Dos Passos, Caldwell and myself. I rated Wolfe first, myself second. I put Hemingway last. I said we were all failures. All of us had failed to match the dream of perfection and I rated the authors on the basis of their splendid failure to do the impossible. I believed Wolfe tried to do the greatest of the impossible, that he tried to reduce all human experience to literature. And I thought after Wolfe I had tried the most. I rated Hemingway last because he stayed within what he knew. He did it fine, but he didn't try for the impossible.

A moment later he adds:

I rated those authors by the way in which they failed to match the dream of perfection. . . . This had nothing to do with the value of the work, the impact of perfection of its own kind that it had. I was talking only about the magnificence of the failure, the attempt to do the impossible within human experience. (New York *Times Book Review,* Jan. 30, 1955)

There are ambiguities in Faulkner's statement, but it strongly suggests that he would consider full coherence a sign of weakness and something to be avoided. That is, he not only places a higher value[4] upon the effort to do the *impossible* than upon accepting human and artistic limitations, but he also seems to measure the effort by the extent of the failure. His works show, in part, I believe, an active quest for "failure."

It is no accident that every one of Faulkner's experiments with form and style—his rapidly shifting points of view, his use of more or less incoherent narrators such as Benjy, Quentin, Darl, Rosa Coldfield, and Gavin Stevens, his disordered time sequences, his juxtapositions of largely independent stories, his unsyntactical marathon sentences, his whole method, as Conrad Aiken puts it, "of deliberately withheld meaning, of progressive and partial and delayed disclosure"—is a movement away from order and coherence. And it is no accident that every one of Faulkner's novels involves one or more of these experiments and that in most of the novels we find all of them.

It is important to recognize, also, that the effects of Faulkner's fragmentation of material are usually quite different from those produced by others who have used similar techniques. In works like *The Ring and the Book* and the

Japanese film *Rashomon* various perspectives are thrown upon the same central event. In *Mrs. Dalloway* and *Ulysses* the seemingly unconnected experiences and events are occurring at the same time or on the same day. That is, either event, time or point of view is held constant. In *The Sound and the Fury, As I Lay Dying,* and *Absalom, Absalom!,* on the other hand, none of these is constant. The various narrators touch upon a few of the same events, but the selection of events seems determined essentially by the particular interests and obsessions of the narrator. In *The Sound and the Fury,* for example, neither Benjy nor Jason throws light on the incest theme which dominates the Quentin section. And Quentin, on the other hand, is dead before many of the events take place which are crucial in the lives of Benjy and Jason. In *Absalom, Absalom!* the various narrators emhasize quite different aspects and periods of Sutpen's history. As a result the reader feels less sense of pattern and equilibrium than in the first named works, is less able to group his thoughts and feelings about a common center.

Particularly indicative of Faulkner's intentions, I think, is the fact that when he does present explicit interpretations of events or analytic commentaries on them he always takes pains to make them either suspect, inconclusive, or incoherent. On many occasions he will narrate or describe an action in perfectly conventional and logical sequence, but his interpretive or philosophic passages are almost invariably disordered. I think we can go so far as to say that the more explanatory or intellectual the content, the less the coherence. The dominant characteristic, in fact, of Faulkner's intellectuals—and it is they, of course, who offer most of the interpretations—is their tendency to be incoherent. The most intellectual character in Faulkner's novels, and probably his favorite commentator, is Gavin Stevens, a Ph.D. from Heidelburg. And, as has been generally recognized, it is his statements which usually provide the greatest resistance to rational understanding. Here, for example, is a part of his final commentary, and the final explicit commentary of any sort, on the meaning of the events in *Intruder in the Dust.* Gavin is talking to his nephew Charles Mallison who has been chiefly responsible for saving the Negro Lucas Beauchamp from being lynched.

. . . what's out yonder in the ground at Caledonia Church was Crawford Gowrie for only a second or two last Saturday and Lucas Beauchamp will be carrying his pigment into ten thousand situations a wiser man would have avoided and a lighter escaped ten thousand times after what was Lucas Beauchamp for a second or so last Saturday is in the ground at his Caledonia church too, because that Yoknapatawpha County which would have stopped you and Aleck Sander and Miss Habersham last Sunday night are right actually, Lucas' life the breathing and eating and sleeping is of no importance just as yours and mine are not but his unchallengeable right to it in peace and security and in fact this earth would be much more comfortable with a good deal fewer Beauchamps and Stevenses and Mallisons of all colors in it if there were only some painless way to efface not the clumsy room-devouring carcasses which can be done but the memory which cannot—that inevictible immortal memory awareness of having once been alive which exists forever still ten thousand years afterward in ten thousand recollections of injustice and suffering, too many of us not because of the room we take up but because we are willing to sell liberty short at any tawdry price for the sake of what we call our own which is a constitutional statutory license to pursue each his private postulate of happiness and contentment regardless of grief and cost even to the crucifixion of someone whose nose or pigment we dont like and even these can be coped with provided that few of others who believe that a human life is valuable simply because it has a right to keep on breathing no matter what pigment its lungs distend or nose inhales the air and are willing to defend that right at any price, it doesn't take many three were enough last Sunday night even one can be enough and with enough ones willing to be more than grieved and shamed Lucas will no longer run the risk of needing without warning to be saved:" (*ID*, 243–244).

Fortunately Faulkner has other voices besides that of Gavin. But these other voices do not negate or encompass Gavin's so much as stand in suspension with it.

Probably the most crucial indication of Faulkner's intentions is the fact that the endings of all his novels not only fail to resolve many of the tensions and meanings provided in the novels but also seem carefully designed to prevent such resolution. Above all, they leave unresolved the question of the meaningfulness of the human efforts and suffering we have witnessed, whether the sound and the fury is part of some larger design or whether it has signified nothing in an essentially meaningless universe.

Consider, for example, the final section of *The Sound and the Fury,* which is perhaps Faulkner's most unified and tightly woven novel. By the end of the first three sections we have seen various parts of the history of the Compson family through the eyes of three of its members—respectively, the idiot Benjy, the sensitive and romantic but neurotically obsessed Quentin, and the practical, materialistic and self-pitying Jason. And we are groping for some larger perspective, context, or pattern under which to view and interpret the unhappy events we have been witnessing. Faulkner has suggested a number of these. The title of the book has suggested strongly that there is no pattern, and Mr. Compson's nihilistic philosophy reinforces this, as does the seemingly chaotic order of events. Opposed to this, however, is our natural disinclination to accept such a view and our awareness of Faulkner's at least partial approval of Benjy, Quentin, Caddie, Mr. Compson, and Dilsey and his disapproval of Mrs. Compson, Herbert, and Jason. And there is also our recognition of several more or less recurrent motifs which encourage us to look for pattern and significance. But the search has sent us in varying directions, none of which has been clearly or conclusively marked. Some of the events have seemed chiefly in accord with a socio-economic antithesis between an old and new culture of the general sort pointed out by the O'Donnell, Cowley, Warren line of criticism. Some of the events and emphases have suggested interpretation in terms of clinical or even specifically Freudian psychology. We have been strongly encouraged, also, to interpret events in relation to Christian myth and ideology, in relation to concepts of time, and in relation to Shakespearian tragedy.

At the same time we are not sure what attitude we are to take toward the disintegration of the family. In the first two sections Benjy and Quentin have reported events in such a way that we see and feel their pathetic rather than ludicrous or ironic side. We are somewhat aware that Benjy is sub-human and that his suffering is not of an order that requires the highest kind of sympathy, and Quentin's posturing and extreme Romanticism at times seem comic, but essentially we are led to see them both as suffering individuals, to feel considerable compassion for them and to take their predicaments very seriously. In the third section, however, narrated by Jason, the tone has been essentially comic and satiric. Not only does Jason come through as a largely comic character but his narration tends to bathe the whole Compson history in a somewhat comic light which at least temporarily blinds us to the poignancy and pathos of it. We are much more detached than in the earlier sections, less serious. We want to see Jason made a fool of and we are not especially moved by the plight of his niece Quentin. Had the novel ended with this section we would view the Compson history largely with a sense of grim amusement, as a tale of sound and fury signifying that the human condition is essentially hopeless and not worth much thought or compassion.

The final section, narrated from an omniscient and objective point of view, begins with a focus and emphasis that seems to offer a kind of implicit interpretation and resolution, one in accord with the sentiments and mood of Faulkner's Nobel Prize speech. The strong emphasis on Dilsey's fortitude, decency, and Christian humility and on her comprehensive view of time, as numerous critics have pointed out, provides a context for the unhappy events, a perspective from which to view them and a way to feel about them. On the other hand, this episode does not so much offer a synthesis or interpretation as a general vantage point and degree of moral affirmation. It does not help us to understand most of the particulars of the Compson story any better, to illuminate, say, the character and motives of Quentin and Caddie. Nor does it in any but a peripheral way relate to the socio-economic context of the story. And although it asserts the relevance of Christianity to the story it does not really clarify the nature of that relevance nor make clear how seriously we are to take the Christian context. Still, its tone and general tenor do provide a general way of looking at and feeling about the story and a sense of resolution.

But—and it is a very crucial "but" which most interpreters of the novel have ignored—the emphasis on Dilsey and her trip to church is at the beginning of the final section, and is only one of several emphases in that section. It is followed by the lengthy description of Jason's vain and tormenting pursuit of Quentin which provides a very different perspective, mood, and set of feelings. We are back in a realm of sound and fury, even of melodrama. We do not see Jason from the large perspective we have just shared with Dilsey, but respond to his frustration and defeat with a grim amusement and satisfaction only slightly leavened by pity. Nor does his defeat appear in any way an affirmative thing, for the "heroine" who has eluded him seems equally doomed. Dilsey and her church recede into the landscape and seem barely relevant to Jason's predicament.

The final part of the last section emphasizes Benjy's misery and the callousness and swagger of Dilsey's grandson, Luster, as he torments Benjy, first by taking his bottle, then by shouting *Caddie,* and finally by driving around the square in the wrong direction. We are reminded for a moment of Dilsey's decency and faith but only to feel its ineffectualness, for neither she nor the church service has touched Luster. The book closes with the carriage ride of Luster and Benjy: with our attention focused on a young Negro whose main desire is to show off, and on an idiot, capable of serenity or anguish but little more than that. Faulkner emphasizes his terrible agony as Luster throws his world into disorder by going around the square in the wrong direction. Jason comes rushing across the square, turns the carriage around and hits both Luster and Benjy. Benjy becomes serene again as the carriage moves in its usual direction and things flow by smoothly from left to right, "each in its ordered place."

It is a powerful ending and a fitting one in its focus on Benjy and its application to the general theme of order and disorder which runs through the novel. But it is an ending which provides anything but a synthesis or resolution, and it leaves us with numerous conflicting feelings and ideas.

We are momentarily relieved and pleased by the cessation of Benjy's suffering but we are troubled by the fact that it has been achieved by Jason who cares nothing for Benjy and is concerned only with maintaining an external and superficial decorum. And we can hardly draw any real satisfaction from the serenity and order because the serenity is the "empty" serenity of an idiot and the order that demanded by an idiot. The general tenor of the episode is in accord with Mr. Compson's pessimism rather than Faulkner's Nobel Prize speech, for everything in it suggests the meaninglessness and futility of life.

This final scene does not negate the moderate affirmation of the Dilsey episode, nor does it really qualify it. Rather it stands in suspension with it as a commentary of equal force. We feel and are intended to feel, I think, that the events we have witnessed are at once tragic and futile, significant and meaningless. We cannot move beyond this. Nor does the final section help us to resolve whether the Compsons were defeated essentially by acts of choice or by some kind of doom, or whether the doom was chiefly a matter of fate or of psychological aberration or of socio-economic forces. And it is worth noting that if we do accept as a primary motif the opposition between an older and newer culture we face the impossibility of choosing between them. Our sympathies, like Faulkner's, are with the old, but the best representatives of it in this book are a drunkard, a suicide, and a lost and lonely woman. And between what they are and what Jason is there seems no middle ground offered.

In short, the ending seems designed not to interpret or to integrate but to leave the various elements of the story in much the same suspension in which they were offered, and to leave the reader with a high degree of emotional and intellectual tension.

The endings of Faulkner's other novels are similar. Two brief illustrations will have to suffice. *As I Lay Dying* ends with Pa's acquisiton of new teeth and a new wife, a cynical, almost farcical note which suggests that all of the pain and struggle and even heroism of the Bundrens was for nothing, that shiftlessness and ineptitude triumph over all, and that we do not take the story very seriously. At the same time, however, the fact that the family did succeed in its task and the emphasis on the patience and sanity of Cash, as well as the presentation of much of the story suggests that what we have witnessed is significant, even epic, and worthy of the highest seriousness of response. The fate of Darl generates further intellectual and emotional conflict, which Faulkner strengthens in a number of ways. He has Cash speculate inconclusively about the question of Darl's insanity, and neither he nor we can get beyond the feeling that we "ain't so sho that ere a man has the right to say what is crazy and what ain't" (*AILD,* 515). But we are far more disturbed than Cash, for unlike Cash we do not misinterpret Darl's bitter laughter when Cash says he will be better off at the insane asylum at Jackson. Our response is further complicated by Faulkner's emphasis on Darl's human concern about Cash's bad leg and by the terrible ambiguity of Darl's laughter and reiterated "yes's" as he is taken away to Jackson. Moreover, these uncertainties reflect back through the novel, for Darl has been the dominant narrator of the book and perhaps the most sympathetic character. As in *The Sound and the Fury* the ending, far from helping us to order or resolve the suspension of multiple suggestions and points of view presented in the book, seems designed to preserve that suspension in all its complexity and even to make it more complex. There is nothing which points firmly or clearly toward any one way of thinking or feeling about the things we have seen. Above all, the ending suggests that the story we have been told is highly significant and worthy of serious contemplation and emotion and that it signifies nothing and deserves primarily a bitter laugh.

At the very end of *Absalom, Absalom!* there are, in effect, four commentaries on the meaning of the whole Sutpen story. The first is provided by the picture of the last Sutpen, the idiot boy Jim Bond, lurking around the ashes and gutted chimneys that are the remnants of Sutpen's mansion, howling until someone would drive him away (376). The second is provided by the end of Mr. Compson's letter, the first part of which we have read two hundred odd pages earlier (173–174), a letter which is obviously and carefully ambiguous and irrelevant so far as any ordering of the story is concerned. The third commentary is that of Shreve, who summarizes the story with brutal and flippant absurdity: " 'So it took Charles Bon and his mother to get rid of old Tom, and Charles Bon and the octoroon to get rid of Judith, and Charles Bon and Clytie to get rid of Henry; and Charles Bon's mother and Charles Bon's grandmother to get rid of Charles Bon. So it takes two niggers to get rid of one Sutpen, don't it?' " (377–378) He then observes that everything is taken care of except that " 'You've got one nigger left. One nigger Sutpen left,' " and he briefly erects this Negro into a symbol of Southern guilt (378, 11, 11–14). Following this he reveals in paradox: the Jim Bonds conquer the western hemisphere and turn white, but still remain Jim Bonds, " 'and so [note the pseudo logic] in a few thousand years, I who regard you will also have sprung from the loins of African kings. Now I want you to tell me just one thing more. Why do you hate the South?' " (378). And the final commentary:

"I dont hate it," Quentin said, quickly, at once, immediately; "I dont hate it," he said. *I dont hate it* he thought, panting in the cold air, the iron New England dark; *I dont. I dont! I dont hate it! I dont hate it!*

It is difficult to conceive of an "ending" which would provide less ordering and resolution. For not only is there no resolution on a cognitive level, but we are also confronted with the differing tones of the four "commentaries," and the terrible emotional ambivalence of Quentin's final outburst. We "end," then, with a psychological oxymoron of simultaneous love and hate, with internal conflict and self-contradiction. It is an intense and powerful ending, and a proper one to seal off and preserve the complex suspension of elements the book has presented. But it is also a pitiful ending. It is pitiful in that Shreve and Quentin seem to have been so little instructed by their immense labor of imagination. It is pitiful (and among many other things, perhaps, Faulkner is saying this, too) in its varied assertions that so much energy, effort, and pain have come to so little: to a lone idiot, an ironic letter, a brutally flippant commentary and act of cruelty to a roommate, and a bewildered cry of pain. It is, above all, pitiful because by it, Faulkner again demonstrates his unwillingness to step beyond the sanctuary of the paradox, to make himself, as do a number of his characters, the clarifying "gesture," which might enable him and us to move beyond that bewildered cry of pain.

Faulkner's other novels exhibit the same avoidance of resolution, the same intent to present suggestive suspensions rather than rationally integrated wholes. In *The Wild Palms,* where Faulkner alternates the chapters of two completely independent narratives, and in *Requiem for a Nun,* where he juxtaposes sections of broad historical narrative with the acts of a play, and in *Light in August,* where he juxtaposes three largely discrete stories, these suspensions become most amorphous. The greatest degree of resolution is offered, perhaps, by *Intruder in the Dust,* whose plot is relatively uncomplicated, and where there is very little doubt cast upon the propriety or justice of the boy's effort to save Lucas Beauchamp. On the other hand, with respect to the motivation for the effort, and the meaning of it, Faulkner is far from conclusive, and in the final chapter of the novel he complicates the context of the entire event by shifting his focus to the evils of mechanization and standardization. His final re-emphasis upon Beauchamp's almost comic pride and pedantry and his own almost comic treatment of the final scene further complicate our reaction to the story. Works whose ambiguities of content and tone have been especially overlooked in critical discussion are *Pylon,* the tall convict section of *The Wild Palms,* "The Bear," and the play in *Requiem for a Nun.*[5]

4

As the reader is undoubtedly aware, I have used the terms "suspension" and "resolution" quite loosely and have made no careful effort to distinguish between what is resolved and what is not or between the kinds of elements left in suspension or between valid and invalid kinds of irresolution. To make these distinctions seems to me a crucial and exceedingly complex problem for future Faulkner criticism. My primary purpose here has been to show that there is a problem, that the irresolution runs both wide and deep. I would like also to suggest some explanations for it.

So far I have written as though Faulkner's ambiguity and irresolution were entirely deliberate, strictly a matter of artistic intent, rather than one of temperament or general irrationalism or mere lack of concern about rational coherence. Up to a point, I think this is actually the case and that we may understand much of the ambiguity and irresolution as serving or reflecting two general intentions.

Conrad Aiken has suggested that what Faulkner is after, in part, is a "medium without stops or pauses," an "image stream" toward which the reader "must be powerfully and unremittingly hypnotized," and he suggests that this intent to hypnotize accounts, perhaps, not only for the length and elaborateness of Faulkner's sentence structure but for his repetitiveness as well.[6] It is very likely that Faulkner's frequent resistance to rational analysis also contributes to this hypnotic effect. Some passages from Edward Snyder's *Hypnotic Poetry*[7] strongly suggest this. Professor Snyder notes that in actual hypnosis the stimuli used "are such as to fix the attention while retarding mental activity," (25) and he concludes that the same retardation of mental activity is helpful in producing the less complete hypnoidal state which he calls "emotional trance," a state in which the subject's emotional susceptibility is highly intensified (32–33). In his Foreword to Snyder's book, the psychologist James Leuba writes that Snyder has "demonstrated the existence of a type of poetry which owes its attraction to a method of composition, the effect of which is to limit the intellectual activity, i.e., to induce a state of partial trance, and thereby to free in some measure the emotional life from the trammel of critical thinking." (x)

Whether Faulkner actually induces a state of partial trance is not especially important here. But it does seem likely that the purpose and effect of much of his presentation is to free the emotional life from the "trammel" of critical thinking, so that like the preacher in *The Sound and the Fury,* who is also in a sense a hypnotist, he might speak directly to the "heart." To some extent, we can say of Faulkner, as McCaslin says was true for God, that he "didn't have His Book written to be read by what must elect and choose, but by the heart" (*GDM,* 260). I do not mean to equate the word "heart" entirely with the words "emotive" or "hypnotic," and Faulkner's own use of the word is ambiguous, but there is no doubt that he sees the heart essentially as an organ of feeling and as antithetic to the head, and that he regards it, and not the head, as the way to truth. "Ideas and facts," he has said in a recent interview, "have very little connection with truth."[8] We give ourselves "mind's reason[s]," says McCaslin, "because the heart dont always have time to bother with thinking up words that fit together" (*GDM,* 348). A generally non-intellectual intention is suggested also by Faulkner's statements that "I must try to express clumsily in words what the pure music would have done better,"[9] and that "I think people try to find more in my work than I've put there. I like to tell stories, to create people, and situations. But that's all. I doubt if an author knows what he puts in a story. All he is trying to do is to tell what he knows about his environment and the people around him in the most moving way possible."[10]

An effort to reach the heart, or to "lift" it, as Faulkner sometimes puts it, by bypassing or retarding mental activity explains certain of Faulkner's obstacles to rational comprehension, but there is much that it does not explain, for Faulkner is not so consistent or complete an irrationalist or even non-intellectual as such an explanation implies. His ambiguity and irresolution must also be understood as asserting and reflecting a view of life. It is a difficult view to define, and the nature of it is such that it is almost impossible to draw a dividing line between the view and temperament. A statement by Warren Beck is helpful toward defining this view of life.

If Faulkner's sentences sometimes soar and circle involved and prolonged, if his scenes become halls of mirrors repeating tableaux in a progressive magnification, if echoes multiply into the dissonance of infinite overtones, it is because the meanings his stories unfold are complex, mysterious, obscure, and incomplete. There is no absolute, no eternal pure white radiance in such presentations, but rather the stain of many colors, refracted and shifting in kaleidoscopic suspension, about the center of man's enigmatic behavior and fate, within the drastic orbit of mortality. Such being Faulkner's view of life, such is his style.[11]

Professor Zink asserts that "at its best, form in Faulkner's art constitutes a living effort to penetrate and to realize in art an ineffable complexity."[12]

Certainly, these critics are right that Faulkner's form often suggests and seeks to communicate a view of life as enigmatic and ineffably complex. To a large extent his shifts in tone and point of view, his avoidance of resolution, and his various obstacles to rational understanding, may be viewed as an effort to present life and experience in such a way as to make facile interpretation impossible. The meaning of the stories of Sutpen and Joe Christmas and others, Faulkner is saying, is largely ambiguous. Whether they are free agents or pawns, heroes or villains, is ambiguous, just as it is uncertain whether the tall convict is a hero or fool, whether Darl Bundren is a seer or madman, and whether the desperate struggles of the convict, the Bundrens, and others are tragic or comic, significant or futile. They are presented as both and neither, just as simple entities like faces are conceived in the both and neither terms of the oxymoron, and just as Quentin's reaction to the Sutpen story, and to the South, in general, is a both and neither combination of love and hate. Whether there is a God or not is problematical, and if there is, whether he is Jehovah, Christ, Satan, Joker, Umpire, Chess Player, or Life Force. The only certainty that exists, Faulkner sometimes suggests, is that man will "endure," but whether he will endure by virtue of his soul or his folly Faulkner does not make clear, not is it clear whether enduring means primarily to suffer or to transcend time.

But these descriptions are inadequate, for they leave out important qualities of Faulkner's feeling about life which are inseparable from his view.

You get born and you try this and you dont know why only you keep on trying it and you are born at the same time with a lot of other people, all mixed up with them, like trying to, having to, move your arms and legs with strings only the same strings are hitched to all the other arms and legs and the others all trying and they dont know why either except that the strings are all in one another's way like five or six people all trying to make a rug on the same loom only each one wants to weave his own pattern into the rug; and it cant matter, you know that, or the Ones that set up the loom would have arranged things a little better, and yet it must matter because you keep on trying. . . . (*AA*, 127)

The words are Judith Sutpen's but the passage communicates more clearly than any other, I believe, the essence of Faulkner's view of life and feeling toward it. The passage suggests not only the complex and enigmatic qualities of life, but the sense of life as conflict, tension, and frustration, which persistently informs Faulkner's presentation. Above all, it suggests the intense contradictory feelings which, more than anything else, I think, explain Faulkner's attitude toward life and toward his own art: "it can't matter, you know that . . . and yet it must matter." It cannot have meaning and yet it must. The statement does not simply describe a dual perspective—"seems sometimes to matter, sometimes not," nor an uncertainty—"may or may not matter," nor even a paradox—"does and does not matter." The simultaneous "can't" and "must" suggests a desperately divided and tormented perspective and condition of mind which tries to move simultaneously and intensely toward both order and chaos, and which understandably seizes upon the figure which most nearly moves in both directions, the oxymoron.

This divided view and feeling about the meaningfulness of life and effort accounts, undoubtedly, for Faulkner's frequent explicit and implicit coupling of terms like "empty" and "profound," "futile" and "tragic," and for statements such as "the substance itself [life] not only not dead, not complete, but in its very insoluble enigma of human folly and blundering possessing a futile and tragic immortality" (*P*, 82), and "profound and irrevocable if only in the sense of being profoundly and irrevocably unimportant" (*P*, 109). It helps us to understand Faulkner's seemingly obsessive assertion and denial of immortality and to account for his often perceptive idiots and incoherent intellectuals. It accounts, in part, for his failure to pursue thoroughly many of the ideas and meanings intensely and then to ignore them or to contradict them with equal intensity, for his use of form both to illuminate and obscure. It is a view and feeling which, in general, makes it necessary for him to try continuously to affirm and deny, to illuminate and obscure, the meaning of his own artistic creations and the significance of the lives and experiences he presents. It accounts, perhaps, for his inability finally to commit himself, and for his ability to treat art both as a plaything and a dedication. Undoubtedly it helps to explain the utterly divergent critical estimates and interpretations of his work. Finally, I believe, it accounts in large measure for the peculiarly compelling and disturbing power of his works, for it reminds us of the similar schizophrenia within ourselves which we have worked hard to bury.

Generally skeptical views of life, or dual perspectives in which life appears in some ways meaningful and in some ways meaningless, are not uncommon, are certainly comprehensible, and have informed much great art, including that of Shakespeare. Metaphysical poetry and Jacobean drama, at times, seem to suggest a division of feeling, as well as of view, about life's meaningfulness which is as intense as Faulkner's. There is still, however, an important difference. Whatever the tensions and opposing suggestions, explicit or implicit, in a poem by Donne or a play by Webster, one feels behind them, I think, a governing mind which never really doubts the validity of its own ideas and perceptions or the possibility if not the existence, of a moral universe in which such ideas and perceptions are relevant, which never abandons the effort to order its thoughts and emotions.

Like many modern artists Faulkner has no such certainty.

Unlike any other moderns of comparable stature, however, Faulkner's uncertainty also embraces his art. Joyce, Virginia Woolf, and even Kafka have never really doubted the validity of art and have used it always to resist and to recreate as well as to reflect the dissolving worlds they saw and felt about them. They remain committed to order and reason. There have been some writers and painters, the surrealists and dadaists, who have not resisted, whose uncertainty or despair has led them to deny reason, whose desperation has led them to protest against disorder with disorder. A part of Faulkner remains intensely committed to art and order, and seeks desperately, and of course, paradoxically to find a way by which art can order equally intense convictions that life and art do and do not matter. A part of him is content with disorder.

Faulkner is more of an irrationalist than many of his critics have been willing to accept, but less of one than he, himself, has often suggested by his numerous explicit antitheses of head and heart and by his varied assertions that "ideas and facts have very little connection with truth." It is only partially true that he "didn't have His Book written to be read by what must elect and choose but by the heart" (*GDM*, 260). For the mere act of reading Faulkner requires a large intellectual effort and much of his appeal is clearly intellectual. Like most of the other elements of his work, his irrationalism is not a consistent or systematic thing, not a clearly governing principle of organization; it, too, becomes part of a suspension and will not fall clearly into place. Perhaps the best term for Faulkner is "non-rationalist."

But finally, I do not think we can adequately explain the kinds of tensions and suspensions we find in Faulkner's work except in terms of temperament. For, at bottom, his works seem governed not so much by a view of life, or by a particular gap in his thought and feeling, or by particular principles of organization as by his temperament;[13] that is, by the particular compound of intellectual and emotional inclinations, tendencies, and responses that characterize his mental life and shape his reactions to experience. It is his temperamental responses rather than any theories or ideas or particular torments, which he undoubtedly trusts to produce and to order his art. One fundamental quality of that temperament is its response to tension and opposition. Another is perhaps best described as a tendency toward profusion. It is this which no doubt helps to account for the remarkable scope of his fictional creation, but also for what surely must be criticized as an overabundance of effects and suggestions. Related to his inability or unwillingness to set limits on abundance, but yet to be distinguished from that quality, is his tendency to avoid commitment. It is this, as has no doubt been apparent, which most troubles me, from a human as well as an aesthetic point of view. For, surely, if there are to be any distinctions in art and life between responsibility and irresponsibility, indeed, any distinctions at all, we must insist that man can and must make choices. In both the form and content of Faulkner's works there is often the assertion or implication that man does not need to make choices. "You don't need to choose," says McCaslin. "The heart already knows" (*GDM*, 260). We do need to choose. There is, of course, also, in Faulkner the frequent implication that we do need to choose, and Ike, himself, does seem to make a terribly important choice by relinquishing his land. By suggesting, finally, that Ike both did and did not choose,[14] Faulkner, too, has made a choice, the choice which he can rarely resist, and which, I feel, seriously limits his stature, the choice not to choose.

1. William Faulkner, *Go Down, Moses* (Random House, 1942), p. 348; hereafter abbreviated *GDM*. Other abbreviations and editions of Faulkner's works used here are as follows. *AA:Absalom Absalom!* (New York: Modern Library, 1951); *AILD: As I Lay Dying* (New York: Modern Library, 1946); *CS: Collected Stories* (New York: Random House, 1950); *H: The Hamlet* (New York: Random House, 1940); *ID: Intruder in the Dust* (Random House, 1948); *LIA: Light in August* (New York: Modern Library, 1950); *MCS: Mirrors of Chartres Street* (Minneapolis: Faulkner Studies, 1953); *P: Pylon* (London: Chatto and Windlus, 1935); *RN: Requiem for a Nun* (New York: Random House, 1950); *S: Sanctuary* (New York: Modern Library, 1932); *SF: The Sound and the Fury* (New York: Modern Library, 1946); *WP: The Wild Palms* (New York: Random House, 1939).

2. Warren Beck, "William Faulkner's Style," see above.

3. *LIA*, 177. Note that the phrasing "had never seen him but once," communicates almost a double suggestion. Compare "had seen him but once," or "had seen him once only."

4. I am aware that Faulkner has said that his rating "had nothing to do with the value of the work." The whole tenor of the statement, however, indicates that he does attach high value to the quest for the impossible and to the magnificent failure. His very choice to rate the authors in those terms is an affirmation of the value of those terms. It may be argued that by saying that his rating had nothing to do with value, Faulkner only intends to qualify his earlier statement. But, in fact, the statement about value contradicts his earlier rhetoric and content, both, and involves an unwillingness to commit himself fully to the meaning of that rhetoric and content or to the consequences of his choice to rate the authors in the terms he did. Similar sorts of self contradiction are present in Faulkner's introduction to the Modern Library Edition of *Sanctuary*, in his Foreword to *The Faulkner Reader*, and a bit less obviously, in his Nobel Prize speech and various other public utterances. That this is true suggests that his literary use of ambiguity may be a matter of temperament as well as of conscious artistic intent.

5. In discussing the end of *RN*, one critic writes: "Stevens is rightly and necessarily silent as the inarticulate, uneducated Nancy says simply 'Believe.' Nancy is herself the visible sign which Temple had sought, the concrete illustration of what is meant by 'Believe' " (Olga Vickery, "Gavin Stevens: From Rhetoric to Dialectic," *Faulkner Studies* II [Spring, 1953], 4). Mrs. Vickery overlooks the final exchange between Temple and Stevens at the end of the book by which Faulkner, characteristically, avoids resolution. Walking out of the jail Temple speaks: " 'Anyone

to save it [reference obscure]. Anyone who wants it. If there is none, I'm sunk. We all are. Doomed. Damned.' " To this Gavin Stevens respond: " 'Of course we are. Hasn't He been telling us that for going on two thousand years?' " (286). If anything, Nancy has believed that man will or can be "saved" (278). Stevens' statement not only qualifies Nancy's by its content and tone but leaves us with what is virtually an oxymoron, for the very use of the "He" contradicts the statement that we are all damned. His statement also suggests that he has not really grown and developed, as Mrs. Vickery has argued.

6. Conrad Aiken, "William Faulkner: The Novel as Form," see above.

7. *Hypnotic Poetry: A Study of Trance-Inducing Techniques in Certain Poems and its Literary Significance* (Philadelphia: University of Pennsylvania Press, 1930).

8. Jean Stein, "The Art of Fiction XII: William Faulkner," see above.

9. Jean Stein, "The Art of Fiction."

10. Cynthia Grenier, "The Art of Fiction: An Interview with William Faulkner," *Accent*, XVI (Summer, 1956), 171.

11. Beck, "William Faulkner's Style."

12. Karl E. Zink, "William Faulkner: Form as Experience," *The South Atlantic Quarterly*, 53 (July, 1954), 384.

13. Any work of art, no doubt, reflects the temperament of its author, and in some ultimate sense is governed by it. In Faulkner's case, however, I am suggesting that the relationship between his art and temperament is a far more immediate, direct, and pervasive one than is true for most novelists.

14. See *GDM*, 288, 309, 310.

WILLIAM FAULKNER:
THE PROBLEM OF POINT OF VIEW

MICHAEL MILLGATE

NOTHING IN FAULKNER'S career is more remarkable than the sheer bulk of his achievement and the extraordinary range of his experimentation, the variety of narrative techniques adopted in successive volumes. Even his earliest novels, *Soldiers' Pay* and *Mosquitoes,* incorporated distinctive experimental elements, and by the time he wrote his fourth novel, *The Sound and the Fury,* he was no longer tinkering with the problems of fictional form but undertaking radical new departures. Three of the four sections of *The Sound and the Fury* take the form of interior monologues; *As I Lay Dying,* his next book is entirely made up of a series of interior monologues radiating from the central "story"

Reprinted with permission from *Patterns of Commitment in American Literature*, ed. Marston LaFrance (University of Toronto Press, 1967), 181–192.

like the spokes of a wheel. In other books of the 1930's and early 1940's the experiments were of many different kinds: chiefly stylistic in *Pylon,* chiefly structural in *The Wild Palms,* both stylistic and structural in *Absalom, Absalom!, The Hamlet,* and *Go Down, Moses.*

After the war, and particularly in his last three novels, *The Town, The Mansion,* and *The Reivers,* Faulkner tended more and more to abandon this experimental exuberance and confine himself to fictional techniques which were less obviously innovatory. It is possible, of course, that the relatively conventional character of the late fiction represents simply a falling-off in energy, but that this may not be the whole answer is suggested by the presence among Faulkner's later work of *Requiem for a Nun,* a kind of play-within-a-novel (or, if you prefer it, a play in which the opening stage direction of each act has the length and indeed the structure of a short story), and also of *A Fable,* an intricately constructed narrative which is, perhaps, not so much a novel as what its title announces it to be—a fable, a moral exemplum, eloquent of general truths. Apparently Faulkner neither rejected experimentation as such nor lost the energy with which to conduct experiments when they seemed to be called for. Is it possible then—and it is to this question that I want to address myself in this paper—that Faulkner may have felt in writing the more conventional of his final novels that he had in fact found not a retreat or a respite from, but actually an answer to, those very problems which had earlier led him into more evidently adventurous paths?

These problems all involved in some degree the question of point of view, an area of technique which is not only of fundamental importance to all novelists but which has characteristically been a major preoccupation of modern novelists, and particularly of Conrad and Joyce, two of the most powerful and most immediate influences on Faulkner himself. The problem of point of view embraces, after all, some of the most crucial questions of literary technique: from whose angle and in whose voice is the story told? Where does authority lie in the novel, and whom, as readers, should we trust? Where does the author himself stand, and how do we *know* where he stands? We have to ask such questions, and answer them satisfactorily, before we can speak with any assurance of the moral patterning of a book or even, in some instances, of what it is, in the broadest sense, about.

What is immediately striking is the rarity of the first-person narrator in Faulkner's work. In a writer who is so often claimed as a direct descendant of Mark Twain and the tradition of Southwestern humour, it is a little surprising to find only two books—*The Unvanquished* and *The Reivers*—which are told entirely from the point of view of a single first-person narrator. And even

in *The Reivers* the first-person narrator is not the final authority: the whole
book is thrust into a frame, set at a distance, by the implications of the two
opening words—"Grandfather said"—and of the colon which follows them.[1]
The content of the book may be Grandfather's story, but clearly we must
suppose that story to have been set down not by Grandfather himself but by
one of his audience, presumably a grandson, and the distinction is crucial to
a proper apprehension of the tone of the whole book. Henry James, of course,
had a horror of "the terrible *fluidity* of self-revelation," and Faulkner, with
his own highly developed sense of form, may conceivably have seen similar
dangers in this particular technique. But obviously there is more to it than that,
and even as one notes the relative absence of direct first-person narrative in
Faulkner's work, one is haunted by the sense that the spoken voice is one of
the dominant elements in almost all of his books. What closer inspection
reveals is that many of his novels have not a single point of view at all but a
multiplicity of points of view and, further, that Faulkner's preference is, in
many cases, for a multiplicity of types of point of view—first person, third
person, stream of consciousness, centre of consciousness, and so on. Perhaps
it would be useful, as a way of clarifying this question, to look in a little more
detail at one particular book, *The Sound and the Fury*, generally thought of
as the most "difficult" and technically adventurous of Faulkner's works.

A reader who comes unprepared to the opening section of the novel may
well be initially at a loss to know into what kind of a fictional world he had
strayed:

Through the fence, between the curling flower spaces, I could see them hitting.
They were coming toward where the flag was and I went along the fence.
Luster was hunting in the grass by the flower tree. They took the flag out, and
they were hitting. Then they put the flag back and they went to the table, and
he hit and the other hit. Then they went on, and I went along the fence. Luster
came away from the flower tree and we went along the fence and they stopped
and we stopped and I looked through the fence while Luster was hunting in
the grass. "Here, caddie." He hit. They went away across the pasture. I held
to the fence and watched them going away.[2]

The reader may well wonder who it is speaking in this curiously formal,
elaborately simple way. It may take some time for him to realize that what he
is hearing is not properly a speaking voice at all; that he is, in fact, inside the
mind of Benjy Compson, a thirty-three-year-old idiot. Benjy cannot talk; nor
is he capable, in even the simplest of ways, of distinguishing the relation of
cause and effect; and what Faulkner does in this whole section of the novel is

establish a convention of pure objectivity. Benjy observes the world around him, but he is incapable of imposing any pattern on that observation, and Faulkner employs him as a kind of camera-eye, recording whatever passes before him.

In that opening paragraph, Benjy is in the garden of the Compson house, looking through the fence and the honeysuckle ("the curling flower spaces") at men playing golf ("hitting") on the adjoining course. When one of the golfers calls out "Here caddie," Benjy howls in anguish ("I held to the fence," he says), and it is not till some time later that we realize he is giving voice to that vague sense of loss he feels at the absence of his sister Caddy, the one member of the family on whom he had depended for comfort. It is only later, too, that we discover that the golf course was formerly Benjy's pasture, one of the few things in the world to which he felt an attachment, and that the land has been sold to pay for a Harvard education for Benjy's brother, Quentin. Later still, we discover that Caddy has left home in disgrace, that Quentin has committed suicide at the end of his first year at Harvard, that Jason, the youngest of the Compson children and the only one left at home with Benjy, is a mean and rapacious small business man. The Compson family had once been a relatively distinguished one in the society of Mississippi, but it is now in the process of rapid disintegration, hastened rather than delayed by the cynicism of a dipsomaniac father, now dead, and the utter selfishness of a neurotic mother, still alive and still complaining.

The reader discovers these things as he gets further and further into the book, as he responds to that experience of progressive discovery and imaginative re-creation to which Faulkner's technique invites and, indeed, compels him. Benjy is narrator of the first section, Quentin of the second, Jason of the third, while the fourth section is told by the familiar method of third-person narration, in which the author puts himself in a position of omniscience. Each of the first three sections is a *tour de force* in its own way: in Benjy's section, as we have seen, there is that brilliantly achieved convention of objectivity and an absolute freedom of movement backwards and forwards in time—the creation of what Faulkner once described in a letter as "that unbroken-surfaced confusion of an idiot which is outwardly a dynamic and logical coherence."[3] Quentin's section is the interior monologue not of an idiot but of a highly sensitive and extremely tortured mind, and we follow, in a variation of the Joycean stream-of-consciousness method, the various experiences, ideas, images, memories which crowd upon his over-active mind during the last day of his life. Jason's section is an extremely successful capturing of a particular personality in terms of a particular tone of voice: "Like I say if all the businesses in a town are run like country businesses, you're going to have a country town" (p. 310). When Jason talks like that, the man and his attitudes come frighteningly alive for us; one might add, too, that although this section, like its two predecessors, is generally spoken of as an interior monologue, the voice evoked is specifically a speaking voice, and it is easy to imagine Jason's words as being spoken out loud. This is much less true of Benjy's and Quentin's sections, and it is perhaps a sign that in this third section we are already moving outwards from the extreme internalization of the first two sections to the overtly social world of the fourth section, in which Faulkner writes as the omniscient author and gives us, for the first time, a physical description of the various members of the Compson family and of the Compson estate, and shows us much more clearly than before the ways in which the Compsons and their Negro retainers relate to the larger society of Jefferson, Mississippi.

But why—it might be asked, and with some passion—why do it this way at all? Faulkner once said that in *The Sound and the Fury* he had told the same story four times,[4] but that will hardly do as a complete explanation: the four sections may illustrate the same fundamental situation, that of the Compson family in its decay, but there is not in fact a great deal of narrative overlapping from one section to another. Indeed, the powerfully evoked individuality of the three first-person narrators, each locked in his own kind of unreality and remoteness, tends to result in a certain lack of over-all cohesion in the novel, and although one of Faulkner's chief purposes seems to have been the creation of Caddy, the Compson daughter, in terms of the viewpoints of her three brothers, there is a sense in which she remains vague and elusive of definition. It would be extremely interesting to know whether Faulkner had originally intended to write the fourth section in the third person, or whether his decision to do so was in some degree the result of a sense that the book was in danger of falling apart and needed a kind of authorial hoop to hold it together. It is not hard, in fact, to see ample justification for Faulkner's decision to write the closing section as he did—it was the most appropriate way of handling a considerable body of narrative material and it gave the reader release from the claustrophobic intensity of the previous sections. But although *The Sound and the Fury* was the book of which Faulkner spoke with most affection in later years, he seems at the same time to have thought of it as at least a partial failure,[5] and one of the sources of his dissatisfaction may have been an awareness that, given the basic technique of the novel, there were other Compson voices that should perhaps have been allowed to make themselves heard: Caddy's, her daughter's, Mr. Compson's, Mrs. Compson's, Dilsey's.

In *As I Lay Dying*, of course, that is precisely what Faulkner did: everyone is given a voice— not only every member of the Bundren family, but also several neighbours and various other people whom the Bundrens encounter on their way to Jefferson. Unity can be said to have been achieved here simply by virtue of the comprehensiveness of the points of view, but it is more specifically achieved by the way in which each of the narrative fragments makes its own contribution to the central "story"—the anecdote of the journey itself. It is a brilliant *tour de force,* but one which could only be achieved, perhaps, with basic material of this limited and essentially anecdotal kind. It is hard to see how the four sections of *The Sound and the Fury* could have been very much shorter than they are, and it seems likely that if Faulkner had attempted to deal in the *As I Lay Dying* manner with material on the scale of *The Sound and the Fury* he would have found himself with a book unmanageable in terms simply of size alone.

There may well have been other reasons, however, why Faulkner did not repeat the kind of experiments in the use of the first-person narrator which he had undertaken in *The Sound and the Fury* and *As I Lay Dying.* He may have recognized a more fundamental limitation in exclusive reliance on first-person narration, however generously proliferated. Use of the first-person point of view can give vitality and immediacy; it allows the novelist both to tell the story, to recount simple narrative events, and, at the same time, to reveal the character of the narrator himself—in terms of the way the story is told, the order in which events are recounted, what is emphasized and dwelt upon, and, certainly not least, the kind of language that is used. But how are we to judge the reliability of what the narrator tells us? How, specifically, does the author dissociate himself from an untrustworthy first-person narrator? Clearly, a skilful author can make a narrator like Jason Compson betray his unreliability by everything he says; an alternative method of ironic self-revelation is to allow the narrative itself to involve patterns of events—or simply passages of dialogue—which irresistibly call in question the narrator's interpretation of them. By such methods the author can invoke in the novel, in however shadowy a form, an ideal standard of value against which the narrator's aberrations can be assessed. The method has its limitations, however, the measurement of human behaviour against abstract standards, whether aesthetic or moral, is not necessarily a particularly sensitive process, and the attempt to enforce judgment of a first-person narrator in terms of standards both abstract and only tenuously implicit may well become oversimplified and much too absolute.

Because Faulkner preferred to judge people in terms not of abstractions but of responses to actual human situations, his view of the world, of human behaviour, and of human values was rather more complex than this, and in writing *Light in August,* his next major novel after *As I Lay Dying,* he attempted to give expression to that complexity. In technical terms this involved considerable modification of his use of first-person narration, which now took a subsidiary rôle instead of the dominant one it had been given in previous books. *Light in August,* indeed, is the novel in which Faulkner first tried to incorporate within a relatively conventional framework the kind of narrative effects he had sought, and in large measure obtained, in *The Sound and the Fury* and *As I Lay Dying*—but perhaps at the cost of drawing disproportionate attention to the techniques themselves. In *Light in August* Faulkner still avoids simple chronological continuity and still deals, as he was to do throughout his career, in large blocks of material so disposed as to achieve maximum effects of ironic juxtaposition or to bring to bear the fullest possible weight of historical, social, and emotional complexity upon a particular moment in time. The long flashback telling the story of Joe Christmas, the man who does not know whether he is Negro or white, is thus poised, in point of time, on the moment just before the final and fatal confrontation between Joe himself and Joanna Burden, the aging white woman who has become his mistress. The novel contains several substantial passages of first-person narrative—by Miss Burden, by Gavin Stevens, by the mad Doc Hines and his wife, by the anonymous furniture dealer in the final chapter, and by a voice identified simply as "they" —the ordinary people of the town of Jefferson and its surrounding countryside. But while these passages often continue uninterrupted at some length, and thus retain a degree of independent identity, they are all incorporated into an over-all narrative framework.

The most remarkable of these passages, structurally speaking, is the final account by the furniture dealer of his encounter with Lena Grove and the doggedly faithful Byron Bunch. The account is essentially a monologue, an extended passage of first-person narration, but it is interrupted from time to time by comments from the man's wife, and we become quickly aware that the telling of this mildly racy story is considerably affected by the presence of this particular audience and by the fact that the two of them are together in bed. At one level, of course, this is very much in the tradition of American anecdotal humour—the humorous story, according to Mark Twain, is essentially American and its point consist primarily in the way it is told—but as one looks at the other examples of first-person narrative in *Light in August* it becomes clear that each of them is addressed to a specific audience and that each of them is affected, to a greater or lesser degree, by the speaker's awareness of that audience (Doc Hines, perhaps, is oblivious of his particular audience, but it might well be argued that this was precisely an aspect of his madness). Our own total experience as we read these passages includes—or should include, if we are reading sufficiently closely—simultaneous awareness of the speaker and of his audience, and of the interaction of the two.

Faulkner's great innovation in *Absalom, Absalom!,* published four years after *Light in August,* was to make this awareness into an organizing principle. He realized that first-person narrative, with all its advantages of immediacy and character revelation, need not be treated in isolation—as separate sections of uninterrupted solo performance—but could be handled in terms of extended dialogue. From this point on, it might almost be said, Faulkner's characteristic way of handling narrative was to present it as a recital to an audience, a monologue with interruptions. The great advantage of interrupted monologue, as Faulkner discovered, was that it permitted interior and exterior views of a character to be much more closely juxtaposed and virtually, indeed, to coexist. Because an audience is present, the characters are quite naturally driven to deal not simply with events but with motivation, to reveal the bases of reason, prejudice, or emotion on which they have acted—or on which they believe themselves to have acted. The listeners, for their part, may abandon silence to protest, argue, cross-examine, or engage in Socratic dialogue—as Gavin Stevens so frequently does, for instance, in the play sections of *Requiem for a Nun.*

In *Absalom, Absalom!* itself, the whole complex structure is built up almost entirely from the interlocking of a succession of interrupted monologues, and Faulkner once described Shreve McCannon, the arch-interrupter, as "the commentator that held the thing to something of reality," adding: "If Quentin had been let alone to tell it, it would have become completely unreal. It had to have a solvent to keep it real, keep it believable, creditable, otherwise it would have vanished into smoke and fury."[6] There is perhaps a hint here of the kind of function performed by the interlocutors in other Faulkner novels: the disgusted interjections of the short convict as the tall convict tells his tale in the "Old Man" section of *The Wild Palms* represent, in one respect, just such an intrusion of the voice of common sense. To put it another way, they are in some degree the kind of interjections which we as readers should be making, and it is almost as though Faulkner had provided the reader with a second self within the very world of the novel.

By methods such as these, the first-person narrator can be judged not simply against standards implicit in his own narrative, but in terms of concurrent commentary from a specific audience. Ironic effects proceed now not so much from verbal jugglery within the monologue itself as from the juxtaposition of monologue and context, the relation between what is said and the situation in which it is said: the tall convict's tale of freedom unappreciated is being related, after all, to an audience of convicts still hopelessly immured. It is in *The Wild Palms*, of course, that Faulkner made the most obviously challenging of his experiments in large-scale ironic juxtaposition, since it seems clear that the story of the tall convict, embarrassed by a freedom he did not seek or desire, was designed by Faulkner as a deliberate counterpoint to the story of Charlotte Rittenmeyer and Harry Wilbourne, who suffered every kind of agony in their search for a freedom they could never attain.[7] Such a juxtaposition relates directly to the question point of view, for our evaluation of the meaning of either story must be profoundly affected by our having been forced to a parallel reading of its companion piece: the meaning of the novel as a whole is precisely the product of our reaction to this experience, our response to the coexistence, the chapter by chapter alternation, of two stories which may look and be quite separate as simple narrative but which Faulkner insists *are* related in significant ways.

The *Wild Palms* was published in 1939; *The Hamlet*, a novel of great beauty and remarkable stylistic virtuosity, appeared in 1940; and in 1942 came *Go Down, Moses,* perhaps the most widely and persistently misunderstood of all Faulkner's works. In *Go Down, Moses,* I suggest, Faulkner is demanding still more of us than he did in *The Wild Palms,* though few critics seem even to have realized that he is demanding anything at all. Misunderstanding of the book began with its first editor, who took it upon himself to call the volume *Go Down, Moses and other Stories;* that "and other Stories" was a quite unauthorized addition which Faulkner later had cancelled but which has bedeviled discussion of the book ever since.[8] The so-called stories which make up *Go Down, Moses* were intended by Faulkner to be read as chapters in a novel;[9] each of them makes a quite distinct statement about white-Negro relations or about the destruction of the wilderness, or about both, and our reading of the book as a whole must depend upon our awareness of the interaction of all these separate statements one with another. We tend to look for neater, more clearly formulated resolutions in most of the books we read, but Faulkner's deliberate choice, here as elsewhere, is to offer as resolution the fact of complexity itself, the frank acknowledgment that there may be situations—such as the white-Negro situation—in which no single standard of right and wrong is universally applicable, and in which men of goodwill can only do what seems to them right and necessary and possible in any given set of circumstances.

The fourth section of "The Bear" is the one point in the novel where Faulkner attempts to bring all his material into narrower focus, and he does so precisely by means of that technique of interrupted monologue we have already discussed. The basic monologue here is Ike McCaslin's, but because Ike is delivering it to his cousin Cass, a man who has adopted different solutions to the very problems which so agitate Ike himself, the whole section becomes a kind of debate, a dramatized presentation of what are essentially abstract issues. Faced with the problem of living as moral men in an immoral world—specifically here, the world of the American South—Ike has chosen withdrawal into idealism, Cass involvement in the sometimes sordid world of actuality; Faulkner is not necessarily here saying that either is right or wrong, but rather that Ike's position, however dignified, looks a good deal less admirable when put side by side with the practical workaday achievements of Cass, while Cass's position, though sensible and practical, certainly lacks idealism and perhaps contributes to the perpetuation of social evils.[10]

Go Down, Moses was the logical culmination of directions which Faulkner's work had been taking for several years previously, and there is no reason to think that he was dissatisfied with it. Nevertheless, its particular solution was not to be his final solution; it is characteristic of Faulkner, indeed, that he regarded no solution as final but tried always to avoid repeating himself in any way, to do something fresh in every book. What he attempted several years later in *Requiem for a Nun* was to isolate the interrupted monologue in the form of a play; his relative failure in this book was perhaps not so much a matter of the basic conception but of the highly artificial dialogue in which he chose to embody it. He did not, at any rate, abandon the idea of disengaging the monologue from the traditional kind of novel structure, even though to attempt to do so was in some sense to retrace the steps he had taken in working towards the integrated structure of novels like *Absalom, Absalom!* and *The Hamlet*.

When, in the middle 1950's, Faulkner resumed the writing of the Snopes trilogy, of which the first volume, *The Hamlet*, had been published many years before, he worked out another solution to the problem of point of view—a solution less dramatic than many of his earlier experiments but precisely calculated to meet the particular demands of his material and themes. In *The Town*, the second volume of the Snopes trilogy, the narration is divided between three first-person narrators, Gavin Stevens, V. K. Ratliff, and Charles Mallison. Gavin Stevens is the central character, and his sections of narrative give expression to his hopelessly romantic attitudes towards first Eula Varner and then her daughter Linda. Ratliff, a man of very different outlook, operates to some extent as the reader's representative within the novel, and his comments on Stevens' romantic notions, though often brief, are extremely pointed.

Charles Mallison, as Stevens' nephew, gives us glimpses of his uncle in domestic situations, but he also speaks specifically as the voice of Jefferson, as a mouthpiece for the local consensus: "So when I say 'we' and 'we thought' what I mean is Jefferson and what Jefferson thought."[11] The novel achieves unity through the continuity of the narrative as it is passed on, relay fashion, from one narrator to another, and through the carefully established sense of Jefferson itself as a place and a society. This unity is also greatly strengthened by the way in which the three narrators, and particularly Ratliff and Charles, seem to engage in a continual conversation. For Ratliff and Charles the conversation is usually about Stevens, and if Stevens, on the other hand, seems often to be taking to himself, that is, perhaps, precisely a sign of his relative isolation from reality.

Although *The Town* is not often thought of as one of Faulkner's major achievements, it perhaps deserves greater recognition as a novel in which Faulkner seems finally to have come to terms with the problem of point of view with which he had wrestled so long. By means of the efficient but quite unobtrusive technique he has here adopted, Faulkner has retained all the normal advantages of first-person narrative; at the same time, he has not sacrificed economy, because he has used only three narrators, each of whom fulfils a major representative rôle, as well as a purely individual one, in the over-all pattern; he has not sacrificed unity, because the successive narrative sections all contribute to a single developing story; he has not sacrificed those advantages of continuing commentary which came with the interrupted monologue, because the placing of many of the sections, particularly those in which Ratliff is the narrator, is designed precisely to fulfil such a function; nor has he sacrificed complexity, since our total response, as in *The Wild Palms* or *Go Down, Moses,* depends upon our awareness not only of Gavin Stevens' view of things but also of the very different views of Ratliff and Charles Mallison and the people of Jefferson. Stevens may operate at some distance from what most of us would regard as the world of practical reality, but we are not allowed to view him in such isolation, any more than we are allowed to view him entirely on his own terms. The characters of the novel include Ratliff and Eula Varner as well as Gavin Stevens, and what finally confronts us here, as in all of Faulkner's works, is not man alone, or man judged against an abstract ideal, but man seen in relation to his fellow men and in the context of his society, doing what he can and must within the inescapable limitations of an actual and highly imperfect world—or, in Stevens' case, refusing, grandly but foolishly, to recognize such limitations at all.

Because of his treatment of such "lost" characters as Joe Christmas in

Light in August and Quentin Compson in both *The Sound and the Fury* and *Absalom, Absalom!*, and because of his recourse in *The Sound and the Fury* and *As I Lay Dying* to the extreme intimacies of stream-of-consciousness technique, Faulkner has often been thought of as a quintessentially "modern" novelist, dealing primarily with the agonies of contemporary man in his desperate search for identity and expression. Unquestionably this element is present in Faulkner's work, and especially in the novels just mentioned. When Faulkner gave his Nobel Prize address, however, these were not the themes on which he dwelt: he spoke rather of "the old verities and truths of the heart, the old universal truths lacking which any story is ephermeral and doomed— love and honor and pity and pride and compassion and sacrifice."[12] If one accepts that the Nobel Prize speech was not an idle rhetorical exercise but a precise expression of what Faulkner believed his work to be about, then clearly one has to see Faulkner's major emphasis as falling not so much on the individual in isolation as on the individual in his relation to other human beings. Faulkner, indeed, seems "traditional," rather than "modern," in his insistence on questions of right conduct, and it might well be argued that the major themes in his work, taken as a whole, are essentially social in character.

Cleanth Brooks has written very persuasively of the importance of responding, in almost every Faulkner novel, to the omnipresent sense of the community, "the powerful though invisible force that quietly exerts itself in so much of Faulkner's work. It is the circumambient atmosphere, the essential ether of Faulkner's fiction."[13] As Brooks goes on to point out, we become aware of the community in a novel like *Light in August* in terms of the minor characters and their reactions to the central characters, and, even more explicitly, in terms of that unidentified voice which speaks for the community as a whole and of the furniture dealer's final picture of Lena Grove and Byron Bunch—a picture which, because of its frankness and humour, serves to place not only the affairs of Lena and Byron but the whole action of the novel in a new perspective. The final section of *The Sound and the Fury* performs a somewhat analogous function, and even in *As I Lay Dying* the passionate voices of the Bundrens in their intensely introspective monologues are counter-pointed against a kind of composite voice of the community, made up of the monologues of the various outsiders who become involved in the story. Even in these most aggressively "modern" of his novels, Faulkner found it necessary to give some direct expression to the social reverberations of individual action, and in subsequent works the presence of society, of the community, becomes even more apparent. The very device of the interrupted monologue, the very presence of an audience for most of the passages of first-person narrative, even the book-length narrative of *The Reivers*—the use of such techniques implies almost automatically the existences of a specific social situation.

Master of technique though he was, Faulkner knew that technique is meaningless if it is pursued simply for its own sake, and in book after book he resisted the temptations of the spectacular and worked towards the perfection of technical devices whose very unobtrusiveness would best subserve his over-all objective of presenting the human condition in all its pain, joy, hope, despair, defeat, and triumph. "Art is simpler than people think," Faulkner wrote to Malcolm Cowley in 1945, "because there is so little to write about. All the moving things are eternal in man's history and have been written before, and if a man writes hard enough, sincerely enough, humbly enough, and with the unalterable determination never never never to be quite satisfied with it he will repeat them, because art like poverty takes care of its own, shares its bread."[14]

1. *The Reivers* (New York, 1962), p. [3].

2. New York, 1929, p. 1. Copyright © 1929 by Random House, Inc. Quoted by permission of Random House, Inc.

3. Autograph letter signed, Faulkner to Ben Wasson [1929], in Massey Collection, University of Virginia; quoted in Michael Millgate, *The Achievement of William Faulkner* (London, 1966), p. 94. Reprinted by permission of Mrs. Jill Faulkner Summers.

4. Robert A. Jelliffe, ed., *Faulkner at Nagano* (Tokyo, 1956), p. 105.

5. *Ibid.*

6. Frederick L. Gwynn and Joseph L. Blotner, eds., *Faulkner in the University: Class Conferences at the University of Virginia, 1957–1958* (Charlottesville, Va., 1959), p. 75.

7. Cf. Jelliffe, ed., *Faulkner at Nagano,* pp. 79–80.

8. For a discussion of this point see Millgate, *The Achievement of William Faulkner,* pp. 202–3.

9. Cf. Gwynn and Blotner, eds., *Faulkner in the University,* pp. 4, 273.

10. For a somewhat similar dramatization of an ideological conflict, see the interview between the Corporal and the old General in *A Fable* (New York, 1954), pp. 342–56.

11. New York, 1957, p. [3].

12. James B. Meriwether, ed., *Essays, Speeches, and Public Letters by William Faulkner* (New York, 1965), p. 120.

13. *William Faulkner: The Yoknapatawpha Country* (New Haven and London, 1963), p. 52.

14. Typed letter signed, Faulkner to Malcolm Cowley, undated, Yale University Library; quoted in Millgate, *The Achievement of William Faulkner,* p. 252. Reprinted by permission of Mrs. Jill Faulkner Summers.

ATMOSPHERE AND THEME IN FAULKNER'S "A ROSE FOR EMILY"

RAY B. WEST, JR.

THE FIRST CLUES to meaning in a short story usually arise from a detection of the principal contrasts which an author sets up. The most common, perhaps, are contrasts of character, but when characters are contrasted there is usually also a resultant contrast in terms of action. Since action reflects a moral or ethical state, contrasting action points to a contrast in ideological perspectives and hence toward the theme.

The principal contrast in William Faulkner's short story "A Rose for Emily" is between past time and present time: the past as represented in Emily herself, in Colonel Sartoris, in the old Negro servant, and in the Board of Aldermen who accepted the Colonel's attitude toward Emily and rescinded her taxes; the present is depicted through the unnamed narrator and is represented in the *new* Board of Aldermen, in Homer Barron (the representative of Yankee attitudes toward the Griersons and through them toward the entire South), and in what is called "the next generation with its more modern ideas."

Atmosphere is defined in the *Dictionary of World Literature* as "The particular world in which the events of a story or a play occur: time, place, conditions, and the attendant mood." When, as in "A Rose for Emily," the world depicted is a confusion between the past and the present, the atmosphere is one of distortion—of unreality. This unreal world results from the suspension of a natural time order. Normality consists in a decorous progression of the human being from birth, through youth, to age and finally death. Preciosity in children is as monstrous as idiocy in the adult, because both are *unnatural*. Monstrosity, however, is a sentimental subject for fiction unless it is the result of human action—the result of a willful attempt to circumvent time. When such circumvention produces acts of violence, as in "A Rose for Emily," the atmosphere becomes one of horror.

Horror, however, represents only the extreme form of maladjusted na-

Reprinted with permission from *Perspective,* Summer, 1949, pp. 239–245.

ture. It is not produced in "A Rose for Emily" until the final act of violence has been disclosed. All that has gone before has prepared us by producing a general tone of mystery, foreboding, decay, etc., so that we may say the entire series of events that have gone before are "in key"—that is, they are depicted in a mood in which the final violence does not appear too shocking or horrible. We are inclined to say, "In such an atmosphere, anything may happen." Foreshadowing is often accomplished through atmosphere, and in this case the atmosphere prepares us for Emily's unnatural act at the end of the story. Actually, such preparation begins in the very first sentence:

When Miss Emily Grierson died, our whole town went to her funeral: the men through a sort of respectful affection for a fallen monument, the women mostly out of curiosity to see the inside of her house, which no one save an old manservant—a combined gardener and cook—had seen in at least ten years.

Emily is portrayed as "a fallen monument," a *monument* for reasons which we shall examine later, *fallen* because she has shown herself susceptible to death (and decay) after all. In the mention of death, we are conditioned (as the psychologist says) for the more specific concern with it later on. The second paragraph depicts the essential ugliness of the contrast: the description of Miss Emily's house "lifting its stubborn and coquettish decay above the cotton wagons and the gasoline pumps—an eyesore among eyesores." (A juxtaposition of past and present.) We recognize this scene as an emblematic presentation of Miss Emily herself, suggested as it is through the words "stubborn and coquettish." The tone—and the contrast—is preserved in a description of the note which Miss Emily sent to the mayor, "a note on paper of an archaic shape, in a thin, flowing calligraphy in faded ink," and in the description of the interior of the house when the deputation from the Board of Aldermen visit her: "They were admitted by the old Negro into a dim hall from which a stairway mounted into still more shadow. It smelled of dust and disuse—a close, dank smell." In the next paragraph a description of Emily discloses her similarity to the house: "She looked bloated, like a body long submerged in motionless water, and of that pallid hue."

Emily had not always looked like this. When she was young and part of the world with which she was contemporary, she was, we are told, "a slender figure in white," as contrasted with her father, who is described as "a spraddled silhouette." In the picture of Emily and her father together, framed by the door, she frail and apparently hungering to participate in the life of her time, we have a reversal of the contrast which has already been presented and which is to be developed later. Even after her father's death, Emily is not monstrous, but rather looked like a girl "with a vague resemblance to those angels in colored church windows—sort of tragic and serene." The suggestion is that she had already begun her entrance into that nether-world (a world which is depicted later as "rose-tinted"), but that she might even yet have been saved, had Homer Barron been another kind of man.

By the time the deputation from the new, progressive Board of Aldermen wait upon her concerning her delinquent taxes, however, she has completely retreated into her world of the past. There is no communication possible between her and them:

> Her voice was dry and cold. "I have no taxes in Jefferson. Colonel Sartoris explained it to me. Perhaps one of you can gain access to the city records and satisfy yourselves."
>
> "But we have. We are the city authorities, Miss Emily. Didn't you get a notice from the sheriff, signed by him?"
>
> "I received a paper, yes," Miss Emily said. "Perhaps he considers himself the sheriff. . . . I have no taxes in Jefferson."
>
> "But there is nothing on the books to show that, you see. We must go by the—"
>
> "See Colonel Sartoris. I have no taxes in Jefferson."
>
> "But Miss Emily—"
>
> "See Colonel Sartoris." [Colonel Sartoris had been dead almost ten years.] "I have no taxes in Jefferson. Tobe!" The Negro appeared. "Show these gentlemen out."

Just as Emily refused to acknowledge the death of her father, she now refuses to recognize the death of Colonel Sartoris. He had given his word, and according to the traditional view, "his word" knew no death. It is the Past pitted against the Present—the Past with its social decorum, the Present with everything set down in "the books." Emily dwells in the Past, always a world of unreality to us of the Present. Here are the facts which set the tone of the story and which create the atmosphere of unreality which surrounds it.

Such contrasts are used over and over again: the difference between the attitude of Judge Stevens (who is over eighty years old) and the attitude of the young man who comes to him about the "smell" at Emily's place. For the young man (who is a member of the "rising generation") it is easy. For him, Miss Emily's world has ceased to exist. The city's health regulations are on the books. "Dammit, sir," Judge Stevens replied, "will you accuse a lady to her face of smelling bad?" Emily had given in to social pressure when she allowed them to bury her father, but she triumphed over society in the matter of the smell. She had won already when she bought the poison, refusing to comply with the requirements of the law, because for her they did not exist.

Such incidents seem, however, mere preparation for the final, more important contrast between Emily and Homer Barron. Emily is the town's aristocrat; Homer is a day laborer. Homer is an active man dealing with machinery and workmen—a man's man. He is a Yankee—a Northerner. Emily is a "monument" of Southern gentility. As such she is common property of the town, but in a special way—as an ideal of *past* values. Here the author seems to be commenting upon the complex relationship between the Southerner and his past and between the Southerner of the present and the Yankee from the North. She is unreal to her compatriots, yet she impresses them with her station, even at a time when they considered her *fallen:* "as if [her dignity] had wanted that touch of earthiness to reaffirm her imperviousness." It appeared for a time that Homer had won her over, as though the demands of reality as depicted in him (earthiness) had triumphed over her withdrawal and seclusion. This is the conflict that is not resolved until the final scene. We can imagine, however, what the outcome might have been had Homer Barron, who was not a marrying man, succeeded, in the town's eyes, in seducing her (violating her world) and then deserted her. The view of Emily as a monument would have been destroyed. Emily might have become the object of continued gossip, but she would have become susceptible to the town's pity—therefore, human. Emily's world, however, continues to be the Past (in its extreme form it is death), and when she is threatened with desertion and disgrace, she not only takes refuge in that world, but she also takes Homer with her, in the only manner possible.

It is important, too, to realize that during the period of Emily's courtship, the town became Emily's allies in a contest between Emily and her Grierson cousins, "because the two female cousins were even more Grierson than Miss Emily had ever been." The cousins were protecting the general proprieties against which the town (and the times) was in gradual rebellion. Just as each succeeding generation rebels against its elders, so the town took sides with Emily against her relations. Had Homer Barron been the proper kind of man, it is implied, Miss Emily might have escaped both horns of the dilemma (her cousins' traditionalism and Homer's immorality) and become an accepted and respected member of the community. The town's attitude toward the Grierson cousins represents the usual ambiguous attitude of man toward the past: a mixture of veneration and rebelliousness. The unfaithfulness of Homer represents the final act in the drama of Emily's struggle to escape from the past. From the moment that she realizes that he will desert her, tradition becomes magnified out of all proportion to life and death, and she conducts herself as though Homer really had been faithful—as though this view represented reality.

Miss Emily's position in regard to the specific problem of time is suggested in the scene where the old soldiers appear at her funeral. There are, we are told, two views of time: (1) the world of the present, viewing time as a mechanical progression in which the past is a diminishing road, never to be encountered again; (2) the world of tradition, viewing the past as a huge meadow which no winter ever quite touches, divided from (us) now by the narrow bottleneck of the most recent decade of years. The first is the view of Homer Barron and the modern generation in Jefferson. The second is the view of the older members of the Board of Aldermen and of the confederate soldiers. Emily holds the second view, except that for her there is no bottleneck dividing her from the meadow of the past.

Emily's small room above stairs has become that timeless meadow. In it, the living Emily and the dead Homer have remained together as though not even death could separate them. It is the monstrousness of this view which creates the final atmosphere of horror, and the scene is intensified by the portrayal of the unchanged objects which have surrounded Homer in life. Here he lay in the roseate atmosphere of Emily's death-in-life: "What was left of him, rotted beneath what was left of the nightshirt, had become inextricable from the bed in which he lay; and upon him and upon the pillow beside him lay that even coating of the patient and biding dust." The symbols of Homer's life of action have become mute and silent. Contrariwise, Emily's world, though it had been inviolate while she was alive, has been invaded after her death—the whole gruesome and unlovely tale unfolded.

In its simplest sense, the story says that death conquers all. But what is death? Upon one level, death is the past, tradition, whatever is opposite to the present. In the specific setting of this story, it is the past of the South in which the retrospective survivors of the War deny changing customs and the passage of time. Homer Barron, the Yankee, lived in the present, ready to take his pleasure and depart, apparently unwilling to consider the possibility of defeat, either by tradition (the Griersons) or by time (death) itself. In a sense, Emily conquered time, but only briefly and by retreating into her rose-tinted world of the past, a world in which death was denied at the same time that it is shown to have existed. Such retreat, the story implies, is hopeless, since everyone (even Emily) is finally subjected to death and the invasion of his world by the clamorous and curious inhabitants of the world of the present.

In these terms, it might seem that the story is a comment upon tradition and upon those people who live in a dream world of the past. But it is not also a comment upon the present? There is some justification for Emily's actions. She is a tragic—and heroic—figure. In the first place, she has been frustrated by her father, prevented from participating in the life of her contemporaries. When she attempts to achieve freedom, she is betrayed by a man who represents the new morality, threatened by disclosure and humiliation. The grounds of the tragedy is depicted in the scene already referred to between Emily and the deputation from the Board of Aldermen: for the new generation, the word of Colonel Sartoris meant nothing. This was a new age, a different time; the present was not bound by the promises of the past. For Emily, however, the word of the Colonel was everything. The tax notice was but a scrap of paper.

Atmosphere, we might say, is nothing but the fictional reflection of man's attitude toward the state of the universe. The atmosphere of classic tragedy inveighed against the ethical dislocation of the Grecian world merely by portraying such dislocation and depicting man's tragic efforts to conform both to the will of the gods and to the demands of his own contemporary society. Such dislocation in the modern world is likely to be seen mirrored in the natural universe, with problems of death and time representing that flaw in the golden bowl of eighteenth-and nineteenth-century natural philosophy which is the inheritance of our times. Perhaps our specific dilemma is the conflict of the pragmatic present against the set mores of the past. Homer Barron was an unheroic figure who put too much dependence upon his self-centered and rootless philosophy, a belief which suggested that he could take whatever he wanted without considering any obligation to the past (tradition) or to the future (death). Emily's resistance is heroic. Her tragic flaw is the conventional pride: she undertook to regulate the natural time-universe. She acted as though death did not exist, as though she could retain her unfaithful lover by poisoning him and holding his physical self prisoner in a world which had all of the appearances of reality except that most necessary of all things—life.

The extraction of a statement of theme from so complex a subject matter is dangerous and never wholly satisfactory. The subject, as we have seen, is concerned not alone with man's relationship to death, but with his relationship as it refers to all the facets of social intercourse. The theme is not one directed at presenting an attitude of Southerner to Yankee, or Yankee to Southerner, as has been hinted at in so many discussions of William Faulkner. The Southern Problem is one of the objective facts with which the theme is concerned, but the theme itself transcends it. Wallace Stevens is certainly right when he says that a theme may be emotive as well as intellectual and logical, and it is this recognition which explains why the extraction of a logical statement of theme is so delicate and dangerous an operation: the story *is* its theme as the life of the body *is* the body.

Nevertheless, in so far as a theme represents the *meaning* of a story, it can be observed in logical terms; indeed, these are the only terms in which it can be observed for those who, at a first or even a repeated reading, fail to recognize the implications of the total story. The logical statement, in other words, may be a clue to the total, emotive content. In these terms, "A Rose for Emily" would seem to be saying that man must come to terms both with the past and the present; for to ignore the first is to be guilty of a foolish innocence, to ignore the second is to become monstrous and inhuman, above all to betray an excessive pride (such as Emily Grierson's) before the humbling fact of death. The total story says what has been said in so much successful literature, that man's plight is tragic, but that there is heroism in an attempt to rise above it.

IV. The Work:

Studies of Individual Novels

MIRROR ANALOGUES IN
THE SOUND AND THE FURY

LAWRANCE THOMPSON

THE CONCEPT OF holding a mirror up to nature suggests an attractive, but thorny, path across the history of ideas, because that trope has lent itself to so many conflicting usages and interpretations. Yet the persistent allusions to mirrors in *The Sound and the Fury* would seem to invite the reader to notice that Faulkner has adapted the ancient literary mirror device and mirror principle to his own peculiar purposes, as a means of reflecting various kinds of correspondences, antitheses, parallelisms, analogues—even as a means of illuminating certain thematic concerns which are implicit throughout the total action. At the risk of oversimplifying Faulkner's elaborately developed meanings, I propose to present in ascending order of significance a few mirror allusions and mirror devices, in the hope that such a progression may increase our awareness of certain basic meanings.

Perhaps the first hint or foreshadowing occurs when the idiot Ben touches a place on a wall where a mirror used to be. During the late afternoon of Ben's thirty-third birthday his Negro guardian, Luster, leads him into this experience:

"We went to the library. Luster turned on the light. The windows went black, and the dark tall place on the wall came and I went and touched it. It was like a door, only it wasn't a door.

"The fire came behind me and I went to the fire and sat on the floor, holding the slipper. The fire went higher. It went onto the cushion in Mother's chair."

Reprinted with permission from *English Institute Essays, 1952* (New York, Columbia University Press, 1953), pp. 83–106.

Although each of those images in that passage has important associations for Ben, this initial allusion to "the dark tall place on the wall" must strike the first reader as being mysterious, even meaningless, except that the tantalizing phrase does have the effect of creating a tension of interest, a focus of attention, which sharpens the response of the reader to later pertinent passages. For example, the superficial tension is completely resolved when Jason subsequently gives his recollection of a similar situation, and views it from a decidedly different angle.

I went on into the living room. I couldn't hear anything from upstairs. I opened the paper. After awhile Ben and Luster came in. Ben went to the dark place on the wall where the mirror used to be, rubbing his hands on it and slobbering and moaning. Luster begun punching at the fire.

"What're you doing?" I says. "We dont need any fire tonight."

"I trying to keep him quiet," he says.

Even this superficial clarification does not help us to understand the significance to Ben of that "dark place on the wall where the mirror used to be" before some of the furnishings were sold. But through Ben's stream-of-consciousness associations evoked by that "dark place" and that fire, Faulkner proceeds to develop a gradually revealing series of analogues, involving Ben and his sister Caddy and his mother at about the time he had been repudiated by his family through the act of changing his name from Maury to Benjamin. Two brief passages may be quoted to suggest the still enigmatic allusions to mirrors.

"Versh set me down and we went into Mother's room. There was a fire. It was rising and falling on the walls. There was another fire in the mirror."

Next, and again by association, Ben is reminded of Caddy. " 'Come and tell Mother goodnight.' Caddy said. We went to the bed. The fire went out of the mirror."

The specific meaning of that final sentence is obvious: as Ben's angle of vision changed, he could no longer see the reflection of fire in the mirror. But the immediate context suggests a symbolic value for that sentence: as Ben turns from Caddy to his mother he suffers a sense of loss which may be symbolized by the disappearance of the reflected fire. His next associational memory dramatizes several reasons why Ben may well have suffered a sense of loss whenever he turned from Caddy to his mother.

I could see the fire in the mirror too. Caddy lifted me up.

"Come on, now." she said. "Then you can come back to the fire. Hush now."

. . . . "Bring him here." Mother said. "He's too big for you to carry."

"He's not too heavy." Caddy said. "I can carry him."

"Well, I don't want him carried, then." Mother said. "A five year old child. No, no. Not in my lap. Let him stand up."

"If you'll hold him, he'll stop." Caddy said. "Hush." she said. "You can go right back. Here. Here's your cushion. See."

"Dont, Candace." Mother said.

"Let him look at it, and he'll be quiet." Caddy said. "Hold up just a minute while I slip it out. There, Benjy. Look."

I looked at it and hushed.

"You humour him too much." Mother said. "You and your father both. You dont realize that I am the one who has to pay for it. . . ."

"You dont need to bother with him." Caddy said. "I like to take care of him. Dont I, Benjy."

"Candace." Mother said. "I told you not to call him that. . . . Benjamin." she said. "Take that cushion away, Candace."

"He'll cry." Caddy said.

"Take that cushion away, like I told you." Mother said. "He must learn to mind."

The cushion went away.

"Hush, Benjy." Caddy said.

"You go over there and sit down." Mother said. "Benjamin." She held my face to hers.

"Stop that." she said. "Stop it."

But I didn't stop and Mother caught me in her arms and began to cry, and I cried. Then the cushion came back and Caddy held it above Mother's head. She drew Mother back in the chair and Mother lay crying against the red and yellow cushion.

"Hush, Mother." Caddy said. "You go upstairs and lay down, so you can be sick. I'll go get Dilsey." She led me to the fire and I looked at the bright, smooth shapes. I could hear the fire and the roof. . . .

"You can look at the fire and the mirror and the cushion too," Caddy said.

In that little dramatic action is ample evidence that Caddy, motivated by her compassion for her younger brother, has eagerly given Ben the kind of motherly attention previously denied to him because of his own mother's inadequacies. Tenderly, solicitously, Caddy has discovered ways of appealing to Ben's limited responses, to satisfy his instinctive and unreasoning hunger for orderliness, peacefulness, serenity. The fire, the red-yellow cushion, the smooth satin slipper are only a few of the objects used by Caddy to provide him with values which are positive to him because they are somehow sustaining. Then Caddy has also taught Ben the pleasure of multiplying these positive values through their reflections in the mirror. Because she has heightened his awareness of all those symmetrical visions of "bright, smooth shapes" which comfort him, it might be said that Caddy herself has become for Ben a kind of mirror of all his positive values, framed in love: her love for him and his love for her.

Ben's seemingly chaotic reverie in Part One of *The Sound and the Fury* is so contrived by Faulkner as to focus attention, not merely on fragments of the entire Compson story, but particularly on Ben's all-absorbing love for the Caddy who was and (like the mirror) is now gone. Her presence was Ben's joy; her absence his grief; her possible return his hope. The arrangement of these fragments in Part One enables Faulkner to withhold conclusive information as to how it happened that the finely sensitive and mothering child Caddy has so completely disappeared. The reader's tension of interest concerning that question is gradually resolved through various later uses of mirror analogues which disclose related aspects of Faulkner's complex theme.

Throughout *The Sound and the Fury* Faulkner employs the convention of using some of his characters to serve as mirrors of other characters, mirrors set at different angles so that they provide contrasting angles of vision. For example, we have already had occasion to observe two contrasting images of Ben: the image reflected in the articulated consciousness of Caddy, as differing from the image reflected in the articulated consciousness of Mrs. Compson. Although various characters in the narrative reflect various images of Ben, all these images may be reduced to two roughly antithetical categories: most of the characters view Ben as a disgrace, a menace, or at least as a slobbering idiot. By contrast, those who genuinely love Ben (particularly Caddy and the Negro servant Dilsey) insist that Ben has certain particular and extraordinary powers of perception. As Roskus phrases it, "He know lot more than folks thinks." Repeatedly Ben is represented as having the instinctive and intuitive power to differentiate between objects or actions which are life-encouraging and others which are life-injuring, and these are used by Faulkner to symbolize the antithesis between good and evil. In this limited sense, then, Ben serves as a kind of moral mirror, in which the members of his own family may contemplate reflections of their own potentialities, their own moral strengths and weaknesses. Most of them naturally refuse to acknowledge this power in Ben, because they do not wish to see themselves in any light other than that of self-justification.

Appropriately, Caddy is represented as having the greatest sensitivity to her brother's power of serving as a kind of moral mirror, and her sensitivity is heightened by her unselfish love for him. Faulkner develops this aspect of

Ben's significance in four episodes which illuminate the progressive phases of Caddy's growth. When she is old enough to be interested in adolescent court-ship, she discovers that Ben's unreasoning reaction against the smell of per-fume gives her a sense of guilt and prompts her to wash herself clean—a primitive ritual repeatedly correlated with Ben's potential for serving as moral agent and moral conscience in his family. Later, when Ben escapes from the house one night, to find Caddy and Charlie kissing in the swing on the lawn, Caddy leaves Charlie, ostensibly to quiet Ben, but also because Ben has again evoked in her a sense of guilt.

We ran out into the moonlight, toward the kitchen. . . . Caddy and I ran. We ran up the kitchen steps, onto the porch, and Caddy knelt down in the dark and held me. I could hear her and feel her chest. "I wont." she said. "I wont anymore, ever. Benjy. Benjy." Then she was crying, and I cried, and we held each other. "Hush." she said. "Hush. I wont anymore." So I hushed and Caddy took the kitchen soap and washed her mouth at the sink, hard.

The third time when Ben is represented as a moral mirror occurs as Caddy returns home immediately after her first complete sexual experience. In that scene Faulkner correlates two implicit analogues which complement each other: first, the analogue of Ben as a moral mirror; secondly, the analogue between simple physical vision and conscious moral vision, suggested by the persistent recurrence of the word "eyes" and the cognate words, "looking" and "seeing," as Ben again evokes in Caddy a deeper sense of guilt.

Caddy came to the door and stood there, looking at Father and Mother. Her eyes flew at me, and away. I began to cry. It went loud and I got up. Caddy came in and stood with her back to the wall, looking at me. I went toward her, crying, and she shrank against the wall and I saw her eyes and I cried louder and pulled at her dress. She put her hands out but I pulled at her dress. Her eyes ran. . . . We were in the hall, Caddy was still looking at me. Her hand was against her mouth and I saw her eyes and I cried. We went up the stairs. She stopped again, against the wall, looking at me and I cried and she went on and I came on, crying, and she shrank against the wall looking at me. She opened the door to her room, but I pulled at her dress and we went to the bathroom and she stood against the door, looking at me. Then she put her arm across her face and I pushed at her, crying.

Each of these three closely related episodes (involving Ben as moral mirror and also involving the symbolic and penitent ritual of washing away guilt with water) is associated in Ben's recollection with his ultimate reaction, at the time of Caddy's fake wedding, where the sense of guilt was ironically washed away with champagne until the celebration was terminated by Ben's unreasoning and bellowing protest. This fourth episode represents the end of the period in Ben's life when Caddy had been able to help him by bringing relative order out of his relatively chaotic experience, and the end of the period when Ben had served as moral mirror for Caddy. Notice that these two endings are obliquely suggested by reiterative mirror imagery in Quentin's recollection of that incident which broke up the wedding celebration.

She ran right out of the mirror, out of the banked scent. Roses. Roses. . . . Only she was running already when I heard it. In the mirror she was running before I knew what it was. That quick, her train caught up over her arm she ran out of the mirror like a cloud, her veil swirling in long glints her heels brittle and fast clutching her dress onto her shoulder with the other hand, running out of the mirror the smells roses roses the voice that breathed o'er Eden. Then she was across the porch I couldn't hear her heels then in the moonlight like a cloud, the floating shadow of the veil running across the grass, into the bellowing.

Caddy goes away after the fake wedding ceremony, leaving a double image of herself as reflected in the consciousness of her family. The reader's initial image of Caddy has been that reflected repeatedly in the consciousness of Ben: the sensitive and mothering Caddy whose love for Ben evoked his love for her and gave meaning to his life. That image remains. Antithetically, the second image of Caddy is that soon reflected (with only minor variations) in the consciousness of Mrs. Compson, Quentin, and Jason: the image of the member of the family whose fall from innocence is said to have brought a peculiar disgrace on the entire family; a disgrace considered equal to, or even greater than, that of Ben's idiocy. Gradually, however, the reader appreciates that Mrs. Compson, Quentin, and Jason, each motivated by different kinds of need for self-justification, have first made a scapegoat of Ben and have then made a scapegoat of Caddy, so that they may heap on these two scapegoats the ultimate blame for the disintegration within the Compson family. Although this suggests one further aspect of Faulkner's complex theme, further elaboration of this central meaning may be postponed until we have considered other varieties of mirror analogues.

In Part Two of *The Sound and the Fury* Faulkner gradually suggests antithetical contrasts between Ben's preoccupation with mirrors and Quentin's preoccupation with mirrors. At one point in his reverie Quentin makes this sequence of observations.

I could smell the curves of the river beyond the dusk and I saw the last light supine and tranquil upon the tideflats like pieces of broken mirror . . . Benjamin the child of. How he used to sit before that mirror. Refuge unfailing in which conflict [was] tempered silenced reconciled.

Quentin is (if we may borrow a phrase which Faulkner affords to Quentin himself) "a sort of obverse reflection" of Ben. By contrast with Ben's instinctive response to objects used to symbolize positive values in human experience, Quentin serves to dramatize a consciously willed and obsessive love for negative values which are life-injuring, life-destroying, and which in turn, are nicely symbolized by his elaborately planned act of suicide by drowning. Throughout *The Sound and the Fury* a recurrent motif, suggested by the title itself, is the traditional convention of conflict between order-producing forces and chaos-producing forces in human experience, here represented in part by the gradual drift of the Compson family from remembered dignity and order toward disgrace and chaos. Quentin is represented as one whose disordering self-love motivates not only his masochistic delight in creating inner chaos but also his erotic lust for his own death. Structurally, then, the juxtaposition of Ben's thirty-third birthday against Quentin's death day accentuates the contrasting life-visions symbolized by Ben (who is ironically the shame of the Compsons) and by Quentin (who is ironically the pride of the Compsons). The two brief passages which constitute, respectively, the end of Ben's day and the beginning of Quentin's day may be quoted to suggest, once again, Faulkner's fondness for the technical principle of antithesis, here used to illuminate obliquely the basic ways in which these two brothers serve as obverse reflections of each other. Ben's day ends with these words:

Caddy held me and I could hear us all, and the darkness, and sometimes I could smell. And then I could see the windows, where the trees were buzzing. Then the dark began to go in smooth, bright shapes, like it always does, even when Caddy says that I have been asleep.

There, implicitly, recurs the thematic suggestion that Ben, with the aid of Caddy, has developed the ability to find within himself the power to convert even darkness into a pattern of meaningful and soothing symmetry, serenity, order: "refuge unfailing, in which conflict [was] tempered silenced reconciled," as Quentin phrased it. By contrast, Quentin begins his day with an irritated resentment of sunlight and with an insistence on finding within himself the power to convert even the life-giving value of sunlight into a reminder of time. After the manner of his father, Quentin has already endowed time with ugly and chaotic significance: "When the shadow of the sash appeared on the curtains it was between seven and eight o'clock and then I was in time again, hearing the watch."

For immediate purposes the pivotal image there is "shadow," an image subsequently enriched by Faulkner to represent Quentin's *alter ego*, his own reflected image of himself, developed by Quentin as an elaborate mirror analogue. Quentin's reasoning, obliquely suggested by his numerous references to his own mirror analogue, may be paraphrased briefly. To achieve his willed act of self-destruction, he is aware that he must cope with that other side of self which is represented by his physical being or body, which intuitively or instinctively clings to life while resisting the death-will of his mind. To insult and belittle that resisting other-self (the body), Quentin identifies his body with his sun-cast shadow. Because the sun is repeatedly represented as creating the shadow of his body, this shadow might be considered poetically as the body's tribute to the life-giving power of the sun. But this is exactly the kind of tribute which Quentin wishes to deny. His inverted attitude toward the instinctive life-wish of his body is nicely reflected in the following poetic sentence, so rich in suggested extensions of meanings: "There was a clock, high up in the sun, and I thought about how when you don't want to do a thing, your body will try to trick you into doing it, sort of unawares."

At first glance, this echo of the traditional body-versus-spirit antithesis suggests Quentin's warped Calvinistic Presbyterian heritage. On reconsideration, it becomes obvious that the thing which Quentin does not want to do is to live; that which his body tries to do is to resist Quentin's obsessive and erotic lust for death. Consequently Quentin perversely views the body's natural death-resistance as the body's attempt to "trick" him. This inverted concept evokes his further conviction that he must counterattack that body-impulse by managing somehow to subdue and "trick" his shadow. Four very brief utterances of Quentin's may be quoted here to demonstrate the ironically enriching effects achieved by Faulkner in permitting this shadow-reflection of Quentin's body to represent Quentin's other-self opponent.

[1] I stepped into the sunlight, finding my shadow again.

[2] Trampling my shadow's bones into the concrete with hard heels. . . .

[3] The car stopped. I got off, into the middle of my shadow . . . trampling my shadow into the dust.

[4] The wall went into shadow, and then my shadow, I had tricked it again.

Obviously, Quentin's ultimate tricking of his "shadow" must be the destruction of his body in the planned act of suicide by drowning. In developing the double significance of this act (as being desired by the will and as being not desired by the body), Faulkner makes pertinent use of Quentin's initial experience on a bridge over the Charles River, where he stands contemplating his own shadow mirrored on the surface of the water below.

The shadow of the bridge, the tiers of railings, my shadow leaning flat upon the water, so easily had I tricked it that it would not quit me. At least fifty feet it was, and if I only had something to blot it into the water, holding it until it drowned, the shadow of the package like two shoes wrapped up lying on the water. Niggers say a drowned man's shadow was watching for him in the water all the time. . . . I leaned on the railing, watching my shadow, how I had tricked it. I moved along the rail, but my suit was dark too and I could wipe my hands, watching my shadow, how I had tricked it.

Later, from another bridge, Quentin blindly contemplates another symbolic shadow: the trout, instinctively fulfilling its potentialities as it swims against the destructive element in which it has its being.

I could not see the bottom, but I could see a long way into the motion of the water before the eye gave out, and then I saw a shadow hanging like a fat arrow stemming into the current. Mayflies skimmed in and out of the shadow of the bridge just above the surface. . . . The arrow increased without motion, then in a quick swirl the trout lipped a fly beneath the surface. . . . The fading vortex drifted away down stream and then I saw the arrow again, nose into the current, wavering delicately to the motion of the water above which the Mayflies slanted and poised. . . . Three boys with fishing poles came onto the bridge and we leaned on the rail and looked down at the trout. They knew the fish. He was a neighborhood character. . . . "We dont try to catch him anymore," he said. "We just watch Boston folks that come out and try."

That little parable or implicit mirror of meaning, wasted on Quentin, helps to correlate several different aspects of Faulkner's steadily developing emphasis on the value of certain kinds of instinctive response in human experience. There is even a suggested analogy between the instinctive action of the trout and the instinctive action of the sea gull which Quentin also blindly contemplates: each in its own discrete element instinctively uses the current or stream of its own element to achieve poise, even as the Mayflies do. Consider these two quotations in their relation to each other.

. . . rushing away under the poised gull and all things rushing.
. . . the arrow again, nose into the current, wavering delicately to the motion of the water above which the Mayflies slanted and poised.

Quentin's element is time, and instead of building on his own innate and instinctive potentialities for achieving poise against the motion of "all things rushing," he is represented as having deliberately chosen to pervert and destroy those potentialities. The trout, the gull, the Mayflies, along with Ben, make available to the reader the kinds of metaphorical "mirrors" of meaning which Quentin refuses to understand. By contrast with Ben, Quentin has a tendency to use all mirrors (literal or figurative) to multiply negative values, particularly those disordered and chaotic values symbolized by the reflection of his own death-obsessed face. On the evening of his death day, as he continues his chaotically systematic ritual of death courtship, Quentin momentarily finds in a window of a trolley car a mirror of things broken: "The lights were on in the car, so while we ran behind trees I couldn't see anything except my own face and a woman across the aisle with a hat sitting right on top of her head, with a broken feather in it."

Having established that mirror-image of the trolley car window, Faulkner subsequently develops extensions of meaning from it. Quentin, after returning to his dormitory room to clean himself up for death, stands before a conventional mirror, brushing his hair, troubled at the thought that Shreve, his roommate, may return in time to spoil his plans. Or perhaps, he thinks, Shreve may be coming in to town on a trolley, just as Quentin is again going out on another trolley, and if so their faces will be momentarily juxtaposed and separated only by the two windows and the space between. The elliptical passage containing hints of these thoughts is of particular interest here, because it suggests a basic mirror principle, namely, Quentin's use of phrases which have only a superficial value for him, but a far deeper thematic suggestion for the reader. Here is the passage.

While I was brushing my hair the half hour went. But there was until the three quarters anyway, except supposing seeing on the rushing darkness only his own face no broken feather unless two of them but not two like that going to Boston the same night then my face his face for an instant across the crashing when out of the darkness two lighted windows in rigid fleeing crash gone his face and mine just as I see saw did I see.

The potentials of meaning which go far beyond Quentin's immediate meaning there may be passed over to let us concentrate particularly on that striking phrase, less applicable to Shreve than to the total action of Quentin: "seeing on the rushing darkness only his own face." That again strongly suggests not only the conflict between Quentin's two opposed consciences but also the total contrast between Quentin's uses of mirrors and Ben's uses of mirrors.

Faulkner's most elaborately contrived mirror analogue, in the presentation of Quentin's death day, stands out as technically different from any mirror analogue we have yet considered. It is a figurative or symbolic mirroring of the meaning of a past action in a present action: the parallelism between the way Quentin plays big brother to the little Italian girl and the way Quentin previously played big brother to Caddy. Another kind of "broken mirror" effect is achieved by scattering through the entire episode involving the Italian girl evoked fragments of memories concerning earlier and related episodes involving Quentin and Caddy. This twofold sequence of analogous actions is much too long to be analyzed here. Yet it deserves to be mentioned as an extremely important example of a mirror analogue, in which Faulkner at least suggests that Caddy's love for her younger brother Ben and for her older brother Quentin was soiled, stained, and perverted by Quentin's self-love until Caddy, trying to keep up with her brother, got into trouble. To a large degree, Quentin is represented as having been personally responsible for the change which occurred in the character of Caddy. Yet, even as Quentin rejects as ridiculous the charge of the Italian brother, "You steela my sister," so he also rejects and ignores even the suggestions made by his own conscious or subconscious associations that he was, indeed, in some way responsible for what happened to Caddy. In this immediate context there is a highly ironic significance in the fact that Caddy should have chosen to name her daughter Quentin, even though her brother was not physically the father of her child.

Faulkner seems to have saved two oblique and "gathering" metaphors or symbolic actions for use in the concluding pages of *The Sound and the Fury;* and in this context it may be permissible to consider those two actions as mirror analogues, figuratively speaking. The first of these occurs in the episode involving Dilsey and Ben at the Easter service in the Negro church, and Faulkner begins it by making technical use, once again, of two contrasting or antithetical attitudes toward one person, namely, the monkey-faced preacher, who undergoes a metamorphosis, as he loses himself in the meaning of an action symbolizing self-sacrificial love:

And the congregation seemed to watch with its own eyes while the voice consumed him, until he was nothing and they were nothing and there was not even a voice but instead their hearts were speaking to one another in chanting measures beyond the need for words, so that when he came to rest against the reading desk, his monkey face lifted and his whole attitude that of a serene, tortured crucifix that transcended its shabbiness and insignificance and made of it no moment, a long expulsion of breath rose from them.

Faulkner would seem to be dramatizing in that symbolic action a key aspect of his central theme, always pivoting, as it does, on various possible meanings for the single word "love." For that reason the responses of Dilsey and Ben to that action are pertinent.

Dilsey sat bolt upright, her hand on Ben's knee. The tears slid down her fallen cheeks, in and out of the myriad coruscations of immolation and abnegation and time. . . . In the midst of the voices and the hands Ben sat, rapt in his sweet blue gaze. Dilsey sat bolt upright beside, crying rigidly and quietly in the annealment and the blood of the remembered Lamb.

The second of these gathering metaphors also illuminates and accentuates the implicit thematic antithesis between two kinds of vision. This time the extensions of meaning are ironically suggested through Luster's saucy analogy between how he does something and "how quality does it." While entertaining Ben by taking him for his customary ride to the cemetery on Easter Sunday, Luster decides to show off, for the benefit of some loitering Negroes. He merely proposes a simple violation of a simple law when he says, "Les show dem niggers how quality does it, Benjy." Instead of driving around the monument in the accustomed way, he starts Queenie the wrong way. Ben, instinctively feeling the difference between right and wrong even in such a trivial situation, begins to bellow and continues until the minor chaos of that situation (ironically corrected by Jason, out of mere embarrassment) has given way to the ritual of orderly return. So the total action of the narrative ends with the implicit and symbolic reiteration of the part Ben has played throughout, in terms of the antithesis between the human power to create chaos and the human power to create order.

Queenie moved again, her feet began to clop-clop, steadily again, and at once Ben hushed. Luster looked quickly back over his shoulder, then he drove on. The broken flower drooped over Ben's fist, and his eyes were empty and blue and serene again, as cornice and façade flowed smoothly once more, from left to right; post and tree, window and doorway, and signboard, each in its ordered place.

Faulkner's choice of title deserves to be viewed figuratively as suggesting one further kind of mirror analogue, because the attitude of Macbeth, as dramatized in the familiar fifth-act soliloquy, nicely reflects an important element in the attitudes of Faulkner's three major protagonists of chaos, Mrs.

Compson, Quentin, and Jason. All of these characters have this much in common: each is intent on self-pitying self-justification. All are certain that they have become victimized by circumstances beyond their control, and all of them project outward on life their own inner chaos, which has its roots in a perversion of love, through self-love. Similarly, in the fifth act, Macbeth is represented as refusing to recognize that he has been in any way to blame, or responsible, for what has happened to him. Instead, he also projects his own inner chaos outward, self-justifyingly, to make a scapegoat of the whole world, even of time, and to view life itself as a walking "shadow." Now consider the ironies of situation implicit in that passage which Faulkner's title suggests as a pertinent mirror of the attitudes not only of Quentin and Jason but also of Mr. and Mrs. Compson.

> Tomorrow, and tomorrow, and tomorrow,
> Creeps in this petty pace from day to day,
> To the last syllable of recorded time.
> And all our yesterdays have lighted fools
> The way to dusty death. Out, out, brief candle!
> Life's but a walking shadow, a poor player
> That struts and frets his hour upon the stage,
> And then is heard no more. It is a tale
> Told by an idiot, full of sound and fury,
> Signifying nothing.

Finally, the meaning of Faulkner's total structure may be suggested by one last mirror analogue. As narrator, he would seem to be intent on achieving a high degree of detachment by arranging his four separate parts in such a way that they do not tell a story in the conventional sense. Faulkner neither invites nor permits the reader to look directly at the total cause-and-effect sequence of events, as such. Instead, each of the four parts provides a different aspect, a different view, a different angle of vision, a different reflection of some parts of the story. Each of these four structural units, thus contiguous, hinged, set at a different angle from the others, might be called analogous to those hinged and contiguous haberdashery mirrors which permit us to contemplate the immediate picture reflected in any single one of those mirrors, and then to contemplate secondary or subordinate pictures which are reflections of reflections in each of the separate mirrors.

In Faulkner's four structural mirrors (the four parts), the first picture (or pictures) may be said to be provided through Ben's reflecting angle of vision. Although the reader's initial impression of Ben's reverie may, indeed, provide a sense that the tale is told by an idiot, signifying nothing, the ultimate impression is that Ben's angle of vision concentrates our attention symbolically on certain basic and primitive powers of perception, available even to an idiot; powers of perception which enable even a severely handicapped individual to create, from his own experience and with the aid of his instincts and intuitions, some forms of order which can give positive values to human experience.

Structurally, the second set of pictures is provided through Quentin's reflecting angle of vision. This time, although the reader's early impression of Quentin's reverie may provide a preliminary sense of a highly sensitive and Hamlet-like character, who views himself as intent on holding up to nature his own idealistic mirror, the ultimate impression is that Quentin's angle of vision reflects, by contrast with Ben's, several important aspects of the negative or obverse side of Faulkner's theme. Psychologically unbalanced by his own inner and outer conflicts, Quentin is represented as being partly responsible not only for what has happened to himself but also for what has happened to some other members of his family. He has permitted his warped and warping ego to invert exactly those basic and primitive and positive values symbolized by that which Ben instinctively and intuitively cherished.

The third set of images is provided by Jason's reflecting angle of vision, and even though Jason sees himself as the only sane Compson, the reader quickly becomes convinced that Jason's sadistic scale of values is more nearly analogous to the values of Iago than to those of the almost Hamlet-like Quentin. The irony of the total situation involving Jason culminates in a ridiculously fine burlesque of poetic justice when Faulkner permits Jason's golden fleece of Caddy to be avenged by Caddy's daughter's golden fleece of Jason. Even as Caddy's brother Quentin has somehow been at least partially responsible for the moral degeneration of Caddy, so Jason is represented as being at least partially responsible for the moral degeneration of Caddy's daughter.

The fourth set of images is provided through Dilsey's reflecting angle of vision. Implicitly and symbolically there is an analogous relationship between Dilsey's emphasis on certain basic, primary, positive values throughout and Ben's intuitive sense of values. Thus, the positive angles of vision, mirrored by Ben and Dilsey most sharply in the first and fourth structural parts of *The Sound and the Fury,* may be considered literally and symbolically as bracketing and containing the two negative angles of vision mirrored by Quentin and Jason in the second and third parts. Taken in this sense, the structural arrangement of these four hinged mirrors serves to heighten the reader's awareness of Faulkner's major thematic antithesis between the chaos-producing effects of self-love and the order-producing effects of compassionate and self-sacrificial love in human experience.

THE WORD
AND THE DEED
IN FAULKNER'S FIRST
GREAT NOVELS

FLOYD C. WATKINS

LYING ON HER deathbed and listening to the shallow moralizings of her neighbor Cora Tull, Addie Bundren in William Faulkner's *As I Lay Dying* thinks "how words go straight up in a thin line, quick and harmless, and how terribly doing goes along the earth, clinging to it, so that after a while the two lines are too far apart for the same person to straddle from one to the other; and that sin and love and fear are just sounds that people who never sinned nor loved nor feared have for what they never had and cannot have until they forget the words."[1] Those who can, Addie says, love and act; those who cannot, talk and speak the words of truth.

Sometimes the mere articulation of a thought may prove its falsity, as when Dewey Dell talks about her communication with Darl: "He said he knew without words . . . and I knew he knew because if he had said he knew with the words I would not have believed that he had been there and saw us" (*AILD*, p. 26). And Caddy asks Quentin, *"do you think that if I say it it won't be."*[2] Along with Frederic Henry's statement about the obscenity of such words as *glory, honor, courage, hallow, sacred,* and *sacrifice,* Addie's speech is one of the most effective rejections of abstraction written in the early twentieth century. Her denial of the efficacy of a moral vocabulary and her reliance on concrete image, fact, and action are reflections of the best aesthetic principles of Eliot, Faulkner, and Hemingway early in their careers. As a standard of criticism, Addie's view provides a sound perspective from which to view the works of these four writers, and it is an especially good clue to Faulkner's themes and techniques in *The Sound and the Fury, As I Lay Dying,* and *Sanctuary.*

Reprinted with permission from Floyd C. Watkins' *The Flesh and the Word: Eliot, Hemingway, Faulkner* (Vanderbilt University Press, 1971), 181–202.

Apparently Addie and Frederic would have regarded Faulkner's own Nobel Prize Speech as embarrassing and obscene because it contains the words "that go straight up in a thin line, quick and harmless." In 1950, twenty years after the creation of Addie, he wrote that it is the writer's duty to remind man "of the courage and honor and hope and pride and compassion and pity and sacrifice which have been the glory of his past." The early Faulkner did not remind his reader, who had to find the moral principles in the work if he could. Later, Faulkner seldom missed an opportunity to walk around his characters and discuss all the ramifications of their meanings. *The Sound and the Fury, As I Lay Dying,* and *Sanctuary,* however, are conspicuously alike in the extreme indirection of the way in which they remind the reader of the "old verities and truths of the human heart."

These three novels are amazingly similar in a number of ways. Each treats the theme of love and the family. Love between the sexes, the lack (or need) of such love, and the perversions of it are significant aspects of the life of almost every mature character. Addie and Anse Bundren, Mr. and Mrs. Compson, Horace and Belle Benbow—a tortured and confused marital relationship is significant in each. The young women in the novels are as confused as the parents—Dewey Bell Bundren and Caddy Compson conceive illegitimate children; Temple Drake and Little Belle Benbow are not pregnant probably because of better luck or more careful precautions. Caddy's fatherless daughter promises to drop a child by the roadside. The nearest thing to a normal and happy family presented in any of the novels is the relationship between Ruby Lamar and Lee Goodwin, a prostitute and a bootlegger. Even their union is cursed with an unhealthy baby. It has "lead-colored eyelids" and a "putty-colored face."[3] "It lies in drugged apathy," and it moves "now and then in frail, galvanic jerks, whimpering" (*S,* p. 123). Darl Bundren and Benjy Compson are committed to the insane asylum at Jackson. Faulkner's treatment of families with insufficient love indicates his anxiety about the problems of the family in the modern world.

Point of view, the author's way of presenting his material, varies a great deal in these three novels. *As I Lay Dying* and *The Sound and the Fury* contain Faulkner's only extended ventures into the technique of stream of consciousness. In *Sanctuary* and the last section of *The Sound and the Fury* Faulkner tells the story himself. But whether the character thinks or the author tells, Faulkner keeps his own views completely out of the fiction except by implication and indirectness. It is easier to tell what he thinks from the talk of his characters than it is from his objective writing in his own person. He either completely reveals the mental processes of a character or refuses to give any glimpse into a mind. In each novel there is a blank mind or an idiot or a confused child: Lee Goodwin's deaf and dumb and blind father (who is so isolated that he has only "one pleasure" and "one sense"—taste—left), Benjy, the insane Darl, and the child Vardaman (troubled by his first encounter with death). At the center of each novel is an ineffectual character with an abstract, intellectual sensibility—Darl, Quentin, and Horace. In all three novels incapacitated females symbolize the weaknesses and failures of the person and the family: Mrs. Compson on her sick bed, Addie on her deathbed, and Temple languishing on her bed in Miss Reba's whorehouse.

At one time, Faulkner refused to acknowledge any relationship between *As I Lay Dying* and *The Sound and the Fury* beyond the fact that the two "together made exactly enough pages to make a proper-sized book that the publisher could charge the regulation price on."[4] But on a different occasion when he was asked whether "Darl is the Quentin of the Bundrens and . . . Cash is the Jason of the Bundrens," he enigmatically agreed that his questioner could say that "if that is any pleasure to you" (*UNIV,* p. 121). And again he admitted a similarity "due to the fact that in each one of them there was a sister surrounded by a gang of brothers" (*UNIV,* p. 207). This is still not an extensive concession, but Faulkner's testimony years after publication is made questionable by forgetfulness as well perhaps as an author's seemly reluctance. Without being particularly conscious of similarities, furthermore, a creative mind may develop significant parallels in different works of art written in a short period of time.

Many minor features reflect the major points of similarities in *The Sound and the Fury, As I Lay Dying,* and *Sanctuary.* A key phrase repeated in *The Sound and the Fury* and *As I Lay Dying* indicates a significant similarity in character relationships. Jewel, Addie says, "is my cross and he will be my salvation" (*AILD,* p. 160). Jason for his mother is "my joy and my salvation" (*SF,* p. 127). Both Quentin and Horace Benbow are haunted again and again by thoughts of the surfeiting odor of honeysuckle, which they associate with the sexual promiscuity of Caddy and Little Belle (*S,* pp. 198, 215). Quentin, Horace, and Darl are all excessively sensitive souls. Not one of them can deal with life in a manly way. If Quentin and Horace share the obsession of honeysuckle, Horace and Darl think of isolation and their longings for an ideal or eternity in terms of the sound of rain. Darl thinks, "How often have I lain beneath rain on a strange roof, thinking of home," (*AILD,* p. 76). Horace thinks "of a gentle dark wind blowing in the long corridors of sleep; of lying beneath a low cozy roof under the long sound of the rain: the evil, the injustice, the tears" (*S,* p. 214). The tortured minds of Quentin and Darl use the same image to reveal their poetic and distorted impressions of reality: Quentin sees "A gull on an invisible wire attached through space dragged" (*SF*, p. 129). Darl watches "cane and saplings lean as before a little gale, swaying without reflections as though suspended on invisible wires from the branches overhead" (*AILD*, pp. 134–135). Loneliness and desire for love in the family are suggested in beautiful images in the thoughts of Addie and Quentin. Quentin remembers a picture in a book: "a dark place into which a single weak ray of light came slanting upon two faces lifted out of the shadow" (*SF*, p. 215). Addie thinks of a similar terrifying image, and, like Quentin, she remembers children isolated from parents: "the cries of the geese out of the wild darkness in the old terrible nights, fumbling at the deeds like orphans to whom are pointed out in a crowd two faces and told, 'That is your father, your mother' " (*AILD*, p. 166).

In each, Faulkner is concerned primarily with the character's ability or inability to communicate love in language. In general those characters who use the words of love are those who have not loved. And those who do not talk of love usually have had profound experiences which, they know, cannot be communicated in language. Olga Vickery has written that "each of the first three sections [of *The Sound and the Fury*] presents a version of the same facts which is at once the truth and a complete distortion of the truth."[5] The theme of the novel, she suggests, "is the relation between the act and man's apprehension of the act, between the event and the interpretation."[6] This statement also describes the theme of *As I Lay Dying*. There is, however, an additional similarity and complexity in the three novels. Those who articulate their interpretations of acts use meaningless words. Those who know and understand do not speak the words. Most of them remain silent in the novel, and emotion and truth are apparent in their deeds. Some reject empty words so much that they not only refuse to speak them but also reject them even in their internal monologues, their stream of thought. To know Faulkner's themes, his meanings, his characters, therefore, one must recognize the difference between truth and statement in each of the characters. Faulkner's techniques enable him to treat each character's relationship to love, fact, deed, and abstract word. The failure of language and the meaning of object and act are keys to the most important ironies and meanings.

The plots of all three novels turn upon the silent woman at the center of the work—Caddy Compson, Addie Bundren, and Temple Drake. In each book the other characters are defined (and they define themselves) by the way in which they are related to these strange women. Caddy is perhaps the most admirable of the three. She may seem to be merely a slut whose maidenhead,

Faulkner has said, was "the frail physical stricture which to her was no more than a hangnail would have been."[7] Actually, she is the heroine and the central figure of the novel. In Faulkner's later years he called Caddy "my heart's darling" (*UNIV*, p. 6), complimented her courage, and especially praised her selfless love.[8] In the appendix first written seventeen years after the publication of the novel, he explicitly stated for the first time his admiration of Caddy. Four times in one sentence he wrote that she loved her brother Quentin, even loved him because he "was incapable of love."[9] In an excellent study, Lawrence E. Bowling has stated that Caddy, unlike the idiotic Benjy, acquires knowledge, but she acquires, he says, "no spiritual depth or worthwhile knowledge." "Because of her moral transgression, Caddy may appear to be active, but she is really passive, for she does not truly act, but only allows herself to be acted upon."[10] This view excessively damns her for sexual promiscuity and ignores her very real virtues.

Caddy only acts. She is the one child of the Compsons who does not talk, who does not tell a section of the novel. She does not use the words, Faulkner has explained, because she is "too beautiful and too moving to reduce her to telling what was going on, that it would be more passionate to see her through somebody else's eyes . . ." (*UNIV*, p. 1). And if she were to speak, her genuine love would sound like only empty and embarrassing words. Indeed, she lies when the facts are unimportant and refuses to speak at all when it is possible to communicate without words. The puritanical Quentin despises disorder. Literally and symbolically, he is shocked when Caddy gets her dress wet playing in the branch. But she says her dress is not wet, because in play its wetness is simply unimportant, just as in love a maidenhead becomes no more significant than a hangnail. People and genuine feelings and needs are all that matter to her. If Frederic Henry gives up words because they obscure the truth, Caddy gives them up for the sake of a greater truth. While Benjy howls his protest, Charlie attempts to make love to Caddy.

"He cant talk." Charlie said. "Caddy."
"Are you crazy." Caddy said. . . . "He can see. Dont. Dont." (*SF*, p. 57)

Caddy does not care for reputation or virtue or herself. She cares only for Benjy and Quentin and her father. And after this scene she promises, purely for the love of Benjy, that she won't "anymore, ever" (*SF*, p. 58).

When Quentin demands that Caddy tell him in words that she loves her seducer, Caddy assumes that words cannot convince him. Twice Quentin asks, and each time Caddy puts his hand against her throat or her heart so that he can feel the fact instead of hearing the word. Quentin feels the "surge of blood

. . . in strong accelerating beats" (*SF*, pp. 187, 203). But even the beat of the pulse is empty like words to Quentin, because he can know only the words— never the love itself. In contrast, the Negroes who hear Brother Shegog's sermon can transubstantiate words into love and reality. Their hearts speak "to one another in chanting measures beyond the need for words . . ." (*SF*, p. 367).

The deeds of the selfless Caddy are Faulkner's triumph in *The Sound and the Fury*. Benjy cannot use a word even so simple and abstract as love unless he hears someone say it. But he remembers Caddy's acts. Three times he remembers how she was kind to him on a cold day. *"Keep your hands in your pockets, Caddy said. Or they'll get froze"* (*SF*, p. 3). No one else is concerned about his cold hands. Caddy's acts show that she actually likes to care for her idiot brother. She feeds him, carries him about, gives him his beloved cushion, defends him from the cruel Jason and his self-pitying mother. When Mrs. Compson weeps over him, Caddy says, "Hush, Mother. . . . You go upstairs and lay down, so you can be sick . . ." (*SF*, p. 78). "I'll feed him tonight." Caddy said. "Sometimes he cries when Versh feeds him" (*SF*, p. 86). But her own daughter, Quentin, asks, " *'Why dont you feed him in the kitchen. It's like eating with a pig'* " (*SF*, p. 86). After Caddy submits to a dishonorable marriage, she no longer has an opportunity to care for others in the family. Time and again, however, she forgets her own despair and asks her brother Quentin to do what needs to be done.

Are you going to look after Benjy and Father. . . . Promise. . . . Promise I'm sick you'll have to promise. . . . (*SF*, p. 131)

But Quentin never promises.

Caddy's loss of virginity and her love affairs apparently are not shoddy like the lust of her daughter, Quentin, with the carnival man. Caddy's heart-beat should prove her love for Dalton Ames, and that Dalton is not a mere mustachioed seducer in a sentimental melodrama is shown in his own concern for Caddy's welfare when Quentin comes to him as an outraged brother: "did she send you to me"; "I want to know if shes all right have they been bothering her up there" (*SF*, p. 198).

In utter selflessness Caddy comforts the stricken Quentin on the night when she is first seduced—a rather curious reversal of the usual roles of brother and sister in such a situation. Her sympathy goes out to anyone in need of understanding. When she believes that her lover Dalton has hurt Quentin, she tells him never to speak to her again. Later, when she learns that he did not hurt Quentin, she wishes to ask his pardon. She stops dressing for a date to lie down with Benjy to get him to sleep. She is willing to commit incest with Quentin, although she never indicates any lustful feelings for him. Her reasoning is never explained, but possibly she sees that such an evil would lead to his self-knowledge and then salvation instead of madness and suicide. Pregnant and unmarried, she marries a man she does not love apparently for the sake of the family's honor, loses her husband, is separated from those she loves (Benjy, Quentin, and her father), and finally gives up her illegitimate daughter to her family in the hope that they will bring up the child in the way she should go. She sends the daughter money, attends her father's funeral wearing a veil so that the family will not be shamed, apologizes to Jason because her divorce from her husband prevented his getting a job in a bank. She visits Jefferson and her daughter once or twice a year.

Caddy has every virtue except wisdom and chastity. Mrs. Compson's only virtue is chastity. Caddy allows an unloving family to rear her daughter, Quentin, who would be better off reared in a bawdyhouse. Jason wishes to keep Quentin so that he can steal the money her mother sends; so he suggests to Caddy that, living with her, Quentin would grow up a loose woman. Jason has touched a nerve and defined Caddy's real fears: " 'Oh, I'm crazy,' she says, 'I'm insane. I can't take her. Keep her. What am I thinking of ' " (*SF,* p. 260). Ironically, Caddy, who placed no value at all on her own virginity, puts too high a value on the chastity of her daughter. And also ironically, Quentin becomes even less chaste than Caddy. But the greatest tragedy of Caddy and of *The Sound and the Fury* is that Caddy and her capacity for love are lost. She loved most of all; she expressed her love in action rather than in word. Two of her brothers mourned her fall for selfish reasons. She falls more than any of the Compsons; the fault is her own; but Faulkner seems to suggest that the Compsons had too little regard for Caddy herself and her love and too much respect for the conventions and proprieties. Only Benjy loves her enough. When he goes to sleep after the long day of regrets for Caddy on April 7, 1928—eighteen years after Caddy has gone—"the Dark," he says , "began to go in smooth, bright shapes, like it always does, even when Caddy says I have been asleep" (*SF,* p. 92). In his limited mind, Caddy still exists in the present tense. The tragedy of the Compsons is that only an idiot remembers the character Faulkner referred to as "my heart's darling."

Caddy does not talk in abstractions. Addie Bundren in *As I Lay Dying* talks not at all except when others quote her and when she makes her one long speech in the novel. Within the "dark voicelessness" of her long monologue however, she condemns abstract words but uses them to describe the facts of her own sin and salvation. Outside the monologue she speaks abstractly only when she is provoked to reply to the sanctimonious preachments of Cora Tull. Addie's philosophy of words and deeds raises immediate questions. Why do her own words not "go straight up in a thin line"? Addie's husband, Anse, is a man of words. "He had a word, too. Love, he called it. But I had been used to words for a long time. I knew that that word was like the others: just a shape to fill a lack; that when the right time came, you wouldn't need a word for that anymore than for pride or fear" (*AILD*, p. 164). Addie herself speaks the words she condemns. In one paragraph of her soliloquy, she mentions *sin* eight times. She discusses *hate, fear, pride, love,* and *duty.* Faulkner seems aware that he and Addie in this speech need to stretch the framework of language and the novel. On the other hand, Addie's interior monologue is hypothetical; these are the words she might have thought. She never says them. The artist formulates the words for us, and Faulkner and Addie explain how she may speak the words which she damns others for using. Addie hears "the dark land talking the voiceless speech." In "dark voicelessness" the "words are the deeds" rather than words (*AILD*, pp. 166–167). Olga Vickery resolves the difficulty by stating that words are not empty if they are based on "non-verbal experience."[11] Perhaps we should add that they must not be spoken aloud. Only in this voiceless sort of language, apparently, may one whose doing goes terribly along the earth express his beliefs.

The meaning of Addie's life is the search for the fact of love. First as a sadistic school teacher she cruelly whips her pupils so that she can make them aware of her: "Now you are aware of me! Now I am something in your secret and selfish life, who have marked your blood with my own for ever and ever" (*AILD*, p. 162). For the same reason she marries Anse after a strange and brief courtship. An affectionate courtship would violate the mores of these hill people, and Addie searches for love. So her premarital love-making with Anse consists of her asking him if he has any "womenfolks" to make him cut his hair and hold his shoulders up. Addie never discusses her connubial bliss or the lack of it in the early days of the marriage. But her sex life apparently did not bring the experience of love, for only when she becomes pregnant with Cash does she realize "that living was terrible and that this was the answer to it" (*AILD*, p. 163). But after the birth of Cash, Anse dies; that is, he becomes merely a word because love for him becomes "a shape to fill a lack." The conception of Darl, Addie thinks, is an accident, as though Anse had tricked her, "hidden within a word like within a paper screen"; she has "been tricked by words older than Anse or love . . ." (*AILD*, p. 164). After love between Addie and Anse becomes meaningless, she turns to sin in search of reality. She hopes that adultery with Preacher Whitfield will destroy her aloneness "and coerce the terrible blood to the forlorn echo of the dead word high in the air" (*AILD*, p. 167). But this affair destroys her isolation only by presenting her with an illegitimate son whom she loves. This son, Jewel, can love his mother, but their love remains as incommunicable in words as any other. After the birth of Jewel, Addie tries to expiate her sin: "I gave Anse Dewey Dell to negative Jewel. Then I gave him Vardaman to replace the child I had robbed him of. And now he has three children that are his and not mine. And then I could get ready to die" (*AILD*, p. 168).

Addie is enigmatic; she seems to be a good mother to Cash and Jewel, but her other children—Darl, Dewey Dell, and Vardaman—suffer from the lack of mother love. Yet even the unloved Darl recognizes his mother's virtues and admires her integrity. He remembers her trying "to teach us that deceit was such that, in a world where it was, nothing else could be very bad or very important, not even poverty" (*AILD*, p. 123). But when he sees his mother weeping by Jewel's bed and intuits the secret of Jewel's birth, he suggests that "she felt the same way about tears she did about deceit, hating herself for doing it, hating him because she had to."

The plot situation in *As I Lay Dying* derives from Addie's making Anse promise that he will bury her with her family in Jefferson. She is not as much interested in being buried by her relatives as she is in what happens to her immediate family while they take her corpse on the long wagon journey to the cemetery. She arranges the odyssey just after the birth of her second child: "I asked Anse to promise to take me back to Jefferson when I died, because I knew that father had been right, even when he couldn't have known he was right anymore than I could have known I was wrong" (*AILD*, pp. 164–165). Her father had said "that the reason for living was to get ready to stay dead a long time" (*AILD*, p. 161). What Addie means in this mysterious clause remains enigmatic: one may achieve immortality by impressing his will on others so much that he continues longer after death to affect the living; or death is oblivion and therefore all definition of the self must come before the eternity of the grave; or life is a constant process of preparation for death and the immortality of the soul. Faulkner does not, I believe, give a basis for choice of a single meaning.

When Addie after the death of her second child gets "ready to stay dead a long time," she extracts Anse's promise to take her corpse to Jefferson; her revenge, she says, "would be that he would never know I was taking revenge." Now there is no question that Addie is bitterly resentful toward Anse, the man of words which "go straight up in a thin line, quick and harmless." Her promise commits him for once in his life to doing which goes terribly "along the earth." The meaning of *As I Lay Dying* hinges on Addie's motive. Does she disrupt Anse's entire philosophy out of pure revenge? Are her motives admirable because she wishes to involve him in life in spite of himself? Does love outweigh revenge? Does Anse transcend himself on the journey and, little as he does, become committed and involved? Or does his selfish motive of buying false teeth in town prevail? Critics take all these views, and evidence may be found for all. Probably *As I Lay Dying* must remain a tantalizing enigma because Faulkner does not seem to have provided enough evidence for resolution.

Hyatt Waggoner has concluded that "unlike Cora . . . , Addie has no faith."[12] But one should not be certain of this. Cora declares her faith again and again in empty words, and Addie has some sort of unorthodox belief. She hears the dark land "talking of God's love and His beauty and His sin"— whatever the sin of God may be and mean. J. L. Roberts maintains that the Bundren family is "doomed by the nihilistic philosophy of an egocentric and selfish mother."[13] Carvel Collins regards Addie as "a failure as a wife and mother, especially in her relations with Darl."[14] The novel itself provides some evidence of love. Human beings must use words, yet words paradoxically betray. Addie's error in part is her inability to voice her love. Certainly motherhood is an admirable virtue even to her. Motherhood, she says, "was invented by someone who had to have a word for it because the ones that had the children didn't care whether there was a word for it or not" (*AILD,* p. 163). She says that she knew this after the birth of Cash. Is it conceivable that she can be as conscious as she is of her duty to Anse and not be aware of her duty to her children? Her last thought before death seems to be a dying mother's concern for the youngest child: "She looks at Vardaman; her eyes, the life in them, rushing suddenly upon them; the two flames glare up for a steady instant" (*AILD,* p. 47). And at this moment of death her great concern is for a child she had spoken of as Anse's and not hers.

Addie and Caddy are profoundly acquainted with the mysteries of life. Addie's monologue reveals an ignorant country mother grasping for meaning; Caddy needs no monologue because her love needs no voice. But Temple Drake can neither think nor feel. She is silent because she never thinks anything worth saying. At times she talks in the garrulous chatter of a teen-ager playing at life, just as Ruby Lamar accuses her of playing at sex. She tries to pray, "But she could not think of a single designation for the heavenly father, so she began to say 'My father's a judge; my father's a judge' over and over" (*S,* p. 50). Words and deeds of love are rare in *Sanctuary.* The focal episode,

Popeye's raping of Temple with a corncob, is a meaningless event in the lives of meaningless characters. Only Horace speaks of truth, and he is weak and the forces of evil are so formidable that he cannot make the truth prevail. One of Faulkner's favorite words, *pride*, appears once in the novel, and significantly it is spoken by the shallow Temple. When Horace visits her in Miss Reba's whorehouse, Temple tells about her experience "with actual pride, a sort of naïve and impersonal vanity" (*S,* p. 209). That Temple should take this attitude toward her deflowering is appropriate in the world of this novel, Faulkner's most pessimistic treatment of the modern Waste Land. If anyone in *Sanctuary* knows love and acts accordingly, it is Ruby Lamar, the commonlaw wife of Lee Goodwin. She has prostituted herself for her lover, and she offers to do so again. She loves; she is capable of courageous sacrifice. She has every virtue on Faulkner's list, but like Caddy, she has the appearance of none.

Darl and Quentin and Horace are insane, mentally disturbed, or simply ineffectual in dealing with the realities of a world of good and evil. Darl is the strangest case of the three. Obsessed by a terrible need for love, he is so clairvoyant that he lays bare the souls and reads the minds of the members of his family. Thus he learns of Dewey Dell's illicit pregnancy and Jewel's repressed love for his mother. Apparently his clairvoyance is a violation of the secrets of the human heart. He learns the things which torture others, but he cannot clairvoyantly see others' thoughts about him. For example, he does not know that Jewel and Dewey Dell plan to send him to the insane asylum in Jackson until they move to capture him. His goading and his secret knowledge make his brother and sister wild with anger. He is a man of the word who never acts except to separate Jewel and Addie or to try to stop the Bundrens' journey to the cemetery with the rotting corpse. Yet Faulkner has made him a lovable character. His monologues, his sensitiveness and his language, Irving Howe has written, reveal Faulkner's "implicit belief that the spiritual life of a Darl Bundren can be . . . important."[15]

Darl's sanity is a question difficult to settle. In 1957 Faulkner said that Darl

was mad from the first. He got progressively madder because he didn't have the capacity—not so much of sanity but of inertness to resist all the catastrophes that happened to the family. Jewel resisted because he was sane and he was the toughest. The others resisted through probably simple inertia, but Darl couldn't resist it and so he went completely off his rocker. But he was mad all the time. (*UNIV,* p. 110)

To Irving Howe, Darl's "sudden crackup comes too much as a surprise."[16] But J. L. Roberts describes Darl as "the sane and sensible individual pitted against a world of backwoods, confused, violent, and shiftless Bundrens."[17] Darl is likeable enough for all who read his monologues to wish he were sane. But his isolation from his family and from life is great enough to cause derangement. He lives without identity and outside any moral order.

Reading the dialogue in *As I Lay Dying* and ignoring all the thoughts of the characters produces startling results. Darl seldom speaks to anyone except his brothers; even his manner of speech is abstract and impersonal—the very opposite of his thoughts. Armstid describes the way he says a sentence: "He said it just like he was reading it outen the paper" (*AILD,* p. 181). He refuses to answer many questions, and he goads and taunts almost everyone to whom he speaks except Cash and Vardaman.

> "It's not your horse that's dead, Jewel," I say. . . . "But it's not your horse that's dead."
> "Goddamn you," he says. "Goddamn you." (*AILD,* p. 88)

His speech reveals little or nothing of the poetry and the depth of his thought.

Darl hopes to thwart the family's commitment to complete the journey and bury Addie in Jefferson. He hauls a load of wood, but his purpose is to separate his brother Jewel from his mother at the time of her death. He sets fire to a barn in the hope that he can destroy the stinking corpse and frustrate Addie's and the family's will. He refuses to help to save the coffin from the flooding river. "'Darl jumped out of the wagon and left Cash sitting there trying to save it and the wagon turning over . . .'" (*AILD,* p. 145). When Cash loses his tools in the flood, Darl goes through the motions of searching for them, but Jewel actually finds them. As the barn burns, he passively watches others save the stock. In all the novel he acts with kindness only twice: with words he stops a fight between Jewel and a man with a knife, and after Cash breaks his leg, Darl brings his tools into Armstid's house.

Darl, then, is thought. He does not speak the words of love aloud because he seeks love but cannot find it. "This world is not his world"; Cash says, "this life his life" (*AILD,* p. 250). Even when he fights Dewey Dell and Jewel to avoid going to the insane asylum in Jackson, he is distant from the action. "It was like he was outside of it too, same as you, and getting mad at it would be kind of like getting mad at a mud-puddle that splashed you when you stepped in it" (*AILD,* p. 227).

The language of Darl's monologues is so beautiful and poetic that there is little wonder that many readers do not understand how Dewey Dell and

Jewel hate him. In concrete and poetic imagery Darl expresses his terrible longings for the love he cannot experience. Whatever he looks on or remembers creates an indelible image. A cedar waterbucket and Cash making his mother's coffin evoke the best of Faulkner's style and Darl's: "Standing in a litter of chips, he is fitting two of the boards together. Between the shadow spaces they are yellow as gold, like soft gold, bearing on their flanks in smooth undulations the marks of the adze blade: a good carpenter, Cash is" (*AILD*, p. 4). Darl's thought processes are also revealed in Faulkner's most exalted vocabulary of sonorous and somewhat onomatopoetic polysyllables—a style like what John Crowe Ransom has called Shakespeare's "conscious latinity."[18] As the funeral procession nears the flooding river, Darl thinks,

Before us the thick dark current runs. It talks up to us in a murmur become ceaseless and myriad, the yellow surface dimpled monstrously into fading swirls travelling along the surface for an instant, silent, impermanent and profoundly significant, as though just beneath the surface something huge and alive waked for a moment of lazy alertness out of and into light slumber again. (*AILD*, p. 134)

The comparison suggests Darl's search for love, for some larger significance in whatever he sees. He is a man of beautiful words who doubts his very existence. In "conscious latinity" and Shakespearian figures he debates whether he is: "How do our lives ravel out into the no-wind, no-sound, the weary gestures wearily recapitulant: echoes of old compulsions with no-hand on no-strings: in sunset we fall into furious attitudes, dead gestures of dolls" (*AILD*, pp. 196–197). Or in stark monosyllables he meditates on the same point: "And then I must be, or I could not empty myself for sleep in a strange room. And so if I am not emptied yet, I am *is*" (*AILD*, p. 76). And when Vardaman asks about his mother, Darl says, " 'I haven't got ere one. . . . Because if I had one, it is *was*. And if it is was, it can't be *is*. Can it?' " (*AILD*, p. 409). Darl and his beautiful words are engaged in a mad search for identity, love, and truth.

   An unsatisfactory relationship with the mother also begins Quentin's problems. A fragmentary sentence suggests that sorrow and suicide might have been avoided if he had had a mother: "*My little sister had no. If I could say Mother. Mother*" (*SF*, p. 117). And again: "*if I'd just had a mother so I could say Mother Mother*" (*SF*, p. 213). And Darl thinks, "I cannot love my mother because I have no mother" (*AILD*, p. 89). The despair of Quentin reduces him to debating his existence almost in the same words which Darl uses. He thinks in confused fragments about the reality of his existence: "thinking I was I was

not who was not was not who" (*SF,* p. 211); "Peacefullest words. *Non fui.*
Sum. Fui. Nom [*sic;* should be *Non*] *sum.* . . . I was. I am not. . . . I am. Drink.
I was not" (*SF,* p. 216). It is almost as if they exist only in the words.

Caddy loves only persons and shows her love only in deeds; Quentin
cannot think of persons and love except in terms of principles. He commits
suicide because of Caddy's loss of her virginity—not because of his loss of
Caddy herself. The person of Caddy hardly matters to him. He is defined by
the absence of love and deep personal feeling. In the appendix to *The Sound
and the Fury* Faulkner wrote that Quentin "loved not his sister's body . . .
loved not the idea of incest . . . , loved death above all, . . . loved only death,
loved and lived in a deliberate and almost perverted anticipation of death as
a lover loves. . . ."[19]

Quentin uses the word *love* only three times, and twice it occurs when he
experiences revulsion as he asks Caddy if she loved her seducers. He is more
distraught than Darl. He recognizes that he has reached an abnormal moral
and psychological state, that he is outside the realm of reality: "It's not when
you realise that nothing can help you—religion, pride, anything—it's when
you realise that you don't need any aid" (*SF,* p. 98). These are the only
instances when Quentin uses abstractions. Frederic Henry and Caddy avoid
speaking them because they know them without being able to say them.
Quentin avoids them because the virtues to him are an abstract code—as
abstract and meaningless as his feeling of duty which makes him complete the
year at Harvard before he puts to death the mind that was supposed to be
educated with the money derived from the sale of Benjy's pasture.

Quentin remembers well his conversations with Caddy, the many questions he asked her; and every single one is concerned with a concept of honor
rather than with Caddy herself. Like Narcissa Benbow in *Sanctuary,* he is too
conscious of reputation. "Why must you do like nigger women do" (*SF,* p.
113), he asks Caddy, and *"Have there been very many Caddy"* (*SF,* p. 142).
He seems to wish to measure her loss of chastity quantitatively as though she
could be either a little bit pregnant or a great deal. Regard for his own shame
is probably the cause of Quentin's opposition to Caddy's taking off her wet
dress before the children playing at the branch. He slaps her, suggesting that
he loves the idea of virtue but not his sister.

Quentin is like a sensitive little child hearing for the first time in some
repulsive fashion how he was made, how babies are born; and all his life he
lives with the child's momentary revulsion and nausea. Once Versh told him
a story about a man who castrated himself. Quentin's recalling the story
suggests that he has considered castration as a solution instead of suicide. But

making himself a eunuch would not remove the stains of dishonor from the world, because even if all men were castrated, sex would still have existed in creation: "But that's not it. It's not not having them. It's never to have had them . . ." (*SF,* p. 143). Quentin's suicide is absurdly idealistic; it is a protest against the way the world is made.

In Quentin and Darl, Faulkner has created characters who exist and live by the empty word. Salvation lies outside the word, but each is incapable of finding the way to life. Darl yearns for love, but does not himself love. He does not act or even speak with kindness. He only thinks. Quentin presumably might define himself first by an act of evil, which would give him identity, and then by knowledge and repentance, which would enable him to accept the world as it is and go on from there—in acts rather than words.

Almost every character in *The Sound and the Fury, As I Lay Dying,* and *Sanctuary* has his own peculiar relationship to Faulkner's governing concepts of abstraction and concreteness and the deed. A great many loquacious users of the word are entirely false, and the falseness of the characters' words is perfectly obvious to everyone except the person who talks and thinks in empty terms. If anyone is worse than a hypocrite, it is the self-deluded soul who does not recognize that the sound and the fury of his own phraseology signifies nothing. Anse, Narcissa, Jason, and Mrs. Compson are evil not only because they represent evil but especially because each one of them believes he is the representative of goodness and truth. Narcissa is an evangelist of status and reputation. She does not care who committed crime nor who is punished so long as Horace does not stain the family honor. "I don't care," she tells Horace, "how many women you have nor who they are" (*S,* p. 178). But the people in Jefferson think he is having an affair with Ruby Lamar. "So it doesn't matter whether it's true or not" (*S,* p. 179). Narcissa resembles Quentin in seeming to care for love and truth, but she does not share his integrity or his longing.

Mrs. Compson makes the sounds of love. But even the idiot Benjy knows how hollow the words are:

Caddy took me to Mother's chair and Mother took my face in her hands and then she held me against her.

"My poor baby." she said. She let me go. "You and Versh take good care of him, honey."
. . . .
"You're not a poor baby. Are you. You've got your Caddy. Haven't you got your Caddy." (*SF,* p. 8)

Mrs. Compson's words are wrong on two counts: that she uses them at all; and that they are the wrong ones. Her sentiments are unworthy. She thinks she pities and loves, but all her pity and love are for herself.

Jason is like his mother—evil but with complete assurance of his own righteousness. His section of *The Sound and the Fury* is often called stream of consciousness;[20] but the main basis of any stream of consciousness is the irrational and poetic associations of a sensitive mind. Jason, however, is too sane and rational ever to make associations which are illogical and poetic. His actions and his words "are the result of clear, orderly thinking in terms of cause and effect. . . ."[21] Like Narcissa, he is concerned with status and reputation. He despises Miss Quentin not because of her lack of chastity but because she has "no more respect for what I try to do for her than to make her name and my name and my Mother's name a byword in the town" (*SF*, p. 291). Love is so alien to his thinking that he cannot even understand why Benjy continues to mourn for the absent Caddy (*SF*, p. 315).

The word is widely separated from the deed in Mr. Compson's talk. He uses abstractions in order to tell his son that truths do not exist: "All men," he tells Quentin, "are just accumulations dolls stuffed with sawdust swept up from the trash heaps where all previous dolls had been thrown away" (*SF*, p. 194). But Mr. Compson loves despite his skeptical denial of the possibility of love. He shows his love when Quentin breaks his leg: "*damn that horse damn that horse*" (*SF*, p. 132), he says in sympathetic anger. He acts with love and kindness to his contemptible wife. He is gentle to his children. His principles will not permit him to accept money from Herbert Head for Caddy's illegitimate daughter. He defends Caddy and wishes to bring her home after her disgrace. True, he drinks himself to death, but love and disappointment are among the causes of his weakness. One cannot be certain that he is so cynical as Quentin thinks he is. Part of his nihilism, perhaps, is the attempt of a wordly wise father to shock an excessively innocent son into an awareness of evil which will lead to understanding and strength.

Other characters in *The Sound and the Fury* and *As I Lay Dying* should be viewed in the same terms. Virtue to Benjy is as physical as the smell of trees. Whatever thoughts or emotions he has are smelled as immediately as the odor of a rose, and they remain just that—immediate and physical. He recognizes love but has no word for it. Words fail Vardaman. He loves his mother and grieves for her, but is too young to know the abstractions which should convey his feelings. Cash reconciles Anse's words with Addie's deeds. He is, writes Olga Vickery, "the one character in the novel who achieves his full humanity in which reason and intuition, words and action merge into a single though complex response."²²

The word in these novels is often the lie of the mouth, and the deed is the truth of the heart. Those who speak are usually false. Those who act are true. "Dilsey, almost as inarticulate as Benjy," writes Olga Vickery, "becomes through her actions alone the embodiment of the truth of the heart which is synonymous with morality."²³ Mrs. Compson believes in words so much that she changes Benjy's name when she learns that he is an idiot. And after Caddy's fall, she refuses to allow her name to be spoken. But for Dilsey words have a different power. *"My name been Dilsey since fore I could remember and it be Dilsey when they's long forgot me"* (*SF*, p. 77). The name and the word for Dilsey have a meaning which transcends the individual, the immediate, and the human. She does not talk of truth, but she knows that the words of truth, like her name, are written in the book of life. They are the facts, the truths of the heart. Long after people have ceased to know her name, she will still be Dilsey. Truth is truth even when it is not spoken and forgotten.

1. Faulkner, *As I Lay Dying,* The Modern Library (New York: Random House, 1930, 1964), pp. 165–166. Hereafter cited in text with abbreviation *AILD.*

2. Faulkner, *The Sound and the Fury* (New York: Jonathan Cape and Harrison Smith, 1929), p. 151. Hereafter cited in text with abbreviation *SF.*

3. Faulkner, *Sanctuary* (New York: Random House, 1931, 1958), pp. 54, 60. Hereafter cited in text with abbreviation *S.*

4. Faulkner, *Faulkner in the University: Class Conferences at the University of Virginia 1957–1958,* ed. Frederick L. Gwynn and Joseph L. Blotner (Charlottesville: The University of Virginia Press, 1959), p. 109. Hereafter cited in text with abbreviation *UNIV.*

5. Olga W. Vickery, *The Novels of William Faulkner: A Critical Interpretation* (Baton Rouge: Louisiana State University Press, 1959, 1961), p. 29.

6. Vickery, p. 29.

7. Faulkner, "Appendix," *The Sound and the Fury,* The Modern Library (New York: Random House, 1946), p. 10.

8. See Catherine B. Baum, " 'The Beautiful One': Caddy Compson as Heroine of *The Sound and the Fury,"* *Modern Fiction Studies,* 13 (Spring 1967), 33–44.

9. *The Sound and the Fury,* The Modern Library, p. 10.

10. Lawrence E. Bowling, "Faulkner and the Theme of Innocence," *The Kenyon Review,* 20 (Summer 1958), 476, 479.

11. Vickery, p. 246. See also Richard P. Adams, *Faulkner: Myth and Motion* (Princeton: Princeton University Press, 1968), p. 106.

12. Hyatt H. Waggoner, *William Faulkner: From Jefferson to the World* (Lexington: University of Kentucky Press, 1959), p. 68.

13. J. L. Roberts, "The Individual and the Family: Faulkner's *As I Lay Dying,"* *Arizona Quarterly,* 16 (Spring 1960), 38.

14. Carvel Collins, "The Pairing of *The Sound and the Fury* and *As I Lay Dying,"* *The Princeton University Library Chronicle,* 18 (Spring 1957), 121.

15. Irving Howe, *William Faulkner: A Critical Study*, Second Edition (New York: Vintage Books, 1962), p. 189.

16. Howe, p. 185.

17. Roberts, p. 33.

18. John Crowe Ransom, "On Shakespeare's Language," *The Sewanee Review*, 55 (April-June 1947), 182.

19. *The Sound and the Fury*, The Modern Library, p. 9.

20. Vickery, p. 28. William R. Mueller, *The Prophetic Voice in Modern Fiction* (New York: Association Press, 1959), p. 111.

21. Vickery, p. 31.

22. Vickery, p. 58. But there is much critical disagreement about Cash. For sympathetic readings, see Waggoner, p. 84; Michael Millgate, *William Faulkner*, Evergreen Pilot Books (New York: Grove Press, Inc., 1961), p. 37; Frederick J. Hoffman, *William Faulkner*, Twayne's United States Authors Series (New York: Twayne Publishers, Inc., 1961, 1966), p. 62; Jack Gordon Goellner, "A Closer Look at 'As I Lay Dying,' " *Perspective*, 7 (Spring 1954), 46; Joseph Warren Beach, *American Fiction 1920–1940* (New York: The Macmillan Company, 1941), p. 134. For interpretations of Cash as a Jasonlike villain, see Edwin Berry Burgum, *The Novel and the World's Dilemma* (New York: Oxford University Press, 1947), p. 215; Edward Wasiolek, *"As I Lay Dying:* Distortion in the Slow Eddy of Current Opinion," *Critique* 3 (Spring-Fall 1959), 19–20. I suggest that Cash's name is not symbolic of money at all, but is a shortening of Cassius. Cassius Gudger, the prototype for a character in Thomas Wolfe's *Look Homeward, Angel*, was called Cash.

23. Vickery, p. 32.

AS I LAY DYING AS IRONIC QUEST

ELIZABETH M. KERR

THE DIFFICULTY OF arriving at any satisfactory and consistent interpretation of *As I Lay Dying* disturbs critics of Faulkner. As one of the most recent, Walter J. Slatoff, says:

> One is uncertain about the qualities of some of the important characters and about how to feel toward them; one is puzzled by the meanings of many of the events; one is far from sure what the book is chiefly about, and above all one is uncertain to what extent one has been watching an epic or tragedy or farce.[1]

Although no approach to the novel can wholly resolve its difficulties and remove its complexities, interpretation of *As I Lay Dying* as an ironic inversion

Reprinted with permission from *Wisconsin Studies in Contemporary Literature*, III (Winter 1962), 5–19.

of the quest romance, rather than as "epic or tragedy or farce," serves to reconcile diverse elements, to clarify patterns of action and functions of characters, and to invest the whole with meaning which corrects sentimental misconceptions and softens the savage irony apparent to those who shun sentimentality. Northrop Frye's analysis of the "Mythos of Summer: Romance," which is part of his "rational account of some of the structural principles of Western literature in the context of its Classical and Christian heritage,"[2] presents so many points which have parallels in *As I Lay Dying* that a systematic comparison of the novel with the traditional structure would seem logical.[3] This comparison proves richly rewarding.

The validity of an interpretation based on a conceptual antithesis between one of the most cherished narrative patterns in Western literature and the unheroic adventures of a family of Southern poor whites is strengthened by Slatoff's well-supported observation that "Faulkner's thought and writing are dominated by thematic and conceptual antitheses of all sorts" (106). But Slatoff fails to note the implicit antithesis exemplified here.

The obscure and difficult technique, with the many short sections in the first person, somewhat conceals the essential simplicity of the central action, the journey of the Bundren family from Frenchman's Bend to Jefferson, beset by perils of flood and difficulties of transportation and supplies, to bury the dead wife and mother, Addie Bundren.[4] The feckless father, Anse, the sons—Cash, Darl, Jewel, and little Vardaman—and the daughter, Dewey Dell, are the central characters. Neighbors, country people along the way, and townspeople in Mottson and Jefferson are the minor characters. The Bundrens have a hill farm from which, with the aid of their kindly but exasperated neighbors, they derive a bare subsistence. Therefore the journey to Jefferson is a major event in their lives, justified only by the extraordinary circumstance that Anse gave Addie a solemn promise to bury her with her family in Jefferson. So welcome is the prospect of the journey to the whole family that one might well suspect the genuineness of the promise were it not confirmed in the one section dealing with Addie's stream of consciousness.[5] The title may be interpreted as a reflection of the irony of the initial situation: as Addie lay dying, the plans for her burial were given impetus by other motives and objectives.[6] Jewel thinks that everyone is "burning hell" to get Addie dead and buried (350). Anse's comment, in Darl's clairvoyant account of Addie's death during his absence, epitomizes the irony: "God's will be done. . . . Now I can get them teeth" (375). As Olga Vickery points out, Anse's "desire for new teeth and Jewel's savage determination to perform the promised act" are all that keep Anse from letting the word serve for the deed.[7]

The diverse dreams for which the characters seek fulfillment and the time of action, July, furnish a parallel to the "Mythos of Summer: Romance," which Frye describes as "nearest of all literary forms to the wish-fulfilment dream" (186). Each of the main characters has a dream, "the search of the libido or desiring self for a fulfilment that will deliver it from the anxieties of reality but will still contain that reality" (193). Barbara Giles neatly sums up the desired fulfillment: "the simple but powerful wish of poor rural folk to go to town."[8] The fact that the dreams are trivial or ludicrous to begin with is the basis of the other ironic inversions. The attempt to read into *As I Lay Dying* the heroic quality that the quest makes one expect is due to a failure to detect this primary inversion. Anse longs for new teeth and, secretly, a new wife. Cash, the carpenter, has saved money for a gramophone. Dewey Dell wants bananas and an abortion. Vardaman wants to look at a toy train in a store window but will take bananas as second best delight. Darl and Jewel, the rejected and the favorite son, are the only ones concerned chiefly with the ostensible object of the quest.

These are the dreams. The "sequential and processional form" (Frye, 186), familiar as it is romantically idealized by a conventional narrator or author, so loses its outlines in the complexities and ambiguities of the multiple views of the characters that events are sometimes not clear. Disagreement among critics on such essential points as whether Darl is really insane, whether Vardaman is merely a small boy or an idiot, and whether the journey is heroic evidence of devotion or a comedy of errors has some justification. If my reading is correct, Darl and Jewel are the central characters, but they are also the most ambiguous ones. Olga Vickery gives the reason for only one section being devoted to Jewel's stream of consciousness: his world "consists of a welter of emotions, centering on Addie, which cannot be communicated." These emotions "are translated immediately into actions" (60). The self revelation of Darl and the contrasting interpretations of him by other characters cause confusion which the reader is left to elucidate as best he may.

And the setting likewise shows ironic inversion. The Mississippi countryside in July should have some idyllic qualities, despite the heat. It is a peaceful region of pine hills and rivers, very sparsely settled. But a flood broke the idyllic summer calm with a destroying fury that seems almost maleficent, and then the heat caused the procession to be enveloped in the stench of corruption. From death to burial, Addie with her attendants became a nine day's wonder. Olga Vickery denies that the journey is "an inspiring gesture of humanity or a heroic act of traditional morality." The journey is rather "a travesty of the ritual of interment" because the individuals do not give meaning to the ritual. Anse and Dewey Dell lack the proper spirit and Cash and Darl are in conflict with it (52–53).

The inversion or the perversion of the idealized quest of the old romances is apparent in the object of the quest, the characters who take part in it, the incidents, the precious objects and symbols associated with the ritual, and the results finally achieved.[9]

Instead of a treasure to be found or a prize to be won, there is a body to be buried. The characters, though not so sharply polarized nor so simply drawn as in quest-romance, are largely ironic counterparts of familiar types.[10] Instead of saving a sleeping beauty, the hero, Jewel, buried Addie, from three to nine days dead, "in summer, and we're running out of ice." Addie, emotionally and structurally the heroine, is also the mother figure. But Addie when alive was not the wise mother of romance, "often the lady for whose sake or at whose bidding the quest is performed" (195), but was an unmaternal mother who rejected her second son and gave Vardaman and Dewey Dell to Anse to make up for the child she had robbed him of and to negative Jewel, a mother who knew that "only through the blows of the switch could my blood and their blood flow as one stream" *(As I Lay Dying,* 467, 463). She was a true mother only to Jewel. "She rejected not only the children she taught and all but one of the children she bore, she rejected life itself. . . ."[11] As Waggoner observes, Addie alive was not a redemptive figure. Dead, she was a peril and an offense. No quest-romance is complete without a distressed damsel, but nowhere in romance is there a distressed damsel like Dewey Dell, who fatalistically lingered with Lafe at the end of the cotton row when the cotton sack was full and who felt "like a wet seed wild in the hot blind earth" *(As I Lay Dying,* 355, 384)—and hoped for a crop failure. If Addie is the "lady of duty" to Anse and her family, a most apt term, Anse's second wife is the "lady of pleasure" (Frye, 196), less seductive than her prototypes. A possible implication of Cash's mysterious first reference to her house as "Mrs. Bundren's house" (509–515), in a passage otherwise limited to the events and, one would suppose, to the consciousness of Cash *before* Anse presented her to the family in the last sentence in the book, is that she was Mrs. Bundren before she married Anse. The lady of pleasure would then suggest a Gertrude-Claudius situation with a hint of the incest feared in connection with the black queen (Frye, 196). Maybe the inversion is inverted!

Anse, as the husband of Addie, the ironic counterpart of the wise mother figure, should be an unwise old man, the white king to Addie's white queen (Frye, 195). And so he is. Though he is inept and helpless, avoiding exertion

for fear that to sweat will kill him (355), Anse is described on one occasion
in terms that definitely recall mysterious sages like Merlin:

> Pa leans above the bed in the twilight, his humped silhouette partaking
> of that owl-like quality of awry-feathered, disgruntled outrage within which
> lurks a wisdom too profound or too inert for even thought. (372)

His ability to secure aid from everyone else while asserting his determination
not to be beholden to anyone suggests a magic power: Armstid said, "I be durn
if Anse don't conjure a man. . . ." (481) Even the other characters regard him
as the special concern of the Lord (402), so contagious is Anse's view of
himself: "I am the chosen of the Lord, for who He loveth, so doeth He
chastiseth. But I be durn if He don't take some curious ways to show it, seems
like" (415). The secret of his power is, as Vickery notes, that "His words create
an image of himself as the meek and magnanimous victim forgiving a cruel and
heartless world" (56): no one dares justify his implications by refusing him
help. What dignity Anse possesses and what grief he might feel would detract
from the irony. But after selling Jewel's horses and taking the helpless Cash's
gramophone money to buy the mules and using Dewey Dell's abortion money
for his teeth, he finally loses all sympathy when, shaved, combed, and "per-
fumed like a milliner," he leads forth his bride, "kind of hangdog and proud
too, with his teeth and all" (530, 531). Through the sacrifice of others he buried
one wife, but he got the second by his unaided efforts and used the "hearse"
to take her home in.

The traditional conflict between father and son occurs between Anse and
Jewel, from the time when, by taking work from his flesh and blood, as Anse
saw it, Jewel earned money to buy the horse (434). The true reason for the
hostility is that Jewel is not Anse's son; though there is no indication that Anse
was aware of the fact, he would be aware that Jewel was Addie's favorite and
his rival.

Cash, the eldest son, is the artificer; he forges no sword, but the care with
which he made the coffin on the bevel to withstand the slanting stress of the
animal magnetism of a dead body (397) recalls the craftsmanship of his legendary predecessors. His concern for his tools, lost in the flood, is like a hero's
concern for an Excalibur.

Darl, the second son, can be viewed in two ways, dependent on whether
one considers him insane or sane: he is either the enchanted knight who is not
released from the evil spell or he is the unenchanted victim of the forces of evil
and sterility which deliver him over to be imprisoned in a dungeon. He is the
son rejected by his mother, as Jewel is the one most dear to her.

Minor characters fall into parallels also. In general they are the equivalent of the characters in romance who aid in the quest.[12] Neighbors or families encountered along the road assist in the quest for various reasons, chiefly the irresistible helplessness of Anse and the noisomeness of the caravan. Each man "describes a stage in the journey . . . in terms of his contribution to it."[13] Vernon Tull helped with the coffin, with the setting out, and with crossing the river. The Armstids offered hospitality beyond the call of duty, as did Gillespie, losing his barn as a result. There is no irony except that Anse's promise costs everyone else more than it does him and that the stench makes everyone eager to speed the Bundrens on their way more expeditiously than is possible. Other individuals, however, offer ironic contrasts to types familiar in romances. Doc Peabody is a combination of the traditional doctor and the awkward, faithful giant, helping and scolding with exasperated kindness and ironically called too late, for both Addie and Cash, to use his skill most effectively.[14] He must be the only "pussel-gutted" giant in literature. The various druggists are the alchemists or magicians, from whom Dewey Dell seeks the ironic equivalent of a love potion. The druggist in Mottson refuses to use his magic powers, being a respectable family man and a church member (487). But MacGowan, the "tricky slave" of the druggist in Jefferson, fearing the return of his boss from lunch before he can complete his deception of Dewey Dell and arrange for her return at night, is vicious, not comic (Frye, 197). He is a kind of sorcerer's apprentice, whose meeting with the naive and desperate Dewey Dell in the cellar at night is left to the reader's imagination, while Vardaman, waiting outside, sees only the moon and the courthouse clock and the red and green jars in the drugstore window (517–525). Dewey Dell is here the ironic version of the simple maiden in the power of the evil magician, for she is both simple and guilty.

Vernon Tull provides another ironic inversion as the faithful, practical helper to the "wise" old man, like Sancho Panza to Don Quixote (Frye, 197). Tull is actually superior to Anse, whom he helps against his own better judgment. His most striking capitulation, however, is not to Anse's fecklessness but to Vardaman's childlike confidence: "Because a fellow can see ever now and then that children have more sense than him" (437). Here the irony vanishes: Faulkner consistently pays tribute to the innate wisdom of children and to their gift for direct action and for making adults act against their own convictions. Perhaps Vardaman has no parallel in romance because he is not ironically conceived.

The parallels between both major and minor characters in quest-romance and in Faulkner's journey explain what seems to Slatoff (114) to be a deviation in *As I Lay Dying* from Faulkner's use of antithesis in characterization: the antithesis exists, but between the characters in the novel and those in romances. Although there is also antithesis between characters within the novel, especially the antithesis between those who respond by words and those who respond by action, providing the structural pattern traced by Olga Vickery, the sharp black and white contrasts of romance are lacking.

In the incidents of the quest, the traditional perils of fire and water are the ones Addie, talking to Cora Tull, had imagined Jewel facing for her sake: "He is my cross and he will be my salvation. He will save me from the water and from the fire. Even though I have laid down my life, he will save me" (460). On the basis of Addie's words and of Jewel's actions, Jewel emerges as the hero, despite the fact that only one passage presents Jewel directly.[15] Slatoff raises the question of what salvation she can mean, "especially if she is going to Jefferson because her father is right or to revenge herself on Anse" (164)[16] Jewel does fulfill the promise Anse made that Addie should be buried in Jefferson. He rescues her from the flood by keeping the wagon from being swept downstream. He sacrifices his horse for a team of mules to pull the wagon. He rescues her from the fire by bringing her coffin out of the burning barn, end over end, himself "enclosed in a thin nimbus of fire" (501). He is the hero of the myth who braves flood and fire to reach or rescue his beloved. The symbolic significance of both the flood and the fire goes back farther than romances, to myth. Interpretation of the flood in *As I Lay Dying* as a rebirth, freeing the sons for their destinies,[17] or as a fable of the testing of the three sons in which the river is the symbol of another world and the journey a journey to salvation[18] relates the story of the Bundrens ultimately to "the archetypal myth of the history of the world," in which the "deluge hero is a symbol of the germinal vitality of man surviving even the worst tides of catastrophe and sin."[19] No dove, no raven marks the end of this flood, but, instead, buzzards. Moreover, the hero sacrifices life to death: Jewel makes good Anse's bargain with Snopes and gives up his horse, the horse which in romance "gets the hero to his quest" and consequently keeps a central place (Frye, 196). The lineage of Jewel's horse, descendant of one of the famous spotted horses Flem Snopes brought from Texas, suggests legendary steeds with noble ancestry. Upon the humble mules, unlike their parallels in romance, the success of the quest depends.

The horse is established as a central symbol identified with Jewel when Darl, in the first section, sees Jewel struggling with the horse, "an epiphany of all that is about to occur" (Waggoner, 73). In Darl's mind, the horse is Jewel's mother (406); thus the loss of the horse repeats the loss of the mother.

Vickery explains Darl's idea by his knowledge "that the horse Jewel caresses and curses is a surrogate for Addie" (59), which "perpetuates Addie's emotional relationship with Jewel" (61) and, one assumes, prevents Jewel from loving another woman. As the horse is an ancient symbol of virility, the fish is "a potent factor ensuring fruitfulness" and a symbol of life.[20] Vardaman, trying to understand the mystery of life and death, confuses the huge fish he caught with his mother and says: "My mother is a fish" (398). Waggoner explains this as a parallel between the Eucharist and the fish, killed, chopped up as "ritual magic" to prevent his mother's death, and ritualistically eaten (66, 83). This symbolism is familiar: "the fish is a Divine Life symbol, of immemorial antiquity," associated with sacramental meals in Jewish, Christian, and Mystery cults.[21] But in the cluster of symbols of death—corpse, coffin, buzzards—the horse of virility and the fish of life and fruitfulness lose their potency: the horse is a substitute for a woman and is lost, and the fish is a child's fantasy, not a sacrament nor a promise that the cycle will pass from death back to life.

Jewel sought no prize but fulfilment of Addie's wishes; he lost the horse he had earned. The prizes sought by the other characters are ironic inversions of the precious objects, often of ritual significance, sought in romance. Anse's teeth, to obtain which Anse impels others to carry out his promise, are grotesque. Furthermore, they are purchased with the ten dollars which was the price of Dewey Dell's most urgent desire, an abortion. Just as the precious objects brought back from the traditional quest are associated with fertility and thus with food and drink (Frye, 193), so Anse's teeth and the other prize won in Jefferson are associated with food: at the end the Bundrens contentedly munch bananas, the one dream realized for the whole family. How Faulkner could have forgotten the cokes, to complete the ritual, I cannot imagine. Mrs. Tull's cakes, the "sacramental" meal of fish and turnip greens, and the basket of food carried on the journey, supplemented by kindly hosts, provide a series of references to sustain the food ritual until the climax, the bananas.

What has the quest achieved? Cash, the artificer son, has suffered the mutilation which for Hephaistos or Weyland the smith was a kind of ritual death (Frye, 193). Cash's analysis of Darl may be the ironic equivalent of the "unusual wisdom or power" gained by mutilation, but it cannot aid Darl. Cash also dwells upon the idea that "nothing justifies the deliberate destruction of what a man has built with his own sweat" (514-515), referring to the coffin which Darl had tried to burn and reflecting his craftsman's pride. Olga Vickery credits his suffering with "the extension of his range of awareness and . . . his increased sensitivity both to events and to people" (57). This is Cash's wisdom;

his only power gained is that of unselfish and silent endurance, at the cost perhaps of the skill he prizes. His only consolation is the music of the "duck-shaped" woman's gramophone. Darl, the most sensitive son, saved nothing in the flood in which Cash saved the horse and had his leg broken and Jewel saved the wagon and coffin and Cash's tools. He is sent to an insane asylum. Dewey Dell wants to destroy the new life within her and will no doubt succeed. True, a bride has been won, Anse's second wife, the "duck-shaped woman" with the "hard-looking pop eyes" (531), like one of the loathly ladies but incapable of magic transformation. Furthermore, she is won by infidelity to the memory of the dead Addie, the heroine for whom the quest was undertaken. Anse's economy in making the borrowing of spades to dig his first wife's grave serve as prelude to his second marriage outdoes the thrift in Elsinore. The lack of hesitation on Anse's part—"it was like he knowed"—would seem to have only one plausible explanation: the bride was an object of the quest, not just a happy coincidence. Jewel, the hero, has lost both his mother and his horse, the substitute for a woman's love as well as a symbol of virility. Whereas the "quest-romance is the victory of fertility over the wasteland" (Frye, 193), *As I Lay Dying* represents the victory of death and sterility and infidelity.

The quest is the third phase of the romance (Frye, 198–199). With the narrative limited in scope and time as it is, one would not look for vestiges of the other phases. But in fact the first two phases, represented in memory of past events, show the significance of the major symbols of the quest in contrast to the symbols associated with the hero's parentage and birth. Again Jewel is the hero. Instead of the familiar symbols of the ark bearing the infant in a watery landscape, *As I Lay Dying* has the coffin bearing the mother. Instead of the embryo, a source of wealth, there is only the corpse, the cause to Jewel of grief and of loss of his horse. The romantic cycle is reversed: the water of life turns to the water of death, and the ravens and doves which herald new life become the buzzards of Jewel's quest.

The paternity of the hero, in light of romance, reveals familiar elements transformed. Son and father are rivals less over the mother than over the horse. The true father, who should be a wise old man, typically a teacher, is, suitably, a preacher, but his wisdom consists in concealing his guilt when the flood providentially substitutes a travail by water for the confession he had intended to make at Addie's bedside. He concludes his rationalizing justification of his silence by praising the "bounteous and omnipotent love" of God which caused the flood—for his exclusive benefit (469, 470). Cora Tull and to a lesser extent Vernon Tull represent "narrow-minded public opinion" (Frye, 199), Cora observing and disapproving of Addie's partiality for Jewel and rejection of

Darl and rightly judging Dewey Dell to be shallow and selfish. Cora's narrow self-righteousness ironically accompanies genuine insight. Dewey Dell, the guilty girl instead of the calumniated maid, takes vengeance on Darl, the only one who knows her guilt, by helping to capture him when the men come from the asylum (513–514).

The second phase, the innocent youth of the hero (Frye, 199–200), is less clearly defined than the birth and parentage phase, but it is suggested by some elements which otherwise seem rather extraneous. The episode of Jewel's earning his horse involves more than the father-mother-son situation. The assumption of the brothers that he has a girl somewhere proves unfounded, but instead of Jewel's showing his erotic innocence by love for his sister (Frye, 200), a favorite theme elsewhere in Faulkner, he loves his horse. The green and gold world of youth in romance becomes instead a world of daytime slumber or grogginess and of night work by lantern light, symbolizing the unfruitfulness of Jewel's passion. Enmity between brothers and sister appears and extends into the quest phase. The fire and river which symbolize a sexual barrier appear, as noted, associated with death and love for the dead; the flood endangers the horse and the coffin and the fire endangers the other horses, the coffin, and Jewel himself.

As is evident, the quest contains some details parallel to those in the first two phases, but the central action is distinct and lends its characteristic pattern to the narrative.

The fourth phase (Frye, 200–201), in which a "happier society" is visible throughout, overlaps the fulfillment of the quest, inverting the traditional theme in romance: "the maintaining of the integrity of the innocent world against the assault of experience." Jefferson, the dream world of the Bundrens, proves to be no "happier society" but a world of tawdry pleasures and pain and deception. The objects of the quest, "instrumental goods perverted into external goals," are accepted by all but Jewel and Darl: "The intemperate mind seeks its good in the external object of the world of experience." The young, the naive, the ignorant should not be censured too harshly: the children of Anse and Addie are all pathetic in various ways. But in Dewey Dell we have no invincible innocence, like that of the Lady in *Comus,* but vincible guilt, combining ignorance, incontinence, and gluttony; we could pity her more if she were not also selfish, cunning, and vindictive. The "integrated body to be defended" is the family, the Bundrens against the world, but it is not defended. Cash's welfare is always secondary to the selfish desires of Anse and Dewey Dell; Darl is betrayed and vindictively delivered over to the authorities. Doc Peabody, still the friendly giant-physician but now also the shrewd and humane townsman, retorts when Cash says it didn't bother him much to ride six days on a wagon without springs, with his broken leg encased in cement: "You mean, it never bothered Anse much. . . . No more than it bothered him to throw that poor devil down in the public street and handcuff him like a damn murderer" (515–516). The most significant indication of the lack of family feeling, the most ironic aspect of the quest, is the omission of any details of the burial itself, which, if it were the true objective, should have been the climax, the emotional peak of the narrative; Cash, the only one to deal with the burial, merely mentions the grave in a pronoun without an antecedent, in relating the seizing of Darl after "we got it filled and covered and drove out the gate" (513). Slatoff suggests that the meager account of the burial and the emphasis on Darl instead of Addie may mean that Darl, not Addie, is the central figure (164).[22] The role of Jewel as hero does not rule out Darl as a vital figure, but his real significance, it seems to me, appears only in the sixth phase.

The fifth phase, the idyllic, reflective view of experience, marked by withdrawal from action, "presents experience as comprehended and not as a mystery."[23] This phase places the true lovers "on top of a hierarchy of . . . erotic imitations" (Frye, 202). Faulkner's only lovers are Anse and his bride; Anse has always withdrawn from action by getting others to act for him; and his comprehension is limited to blaming the road for all his bad luck, on the assumption that if God had intended men to move around He would have "put him longways on his belly, like a snake" (362). The complete irony of this phase is broken only by its un-ironic conformity to pattern in dealing "with a world very similar to that of the second phase" except in mood; in fact, it is the same world, inhabited by the same people except Addie and Darl.

The sixth phase (Frye, 202–203) can be discerned by a further projection into the future: "the central image . . . of the old man in the tower" is supplied by Anse on top of his hill, letting the rest of the world go by while he listens to the gramophone and eats with the new teeth, pleasures which supply the typical note of comfort. Lacking, of course, are the "occult or magical studies" and the "contemplative haze." As Vickery notes, Anse "avoids agony and insight alike," by taking words for deeds (57).

Only one more element remains to be sought in ironic counterpart, the "point of epiphany" on a mountain top or tower. I find a kind of epiphany, but on a train: after contrasting money with two faces with a French souvenir with two backs, Darl's last words, "Yes yes yes yes yes yes yes yes," seem to me to signify both his acceptance of the frankly insane world to which he is going from the supposedly sane world, given over to money and sex, which condemns him and his rejection of the family who sit in the wagon and munch bananas (527).[24] Cash also experiences an enlightenment, without a vision or image, when he tells Darl that the asylum will be better for him, "quiet, with none of the bothering and such" and questions the right of a man "to say what is crazy and what ain't. It's like there was a fellow in every man that's done a-past the sanity or the insanity, that watches the sane and the insane doings of that man with the same horror and the same astonishment" (514, 515).[25] Slatoff considers Darl's laughter and *Yes's* "highly ambiguous" and comments on the "note of peace and even affirmation" in the last glimpse of him (168). The truly insane world is that in which the banana eaters, heedless of the patient, suffering Cash, are joined by Anse, spruced up and grinning with his new teeth, accompanied by his duck-shaped wife, and all drive off in the wagon which, one imagines, still reeks of its late cargo. Though Darl was insane to begin with, he was also, as Slatoff puts it, the victim of the family's "hate and stupidity," of "Jewel's and Dewey Dell's hatred and of Anse's self-indulgent ineptitude," and one agrees with him that the quest concludes with "one of the most grim and cynical endings in literature" (169). It is part of the irony that Cash gained his wisdom through suffering due to the family's incompetence and insensitivity and that Darl, who had the greatest insight, was driven completely mad and was cast off by the family.

The extent to which *As I Lay Dying* ironically parallels the quest romance and the other phases of romance proves to be much greater and more impressive than first anticipated. The explanation for the central pattern and chief characters may be simply that, as Frye says, "Of all fictions, the marvelous journey is the one formula that is never exhausted" (57) and that Faulkner's propensity for archetypal forms attracted to the central journey other traditional elements. His use of these traditional elements may explain the unique facility of composition. *As I Lay Dying* "was written in six weeks without changing a word" because he "knew from the first where that was gonig."[26] But certainly Faulkner was not deliberately trying to work out a systematic synthesis of such myths and patterns as are analyzed by Frye, and the multitude of parallel details should not be given exaggerated significance as revealing deliberate intent. The vital point is that the consistency of the inversion would seem incompatible with any sentimental or heroic concept: it is rather the essence of ironic mockery. Therefore interpretation of the novel must be based on this inversion, placing it squarely in the category of irony and satire, of which the "archetypal theme" is *"Sparagmos,* or the sense that heroism and effective action are absent, disorganized or foredoomed to defeat, and that confusion and anarchy reign over the world" (Frye, 192). The tendency of Faulkner to use mythical themes in a realistic framework, illustrated by this

novel about Yoknapatawpha County, also furnishes support for Frye's observation that *"displaced* myths" and plot formulas move "over towards the
opposite pole of verisimilitude, and then, with irony," begin "to move back"
(52). Faulkner's involvement with Yoknapatawpha County and its people is
such that irony cannot exclude sympathy; the Bundrens are never wholly
despicable, as few of his characters are except Flem Snopes and Jason Compson. The technique of having the characters reveal themselves further contributes to the complex emotions they arouse in the reader. Recognition of the
pervading irony does not eliminate ambiguity, but at least such recognition
excludes some of the possible meanings and enables one to say that of Slatoff's
two interpretations of the last paragraph of *As I Lay Dying*—"a kind of comic
affirmation" or the idea that "life is so meaningless and even vicious that any
kind of affirmation is a mockery" (173)—the second is supported by the ironic
inversion.

1. *Quest for Failure: A Study of William Faulkner* (Ithaca, New York, 1960), 159. Mr. Slatoff's
book is the most recent full-length work on Faulkner and, with its emphasis on "polar imagination," has particular relevance to my study of *As I Lay Dying*, which was planned before the book
was published.

2. *The Anatomy of Criticism* (Princeton, New Jersey, 1957), 133.

3. Although Hyatt Waggoner's interpretation of *As I Lay Dying* fails to take fully into account
the grotesque humor and the irony, he finds in it "added dimensions in . . . association with the
basic Western myth." It is difficult to accept his next statement: "The novel not only re-enacts
the Eucharist, it is incarnational in its very form." He sees Cash as a human Christ and Jewel
as " 'divine' champion." Chapter 4: "Vision: *As I Lay Dying,*" *"William Faulkner: From Jefferson
to the World* (Lexington, Kentucky, 1959). The basic Western myth as it appears in traditional
romance lends itself better to ironic treatment than does ritual fundamental to Christian doctrine
and faith. Waggoner's interpretation approaches sacrilege.

4. Although "the structural metaphor" may be, as Waggoner says, "a journey through life to
death and through death to life" (62), the return to a narrow, impoverished, and fruitless life gives
an ironic twist to the cycle.

5. William Faulkner, *As I Lay Dying* (New York, Modern Library, 1946), 464.

6. Roma King describes the Bundren piety and respect as superficial or even hypocritical: "The
Janus Symbol in 'As I Lay Dying,' " *University of Kansas City Review,* XXX (June, 1955), 288.
Jack Gordon Goellner similarly denies that the motivation is noble or the effort heroic, since Anse,
who contracted the obligation, does least to fulfill it: "A Closer Look at 'As I Lay Dying,' "
Perspective, VII (Spring, 1954), 47.

7. Chapter 4: "The Dimensions of Consciousness," *The Novels of William Faulkner* (Baton
Rouge, 1959), 56.

8. "The South of William Faulkner," *Masses and Mainstream,* III (February, 1950), 29.

9. The traditional elements referred to in the quest-romance are those presented by Northrop
Frye, *The Anatomy of Criticism,* 186–206. Specific passages are indicated by page numbers in
parentheses in context.

10. Valery Larbaud discusses the burial of Addie as an epic episode, like the obsequies of a

Homeric queen, and cites these parallels to epic or traditional characters: Cash, Hephaistos; Darl, prophet; Dewey Dell, princess; Anse, a peasant Ulysses: "Un Roman de William Faulkner. 'Tandis que j'agonise,' " *Ce Vice impuni, la lecture . . . domaine anglais* (Paris, 1936), 302. Carvel Collins finds a source for the title in translations of Agamemnon's words to Odysseus, the *Odyssey*, Book XI, and lists parallels with characters in Greek mythology: Addie, Demeter; Jewel, Dionysus; Dewey Dell, Persephone; Anse, the King of Hell; Bundrens' farm, the underworld; Jefferson, Heaven: "The Pairing of 'The Sound and the Fury' and 'As I Lay Dying,' " *Princeton University Library Chronicle*, XVIII (Spring, 1957), 114–123. Frye's analysis of romance provides more consistent parallels with character types than does either Larbaud's or Collins' identification with single, specific characters, in which there are numerous logical discrepancies.

11. Waggoner, 81.

12. Larbaud recognizes a dramatic aspect as well as an epic one, and refers to the neighbors as the chorus. Since the minor characters play an active part, the analogy with characters in romance who aid in the quest is much the stronger.

13. Vickery, 63.

14. Collins identifies Peabody as Hermes. Jessie Weston shows that the doctor was a traditional character also in Fertility ceremonies, Greek Classical Drama, mumming plays, and medieval Romance: Chapter VIII, "The Medicine Man," *From Ritual to Romance* (New York, 1941).

15. See also Kenneth B. Sawyer, "The Hero in 'As I Lay Dying,' " *Faulkner Studies*, III (Spring-Summer, 1954), 30–33. In an M.A. thesis, "Empathy in Faulkner's 'As I Lay Dying' " (Vanderbilt University, 1954), Lloyd Moore Davis recognizes Jewel as "the guiding force of the burial procession" (82).

16. The revenge motive is specified also by J. L. Roberts, "The Individual and the Family," *Arizona Quarterly*, XVI (Spring, 1960), 29. William J. Handy suggests that Addie seeks revenge for the destruction of her life by the false values of Anse: " 'As I Lay Dying': Faulkner's Inner Reporter," *Kenyon Review*, XXI (Summer, 1956), 449.

17. Donald Dike, "The World of William Faulkner's Imagination," Ph.D. thesis, (Columbia University, 1954), 96.

18. Melvin Backman, "The Pilgrimage of William Faulkner: A Study of Faulkner's Fiction, 1929–1942," Ph.D. thesis, (Columbia University, 1960), 69–73.

19. Joseph Campbell, *The Hero with a Thousand Faces* (New York, 1956), 37.

20. Weston, 127.

21. *Ibid.*, 117, 123.

22. Julia Randall considers "Darl's observation, his knowledge, his cast of mind . . . central in the novel" because of the space allotted to him: "Some Notes on 'As I Lay Dying,' " *Hopkins Review*, IV (Summer, 1951), 49. Olga Vickery explains Darl's complexity and madness by his encompassing "all possible modes of response and awareness without being able to effect their integration" (51).

23. Frye, 202. This phase represents the third of Vickery's three modes of response to experience: "words, action, contemplation" (51).

24. J. L. Roberts regards Darl as sane, on the basis of subjective evidence and the objective testimony of the Tulls, Dr. Peabody, and Gillespie (36). Faulkner says, "Darl was mad from the first. He got progressively madder because he didn't have the capacity . . . of inertness to resist all the catastrophes that happened to the family." *Faulkner in the University* (Charlottesville, Virginia, 1959), 110. Darl's madness obviously does not prevent his having genuine insight.

25. Waggoner regards Cash as an artist, a "committed character who has a sacramental view of nature" (84). Goellner considers Cash the only one to gain understanding, and that limited (46), but he is the finest character and provides the final perspective (54). Vickery describes Cash as "the one character in the novel who achieves his full humanity in which reason and intuition, words and action merge into a single though complex response" (58).

26. *Faulkner in the University*, 87.

AS WHIRLWINDS IN THE SOUTH:
AN ANALYSIS OF LIGHT IN AUGUST

PHYLLIS HIRSHLEIFER

Light in August differs rather strikingly from such novels as *Absalom, Absalom!* or *The Sound and the Fury* in which a central family relationship provides a convenient and effective dramatic focus. This sort of family framework is not merely absent in *Light in August;* a positive effort has been made to remove or obscure all suggestion of family ties, so that we see the characters as conspicuously solitary individuals. Even Lena, who is so much a symbol of family potentialities, is first seen as a single figure on the road, distinct from the society through which she is moving. Byron Bunch has lived and worked in Jefferson for seven years, yet the town has never discovered that he spends his Sundays leading the choir in a country church, or that he visits Hightower. Through Byron we encounter the baleful stranger Christmas, whose name and complexion make him seem a foreigner, who deliberately isolates himself in every way. Brown, the second stranger who appears at the mill, is a man with an obviously false name, of whom Byron thinks—

. . . there was no reason why he should have had or have needed a name at all. Nobody cared, just as Byron believed that no one (wearing pants anyway) cared where he came from nor where he went nor how long he stayed. Because wherever he came from and wherever he had been, a man knew he was just living on the country, like a locust. (p. 33)

Miss Burden, though a native of Jefferson, is a single lonely Northerner living in her large empty house. The town takes no interest in her until her death provides it with "an emotional barbeque, a Roman holiday." Hightower, also a resident of long standing, is a social outcast whose house no one but Byron has entered in twenty-five years. Doc and Mrs. Hines are strangers to Mottstown and, in large measure, to each other. Percy Grimm, Christmas' "executioner," is at once a leader of society and a personality estranged from

Reprinted with permission from *Perspective* II (Summer 1949), 225-238.

it. He can never forgive his parents for his having been born too late to be in the war. His relation to the town is manipulative, his dream something in which the townspeople become involved scarcely realizing its implications.

I wish to stress the isolated, or as Faulkner would put it, "isolant" nature of the figures of *Light in August* because it seems to me essential to Faulkner's purpose and because it involves a narrative complexity and apparent lack of structural co-ordination which has troubled many readers. There has been almost unanimous agreement among critics that *Light in August* is one of the most beautifully written and strikingly conceived of Faulkner's novels, but that it is structurally defective. It seems to me, however, that thematic integration is quite effective and that apparent flaws of the plot often disappear entirely when the novel is approached in terms of meaning.

The plot itself is, of course, complex and bulky. The primary action, which takes place in and around Jefferson during the week in August beginning with Miss Burden's death and ending with Christmas', takes on its full significance only in terms of the background of the figures involved. Because they are isolated figures, each with a distinct history separately revealed, the sheer weight of the narrative is considerable. Time dislocations add to the complexity of the plot, but serve to emphasize the continuity of past and present by movement back and forth to related events at different points of time. They also enable Faulkner to juxtapose personalities and situations he wished to compare or contrast.

Thus, as the first chapter closes we see Lena approaching Jefferson. Chapter two opens with the stranger's arrival, but the stranger is neither Lena nor Burch (for whom we might reasonably have been prepared) but Christmas, who stands in important symbolic contrast with Lena. The time of Christmas' arrival is, of course, three years before Lena's. We are then told briefly that Byron arrived seven years earlier—than Lena, not Christmas. This brings together the comparable personalities of Byron and Lena. Burch, arriving rapidly in the narrative after his "master" Christmas, has actually reached Jefferson two and a half years after Christmas, and only six months before Lena.

These are only the first of a series of complex time dislocations which seem to me to arise necessarily in a story based on the interaction of strangers and, as almost all Faulkner's novels are, on a gradually deepening perception of the meaning of actions by repeated examination of them. We are carried back into the past (and different points in the past) in order to understand it and its influence on the motivations of the present. And because the essential points of similarity and contrast between the isolated figures of *Light in August* might easily be obscured in direct chronological presentation, there is a unifying rather than a disrupting effect in the juxtaposition of similar characters and situations apart from the particular time involved.

This may not be what the critics find objectionable, however. It is a technique characteristic of almost all Faulkner's work, though the chunks of the past which interrupt the main action of *Light in August* may seem particularly lengthy and various. The failure of the two main characters, Christmas and Lena, to meet at any point may be considered a structural defect, but thematically it is utterly appropriate. They represent contrasted worlds, extremes of two utterly opposed faiths, and their not meeting is significant in a way in which no encounter could be. The symbolic value of each is intensified by this apparent plot defect.

It is not, after all, the plot which is the center of interest in a Faulkner novel, as Robert Penn Warren points out, though the stories are so well told that they become extremely engrossing in themselves. The structure of the novel must surely be approached in regard to its theme or meaning. This use of the term "theme" should, incidentally, be distinguished from Malcolm Cowley's. In discussing the structural defects of Faulkner's major novels, Cowley specifies that there is a shift halfway through *Absalom, Absalom.* "from the principal theme of Colonel Sutpen's ambition to the secondary theme of incest and miscegenation." *(Viking Portable,* p. 18) This seems to me misleading. "Incest and miscegenation" represent the working out of Sutpen's doom stemming from his ambition and do not constitute a separate "theme" any more than violence, flight from women, consciousness of the negro world are separate "themes" in *Light in August.* They are various ways of looking at the central theme of the plight of man cursed by the evil of the past and his own alliance with that evil—a theme which is intensified rather than disorganized by the different areas of symbolic reference which are associated with it.

Thematic integration is achieved by Faulkner in a variety of ways. The recurrence of descriptive terms suggests that certain figures are to be viewed in a similar light. Also, though each story in the novel is different from the others, there is a recurrence of such situations as that of a person suffering savagely deliberate blows on the face. McEachern abuses Christmas in this manner in connection with the sale of the hiefer, and the waitress' friends beat Joe in the face after he has killed McEachern. Christmas himself repeatedly strikes Brown's face with ritualistic viciousness. Doc Hines strikes his wife when she tries to stop him from going after the circus man. There are related situations involving injuries to the head. The savage fight between Burch and

Byron leaves the latter with a bloody head, Christmas' attack on Hightower leaves him with a bloody head, and the decapitation of Miss Burden may be taken as the "type" of such injuries.

The pattern of violence, of man's inhumanity to man, is of course expressed in other ways as well, but the injuries to head and face are important because they involve almost every major personality of the book (and such minor ones as Halliday, the man who captures Christmas in Mottstown and quite unnecessarily hits him in the face several times). The recurrence of the situation suggests recurrent human attitudes and a similarity of character and outlook among the otherwise isolated figures of the novel.

The preoccupation with faces is of considerable symbolic importance not only in the situations already mentioned, but also as a recurrent image. Hightower sees his congregation, and later the townsmen who mob Christmas, as "faces which seem to glare with bodiless suspension as though from haloes." His final vision is of a wheel in which all the faces he has known are suspended peacefully at last. God, for Hightower, is "the final and supreme Face Itself." The face is identified with the whole being (or perhaps with the essence) and human faces are seen in a "suspension" which suggests both crucifixion and the ascension through death into peace. The bodiless suspension of faces also indicates a cleavage between mind and heart, conscious principle and human feeling, which characterizes the crucified figures of the book, particularly Christmas and Hightower himself. (This was first suggested by Miss Ruth Lottridge of Radcliffe in a discussion of this essay.)

Injuries to head and face, to the essential being, are received and inflicted by almost all the major personalities (except Lena who represents a contrasted way of life—indeed, the way of life rather than death) and provide an important link between them. *Light in August* is far less a novel about distinct human beings with varied attitudes, compulsions, hopes and fears than it is a picture of man in a thousand alternate situations which are critically alike, living out a more or less inescapable pattern. It is not really inescapable, for Byron manages to ally himself with Lena, but the pattern is so nearly binding that the tragic figure of Christmas is the symbol of man. Hightower, when first told of the murder, says of Christmas—"Poor man, poor mankind," and the exclamation does not seem accidental. Christmas is, of course, a Christ figure, but he is so not as the Son of God, but as the Son of Man. He is Joe, son of Joe, as Doc Hines says, the figure of everyman driven by a violent past into a violent present, burdened by the curse of his ancestry, crucified as Hightower (and possibly Faulkner) sees every man crucified.

The isolated individuality of the personalities of the book, in view of the

crucial similarities of their behavior and of the imagery by which they are
depicted, suggests that almost any figures of the town—and the town is surely
representative not only of the South but of human society in general—would
exhibit similar tendencies. Faulkner has achieved a picture of the human
family all the more striking in his having eliminated the immediate family
background of his characters. Doc Hines is Christmas' grandfather, but
primarily in the sense that man with his cruelties and evil is the progenitor of
the next generation with its evil and despair. (If Christmas is a kind of Christ
Doc Hines may be considered an "old Adam.") Mrs. Hines' illusion that
Lena's baby is "Joey," the son of Christmas, and Lena's own confusion at this
is of some significance. The baby is a kind of Christ child (to the circumstances
of its birth may be added Hightower's impression of the child at Lena's breast
as a face "which seems to hang suspended") and basically as much the heir
of Christmas as Christmas is of "Grandad Hines." Christmas himself is as
genuinely the son of McEachern, in spite of the accident of adoption, as
Nathaniel is the son of Calvin Burden, who beats him as ruthlessly as McEachern beats Christmas. Miss Burden's corruption is the product of her grandfather's evil as surely as Christmas' savagery is his response to the code of
brutality Hines and McEachern force upon him.

II

If *Light in August* is in a sense a novel about everyman, everyman is not
without diverse potentialities and responses; and these are seen by Faulkner
largely in terms of faith. Hightower is an ex-minister, Doc Hines is thought
to be one. McEachern and Calvin Burden are religious fanatics. (The names
"Calvin" and the Scottish McEachern are pointedly suggestive.) If the avowed
faith of these men is Christianity, the actual one is a faith in violent self-
assertion and almost grateful acceptance of the violence of others. McEachern
that righteous Christian, beats the boy to unconsciousness on a Sunday, forgetting to go to church. His recollection of the omission comes with the ironic
description—

McEachern began to pray. He prayed for a long time, his voice droning,
soporific, monotonous. He asked that he be forgiven for trespass against the
Sabbath and for lifting his hand against a child, an orphan, who was dear to
God. He asked that the Child's stubborn heart be softened and that the sin of
disobedience be forgiven him also, through the advocacy of the man whom he
had flouted and disobeyed, requesting that the Almighty be as magnanimous
as himself, and by and through and because of conscious grace. (p. 143)

McEachern, the advocate, is surely the most inverted Christ of them all. His real religion is, of course, one of injure and be injured. After Joe has fought with the boys McEachern says, "I hope you left marks on them"; and he receives his death at Joe's hands with "the furious and dream-like exaltation of a martyr." He is killed, it may be noted, by a blow on the head, just as he is about to strike Christmas' face as the representative of "the wrathful and retributive Throne."

Doc Hines, who also considers himself the instrument of God's retribution against "bitchery and abomination" is an ironic figure in the light of "He that is without sin among you, let him first cast a stone at her." In a sense, Hines and McEachern may indeed be God's instruments, but not as they conceive it, as righteous men, but as the unrighteous who originate and perpetuate the curse of evil which is on all mankind. The faith of Joe Christmas, the man who professes hatred of religion and who is taken for Satan by the negroes whose church he breaks into—again to beat the minister about the face —is in fact the same faith in violence as a return for violence which the supposedly Christian Doc Hines holds. (The latter also breaks into negro churches to preach hatred—white supremacy!—instead of love.) In contrast with these figures who do have a positive faith, however perverted, there is the figure of Burch, who has no faith at all, not even the merest pride in himself. When he has called the men at the mill *bastards,* he is forced to retract in regard to each one until there is no one left to whom the term can be applied but himself. Burch's faithlessness is involved, of course, not only in his flight from Lena, but also in his enactment of the role of Judas to Joe Christmas. He is called a "disciple" and described as betraying the man who befriended him for the thousand dollar reward.

The central contrast of the book is, of course, between the figures like Christmas who can respond to evil only with further wrong and who cannot come to terms with the earth or themselves except through martyrdom, and the figures of Lena and Byron who have a faith which enables them to endure. Both types of faith stem from the past. They represent a heritage available to every man, but the choice must be made between perpetuating the curse of the past by further violence or enduring evil and holding on to what has been good in the tradition, to human dignity, kindliness, and fidelity, which to some extent mitigate the evil.

Lena's roots in the past are emphasized like Dilsey's. The floor of her family's log house is also "worn smooth as old silver by naked feet." She has faith and true humility before God. She reckons the Lord will see to it that a family will be together when a chap comes. She is not embittered or even more than momentarily frightened by Burch's desertion; for her faith gives her the strength to endure injury and in a way, to transmute evil to good. The society through which Lena moves, the people who give her food, lodging, money, and transportation because of her patient, undemanding modesty are, after all, the same people who crucify the Christmases whose evil arouses their own.

Byron, in spite of Hightower's influence and his own impulses to run away, is sufficiently secure in his faith, even after his humiliation by Lena, to come back saying, "I done come too far now. I be dog if I'm going to quit now." The hillbillies, Byron and Lena, are, as Hightower recognizes, "fine people," "the good stock peopling in tranquil obedience to it the good earth." Their simple, unobtrusive faith in God expresses itself in their kindly, courteous relations with their fellow human beings. Byron offers his lunch pail to the destitute Christmas "as reflex." He is as brave (in fighting Burch) as he is generous, but his courage does not involve a desire for either revenge or martyrdom; it represents only the acceptance of a painful responsibility on behalf of Lena.

The sense of responsibility and of human dignity which distinguishes Lena and Byron from the other figures of the book is treated with some humor by Faulkner, but is nonetheless genuine Lena, sucking the sardine oil from her fingers as she remembers that she "et polite" at the Armstids, may seem ludicrous, yet she really is a lady. She is unfailingly courteous and thoughtful. She sweeps out the truck with a gum branch (the branch itself is a symbol both of her relation to God and her closeness to the earth) as responsibly as any lady would set in order the family manor. For the earth is Lena's home. However humorous her sense of the proprieties by which one lives comfortably and considerately on it, the sense is basic; she is in striking contrast with Burch who is a locust on the land, a contemptibly humorous figure, and with the tragic Christmas about whom

there was something definitely rootless . . . as though no town nor city was his, no street, no walls, no square of earth his home. (p. 27)

The humorous presentation of Lena and Byron, which at least in part represents a consciously humorous view they take of themselves ("Byron Bunch who weeded another man's laidby crop . . .," and Lena in climbing through the window to leave home—"If it had been this hard to do before, I reckon I would not be doing it now."), is of two-fold importance. Their sense of humor, their lack of self-centered seriousness is perhaps part of the ability of these good, simple people to endure. For the total effect of the novel, the humorous handling of what are essentially the righteous figures makes them far more agreeable than a serious treatment. Sympathy is engaged for the tragic personalities while principle is unobtrusively all on the side of Lena and Byron. Were they self-righteous as well as right, the balance of the novel would be destroyed. Faulkner's ironic view of the ideal (for it is this that Lena largely represents in contrast with the tragic reality of Joe Christmas) creates an element of surprise which he no doubt values, and also provides an essential artistic balance.

The central contrast between the sincere, unpretentious faith in God which characterizes Lena and Byron and the fanatic faith in violence clothed in the language of Christianity which constitutes the religion of Doc Hines, McEachern, Calvin Burden is a contrast most strikingly exemplified in Hightower's life. Hightower is Byron's friend and advisor, assuming the role of a father confessor and conceiving of his house almost as a church where Byron stumbles on the first step whenever he enters, except when he enters in pride. However, Hightower is not really Byron's guide in relation to Lena, and Byron the good man, the sincere Christian, has little understanding of Hightower's character or the meaning of his life. The bad odor of Hightower's "unwashed flesh" is called by Byron in a moment of inspiration "the odor of goodness," but in fact it relates the ex-minister to Doc Hines who has a "quality of outworn violence like a scent." (Bad smells are characteristically used by Faulkner in this biblical sense as the outward sign of moral corruption. The romeo who by any other name would smell as sweet in "A Rose for Emily" and Charlotte's figurine named the Bad Smell in *The Wild Palms* are the most notable example of the device.) Byron is also mistaken in his interpretation of Hightower's passiveness. He thinks that Hightower has remained in Jefferson—

... because a fellow is more afraid of the trouble he might have than he ever is of the trouble he's already got. He'll cling to trouble he's used to before he'll risk a change. Yes. A man will talk about how he'd like to escape from living folks. But it's the dead folks that do him the damage. It's the dead ones that lay quiet in one place and don't try to hold him, that he can't escape from. (p. 69)

But this oddly distorted version of the "To be or not to be" soliloquy by no means explains Hightower's motives. He is indeed held in Jefferson by his dead grandfather, but far from wishing to escape this influence, he considers it the great satisfaction of his life—which makes the very worst ills not only bearable but positively welcome. It is not because he fears death, but because he has made the same covenant with it that Christmas has made, that Hightower refuses to leave Jefferson. The name "Hightower" itself may echo the threat in Isaiah that on the day of judgment "every high tower . . . shall be bowed down, and the haughtiness of men shall be made low," and Hightower is assuredly one of those who have chosen the way of death. If Christmas' denial of life, of normal human responsibility, is expressed in his continuous irrational flight, Hightower's is no less explicit in the irrational refusal to flee. Both prefer a "voluptuous martyrdom" to the danger of involvement in ordinary human relationships.

Hightower is the most reflective figure of the book, and the next-to-last chapter in which his background is finally revealed through his own despairing consciousness is not anti-climactic after Christmas' death, but the vital philosophical counterpart of it. The moral alternatives are particularly clear in Hightower's life. His father and grandfather represent the two principles of man's heritage, indeed of his nature. The bluff heroic grandfather is identified with slavery and war, the father "was an abolitionist almost before the sentiment had become a word to percolate down from the North." He is a man of peace, yet when war comes, he takes part as a doctor (self-taught, for in peace he was a minister)—and is fully as heroic as the grandfather. Hightower's one feeling of admiration for this father is that the blue patch on his coat may have meant that he killed a Yankee, and this, of course, represents an utter rejection of the whole meaning of the father's life. It is not the heroism that Hightower values in his grandfather, but the wanton self-destructiveness, as exemplified in the moment of his death (breaking into a hencoop). It is this principle with which the grandson allies himself thinking, "It is any man's privilege to destroy himself, so long as he does not injure anyone else . . ." But the final horrifying recognition is that Hightower has not only sacrificed his own life in devotion to his grandfather but has driven his wife to despair and death. And because Hightower had turned himself into the grandfather at that single instant of the latter's career, the grandfather himself has destroyed the wife. The grandfather has become a murderer through the effect of Hightower's worship of him, the dream itself corrupted by its influence. This is perhaps the most complex statement of the theme of sowing the wind and reaping the whirl-wind, which runs through the novel. Hightower's first name, Gail, which he shares with his grandfather, suggests this theme, incidentally. He enters the church because it is "like a classic and serene vase, where the spirit could be . . . sheltered from the harsh gale of living."

The rejection of his wife links Hightower with McEachern and Doc Hines, both of whom reject and abuse their wives in order to follow their false ideal, with Burch, whose rejection of Lena and the child is the type of all denial of family love and responsibility, and with Christmas, whose relationship with Miss Burden (a grotesque survey of a whole lifetime of sexual experience) demonstrates his utter unwillingness to become involved in love. The religious significance of this rejection of women is clear to Hightower. God created Woman, he thinks, "to be not alone the recipient and the receptacle of the seed of his body but of his spirit too." When Hightower declines to make his wife the partner of his dream, the receptacle of his spirit, "the face of God turned away in very shame." Hightower is doomed because on the stage of the church he has offered the idol of his grandfather instead of "the crucified shape of pity and love," because he has taken a wife not for love—"not for My ends," the accusing Face of God tells him—but for his own, namely to get to Jefferson.

It is perhaps worth noting that the conflict between the "galloping hooves" of Hightower's dream and his wife has the symbolic force of a contrast between normal and abnormal sexuality. Horses are characteristically used by Faulkner in reference to abnormal sexual experience in contrast with cows which represent normal love and fecundity. (This is, of course, most fully developed in *The Hamlet.*) Christmas' statement, "Why in hell do I want to smell horses? . . . It is because they are not women. Even a mare horse is a kind of man," suggests the meaning of the horse symbol; and the relation of Christmas to the rather masculine Miss Burden is in many ways similar to the relationship between Jewel and his horse (the obscenity, mingled caresses and blows) in *As I Lay Dying.*

The sexual aspects of Christmas' story have the symbolic importance of a failure of love in the most general sense, not only the love between man and woman, family affection, and that between man and his fellows, but the love between God and man which is expressed through human relationships. Food, it may be noted, is a recurrent sexual symbol (Miss Burden, the waitress, the dietitian all supply Christmas with edibles, and the motif is concluded with his discovery shortly before death that he no longer has to eat), but the rejection of "women's muck" is the same when Miss Burden tries to entangle him as when Mrs. McEachern tries to mother the boy, and both situations are comparable to the rejection of the muck in Byron's lunch pail. Christmas systematically refuses every form of personal tie. The only thing he consumes willingly is the toothpaste, significantly enough called the "worm," and suggestive of the original falling off from God.

The imagery of *Light in August* stresses the dominating religious motif. The Christ image, as seen primarily in Joe Christmas, is a fundamental device of the book. The three years Christmas spends with Miss Burden may be taken as an enlarged three days of involvement in life (an ironic inversion of the three days in the tomb) from which he gains release by the more explicit crucifixion which begins with the arrest on Friday and ends with his death on Monday. This is specifically described in terms which suggest resurrection—

It (his blood) seemed to rush out of his pale body like the rush of sparks from a rising rocket; upon that black blast the man seemed to rise soaring in their memories forever and ever. (p. 440)

The three days in which Doc Hines removes Christmas from the orphanage are perhaps a minor death for him which concludes with his resurrection as Joe McEachern. Also, the three days of waiting after Joe has watched the dietitian represent a kind of martyrdom for her as well as for him. Hightower's final vision comes as a kind of crucifixion for him and is described in terms of ascension.

Then it seems to him that some ultimate damned flood within him breaks and rushes away. He seems to watch it, feeling himself losing contact with the earth, lighter and lighter, emptying, floating. (p. 466)

"Ultimate damned flood" indicates the nature of this and the other crucifixions of the book. If Faulkner constantly draws the figure of Christ before us, the image is characteristically grotesque. Christmas' "slashed garments" after Grimm has emasculated him may be a reminder of "They parted my garments," but the scene involves monstrous irony. The whole use of the Christ symbol is ironic. Christmas is identified with hatred; he is the instrument of destruction (for McEachern, Miss Burden, Hightower, as well as himself).

There is the most striking recurrence of religious similes and metaphors throughout *Light in August* which links similar personalities and provides a sustaining atmosphere for the Christ symbol. Grimm's voice is "clear and outraged like that of a young priest." Max, the man in the restaurant, has "an inscrutable and monklike face." The townsmen have "almost the air of monks in a cloister." When McEachern is beating him, Joe has "a rapt, calm expression like a monk," "save for the surplice he might have been a Catholic choir boy." The barn in which they stand is described almost as a church and the snorts of the beasts bring to mind the manger in which Christ was born. Incidentally, McEachern's statement, "You would believe that a stable floor, the stamping place of beasts, is the proper place for the word of God. But I'll learn you that too," has special pointedness since a manger was a suitable place for the Son of God. McEachern's feeling that Christmas was a "heathenish name" involves similar irony.

Various images other than the religious ones are reiterated with symbolic force. The "gale" suggested by Hightower's name appears frequently in other connections as well. Christmas feels the wind "dark and cool" as he goes to kill Miss Burden. After her death, however, the pillar of smoke left by the burnt house stands "tall and windless above the trees." When the boys fight after Christmas has kicked the negro girl, "it was as though a wind had blown among them, hard and clean." Hightower's dream is, of course, a "cyclone"; his phantoms come "like a long sighing of wind in trees." The wind is life, the harsh life of crucified man and the harsh continuity with the past. (Though it is not a religious image in the same sense as the Christ symbol, the biblical suggestiveness of the wind motif is clear.)

There is a consistent use of shadow imagery in connection with Christmas and the figures like him. Hightower sees himself as a "shadowy figure among shadows," and, of course, his past is seen in terms of phantoms. Between Miss Burden and the town is "the phantoms of the old spilled blood and the old horror of anger and fear." Christmas, as he goes through the negro world of Freedomtown,

. . . contrived to look more lonely than a telephone pole in the middle of a desert. In the wide, empty, shadowbrooded street he looked like a phantom, a spirit, strayed out of its own world and lost. (p. 106)

In the orphanage Christmas was "sober and quiet as a shadow." He sneaks from McEachern's house "with the shadowlike agility of a cat." When the waitress tells the outraged, furious Christmas she is "sick," he flees, "the shape, the shadow" fading down the road from her.

The image of the road and the pattern of flight and pursuit are, of course, strikingly reiterated. Christmas is perpetually in compulsive flight—from the waitress, McEachern, Jefferson—essentially from himself. The hopelessly slow motion of the horse he rides from the dance hall registers the futility of all his frantic running. The street of Christmas' life offers no escape except through death for, as Gavin Stevens says, "there was too much running with him, stride for stride with him. Not pursuers: but himself: years, acts, deeds omitted and committed. . . ." Like Christmas, Burch seems to be in constant motion throughout the novel, fleeing from Lena, running with the dogs to capture Christmas, and finally fleeing from Byron with a practised agility in hopping trains. Lena's motion, in contrast with the frantic flight of the men, is, of course, slow, measured, peaceful, "like a change of season." She advances "like something moving forever and without progress across an urn," for her life is "a peaceful corridor paved with unflagging and tranquil faith." (There is, of course, an ironic inversion of the "mad pursuit" and "struggle to escape" of the figures on Keats' Grecian Urn in Faulkner's use of the image.) Lena's slow motion reflects the assurance of Isaiah that "he that believeth shall not make haste."

The title of the novel (like the symbolic names of so many of the characters) emphasizes a number of important motifs. *Light in August* may refer primarily to Lena, who is to give birth, but also suggests the lightness of the ascension and the Light of God and of religious insight. In addition to the lightness of release which appears in connection with Christmas and Hightower (and surely the contrast between the lightness of Lena in bringing forth life and that which involves passage into death is a crucial suggestion), there is a great deal of emphasis on light and dark throughout the book. We are shown houses that are dark, ones with one lamp or two—and street lamps are specifically called "Augusttremulous lights," so that comments on light and dark which might otherwise seem casual are caught up in the title. A chiaroscuro pattern is a definite part of the artistic organization of the book. (I think Richard Chase is quite right in this and some of his other interpretations, though his notion that Faulkner's technique is a poetry of physics seems a little far-fetched.)

The light-dark pattern is caught up with negro and sexual symbolism in such a passage as:

He (Joe) was standing still now, breathing quite hard, glaring this way and that. About him the cabins were shaped blackly out of blackness by the faint, sultry glow of kerosene lamps. On all sides, even within him, the bodiless fecundmellow voices of negro women murmured. It was as though he and all the manshaped life about him had been returned to the lightless hot wet primogenitive Female. He began to run, glaring, his inbreath cold on his dry teeth and lips, towards the next street lamp. (p. 107)

Joe's death, the soaring or lightness with which his peace comes, is very basically an escape from the female world which has tried to entangle him (in life itself) and the negro world whose symbolic meaning is much the same. The association of visual light and dark with male and female and negro and white (Joe's light shoes coated with black mud symbolize the negro and white aspects, as do his white shirt and dark pants) draws together the implications of "light" in regard to Christmas' plight, which is every man's. Faulkner's titles are always good, but seldom better than this, I think.

Christmas' negro aspect, it is worth noting, is primarily a matter of psychology. He does not know that he is a negro, but finds it useful to believe. His negro blood is the symbolic source of his homelessness in the white world just as his white blood would "make him look like a pea in a pan full of coffee beans." He rejects the negro girl presumably to reserve himself for the white world, but deliberately tells the waitress he is a Negro to avoid acceptance in her world. The tragedy of Christmas' being both negro and white is that not one but two worlds are open to him, in either of which he could find a way to endure. But Christmas is utterly a lost soul who has no place on earth and wishes none.

The negro in Christmas is, of course, also the curse of slavery (perhaps of human injustice in general) which the white man must bear, the black cross on which Miss Burden sees every white child crucified; but the curse is on black and white alike. Nathaniel Burden says,

> The curse of the black race is God's curse. But the curse of the white race is the black man who will be forever God's chosen own because He once cursed Him.

and Christmas is doomed both as a black man who has injured and rejected his brothers and as a white—as man, in short. I have seen him as everyman, but he might be called ultra man, since his character and experience involve such concentrated symbolism.

The central theme of *Light in August* is that of man's inhumanity and the ruin it brings upon him. It is a theme seen on several levels, historically in terms of slavery and the Civil War, on the personal level as violence between man and his fellow man and the revulsion between man and woman which is generally symbolic of the rejection of divine love. The richness of symbolic reference and the diversity of the personalities involved make for a complex, but not, I think, for an uncoordinated novel. The isolated figures of *Light in August* are drawn together by the most striking parallels of imagery and situation, and the result is a novel of great dramatic intensity. Christmas, Hightower, Miss Burden, McEachern, Grimm—the doomed generality—stand together in contrast with Lena and Byron, the faithful who are no more than a remnant, possibly only an ideal.

THEMATIC DESIGN IN
LIGHT IN AUGUST*

CARL BENSON

OF ALL THE readers who have sought the thread which would afford safe
entrance into *Light in August,* a labyrinth of tangled lives, creeds, fates, and
destinies, Cleanth Brooks seems to me to have come closest to comprehending
the novel in its totality. He says, "The Community is everywhere in this
novel." And he says, "Unless the controlling purposes of the individual are
related in some fashion to those which other men assume, the individual is
indeed isolated, and is forced to fall back on his own personal values with all
the liability to fanaticism and distortion." I subscribe fully to these statements,
but it seems to me that Mr. Brooks may be oversimplifying and limiting *Light
in August* when he says: "The various characters who act and suffer in this
novel are all people outside the community, and whatever their special psychological isolation, it is given objective reference and dramatic meaning by their
alienation from the community in which they live or into which they have
come."

Solidarity within the community is certainly the central subject, but the
characters are not all outside the community. Furthermore, those who are
outside are outside in different degrees, and the book achieves its particular
form because the different degrees are so intermeshed as to constitute a narrative and dramatic presentation of an essentially thematic structure. If we are
to attain a Coleridgean ideal and account for the work as a structural whole,
we must account for the presence in the novel of these "special psychological

*Read before the American Literature Section of the South Atlantic Modern Language
Association, November, 1952. In addition to the critics of Faulkner cited in the text and many
others, I am indebted to Irving Howe for the Anderson parallel. There are many points of
agreement between my reading and the essay of Robert D. Jacobs, "Faulkner's Tragedy of
Isolation," and William Van O'Connor. "Protestantism in Yoknapatawpha County," both avail-
able in *Southern Renascence.* Indeed, there is general agreement as to the central moral issues in
Faulkner's work: the problem is to relate the narrative structure to the pervasive moral concerns.
Reprinted with permission from *The South Atlantic Quarterly,* LIII(1954), 540–555.

isolations" and the battles which the characters fight, or refuse to fight; and we must so phrase a statement of theme as to account for the presence and the relationships of these particular lives.

Light in August rises out of Faulkner's tragic vision of man as inescapably dual in nature. In the psychological dialectic sustaining it the thesis is: the world in which we live is a chaos of mixed evil and good, a chaos which stems from (1) limited or lip service to moral (community) orders which are selfishly conceived and so corrupted, (2) human incapacity to adopt any code without its ultimately becoming rigid—humane conviction inevitably hardens into inhumane convention. The antithesis: despite the moral anarchy arising necessarily from this thesis, the individual realizes himself only in terms of community values, and he must submit himself to the larger good or perish.

The dramatically demonstrated impossibility of molding a compassionate community of isolative and selfish motives and ideals makes *Light in August* Faulkner's most pessimistic novel. As the theme is worked out, we are made increasingly aware of the ultimately insoluble ethic problem which is the core of the tragedy: Man is not simply a moral being with dual leanings towards self-realization and communal obligations; the two become in actual life (in the microcosm of Jefferson in *Light in August*) so interwoven that one may convince himself that his own private demands are, or should be, those of the community; or he may seize upon certain commonly esteemed values with such fervor that he cannot allow his views to be questioned. We are reminded of Sherwood Anderson's story of the old writer with his theory of how truths become grotesque. "It was his notion," says Anderson, "that the moment one of the people took one of the truths to himself, called it his truth, and tried to live his life by it, he became a grotesque and the truth he embraced became a falsehood."

In *Light in Augsut* Faulkner is dealing with a group of such grotesques; but Faulkner cuts deeper than Anderson's old writer, because Faulkner's grotesques, despite their strangeness and despite the illusions which render them grotesque, are all too human to allow us to conclude that Faulkner is simply asserting the overriding importance of community obligation. He is insisting that there are within man and within the community itself forces that are inherently divisive. He accomplishes his intent by exploring the rationale of various types of alienation and illusion and by postulating a graded scale of illusions and their effects upon their possessors as communal beings. This graded scale constitutes the complex of ethic judgment upon which the comprehension of the novel as a whole depends.

What we have to deal with in *Light in August* is the peculiar collocation in Jefferson, Mississippi, of various lives whose stories cannot be accounted for on the basis of narrative alone. If, however, we see that the thematic conflict is between rigid patterns of self-involvement on the one hand and commitment to a solidarity that transcends self on the other, we must see that the chief character, the moral protagonist, because he alone can serve as an ethic slide rule by means of which we can compute the relative failures and successes of the other characters, is Gail Hightower, the old unchurched minister who is, as we open the story, ironically "Done Damned in Jefferson." It may be that at the end he is still damned as far as Jefferson is concerned, but through him the reader who inhabits a larger, though not dissimilar, community is enabled to estimate the relative moral worth of the other characters and the fixations which inhibit or limit their participation in society.

Actually, it might reasonably be argued that Hightower is also the central figure in a strict narrative sense and that far too many readers have been misled by the seemingly simple opposition of the violent Joe and the placid Lena. After all, Byron brings to Hightower the problems of Lena and Joe as well as his own. Joe's grandmother also comes to the old minister for assistance. Indeed, a good part of the action of the entire book seems designed to evoke the action or the response of Hightower. But it is his function of moral hero with which we are principally concerned. My argument is that he is a Yoknapatawpha Heyst who, like Conrad's hero, achieves a victory by traveling the moral distance from selfish immunity to redemption by the conviction that immunity cannot be bought. We have hints that his redemption is of major importance almost from the beginning. As soon as Byron Bunch brings him the problem of helping Lena, he breaks into a sweat of fear of being drawn from the isolation he thinks he had paid for. Thereafter, as Byron continues to ask his aid, though he replies, "I won't," and "I have paid," his compassionate nature gradually asserts its mastery; by the end he is so involved with "poor mankind" that he has delivered Lena's child and has tried to save Joe Christmas from Percy Grimm.

If it be objected that Hightower is no fit candidate for the role of moral hero, it may be said that Faulkner is aware of this irony, because he made it. Indeed, Faulkner's profound pessimism and his ultimate idealism both find witness in the use of Hightower as moral standard: pessimism, because we are given no better than Hightower as the slide rule for solidarity; idealism, because Hightower rises from the most foolish and inhumane illusion of all to tremendous heights by the abnegation of the illusion. He achieves moral stature in the only way possible for him—by descending into the pit of himself and ripping from his heart his dearest sin.

It is significant that Hightower's recognition of the true nature of his cherished illusion should be saved for the magnificent penultimate chapter— a chapter which, despite its strategic position and rhetorical splendor, has been generally neglected. Faulkner has cunningly withheld the key piece of his ethic jigsaw puzzle until the end so that the reader can contemplate the finished lives of the characters with the Hightower compassion in which the novel was conceived. The very imagery of the chapter compels this reading.

We have seen Hightower earlier get on the road back to the community. We have seen him first as the village "they" describe him to Byron Bunch: the young preacher came to Jefferson with a frustrated wife and a bewildering confusion of God and a heroic grandfather. We have seen how the natural outrage of his parishioners has deprived him of his church. But we have also seen the sensitive though reluctant response he made to Byron's overtures to interest him in action for others. Shortly before this final chapter, his heart has been so engaged by the need of others that he has delivered Lena's baby and experienced a great satisfaction ("I showed them"); his sympathy has gone out to Joe's grandmother; he has even tried, with an obvious lie, to save Joe. But all this is mere prelude; and it is important to note that he has not yet seen the rightness in Byron's love for Lena: he has not come from his selfishness enough to do that, for it would imply a recognition of his own failure for his wife, a self-discovery reserved for his last scene.

In this last scene we finally understand the childhood obsession that formed the original cause of his desire for immunity: the growing-up in a house populated by three phantoms (the sick mother, the harshly rigorous yet tame father, the old Negro woman) and a ghost, the heroic grandfather about whom the Negro woman told him stories, who was shot with a fowling piece while he was engaged in the very unmilitary, and yet somehow grand, prank of robbing a chicken coop. Brooding over this image of selfless, magnificent folly has caused the young Gail Hightower to become convinced that "I had already died one night twenty years before I saw light," and has compelled him to believe that "My only salvation must be to return to the place to die where my life had already ceased before it began." To this freakish illusion he has subordinated his entire life. When, for instance, he receives a call to the ministry, which should be a way to spiritual life (a community), it is for him merely a shelter, wherein

he could see his future, his life, intact and on all sides complete and inviolable, like a classic and serene vase, where the spirit could be born anew sheltered from the harsh gale of living and die so, peacefully, with only the far sound of the circumvented wind, with scarce even a handful of rotting dust to be disposed of. That was what the word seminary meant: quiet and safe walls within which the hampered and garmentworried spirit could learn anew serenity to contemplate without horror or alarm its own nakedness.

He uses the call to the ministry, the influences of the seminary and of his wife, to "shun the harsh gale of living," to get the pastorship in Jefferson, where his grandfather had died. Now, in his last revery as he sits dying, he perceives that by using the church to forward his own selfish desire he has participated in the hardening of the church into doctrinal inhumanity:

That which is destroying the church is not the outward groping of those within it nor the inward groping of those without, but the professionals who control it and who have removed the bells from its steeples. . . . He seems to see the churches of the world like a rampart, like one of those barricades of the middleages planted with dead and sharpened stakes, against truth and against that peace in which to sin and be forgiven which is the life of man.

Hightower is finally beginning to see the enormity of his moral shortcomings, for he says, "I acquiesced. Nay, I did worse: I served it. I served it by using it to forward my own desire."

Here Faulkner introduces his effective turning-wheel imagery. Hightower's awakened moral consciousness turns slowly, like a wheel in heavy sand, as he unwillingly accepts the implications of his misspent life. He sees that he has been

. . . a charlatan preaching worse than heresy, in utter disregard of that whose very stage he preempted, offering instead of the crucified shape of pity and love, a swaggering and unchastened bravo killed with a shotgun in a peaceful henhouse. He sees that in his search for immunity he has created a humanly and religiously false martyrdom for himself; but he still tries to find excuses: "But I was young then. . . . And after all, I have paid. I have bought my ghost even though I did pay for it with my life. . . . It is any man's privilege to destroy himself, so long as he does not injure anyone else, so long as he lives to and of himself."

And now the final horror, still in terms of the turning wheel:

He is aware of the sand now; with the realization of it he feels within himself a gathering as though for some tremendous effort. Progress now is still progress, yet it is now indistinguishable from the recent past like the already traversed inches of sand which cling to the turning wheel, raining back with a dry hiss that before this should have warned him: ". . . revealed to my wife my hunger, my ego . . . instrument of her despair and shame . . ." and without his having thought it at all, a sentence seems to stand fullsprung across his skull, behind his eyes: *I dont want to think this. I must not think this. I dare not think this.* As he sits in the window, leaning forward above his motionless hands, sweat begins to pour from him, springing out like blood, and pouring. Out of the instant the sandclutched wheel of thinking turns on with the slow implacability of a medieval torture instrument, beneath the wrenched and broken sockets of his spirit, his life: "Then, if this is so, if I am the instrument of her despair and death, then I am in turn instrument of someone outside myself. And I know that for fifty years I have not even been clay: I have been a single instant of darkness in which a horse galloped and a gun crashed. And if I am my dead grandfather on the instant of his death, then my wife, his grandson's wife . . . the debaucher and murderer of my grandson's wife, since I could neither let my grandson live or die. . . ."

Thus, in the moment of final recognition, Hightower sees destroyed his cheating martyrdom, his justification for his behavior to his wife and the church, his immunitiy, and the cherished ghost itself.

In order to accentuate the significance of Hightower's moral struggle and victory, resulting in the abnegation of the illusion, Faulkner says, "The wheel, released, seems to rush on with a long sighing sound. . . . It is going fast and smooth now, because it is freed now of burden, of vehicle, axle, all. In the lambent suspension of August [here perhaps is the moral significance of the title] into which night is about to fully come, it seems to engender and surround itself with a faint glow like a halo." The function of the wheel imagery shifts. The wheel is disengaged from the private conscience of Hightower and spins before him carrying on its circumference the faces of the people who have populated the novel. It is as if the old minister, freed at last of his morally debilitating illusion, has earned the right to pass judgment on the people he has ignored, misunderstood, or wronged. He sees all the chief figures of the novel and even some individually insignificant members of his congregation. And in the compassion he has attained by his acknowledgment of the ubiquity of human responsibility, he perceives that the faces of all suffering humanity are pretty much alike.

In summoning before himself for review and rejection his past life, Hightower reveals the source of moral achievement: he manifests the power of choice, of free will. Just as it was within his power as moral agent to reject the community for immunity, so also it is within his power to reject immunity—to earn his redemption, as Robert Penn Warren might say, by being judge at his own trial before the bar of communal justice. In exercising the power of choice and in becoming the compassionate observer, Hightower seems to speak for Faulkner and to be raised out of himself into a sort of mediate figure between the community, including the readers, and the more alienated figures of the novel. I think Warren Beck has something like this in mind when, in speaking of the "Compassionate troubled observers" of several of Faulkner's works, he says, "It is no doubt significant of Faulkner's own attitude that these compassionate observers so largely provide the reflective point of view from which the story is told and thereby determine its moral atmosphere."

If we reflect now on the story of Joe Christmas, we will see that it is, in a sense, precisely antithetical to that of Hightower. This Christmas story is of a man who has no choice in any meaningful sense of the word. His responses are entirely conditioned by exterior forces; though he tries to attain selfhood as a moral agent, he is doomed to failure, because he cannot break out of the circle of conventional attitudes towards his being the son of a white mother and a mulatto father. The fact that he may have no Negro blood (Doc Hines is not exactly a reliable witness) only intensifies the moral nature of his struggle. He is convinced he has, and it is his consciousness of being a misfit between two worlds, of being unable to attain true human status in either, that is determining. He tries to lie alternately as white with white, as black with black; but always, we are given to understand, the other side of his being, his other blood, rebels at not finding its realization.

But Faulkner is not content to explain the isolation of Christmas, his failure to find a community, in terms of conflicting blood strains alone. The isolation is reinforced by derivative and ancillary conflicts. Christmas is delivered as an infant to a mechanically administered orphanage, where, in the strict uniform of the wards of the community, he hears himself called "nigger" as early as he can understand the word. This psychic wound sets him apart from the other wards. Then, when we might expect at least some love from his foster parents, we discover that he has been adopted by a sadistic Calvinist, whose rigorous exactions of religious duties seem to Joe but a continuation, in slightly different terms, of the harsh treatment of the orphanage. He accepts the cruelty of his foster father, McEachern, rather than the love of Mrs. McEachern because of this continuity; the emotion of love or sympathy confuses him. In short, he reaches maturity in a world which has shown him so little compassion that he does not know how to deal with it. It is no wonder that his first love affair should be with the tough little prostitute, Bobbie Allen; and it is no wonder that Faulkner describes him, as he first appears in Jefferson, as having "something definitely rootless about him as though no town nor city was his, no street, no walls, no square of earth his home."

He is doomed to remain rootless, to find no home, but the point is that his failure to become integrated in a community derives from the fact that his world is deterministic; it denies choice, and it is deterministic because the conventionalized attitude others maintain towards him denies his individuality. Faulkner records this determinism and Christmas's pitiable attempt to become a human entity with sharpest distinction in a rather subtle passage. A week after his murder of Joanna Burden, Christmas is riding in a wagon towards Mottstown:

"I have been farther in these seven days than in all the thirty years," he thinks. "But I have never got outside that circle. I have never broken out of the ring of what I have already done and cannot ever undo," he thinks quietly, sitting on the seat, with planted on the dashboard before him the shoes, the black shoes, smelling of Negro: that mark on his ankles the gauge definite and ineradicable of the black tide creeping up his legs, moving from his feet upward as death moves.

Here Joe is attempting to assume responsibility for his own acts (Faulkner always insists that responsibility is the measure of the human condition), and it is in a way true that in the seven days since the murder Joe has come closer than ever before to attaining an independent being; at least society has recognized him as an individual. But the circle was not, as he would like to believe, constructed by his own acts; it was, rather, composed of the loveless and mechanistic societal patterns which surrounded all his years; and in the fine rhetoric of the last sentence Faulkner has expanded the synecdoche of the black shoes into a symbol which suggests the true nature of the circle.

At one point Faulkner phrases the human nonhuman limbo in which Christmas lives even more pointedly. Just before the murder of Miss Burden, Faulkner says of him, "He believed with calm paradox that he was the volitionless servant of the fatality in which he believed he did not believe." "Volitionless servant of fatality" is precisely the right phrase for Joe Christmas, for the central contrast of the book between Gail Hightower and Christmas is based upon an assumption which reminds one forcibly of the distinction Yeats makes between Fate and Destiny. Destiny is from within the very being of the individual whereas Fate is imposed from without. In *Light in August* the man of destiny, Hightower, shapes his own destiny by acts of will, and he is, therefore, morally accountable for his choices. Christmas, shaped by exterior forces and attitudes, has no power over fate and can, therefore, never be responsible.

Some such distinction is what Faulkner has in mind when he speaks through Joanna Burden and in his own voice as omniscient narrator of the black curse every white child bears from birth and when he speaks of the Player who moves Percy Grimm, as if Grimm is only the instrument of fate, implacably into the pursuit, shooting, and emasculation of Christmas. The Player, as opposed to the "crucified and suffering Christ" who enters Hightower's last revery, is mentioned only in this context; and I believe that the Player imagery and the black curse mean that we have laid a curse upon ourselves by depriving any man for whatever reason (black blood or other) of his destiny. Such an intent would account for Faulkner's description of the effect of the death of Christmas upon the representatives of the community who have joined in running him to earth:

For a long moment he looked up at them with peaceful and unfathomable and unbearable eyes. Then his face, body, all, seemed to collapse, to fall in upon itself, and from out the slashed garments about his hips and loins the pent black blood seemed to rush like a released breath. It seemed to rush out of his pale body like the rush of sparks from a rising rocket; upon that black blast the man seemed to rise soaring into their memories forever and ever. They are not to lose it, in whatever peaceful valleys, beside whatever placid and reassuring streams of old age, in the mirroring faces of whatever children they will contemplate old disasters and newer hopes. It will be there, musing, quiet, steadfast, not fading and not particularly threatful, but of itself alone serene, of itself alone triumphant.

The "they" will remember because though Percy Grimm alone committed the culturally sanctioned murder and atrocity, "they" are implicitly involved; and they will never forget because the symptomatic act in which they are involved is an act that denies not only human justice, but also, as far as Joe Christmas is concerned, moral being. This interpretation, incidentally, is reinforced by the contrasting treatments of the deaths of Hightower and Christmas. We are given the last moments of Hightower and the rehabilitation of his moral consciousness in his own interior monologue; the death of Christmas, on the other hand, is handled steadily from without.

Joe Christmas and Gail Hightower are the extreme poles of morality between which all the other major and minor characters fall. But, as I have pointed out, since Christmas is blamelessly irresponsible, communally impotent, we have to fall back on Hightower, who moves from selfish immunity to compassion, as encompassing within the bounds of his single being the range of communal morality. It is not Joe's tragedy, because Joe is never truly an agent; he is always played upon; despite his frenzied efforts to attain selfhood, his is a fate he never made. Christmas and Hightower are in ethic terms the most complex figures of the novel, and perhaps that is the reason they have been commonly misunderstood, despite the relatively much more elaborate treatment Faulkner has given them. The other characters can be more quickly accounted for.

In terms of a graded scale of community participation, Lena Grove is not communityless at all; in fact, wherever she goes she relies on human fellowship; and it responds to her trust by giving her what she needs—a night's rest with the Armstids, Byron's room, a place to have her baby, and finally even, we are led to believe, a decent man for a husband. She always finds people "right kind" and sets out afoot to find the man who seduced her, serene in her conviction that "A family ought to be all together when a chap comes. Specially the first one. I reckon the Lord will see to that." Many of the good simple folk of Yoknapatawpha County are lucky enough to possess such a feeling of thoughtless trust, and it is good that such people should make happy communal adjustments; but Lena's assurance does imply a high degree of moral unawareness, to which Faulkner calls attention by observing that she possesses a "tranquil and calm unreason." It is aesthetically fitting that her career should open and close the novel, for she is the representative of the ordinary folk who possess so easily the solidarity which is the focal point of the novel and the goal, in some terms, of the more violent figures. But to think of her as the moral standard of the novel is, it seems to me, to ignore the careful elaboration of Hightower and to create an ideal of uncritical simplicity. In truth, she can no more break out of communal patterns of behavior than Christmas can break into them; and it may be said that she experiences no moral change or achievement.

At the opening of *Light in August* Byron Bunch is morally neutral. He observes certain conventions faultlessly: for instance, he rigorously minds his own five-minute rest periods on Saturday mornings when there is no one around to check on him, and he sings in a rural church every Sunday; but all he does is done habitually, mechanically, without conviction; and so, though he lives a life approved by community conventions, he may be said to be morally unawakened. When he falls in love with Lena, however, he undergoes a transformation and tries to become a part of the living community, not just a clock-punching machine. To be sure, after years of noncommitment, he finds that life comes haltingly hard; but by the end Byron, as the salesman sees, is making progress toward union with Lena, and, through Lena, with life itself. The end of his achievement will be, on an absolute scale, higher than that of Hightower but Byron has not had so far to go, and his moral victory is far less significant.

We must consider now those characters who remain alienated from the community because their ideals, despite their origins in genuinely human feelings, have become inhumane by being codified into rigid patterns, and, persisting as codes, have rendered their possessors incapable of true participation. Joanna Burden, for example, because of a devotion to abolition on the part of her forebears, continues in the abolitionist tradition. But her adherence to the ideal of her grandfather is, in her time, unreasonable, academic, and blighted by the revenge motif which attends it from the begnning. She is like Hightower in her devotion to the past, but unlike him in that her moral enslavement to her Calvinist-abolitionist family is so complete that the quintessential compassion, which finally redeems Hightower, is absolutely lacking. She does not mesh her life with that of Jefferson at all; and the town has set up its own pattern of ignoring her, that is, until the residents learn that she has been keeping house for a man of Negro blood, whereupon, ironically, she fits into another pattern, this one worthy of interest. In sum, her servitude to the codes of the past has blotted out natural human affection (her unnaturalness Faulkner insists on by recurrent references to her masculinity); so that when life is offered to her in the form of a passionate union with Joe Christmas, she responds unnaturally and slips into a prolonged and aberrant sexual frenzy, which she attempts to maintain by asserting falsely that she is pregnant. That failing, she turns violently from the puritanical hell in which she has been wallowing and attempts to bludgeon Joe into praying with her, whereupon Joe kills her. So three means of transcending self fail Joanna Burden—a great human ideal, sex, and religion; and they fail her because she fails them.

Two other characters have converted the object of worship from "the crucified shape of pity and love," to use Hightower's phrase, to vindictive demanding gods constructed in their own image and compounded of bigotry and ignorance. Doc Hines, who frequently "gets in touch with God," feels that he is in a private league with an Almighty who is the supreme proponent of white supremacy and the supreme opponent of "woman flesh," categorically assumed to be nothing more than "bitchery and abomination." And Simon McEachern is so convinced of his own stern righteousness that he cannot condone the slightest human frailty. He is completely lacking in the pity that characterizes Hightower and that led Hightower to perceive that the church, as a McEachern would understand it, stands "against truth and against that peace in which to sin and be forgiven which is the life of man." It should be said, at least parenthetically, that there is a great deal about the failure of religion for the modern world in *Light in August*. The recognition of this failure is present most succinctly in the final revery of Hightower, but it is dramatically handled, as I have suggested, in the lives of McEachern, Joanna Burden, Doc Hines, and to some extent in the congregation which ousted Hightower. I am not certain as to just how far we may push the Christ-Christmas parallel (which has often been recognized as a troublesome problem in the book), but it seems reasonably clear that the forces and conventions and people that prevent Joe from attaining the humanity he seeks and that ultimately "crucify" him are not spiritually responsive to "the crucified shape of pity and love." Perhaps it may be said that the use and abuse of religion as related to the maintenance of community solidarity constitutes a sort of leitmotif for the novel.

The illusion that separates Percy Grimm from the community is of an entirely different order. Born too late to achieve military glory in World War I, he becomes officious in the exercise of his National Guard captaincy. Of course, the pursuit of military honor has been at times the means of maintaining a social order, but not as Grimm conceives it, for he takes what he is pleased to call "law and order" into his own hands. When his desire to play the heroic soldier, which causes him to ignore the explicit orders of the shrewd and community wise sheriff, combines with his irrational hatred of Negroes, he becomes less than human, just as bigoted in the certainty of his own rectitude as Hines (Faulkner says of him, ironically, "His face had that serene, unearthly luminousness of angels in church windows") and the fit instrument for the Player to use for the destruction of Christmas. The linkage of this pair by fate is emphasized by the fact that in Hightower's vision of suffering humanity as the figures of the novel turn before him on the wheel, only the faces of Christmas and Grimm are indistinct; they blur together before they come clear.

Lucas Burch is a representative of the Snopes class in the sense that O'Donnell defines that class. In the terms of this essay, the illusion which precludes his participation in the community is the inhuman conviction that money is the only worthwhile goal, a conviction grasped with such single-minded rigor that he has no interest in others except to exploit them. Byron Bunch recognizes Burch's lack of humanity by describing him in the imagery of a mechanical contrivance; Burch, he says, is like "one of these cars running along the street with a radio in it. You can't make out what it is saying and the car aint going anywhere in particular and when you look at it close you see that there aint even anybody in it." In terms of a graded scale of moral being, Burch is at the bottom. Hines, McEachern, and Grimm have so warped the once communal orders to suit themselves that *communal* is no longer a proper attributive, but at least the codes which their particular self-involvements render horrible travesties had their origin in the community. The materialism which motivates Burch, on the other hand, has always been nonmoral and consequently lacking in human ideals.

But what of the community itself, in which these versions of humanity *manqué* move? What in it is worthy of devotion? It must be said at once that Faulkner is too committed to bitter reality and to the tragic view to make human solidarity an obvious and unequivocal proper aim. As we have already seen, the church, the spiritual community, has in Hightower's view failed of its essential mission by being reduced to the doctrinaire tenets of some of its members; and simple human pity can largely be abandoned if conventional attitudes towards miscegenation and white supremacy are questioned. But Faulkner is even more explicit about the hardening of convention; his criticism gains a cutting edge when exploited by a sardonic humor. For example, the composite "they," the voice of the community, makes a judgment on "good" women:

The town believed that good women dont forget things easily, good or bad, lest the taste and savor of forgiveness die from the palate of conscience. Because the town believed that the ladies knew the truth, since it believed that bad women can be fooled by badness, since they have to spend some of their time not being suspicious. But that no good woman can be fooled by it because, by being good herself, she does not need to worry any more about hers or anybody else's goodness; hence she has plenty of time to smell out sin. That was why, they believed, that good can fool her almost any time into believing that it is evil, but that evil itself can never fool her.

Again, the men of the town, when they were boys, followed Miss Burden about, yelling "Nigger lover" at her, as their fathers had before them; but at the time of the discovery of her dead body, they want to catch and lynch the black son who murdered and (they hope) ravished her. They shift thoughtlessly from one conventionally inhumane attitude to another. Hightower's congregation has always been shocked and amazed at his sermons, but does not move to oust him until the particular circumstances of the death of his wife bring notoriety to the church; the members even have to be conventionally shocked. Thereafter Hightower is unable to keep a Negro cook, for the people of Jefferson, led by the Ku Klux Klan, having picked up the habit of believing evil of the minister, insist on believing that he is having "unnatural" relations with his cook. In truth, as Byron says, "When anything gets to be a habit, it also manages to get a right good distance away from truth and fact."

The community, we may safely say, is not an unqualified good. But in spite of its suspicions, bad habits, mixed good and bad conventions, it is the arena in which moral battles are to be fought. And the behavior of some of its citizens offers some hope that the moral struggles will be recognized for what they are: Martha Armstid gives her hard-earned money to Lena; the sheriff, though he is willing to have a Negro whipped to get information, is truly sympathetic towards Byron when he thinks that Byron is having bad luck in love. Even the most isolated characters, except Burch, are in their own minds, striving for good. The sin they have in common is a failure in common kindness.

In attempting to abstract the moral significance of the characters of *Light in August,* I risked the accusation of forgetting that Faulkner is a novelist and that his success must finally be gauged in terms of fiction. But I hope I have suggested also that the moral essence is caught and realized by Faulkner in the bewilderingly complicated yet convincing web of created lives so brilliantly, profoundly, and passionately delineated. Yet the characters, while they live their own lives, are the creations of a novelist of strong ethical preconceptions; and only the complex of ethic judgment will enable us to see why we have this assortment of lives and just these treatments of the lives.

Faulkner is sometimes willing to voice his own moral convictions; this is true in the case of a bit of literary criticism which appears in the midst of *Light in August.* When Byron first tells Hightower that he has taken Lena to the cabin on the Burden place and asks for Hightower's aid, the old minister's desire for immunity still rules; when Byron leaves, he tries to escape into Tennyson. Then Faulkner says:

It does not take long. Soon the fine galloping language, the gutless swooning full of sapless trees and dehydrated lusts begins to swim smooth and swift and peaceful. It is better than praying without having to think aloud. It is like listening in a cathedral to a eunuch chanting in a language which he does not even need to not understand.

I do not believe that this is willfully capricious denigration. It is in keeping with Faulkner's conviction that a relevant moral order must be applicable in a world of hardened convention, of men and women of selfish desires, self-deception, and chicanery. Instead of a reaffirmation of new or old community ideals, the best Faulkner can offer is a Hightower compassion, grounded on an understanding of the need to recognize human weakness. As another of Faulkner's characters has phrased it elsewhere, all that God Himself asks of man is that he "hold the earth mutual and intact in communal anonymity of brotherhood, and all the fee he asked was pity and humility and sufferance and endurance and the sweat of his face for bread." So the moral power of Tennyson's never-never land is meaningless, does not answer to man's nature and needs as they are; it is significant that after delivering Lena's baby, Hightower reads *Henry IV,* which Faulkner calls "food for a man." By then Hightower's compassion is in the ascendant, and it is capable of causing him to struggle to transcend himself. In the final analysis it is the struggle that is important, and perhaps its importance is emphasized by the fact that it takes place within the unlikely breast of Hightower. At any rate, through Hightower we see that even moral splendor is relative and can be achieved by a man who rises from the stench of selfish isolation to assert the absolute value of pity. Of course, the proper understanding comes too late for much social efficacy; and as Hightower sits before his window awaiting death, the habitual thundering horses and flashing sabers tumble again into his revery. But before that there has come his realization of his sins and of his duty as communal man; and this realization for a moment triumphs, though the one man dies.

THE DESIGN AND MEANING OF
ABSALOM, ABSALOM!

ILSE DUSOIR LIND

ABSALOM, ABSALOM! is a unique fictional experiment—unique in relation to Faulkner's other novels and to modern fiction generally. Indeed, it is not too much to claim that in point of technique it constitutes the last radical innovation in fictional method since Joyce. A "difficult" work, its difficulties do not inhere in verbal subtleties or in excessive refinement of perception, but in the strain imposed upon attention and sensibility in comprehending its monumental design.

Broadly stated, the intention of *Absalom, Absalom!* is to create, through the utilization of all the resources of fiction, a grand tragic vision of historic dimension. As in the tragedies of the ancients and in the great myths of the Old Testament, the action represents issues of timeless moral significance. That

Reprinted with permission from PMLA, December, 1955, pp. 887–912.

Faulkner here links the decline of a social order to an infraction of fundamental morality cannot be doubted. Sutpen falls through innate deficiency of moral insight, but the error which he commits is also socially derived and thus illustrates the flaw which dooms with equal finality the aspirations of a whole culture. Events of modern history, here viewed as classic tragedy, are elevated through conscious artistry to the status of a new myth.

Every reader of the novel is struck by its curiously heightened pitch, its brooding intensity, its poetic language, and the endless recapitulations which have the effect almost of incantation. What has not yet been studied is the relation of style and structure to the larger plan of execution. And exploration of unprecedented depth and scope into the meaning of history, the novel possesses throughout techniques proportionate to its ends. Only by considering form and meaning in organic interrelationship can we hope to discover the conception underlying this vast and strangely compelling tragic vision.

1

The characters themselves are projected on a scale larger than life. As Mr. Compson puts it, musing on the differences between then and now, we see "in this shadowy attenuation of time [people] possessing now heroic proportions, performing their acts of simple passion and simple violence, impervious to time and inexplicable." Sutpen "abrupts" onto the scene as "demon," devil, with "faint sulphur-reek still in hair, clothes and beard," "ogre-shape," "fiend," "blackguard." His stature is heroic: the townspeople feel that, "given the occasion and the need, this man can and will do anything." His face is "like the mask in Greek tragedy." He is the chief actor on the stage, "still playing the scene to the audience, [while] behind him Fate, destiny, retribution, irony —the stage manager . . . was already striking the set and dragging on the synthetic spurious shadows and shapes of the next one." Community opinion chants the chorus to his actions: ". . . in steady strophe and anti-strophe: *Sutpen. Sutpen. Sutpen. Sutpen.* "

Even in his decline, his proportions are projected on a scale enlarged by wide mythological reference. He is not the "widowed Agamemnon" that he should be, but "ancient, stiff-jointed Pyramus." He is an "ancient varicose and despairing Faustus," and enfeebled Abraham relegating the punishment of his sins to his children's children. His death is by the scythe, "symbolic laurel of a Caesar's triumph." And not least, in his anguished recognition of the unavailability of his rightful heir for the fulfillment of his design, he is, by ironical allusion to the title of the book, King David of Jerusalem, to whom it was promised that God would build him a house and establish his kingdom forever.

Of his brood, "begot with the fecundity of dragon's teeth," it can equally be said that they were "not articulated into this world." They are drawn with a curious flatness; their gestures are formalized, almost choreographic, wholly determined by the exigencies of the theme. Behind Judith's mask we never penetrate. Credited with her father's demonic will, she enacts her role for motives that we are not given to know. Like Antigone, she dignifies the rejected brother with the appropriate rites of burial; as with Greek tragic heroines, generally, her individual psychology is not explored. She is the righteous Judith of the Old Testament, "the same as a widow without ever having been a bride," dedicated under self-assumed and uncommunicated compulsion to single-handed restoration of the moral order.

Henry Sutpen and Charles Bon exist only to perform the parts assigned to them—Bon to pursue the acknowledgment which can never be his; Henry to commit, under circumstances which convey its poignancy to the fullest, the inevitable fratricide. They are the Biblical Absalom and Ammon in mortal conflict over a sister; they are Polyneices and Eteocles, sons of the cursed family of Oedipus, separated by their claims to power and doomed to mutually inflicted extinction.

The literary associations here suggested for Judith, Henry, and Charles are not, as in the case of Sutpen, made by direct allusion, but that such association is intended to magnify the tragic aura is evident in the choice of a name for Sutpen's Negro daughter. Sutpen called her Clytemnestra, Mr. Compson tells us, in confusion with the more appropriate Cassandra. Remote, inscrutable, unspeaking, she exists as the pure, abstract embodiment of the theme, "in the very pigmentation of her flesh representing that debacle which [says Miss Rosa] had brought Judith and me to what we were and which made of her (Clytie) what she declined to be just as she had declined to be that from which its purpose had been to emancipate her." Identifying herself with Sutpen worth while still fulfilling the menial role allotted to one of her blood, she is the essence of that division which spells disaster for the man and social order which begot her: ". . . presiding aloof upon the new, she deliberately remained to represent . . . the threatful potent of the old." As an individual she remains unknown. Her actions, like those of Charles Bon, Charles Etienne Bon, and Jim Bond, serve primarily to illuminate—not her own psychology—but the psychological, social, and moral aspects of the Negro-white conflict.

To be sure, Charles Bon and his son became better known to us than do Clytie or Judith, but the compulsions which drive them are sketched with bold strokes; the Bons are not rounded characters. Comparing Charles Etienne Bon with Joe Christmas of *Light in August* (they are identical types), the deliberate chiaroscuro of Faulkner's characterization becomes apparent. An intimate and compassionate understanding of the psychodynamics of Joe Christmas is a major goal of *Light in August;* his "case history" is therefore minutely documented. For Charles Etienne Bon, however, the psychodynamics are indicated in almost code form. The reader, crediting the unalterability of inner psychological drives as such, accepts his strivings as inevitable. Our compassion for him derives from the recognition of the conflicts by which he is torn, rather than from personal identification with him as an individual.

If the characters in the Sutpen story remind us of Greek actors and epic Biblical figures, so does the action itself recall the events of ancient tragic myth. A synopsis of the Sutpen legend would read like one of the summaries of Greek myths conveniently placed as prologue to modern translations of Greek plays. The continuing (though loose) analogies which exist between Sutpen and Oedipus, Sutpen's sons and Eteocles and Polyneices, Judith and Antigone, suggest that the Oedipus trilogy might have served as a general guide in the drafting of the plot.[1] At the same time, Sutpen's fall and the obliteration of his house bring to mind the great myth of man's original fall from innocence and the visitations of Divine justice upon third and fourth generations. Old Testament violence evoking God's wrath is recaptured here in a legend of father turning against son, son against father, and brother against brother.

What endows the novel as a whole with a sense of overpowering urgency is its surcharged atmosphere of doom. This pressure derives in part from the blind psychological forces by which all the characters are driven. But fate itself is felt to be the agent of personal and historical doom. The Greek sense of fate, specifically, is invoked. Slavery goes against the will of the gods; or, as it is stated in more exact terms, slavery goes against nature. In Haiti, where the earliest instance of this moral violation takes place, it is "as if nature held a balance and kept a book and offered recompense for the torn limbs and outraged hearts even if man did not." Buried in the soil, the bones and blood of the first Haitian slaves "still cried out for vengeance." The undoing of Sutpen's false ambition illustrates the operation of retributive justice in the human drama; the fall of the South is its larger social representation.

2

The Sutpen tragedy as communicated in the novel has no "objective" existence. It is the collective product of the workings of the minds of three major narrators, abetted by the collaboration of a fourth. The Sutpen tragedy is the novel's center of dramatic interest, but the narrators are the center of the novel. In the execution of this double focus Faulkner exercises the full play of his genius.

The story of Sutpen exists in local recollection. The four narrators take the local story and transmit it through what they are and through their relation to it. The Sutpen tragedy, with its magnitude, power, and intensity, is thus synthesized by Faulkner from the psychic bias of each narrator. Projecting their distortions upon their narrations, he achieves a reality which rests upon unreality. When the reader first encounters Sutpen and his kin, he suspects a distortion in the manner of Miss Rosa's presentation of the story, but he cannot measure its degree because he knows as yet so little about her. As the legend grows through the narrators' successive contributions, his capacity to estimate the various degrees of distortion increases. However, such is the ordering of the narrative that the magnification of events occurs always in advance of an understanding of the distortions which cause it. The reader is consequently affected sensibly before he can react intellectually. He knows that the narrators' conjectures are often in point of literal fact impossible, but he is forced to give them provisional credence; in so doing, he is taken in despite his reservations. Thus it is that the incredible tragedy of Sutpen's ambition and fall is brought into being. The heroic enlargement, the urgency, and the aura of relentless doom, are endowed by the narrators who create it.

Miss Rosa, whose shrill, belated, and misguided cry for vengeance opens the tale at its highest pitch, is a frustrated spinster. She is both physically and psychically misshapen. Venting upon Sutpen's image the accumulated tension of a lifetime of hallucinated isolation, she pictures Sutpen as the incarnation of demonic energy, positing horrendous crimes, "too dark to talk about," as the cause of the disasters which have overtaken Sutpen and his kin. A belief in his foredoomed obliteration is to her a pychological necessity, a means by which she can visit upon Sutpen vicariously her unquenchable private outrage and relieve her preternaturally developed sense of guilt. A Methodist steward's daughter, she endows her notion of an avenging fate with the coloration of a wrathfully righteous Lord, pondering "what our father or his father could have done before he married our mother that Ellen and I would have to expiate . . . what crime committed that would leave our family cursed to be instruments not only for that man's destruction, but for our own." Her portions of the narrative, hysterical and disordered, generate the tension and fatality which span the entire legend. It is her madness which endows Sutpen with supernatural vitality and her perverted moralism which invokes the certainty of his destruction.

Mr. Compson brings to his narration a seeming repose and expansiveness which is a welcome counterbalance to Miss Rosa's blind subjectivity. Enlightened, informed, comprehensive in his judgments, Mr. Compson at first arouses the confidence of the reader as an unbiased narrator. His ironic eye easily pierces the romanticisms, enthusiasms, and self-deceptions of others. A skeptic in religion, a rationalist in his general approach to life, a shrewd analyst of the social scene, his elaboration gives the legend an apparent foundation in fact. But his observations have dubious validity; they are the projections of a profound spiritual resignation. His world-weariness, his love of paradox, his fascination with the exotic, all suggest that he has absorbed the *malaise* of *fin de siècle* decadence into his private philisophy. The cast of his imagination is unhealthily voluptuous. Only his love for the refinements of eroticism could do justice to the institution of octoroon mistresses in New Orleans. His skepticism is bottomless; he is a fatalist because he is at heart a defeatist. His grandiloquent allusions to "the horrible and bloody mischancing of human affairs," and to the "blank face of oblivion to which we are all doomed," endow his narrations with the atmosphere of moral gloom. He sustains the aura of catastrophe which Miss Rosa's forebodings initiated.

Quentin's efforts at legendizing are marked by a febrile intensity which charges the entire last section with renewed emotion. The passionate delivery of the Bon-Henry conflict derives wholly from Quentin's morbid involvement. Aroused by the question of incest which the Bon-Henry-Judith relationship poses, Quentin shapes the story in the terms of his own vicarious incest wishes and creates the doomed Henry as an image of himself.

Shreve, whose youthful curiosity and romanticism make him a suitable collaborator in the Bon-Henry legend, projects the fraternal affection, mildly homosexual in basis, which exists between his roommate and himself. Not otherwise involved, he serves chiefly as instigator, prodding his curiosly obsessed Southern roommate into the reluctant fulfillment of his narrative function.

Through their acts of narration, the narrators reveal themselves. Miss Rosa's impossible romanticism is betrayed by her image of the ideal lover (the Bon-Judith courtship), her obsession with sin in her ascription of evil to Sutpen. Mr. Compson's effeteness is established in the very play of his rhetoric, in his perverse delight in what is mildly shocking, and in his sardonic asides. Quentin's psychology is depicted through his creation of Henry to no less degree than Henry's through Quentin.

The narrators frame the legend as well as relate it. Their unhappy condition arouses the question which the tragedy they create must answer. They live in a world of ghosts—the shades of the past. Miss Rosa is in pursuit of a ghost.

Mr. Compson has surrendered himself to them; he has nothing to give his son except tales of the past, redolent of grandeur and defeat, but without meaning. During the period over which the legendizing takes place, we see Quentin sink progressively into self-willed oblivion. The past engulfs him; he cannot stay its flood. Miss Rosa drags him on her mission; his father refuses to stop talking. Quentin makes feeble efforts at resistance: he doesn't want to accompany Miss Rosa; he would rather not hear any more about Sutpen; he shuts his ears to his father's endless hypothesizing. During much of the legendizing he is "not even listening." But he is propelled by a momentum which is beyond his own power to check.

It is Quentin's tragedy, above all, which the Sutpen tragedy must finally illuminate. "Too young to deserve yet to be a ghost, but nevertheless having to be one for all that, since he was born and bred in the deep South," he is doomed through some cause antecedent to his own existence, the victim of some larger fatality marked for the deep South itself.

All of the major narrators are born and bred in the South. Their relationship to the Sutpen tragedy is immediate: their own ancestors appear in the background. Mr. Compson and Quentin are descended from the General Compson of the tale, whose independence and humanity set him apart from his fellow citizens of aristocratic status. In the Sutpen story, he transcends the narrowness of his class, accepting Sutpen into the community, attending his wedding, and befriending him in his crisis. He comprehends the limitations of Sutpen's nature, yet he is not alienated from him in human affection. To Charles Etienne Bon, Sutpen's Negro grandson, he accords equal sympathy. He knows the hopelessness of his plight, yet intercedes for him with the law and attempts personal assistance. In him the best of the Old South, as opposed to the "minimum of logic and morality," which governed the aspirations of the class of men represented by Sutpen, is symbolized.

Quentin and Mr. Compson are General Compson's heirs, the inheritors not only of his broad intelligence and conscience, but also of the altered social status which the Civil War brought about. Retaining the refinements of culture and sensibility perpetuated in family tradition, but deprived through historical circumstance of a proper field in which they may be exercised, Mr. Compson and Quentin are both rendered incapable of action. Their feelings towards Negroes are, like their ancestor's, personal and humane; no trace of prejudice or condescension is to be found in their narrations or conversational interchanges. They lack aggressiveness completely. Mr. Compson's manner of coping with life is through intellectual analysis undertaken from the refuge of personal retreat; Quentin, as the unfortunate heir of his spiritual bankruptcy and further declined status, is equipped only with excessive sensibility and illusion.

Miss Rosa is implicated in the legend in a different way, through the direct impingement of Sutpen's drives upon her life, and through the place of her father in implementing Sutpen's design by providing him with an acceptable marital alliance. The part played by Southern Protestantism in lending support to caste ambitions is depicted in the behavior of Mr. Coldfield. Denying slavery in principle, abetting it in practice, and in general substituting morbid righteousness for warm humanity, Mr. Coldfield's religiosity—and its contribution to Negro-white tensions—is a representation, in condensed form, of all that was set forth on this theme in *Light in August.* He lends money for Sutpen's dubious financial speculations (symbolizing the involvement of Southern planters with Northern finance), while detaching himself from the consequent moral responsibility. His impossible stand on the issues involved in the War leads to his complete withdrawal and ultimate self-annihilation.

From the atmosphere of cold abstraction and proud near-poverty in which she was raised, Miss Rosa derives not only her distorted view of life, but the social pretentiousness of a would-be aristocrat. Her repeated assertions that Sutpen "wasn't even a gentleman," and her claim that "the Coldfields are qualified to reciprocate whatever particularly signal honor marriage with anyone might confer on them," betray her actual social position. Her prejudices against Negroes are intensified by her repressions and by her need to sustain a false sense of social superiority. In youth, she refused to touch the objects with which Clytie had come in contact; at one point in the story, the shock of physical contact with Sutpen's Negro daughter sickens her with revulsion. Time does not lessen her snobbery or her prejudices; it merely fixes them into reflexes. The form of address she employs to the last of Sutpen's enfeebled kin: "You nigger. . . . You ain't any Sutpen," reveals that even as late as 1913 there was no end in sight of the vicious continuum of Negro-white tension. If the Compsons survive as the undeserving victims of the conflict brought on over the Negro issue, Miss Rosa remains as a pitiable reminder of the persistence of its causes.

The thematic link between the created tragedy and the narrators who project it is reinforced by many interspersed observations about the present-ness of the past and the pastness of the present. There is, to begin with, the identity of place: "Quentin breathed the same air in which those church bells had rung on that Sunday morning in 1833." There is continuity of blood: Mr. Compson recognizes, in these figures from an earlier era, "people in whose living blood and seed we ourselves lay dormant and waiting." Most binding of all is the psychic bond with a dead past. The cord which ties Quentin to the past has never been severed. Struggling futiley to free himself, Quentin succumbs in a hopeless concession to interrelatedness in which no individual identity remains: "Maybe nothing ever happens and is finished . . . maybe it took Father and me both to make Shreve or Shreve and me both to make Father or maybe Thomas Sutpen to make all of us."

The narrators themselves, lost in their private obsessions and viewing the Sutpen story only partially through their individual distortions of vision, do not see the meaning of the tragedy in which they play a part nor its relation to the one they have made. Only the reader has a full view of the stage. He sees, as it were, two tragedies on a single theme, simultaneously enacted. The curtain lifts on a play within a play: on the inner stage, the Sutpen drama; on the outer, the larger social tragedy involving the narrators. The second creates the first, and the first serves to convey the second. They are brought to their overwhelming finale together, but not without the reminder that, although catastrophe has been portrayed, life goes on. Shreve, the Canadian, remote from the involvements of either South or North, remains to the last uncomprehending and unaffected. His levity intensifies Quentin's ordeal by contrast, but it also affords a means by which the conjoined tragedies can be placed in detached perspective. The inclusion of his "normal" view toward the end of the novel is analogous to the placement of the Dilsey section in *The Sound and the Fury* and the furniture dealer's story in *Light in August*. Subtly mediating the return to reality, Faulkner demonstrates his own hold upon it and proves his absolute command of the means by which imaginative reality is brought into being.

3

One of the most remarkable achievements of the novel is the maintenance of suspense. The reader knows the outlines of Sutpen's history from Miss Rosa's first account; in each subsequent narration the local myth of his strange rise and fall is told again and again, until through sheer repetition it takes on the quality of a familiar legend. Yet knowing the outcome of Sutpen's ambition, the reader's anticipation of what each new redactor will bring to the tale is not diminished. In fact, suspense mounts steadily.

The problem of creating suspense when treating well known legendary characters was a crucial one for Greek dramatists. Individual playwrights met the challenge by providing new details of interpretation or by selecting, from among the wealth of divergent stories already existing about the same figure, a new conclusion which resolved the contradictions of varying versions or which embodied the particular moral which the dramatist wished to illustrate. "The element of uncertainty which could be produced by these means," one classical scholar has asserted, was "perhaps the most important single factor in the suspense of any Greek play."[2]

We cannot know whether Faulkner availed himself of the scholarly hints which might have been serviceable to his purpose; nor is it our present object to inquire into his sources. The value of the analogy which can be drawn between Faulkner's method of creating suspense and the practise of the Greek dramatists is that it enables us to see how the sequence of narrations gains momentum.

If we grant, as indeed we must, that Miss Rosa, Mr. Compson, and Quentin are the creators of the Sutpen myth, each spinning his version of the legend out of his own psyche, then their three differing interpretations might be compared to a display of the talents of the three Greek dramatists composing tragedies about the same mythical figure, each poet having access to his predecessor's interpretation and adding new insights and flourishes of his own. The last composer would be in the position to contribute the most; suspense would consist in the expectation that he solve the questions which earlier versions had raised.

The most prominent inconsistence in the three narrators' versions relates to Sutpen's motivation for the act which brought about his downfall. The question upon which all the narrators brood successively is: Why did Sutpen forbid the marriage of Bon and Judith? (The motive of Henry's murder of Bon hinges on the answer to this question.) It was the mystery of Sutpen's opposition to Bon which confounded Miss Rosa. "I saw Judith's marriage forbidden without rhyme or reason or shadow of excuse," she says, hinting at demonism as the only possible explanation. Mr. Compson gropes in equal futility for an answer to this question; he guesses that an "eighth part negro mistress" was the basis of Sutpen's denial and Henry's subsequent murder of Bon. It was the "morganatic ceremony" which—he conjectures—aroused Sutpen and shocked Henry. Elaborating this theory in fond detail, he nevertheless is forced to abandon it as wide of the mark. "It's just incredible," he finally concedes. "It just doesn't explain. . . . They are there, yet something is missing."

We thus await Quentin's resumption of the task of providing a more satisfactory account of Sutpen's motivation. Bringing the new information that Bon was Sutpen's son (a fact which he had been told by his grandfather but had not shared with his father), Quentin constructs with Shreve the legend of the outcast brother, the son who renounced his birthright, and the incestuous love triangle.

But even this will not wholly serve. Assuming that both Henry and Bon guess their blood relationship, Quentin explores the incest theory with an intensity of interest possible only to one of his morbid sensibility and finds it still insufficient. Suppose Bon and Henry surmised the incestuous objection, Quentin considers, how would Henry react? He would oppose the sin at first, but he would reconsider. His identification with both Bon and Judith would cause him to override the objections of conscience. He would sanction the unlawful union between his idolized older brother and his adored female counterpart. Thus, the basis of Sutpen's objection must have exceeded even this, to account for Henry's strange and abrupt reversal. Quentin and Shreve continue their conjuring.

They reinvoke Sutpen, and five fatal words dropped from his lips serve at last to resolve everything. They are spoken to Henry and relate to Bon: ". . . his mother was part negro." This final revelation, held for the very close of the legend, casts into sudden order all the hitherto unaligned clues in the versions of the various narrators and clinches the moral of the tragedy. That scene in the cold early dawn in which Charles, now knowing the news Henry has brought from Sutpen, places his cloak about his younger brother's shoulders in the last gesture of tenderness which can ever be possible between them, is the high point of pathos in the entire drama. The love of a brother for a brother, represented as so ideal in quality that it could surmount even the test of the incest conflict, is altered in an instant to blindly obliterative hate. The slight fraction of Negro blood, whose denial was Sutpen's crime, is sole cause. Now at last we know what turned father against son, son against father, and brother against brother. The language and allusions which elevate this compassionately rendered Cain-Abel conflict are appropriately Biblical.

The placement of the narrations in a sequence of cumulative revelations is supplemented by more familiar suspense-building devices. Accomplished action precedes cause throughout. In Chapters I through VI, Sutpen appears as heroic, demonic, purposive and inscrutable; Chapter VII first presents him as the baffled, limited and compulsive mortal that he is. Henry's murder is cited as fact beginning with Chapter I; the circumstances and motive are not provided until Chapter VII. Miss Rosa's ravings are suspect as hysterical from her earliest remarks in Chapter I; not until Chapter V do we learn how to discount her assertions in the light of her own psychology. Sutpen is buried (Chapter VI) before we are admitted to a view of his murder (Chapter VII); the murder itself is recounted in all its violence without our knowing what really provoked it (the sex of Milly's baby). Effect-cause sequence is worked into all the action and characterization.

The promise of an easy moral also lures the reader on from the opening pages. Quentin's first thought is that Sutpen's story will tell him (italics his): *"why God let us lose the war: that only through the blood of our men and the tears of our women could He stay this demon and effact his name and lineage from the earth."* We must make our way through almost the entire novel to modify this view and to extend it properly to the whole social class which Sutpen and his design epitomize. The most direct statement of this modification is made when Wash awaits the citizenry who will pass judgment on his murder of Sutpen. He "felt them gathering . . .—the curious and the vengeful —men of Sutpen's own kind, who used to eat at his table . . .—men who had led the way, shown the other and lesser ones how to fight in battles . . .—who had galloped also in the old days arrogant and proud on the fine horses about the fine plantations—symbol also of admiration and hope, instruments too of despair and grief." In his profound and tragic disillusionment, he sees them with new eyes: ". . . and maybe for the first time in his life [Mr. Compson comments] he began to comprehend how it had been possible for the Yankees or any other army to have whipped them."

Gothic mystery is also used to engage our curiosity and heighten our sense of horror. The entire novel is framed in a macabre search. When the book opens, Miss Rosa asks Quentin to help her find out who is now living in that decaying, almost-deserted old house. The answer to this question, bringing before us the sight of Henry's "wasted yellow face . . . wasted hands crossed on the breast as if he were already a corpse," closes the legend. As a device it is melodramatic, excessive. But it achieves its purpose without taking us off our course. The rotting mansion is the house of the past; the death-in-life of Henry is Quentin's own.

4

The literary style of the novel is in keeping with its high tragic aim. We habitually think of Faulkner as having a single style because all of his writings bear his markedly individual stamp, but this is to overlook the consciously contrived effects within his various works. In *The Sound and the Fury,* four distinct styles are employed, all scrupulously differentiated, and the short stories are a record of endless stylistic experimentation.

All the narrators speak in two voices—their own idiom, when engaged in casual conversation with each other, and the highly stylized orations in which they serve as narrators of the legend. (For Quentin, a third style, stream-of-consciousness, is also maintained.) Miss Rosa's decorum as a Southern maiden lady is conveyed in her initial address to Quentin: "Because you are going away to attend the college at Harvard. . . . Maybe you will enter the literary profession as so many Southern gentlemen and gentle women too are doing now and maybe some day you will remember this and write about it." When later she deviates from this drawing-room propriety to use such overt sexual imagery as "a metabolism of the spirit . . . in which the stored accumulations of long time burn, generate, create and break some maidenhead of the ravening meat," or to describe herself in adolescence as "all polymath love's androgynous advocate" (which simply means that she fell in love with love)—we may well wonder what has happened to dictional verisimilitude.

The difference is consistent, however; the actual Quentin is represented by his polite "Yessums" and "Nomes"; the narrator Quentin by Faulkner's own characteristically sonorous, Latinate prose. Shreve, as the Canadian and college youth, speaks an amusingly bluff, deprecating slang. When he collaborates in the creation of the Bon legend, however, the distinguishing features of his personal idiom disappear. The differences are not arbitrary. By means of a few strokes of realistic dialogue, the narrators are established as real; once established, they become the instruments for Faulkner's own poetic formulation of his material. Thus, while we must take each narration in its own terms, making allowance for the disposition of the teller, all the mythologizing is unified by the dominance of a single rhetorical style.

Decanting the poetic essence from his carefully wrought vessels, Faulkner himself is everywhere and nowhere. As in the great tragedies of Shakespeare, poetized philosophy—observations upon love, life, death, nature—finds, as it were, objective utterance through *dramatis personae* who speak in elevated poetic diction. Such diction—the blank or heroic verse appointed for tragedy—was an established convention in the sixteenth and seventeenth centuries. For modern writers, however, no such resource exists; original expedients have had to be devised to suit the needs of heroic enlargement. Melville's rhetorical prose was one such device; Maxwell Anderson's modernized blank verse another. If, as Emily Dickinson has observed, "the abdication of belief/ makes the behavior small," so too, it may be argued, does the use of a realistic prose style in compliance with an outlook of "scientific" objectivity. The declining vitality of much realistic writing of the twenties and thirties—of Farrell's fiction, for example, which was also intended to convey the power of relentless forces—is in part a reflection of the inadequacy of realism for tragic themes.

The rhetorical style of *Absalom, Absalom!* is essential to its conception, excessive as it may at times appear when it fails in that perfect felicity in which rhetoric is never questioned. The use of polysyllabics and involved—usually periodic—sentences, while natural to the author, is not a surrender to the line of least resistance. Prefixes and suffixes, especially those containing liquids and nasals in combination with vowels, lend sonorous enrichment; sentence units into which are enfolded a series of phrases and clauses which must be gathered sequentially into the mind before the release of meaning afforded in a final verb, are a means of approximating poetic rhythm in prose medium.

The unceasing flow of language gives the effect, as in *Moby-Dick,* of being tapped under pressure from unconscious or supraconscious sources; the richness of poetic imagery and literary association enlarges its power at every turn. In addition to the allusions already cited, Faulkner echoes familiar lines of deeply tragic import from *Hamlet, Macbeth* and from A. E. Housman. The intention of heroic enlargement is discernible throughout: Sutpen's wife is a Niobe; Bon a Lothario, a Lancelot, and a hero out of the Arabian Nights; the young Confederates are the Virgins of Priapus; Sutpen builds "Camelots and Carcassonnes," and performs "Herculean" labors.

The many memorable utterances, taking the form of maxim-like gems or sustained metaphors, will perhaps remain as the novel's greatest permanent attraction. Miss Rosa's sections particularly reflect this poetizing tendency. Her incisive capsule definitions of hope, defeat, sanity, madness, penury, endurance, etc., dropped parenthetically into the pauses of her breathless self-justification, are poetry in all but metre. They are reminiscent, in manner as well as idea, of the penetrating formulations of Emily Dickinson. And indeed, the concept of Miss Rosa as a kind of Emily (one is reminded of that cryptic title, "A Rose for Emily"), may have entered into Faulkner's creation of her: Miss Rosa was the local poetess. Mr. Compson's *bon mots* tend more toward the definition of social concepts and customs, through his range, too, includes timeless psychological verities.

Such imaginative reaches are attained variously by almost all the speakers: Gen. Compson on morality viewed as a baking recipe, Judith on life as the weaving of a pattern into a carpet, Bon on existence as a conjugation of the verb *to be,* Quentin on the interpenetration of all historical events—these are eternally pertinent and consummately expressed.

Many general observations of a philosophic nature are stated in such a way as to reinforce the tragic theme directly, as the definition of the verbal communication, for example, which is brief enough to cite by way of illustrating the aphoristic quality that is often attained: ". . . language, that meagre and fragile thread . . . by which the little surface corners and edges of man's secret and solitary lives may be joined for an instant now and then before sinking back into the darkness where the spirit cried for the first time and was not heard and will cry for the last time and will not be heard either." Spoken

by Gen. Compson to Quentin in connection with Sutpen's regret at not having
learned French before going to Haiti, it arises so naturally from the situation
that the reader has no special sense of the intrusion of the author's eloquence.
Placed within the dramatic frame, made to flow from narrations which are
maintained at a consistently elevated level of expression, such *sententiae* belong, like the novel itself, to a grand tradition of noble utterance.

5

Nothing which is told or conjectured by the narrators, however distorted,
is without thematic relevance. Since their projections are determined by their
own psychological and social past, and since the Sutpen story throws additional light upon that past, the meaning of what they tell reflects at least doubly
and must be read throughout for its multiple import. Even the false leads,
while they delay our otherwise too hasty discovery of Sutpen's motive, are
significant. They tell what *might* have occurred; their usefulness lies in their
conjectural plausibility. For example, although in actuality Henry did not
object to Bon's marriage to the octoroon mistress, it is likely that as a young
Sutpen he would have. This theoretical probability—raised by Mr. Compson
and later disproved by other facts—in its very error is valuable as a thematic
datum. For "there is a might-have-been which is more true than truth," as
Miss Rosa symptomatically puts it. Out of guess and conjecture, snatches of
old story, the narrators build their tragedy. Perhaps none of it is true; or
perhaps it is the only truth. How can truth be known except by conjecture?
Quentin remarks, "If I had been there, I could not have seen it this plain."
    Through the reciprocal interplay of narrators and the story they tell, the
issues created by racial subordination are considered in many aspects and
driven home through the working out of numerous parallels and recapitulations. For purposes of analysis, two coordinate levels of the theme may be
differentiated: the problem of blood as it figures in the Sutpen tragedy, and the
issue of slavery as it affected the history of the South.
    In the Sutpen tragedy, one of the most striking recurrent patterns express-
ing the theme is the problem of legal marriage, an obvious crux in a society
where continuing class superiority depends on strict differentiation of blood.
In fact, as Mr. Compson reminds us, sexual relationships between Negro
women and white men were never honored by law. The license which recorded
the marriage of Bon and his mistress was a meaningless document, "vesting
no new rights in no one [*sic*], denying to none the old." For, as Compson has
Bon explain to Henry during the time when both young men assume that Bon
is white, the ceremony was a mere romantic ritual, unenforceable by the

octoroon. For "this woman, this child, are niggers."

When Sutpen, in conformity to the "design," dishonors his legal tie to his first fractionally Negro wife, convincing himself that the claims of morality have been appeased by a financial settlement, his first crime against humanity is committed. According to law he has done, as he repeatedly argues, more than was demanded of him. But there are obligations of heart and feeling of which Sutpen is unaware. The true nature of his "abysmal and purblind" innocence is appropriately commented upon by Gen. Compson (speaking through Quentin): ". . . because it was that innocence again . . . which believed that the ingredients of morality were like the ingredients of a pie or cake and once you had measured them and balanced them and mixed them and put them into the oven it was all finished and nothing but pie or cake could come out."

That innocence, a "minimal" response to the human spirit and its needs, Sutpen never outgrows. He marries Ellen not for love, but because he is ready to acquire the furniture for his house, "not the least of which furniture was the wedding license."

When Bon appears as the suitor to Judith, he comes as the instrument of vengeance for the outraged heart of his mother. Sutpen immediately knows him for his own son, and worse, knows that he is part Negro. Acknowledge him he feels he cannot; yet without acknowledgement there is no basis for objection to his marriage to Judith. "Fogbound" in this dilemma, Sutpen forbids the marriage without any reason, hoping that time itself will veer the curve of events within the orbit of his ambition.

But he fails to reckon with love. Judith and Henry both love Bon, and their self-sacrificing loyalty is as fixed as Sutpen's will. Alienated from his father because of the seeming unreasonableness of his opposition, Henry renounces his patrimony in favor of Bon, and in so doing deprives Sutpen of the sole object of his matrimonial endeavor—a subtle heir. Desperate, Sutpen plays his trump card (the information that Judith's suitor is part Negro), but again he miscalculates. Henry's prejudices are more deeply ingrained than his own, which have a purely practical basis in his ambition. What Sutpen had wished was merely to have Bon stopped; Henry murders him. Now both sons are lost, and Sutpen's incapacity for feeling has caused the death of Charles, the exemption of Henry from meaningful existence, the unbrided widowhood of Judith, and all the ills which are yet to befall the remaining Bon descendants.

His inability to locate his error dooms him to a repetition of his sins. At best, he can think only in terms of some practical mistake, some miscalculation in "strategy" which threw him off the "schedule" he had set himself for the completion of his project. The actual source of his frustrations remains concealed from him; he questions neither the limitations of his own rationalism nor the justice underlying the design itself. "Whether it was a good or bad design is beside the point," he tells Quentin's grandfather; "the question is, Where did I make the mistake in it . . .?" After the destruction of the design in Henry's flight from justice, he is chary of any new marital commitment which does not guarantee in advance the suitable heir of which he feels that he has been defrauded. Hence his retraction of his proposal to Miss Rosa. His cold-blooded proposition—"let's try it and if it's a boy and it lives, we'll get married"—enkindles in her the wrath which still burns after forty-three years. Hence, too, his holding off with Milly until after he knows the outcome of her delivery. When Wash is compelled to absorb the finality of Sutpen's dishonorable intentions toward Milly, the bottom drops out of his world. His smiting down of Sutpen at this point is an appropriate vengeance against an overstepping—almost beyond credibility—of the bounds of generally understood humanity.

In their attitudes toward Negro-white marriages, Sutpen's children reflect the views of the class in which they have been reared. At least so Mr. Compson, reasoning from the axioms of Southern upper-class mores, offers for conjecture. His mythologizing completes the symmetry of the marriage pattern. According to him, the puritanical Henry was less offended by the voluptuousness of Bon's erotic tie to the octoroon mistress than by the implied insult to Judith of even a "morganatic" ceremony. Judith herself is pictured years later as reminding Etienne Bon that the "paper . . . between you and one who is inescapably negro . . . can be put aside." The point is clear: where caste rules prevail, affection and intimate relationships between "whites" and those of "tainted" blood cannot be recognized or sanctioned. The effect of such denial to those involved is, of course, vicious. Arbitrary rejection from those most binding of all ties, familial and marital love, breeds psychic outrage, and psychic outrage breeds personal revolt. The human psyche has its own mechanics of vengeance.

The exclusion of the Negro from another fundamental relation, participation as an accepted member in the social community with his fellow, adds further impetus to negative compulsions. This variation of the theme is also elaborately patterned. All the Sutpens accept the doctrines of racial supremacy as such, with no thought as to their origins, rightness, or possibility of modification under special circumstances. When Sutpen learns of his wife's part-Spanish, part-Negro ancestry, he ousts her without entertaining even momentarily the possibility of suppressing the knowledge of her origins, the traces of which were so invisible as to have successfully deceived him.

Judith, Clytie, Henry, and Miss Rosa similarly perpetuate the race assumptions derived from plantation culture. Clytie and Judith keep young Charles Etienne Bon scrupulously isolated from Negro companions, in an excess of good intention which has dire results. Clytie is depicted as trying literally to scrub the faint ivory tinge from his young skin. Henry, for all his delicacy of conscience, succumbs ironically at the last to the simple murderous reflexes of his class: his brother may marry his sister, but a "nigger" must be shot dead. Miss Rosa's prejudices are rabid, as has already been shown.

The indignation of the denied Sutpens, exhausting itself for lack of a more assailable object in wanton violence or destructive self-spite, is traced to its final obliteration from consciousness in the idiocy of Jim Bond. The well-bred mother of Bon never comes to terms with her dismissal. "Paranoic" in her enraged irreconcilability, she lives as the true Clytemnestra of the tale, appeasing her lust for vengeance at last. The genteel Charles Bon does not leave the scene without making final show of his outrage, in terms appropriate to his upbringing. His sudden determination to marry Judith against Henry's command, after his long submission to the outcome of Henry's internal debate, is touched off by the realization that he has been rejected by Sutpen and Henry, not as a man, or even as Judith's brother but *in toto*—as Negro. "So it's the miscegenation, not the incest, that you can't bear," he reasons summarily, freezing in the instant of this awareness into stony recalcitrance. Defiance and counter-retaliation are the cause of his removing Judith's picture from his wallet and replacing it with that of his octoroon wife. (Shreve's foolish interpretation of this act gives ironic heightening to its real poignance.) Charles's gesture says, in effect, that if he is to be none of theirs, they will be none of his. In flaunting Henry's will, Charles invites his own death; yet before he is killed he succeeds in giving at least token return for the psychic blow he has received.

Charles Etienne Bon, whose spiritual rebellion is signalized in his establishment at Sutpen's Hundred of an anthropoid wife and in his rampages of uninhibited inebriation, reenacts his father's symbolic gestures with greater vehemence, in response to the more sustained psychic and social pressure which he has had to endure. Raised as white but self-identified as Negro, he treads that special path to Gethsemane which is reserved for the Joe Christmases of this world.

The blight of slavery is rendered with supreme effectiveness in terms of another pattern which appears recurrently in the Sutpen legend—the effect of race division upon the "common man" in the South—the poor white. Sutpen and his father were of this class; so too were Wash and Milly. The power of caste aspiration to blot the true ties of human kinship from recognition is brought fully home when it is remembered that Sutpen, who was incapable of according to Milly the accommodations provided even for a beast, had himself had a sister whose illegitimate child was born in an outbuilding. In Sutpen's sister's case, however, no vengeance was sought upon the defaulting male; the girl simply climbed back into the wagon with her child and rejoined the family.

But the mountain society from which the Sutpens descended lacked the conditions which fostered perpetual tensions of social status. A primitive community, men within it were judged on the basis of individual strength and courage, not upon the ownership of goods or upon spurious differentiations between the quality of their blood and that of certain of their fellows. In the mountain where young Sutpen lived "the land belonged to anybody and everybody and so the man who would go to the trouble and work to fence off a piece of it and say 'this is mine' was crazy; and as for objects, nobody had any more of them than you did."

The gradual descent from this mountain paradise to a society, "where a few men not only had the power of life and death and barter and sale over others, but had living human men to perform . . . [those tasks] which no man ever has or will like to do," constitutes the fall of the Sutpens and their kind from grace. The Biblical allusions which pervade the descent heighten the contrast between mountain "innocence" and the spiritual depravity of a slave society.

The gradual corruption of the mountain-folk is traced step by step. When Sutpen's hard-drinking father enters a tavern now, he is "not even allowed to come in by the front door." At one place "a huge bull of a nigger, the first black man, slave, they had ever seen," ejects him. (The doorway barred to inferior whites, with a Negro standing in enforcement of the distinction, is itself a recurrent symbol. Just so, the Negro butler turns away young Sutpen, and Clytie later bars admission to Wash.) Soon Sutpen's father needs to find outlet for inexplicable tensions in the empty triumphs of "whupping Pettibone's niggers." The passive, seemingly mocking docility of the slaves challenges in the white man his sense of personal worth, causing him to strike out in random violence, not against Negroes as individuals, but at their "balloon faces." The women, too, are affected; it shows in a "certain flat level silent way" Sutpen's sisters and other women of their kind had "of looking at niggers . . . with a kind of speculative antagonism."

Young Sutpen's own loss of "innocence" takes place before that white door of the great house of the plantation owner, where—under the stare of the "nigger monkey"—he first felt, like Adam in Paradise, the shameful inadequacy of his natural garb ("his patched overalls and no shoes"). That single, contemptuous glance of the slave at the door altered his whole spiritual condition. The refusal of the Negro to hear his message or give him admittance provided the negative impetus upon which his entire design was constructed. Indescribably moving is the account of young Sutpen's attempt, in his retreat to the woods for clarity of thought, to adapt himself to his new sinful awareness by the use of his logical faculties. What makes this effort all the more touching is that the labored advances of his circumscribed reason are logical, undeflected by self-commiseration, and brought to a conclusion leading to action.

In his ordeal of social initiation, Sutpen learns—at a rate faster than his capacity for emotional assimilation—that there are differences "not only between white men and black ones," but between "white men and white," not measurable in the rudimentary tests of manhood with which he is familiar, like "lifting anvils or gouging eyes or how much whiskey you could drink." Sensing exactly where his own naked worth places him in this new system of values, Sutpen is outraged to the very depths of his being. His first impulse is to shoot the "man in the hammock," whose indifferent luxuriousness is the symbol of everything which has disordered his simple world. But his reason tells him that nothing can be accomplished by direct assault. It "ain't a question of rifles," he painfully concludes: ". . . to combat them you have got to have what they have that made them do what that man did." Accepting the fruits of this logic, Sutpen sets himself to the labors indicated. The path of social conformity which he chooses, however, proves a straight descending route to perdition.

After our imaginative participation in Sutpen's ordeal, we can never be wholly alienated from him in sympathy. We cannot hate him, any more than Quentin can "hate" the South. The family stock from which Sutpen derived was the class of settlers released to American from penal servitude in Old Bailey, and from this bit of genealogy we may assume for young Sutpen a meager heritage of humanistic values. The governing influence of his mother upon the movements of the family (it was she who directed them westward, and it was not until after her death that they "slid" down the mountain), ceased in Sutpen's early adolescence. The effects of caste splendor upon his impressionable mind shortly thereafter were fatal. The ideals which guided him in life were thus inadequate in their origins and too soon crystallized from experience. "Courage" and "shrewdness" without humanity will not serve to found a family any more than they will afford a stable basis for a culture.

Within their understandable limitations, however, Sutpen's qualities are admirable. His private integrity, manifested in innumerable small ways—his refusal to malign his first wife, his unwillingness to accept favors he cannot return, his establishment of man-to-man superiority over his slaves in sportsmanlike physical combat (as opposed to anonymous raids in the darkness, typical of others of his class), his searching for faults in his own acts rather than blaming others or Fate for his disappointments, his purposive adherence in conduct to the illuminations of his reason—these virtues confirm the largeness of his stature.

To be sure, he never becomes an integrated member of his community. Yet this is an adverse reflection upon the community as well as upon Sutpen. Their first response to his entry was a watchful defensiveness of their own privileged status: they attempted to halt his architectural enterprise by having him placed under arbitrary arrest, and they incited a mob (which later dispersed "like rats") to bombard his bride with vegetable refuse. Over the years "the town . . . had merely assumed armistice rather than accepting and assimilating." Only General Compson gives his friendship, and it is he whom Sutpen honors with his confidence. Sutpen fights in the war for "four honorable years"; afterwards, he refuses flatly to be coerced into joining one of the armed secret groups which terrorize the country. To the deputation which calls upon him he speaks his mind with fearlessness and essential rightness: ". . . that if each man in the South . . . would see to the restoration of his own land, the general land and South would save itself."

In his independence and strength, he is truly heroic; in the tragic flaw of his nature he resembles the great tragic heroes of literature. Unlike Macbeth or Lear, however, he never gains insight into his fault. Like Oedipus, rather, he is driven to new evils by forces which antedate his birth and which are beyond the sphere of his conscious governing. He is the modern tragic hero, insofar as art can represent him, a man felt to be circumscribed by psychological and social conditions, however large his abilities and aspirations.

His tragic fate is reiterated in the plight of his unheroic foil, Wash Jones. Weak, cowardly, compliant, Wash nevertheless also knows the longings of the poor white to rise above his class and senses the derision of the Negroes for his familiarity with the plantation owner. Sutpen he takes for no less than "God himself." Wash, too, has an innocence to lose—the belief that because Sutpen is brave and a big plantation owner, he is capable of being human in considerations touching his design. ("But you are brave," he says to Sutpen prayerfully in submitting to the aged man's seduction of his granddaughter. "That's where it's different.") In his childlike adulation he believes that whatever the aged Sutpen driven to madness by the frustrations of his ambition may do, he will "make hit right" with the fifteen-year-old Milly.

The incredulity of his disillusionment equals that of the boy not accepted as a simple human boy by the "monkey" at the white door: "I kaint have heard what I know I heard," he utters. "I just know it. I just know I kaint." Wash's thought, before he cuts his swath of corpses, is the despairing cry of a heart too young in the knowledge of this world's treachery to support the staggering burden: "Better if his kin and mine too had never drawn the breath of life on this earth. Better that all who remain of us be blasted from the face of it."

Thus the results of caste ambition, as they affect the relations of whites to whites as well as of whites to Negroes, are illustrated in the Sutpen tragedy.

6

The Sutpen tragedy is the means of conveying the larger social tragedy. In its broader outlines, the Sutpen tragedy is in many ways analogous to the social. Sutpen had two sons: one white, the other Negro. He denied the Negro; fratricide resulted. The Civil War, too, was a fratricidal conflict caused by denial of the Negro. In the passage which designates the Mississippi River as the "geological umbilicus" of the continent, uniting Quentin and Shreve in a "sort of geographical substantiation," the brotherhood of North and South is established explicitly.

Sutpen's sin, his failure of humanity, is the equivalent in personal terms of the sin of plantation culture, its failure to accept the brotherhood of all mankind. Both failures are provided with the suggestion of an ancestry. Sutpen's progenitors go back to the criminal element in England; slavery, when first introduced into the West Indies, was begun by men "whom the civilized land and people had expelled": "whose thinking and desires had become too crass to be faced and borne longer," and who had been set, "homeless and desperate upon the lonely ocean." In the description of Haiti as "the half-way point between what we call the jungle and what we call civilization," we are not far from Mr. Compson's description of the half-civilized Methodist South: "(. . . Sutpen and Henry and the Coldfields too) who have not quite yet emerged from barbarism, who two thousand years hence will still be throwing off the yoke of Latin culture and intelligence from which they never were in any great permanent danger to begin with."

The social tragedy is conveyed through the Sutpen tragedy concretely as well as abstractly. As the biggest single plantation owner in the country, Sutpen is the very incarnation of the Old South. In describing the conception, attainment, and destruction of Sutpen's design, Faulkner shows the tragedy of that society in terms of the presiding theme.

The social panorama which first unfolds itself to young Sutpen's eye when he descends the mountain is of "a country all divided and fixed and neat with people living on it all divided and fixed and neat because of what color their skins happened to be and what they happened to own." The division upon which the plantation system rests is seen as already established. He sees "niggers working in the fields . . . while fine men sat fine horses and watched them." Poor whites find miscellaneous work in connection with the plantations, getting their overalls and calico dresses from the "plantation commissary," or on store credit, and taking shelter in cabins "not quite as well kept up and preserved as the ones the nigger slaves lived in." The poor whites are physically less well provided for than the Negroes, but their dwellings are "nimbused with freedom's bright aura." In the theoretical concession to worth which freedom implies lies their torment. Only the exceptionally strong and ruthless of purpose, like Sutpen, could accept the challenge to equality with the men who sat the fine horses. Their more typical responses of indignation, blocking the road to an oncoming carriage or throwing dust after its proud wheels, were purely symbolic.

During the years in which Sutpen completes his house, obtains the appropriate wife, and raises to near adulthood the two perfectly suitable heirs of his caste ambitions, plantation society is depicted as reaching the pinnacle of civilized refinement in manners, arts, dress, ceremony and entertainment. The exquisiteness of these attainments is in part symbolized in the beauty of the house itself, its grace deriving from the enforced labors of the French architect and from the objects which go to furnish it: the crystal chandeliers, the candelabra, the tapestries, silver, linen, Damask, crystal, Wedgewood, carpets, and —above all—the great formal white door with its fanlight "imported pane by pane from Europe." (Shreve's garbled review of "crystal tapestries and Wedgewood chairs" is final evidence of the hopelessness of his ever comprehending this aspect of Quentin's cultural past.) Sutpen's marble monument, imported from Italy and brought past the Civil War blockade to be toted in the regimental forage wagon all the way from Charleston, symbolizes a sense of social grandeur and dignity which had become so completely assimilated by the upper classes as to be projected for immortality.

Sutpen's wife, Ellen, the vacuous "butterfly" who chaperones for Judith and Bon a courtship of patterend walks in a formal garden, is the female who presides over the rituals of refined existence. The shopping expeditions with her marriageable daughter, during which she would "finger and handle and disarrange and then reject . . . the meagre fripperies and baubles" of local shops, conveys the luxury of taste made possible by plantation prosperity. Henry's social experience, a round of hunting and cockfighting, amateur horse racing, and dancing at "other plantations almost interchangeable with his own," is the model of socially prescribed leisure. Judith's pattern, likewise, is conveyed by "riding habits" and "ball gowns." The library of the magnificent house, decked in the consummate festiveness of Southern Yuletide, is the scene where the gentlemanly young Henry renounces his birthright in favor of the even more gentlemanly, New Orleans-bred Bon, whose posed indolence and silken dressing gown had first won him his country brother's idolatry.

The image of that society is captured in briefly-sketched word pictures which are as conventional and set as old-time calendar prints. The slave belongs in this picture, and he is never omitted. There are the ladies going to church "with house negroes to carry the parasols and flyswishes . . . moving in hoops among the miniature broadcloth of the . . . little boys and pantelettes of the litle girls." There is the evocation of Southern Christmas in a view of the plantation houses "with . . . holly thrust beneath the knockers . . . eggnog and toddy . . . and blue unwinded wood smoke standing above the plastered chimneys of the slave quarters." There is "music at night—fiddle and triangle among the blazing candles." On such occasions the best champagne is "dispensed out of the burlesqued pantomime elegance of Negro butlers." When the young Confederates make their farewells for battle, after an evening of waltzing with their crinolined ladies, the view of their departure includes their grooms and "body servants." The glory and romance are conveyed unforgettably, but the shadow of the slave haunts the scene. As Ellen and Judith return in their carriage from a triumphant shopping expedition, they ride with "an extra nigger on the box with the coachman to stop every few miles and build a fire and re-heat the bricks on which Ellen and Judith's feet rested."

The extent to which the entire social superstructure is set upon treacherous foundations is hinted at repeatedly. Graciousness prevails, but at too great a remove from the elementary facts of life. Private and colonel, on the eve of enlistment, are united in honor and pride. They "call each by their given names . . . one man to another above the suave powdered shoulders of the women." But they do so as gentleman to gentleman, "not . . . as one farmer to another across a halted plow in a field."

The delicacy of consideration accorded the young gentlewomen is not truly earned. Mr. Compson distinguishes three types of females in the society: "the virgins whom gentlemen someday married, the courtesans to whom they went while on sabbaticals to the cities, [and] the slave girls and women upon whom that first caste rested and to whom in certain cases it doubtless owed the very fact of its virginity." He describes the simple commandeering of the slave girls from the fields; no more respect was accorded the well kept octoroon mistresses, like Bon's, who for all their loyalty and careful nurturing were valuable only as "commodities." Except for the selective interest of the white man in these few, Mr. Compson has Bon explain to Henry, they "would have been sold to any brute for the price . . . body and soul for life . . . [to be used] with no more impunity than he would dare to use an animal." In their incredible beauty and helplessness, these women are "the supreme apotheosis of chattelry." ⟍

Upon the maintained difference between slave-girl and gentlewoman, slave laborer and gentleman, plantation society rested. Yet how different were Henry and the young men of his class from their darker-skinned contemporaries? It is Mr. Compson who asks this question and gives the answer: ". . . only in the surface matter of food and clothing and daily occupation any different from the Negro slaves who supported them—the same sweat, the only difference being that on the one hand it went for labor in the fields where on the other it went for the spartan pleasures which were available to them because they did not have to sweat in the field."

From the utmost heights comes the fall to utter devastation, economically, socially and spiritually. The war is lost, and not merely because of the superior strategy and numbers of the enemy, but through the transposition into military terms of the very flaw by which the society was marred, through "generals . . . who should not have been generals . . . who were generals not through training or aptitude . . . but, by divine right to say 'Go there' conferred upon them by an absolute caste system."

Girls of Judith's kind, created by "a hundred years of careful nurturing . . . by the tradition in which Thomas Sutpen's ruthless will had carved a niche," must now dress the "self-fouled bodies of the strange injured and dead," must learn to tend household without money or servants, to harness the mule, and go clad in faded gingham. The house, too, must surrender its objects of beauty and pride, "giving of itself in slow driblets of furniture and carpet, linen and silver."

Sutpen comes home to find "his plantation ruined, fields fallow . . . taxes and levies and penalties sowed by United States marshals . . . and all his niggers gone." Defeat has brought about a leveling of whites; Wash Jones, who never before would have dared, now freely crosses the threshold. Sutpen is reduced to running a country store with Wash. His persistence in his design becomes fantastic.

Most devastating is the spiritual alteration in the people. The gallantry of those who were the first to go is contrasted strikingly with the sullenness of those who were the first to come home: ". . . not all of them tramps, ruffians, but men who had risked and lost everything, suffered beyond endurance and had returned now to the ruined land, not the same men who had marched away but transformed . . . into the likeness of that man who abuses from very despair and pity the beloved wife or mistress who in his absence has been raped." Frustrated and embittered, these men strike fear into their compatriots who remained. During the era of carpetbaggers, they organize into night raiders, draining off in these excesses the "suppurations" of defeat. The more reflective exist, like Bon, "mindless and irrational companion and inmate of a body which . . . is still immersed . . . in recollection of old peace" but in whom consciousness enforces the knowledge that "what was is one thing and now it is not because it is dead, it died in 1861."

Forty years later the Sutpen mansion, symbol of a social design, still stands. Its "rotting portico and scaling walls" bespeak "some desolation more profound than ruin." Three generations of Sutpen had met doom within it; three generations of Southerners, brooding upon the mystery of its decay, had lived within the shadow of its prefigured annihilation. The desolation of the mansion is the key to Quentin's own, and in the story of a design that failed we may read the meaning of the decline of the South. And more: this novel, which holds an instant in history timeless and infinite in sombre implication, is a new revelation of "the dark and simple heart of things,"[3] pulsing forever in the world. All human history in its recurrence of error and anguish is represented in the myth of Quentin, Sutpen, and the South. In this fall of a man, a house, a class, and a culture, we know again, with terrifying nearness, the inexorability of "fate." Hybris and its punishment, sin and atonement, psychological compulsions and their proliferating destructiveness—these concepts, ancient and modern, endow *Absalom, Absalom!* with the poetic reality of classic moral tragedy.

---

1. Eugene O'Neill, 5 years earlier, had discussed the possibility of using "one of the old legend plots of Greek tragedy as the basis for a modern psychological drama" in which he hoped to "achieve a modern psychological approximation of the Greek sense of fate which would seem credible to a present-day audience and at the same time prove emotionally affecting." Introd. to *Mourning Becomes Electra,* Wilderness Ed. (New York, 1934), ii, xiii.

2. William Flint, Jr., *The Use of Myths to Create Suspense in Extant Greek Tragedy* (Concord, N. H., 1922), p. 6.

3. *Mosquitoes* (New York, 1927), p. 340.

THE UNVANQUISHED: FAULKNER'S ORESTEIA

GORMAN BEAUCHAMP

A CCOMPARISON OF FAULKNER TO AESCHYLUS will strike some as strange; by way of justification let me offer a comment of T. S. Eliot's from his influential essay, "Tradition and the Individual Talent":

No poet, no artist of any art, has his complete meaning alone. His significance, his appreciation is the appreciation of his relation to dead poets and artists. You cannot value him alone; you must set him, for contrast and comparison, among the dead. I mean this as a principle of aesthetic, not merely historical, criticism.[1]

By calling *The Unvanquished* Faulkner's *Oresteia,* I want to point up a thematic similarity between the two writers, the similarity of artistic moral vision. If, as the Greeks believed, the movement of history is cyclical, both artists present in their work that stage in the cycle when their societies are faced with radical dilemmas concerning the nature of justice and its relation to morality. Aeschylus deals with the socio-historical transformation of Greek culture from a tribal to a civil way of life—from *phylia* to *polis.*[2] Faulkner deals with the similar transformation of Southern society in the violent period of the Civil War and Reconstruction.

The conflict of the *Oresteia* grows out of the code of justice, the *lex talionis,* that obtains in primitive society: blood demands blood. The eye for an eye, tooth for a tooth retribution of the Old Testament Deuteronomists, of the Greek epics and the Norse sagas is based upon an uncompromising, even mathematical, belief that violence must answer violence if law and order are to be maintained. This is the argument of the Furies.[3]

However, a point is reached in the evolution of civilizations when, for at least their thoughtful and humane members, the moral inadequacy and destructiveness of the code of revenge is realized. Aeschylus dramatizes this moment by presenting the dilemma of Orestes, caught between two conflicting

Reprinted with permission from *Mississippi Quarterly* XXIII, No. 3 (Summer 1970) 273–277.

numinous demands, Olympian and Chthonic. He is damned by Apollo if he does not avenge his father's murder and damned by the Chthonic Furies if he sheds his mother's blood. Clearly the moral order is out of kilter; the vicious cycle of vengeance allows him no escape. As H. D. F. Kitto writes, "the law of Dikê has ended in a knot which cannot be untied: it can only be cut."[4]

In the *Eumenides,* the final play of the trilogy, Aeschylus presents a parable of the coming of the concept of justice into the affairs of men. The two conflicting orders, Olympian reason and Chthonic emotion, meet to lay their claims before a court. The debate, personified in Apollo and the Furies, involves the deepest questions concerning the social and moral nature of man; and each in defending something essential in man's being ignores something equally essential. The power of Aeschylus' vision lies in his ability to harmonize the conflicting demands of reason and emotion in a moral *via media* which comprehends both. He does so with a symbolic gesture—the establishment of the rule of law in the form of the Agora, along with Athena's power of Holy Persuasion by which she induces the terrorizing Erynnyes to become the Eumenides, servants of a justice based on reason but imbued with the awe of power.

The *Oresteia* represents unquestionably one of the great moments of illumination in man's ethical history, comparable to the final book of the *Illiad* or the Sermon on the Mount: each a denial of the validity of retributive vengeance. When we turn to *The Unvanquished,* we find the same attempt to resolve the conflicting claims, one social, one religious.

Edmond Volpe writes of *The Unvanquished,* "Faulkner powerfully expresses the binding force of tradition by giving the story the framework of Greek tragedy. Bayard becomes Orestes, and Drusilla becomes Electra."[5] Volpe carries this suggestion no further, but I want to elaborate on his two sentences. Certainly the second sentence is true, not in terms of formalistic parallels—Drusilla is not Bayard's sister but his cousin-stepmother—but in a wider ethical-existential sense. Faulkner describes Drusilla as "the Greek amphora priestess of a succinct and formal violence" (p. 252).[6] In each of Aeschylus' plays there is such a "priestess": Clytemnestra in *Agamemnon,* Electra in *Choephori,* and the Furies in *Eumenides,* each demanding a "succinct and formal violence." Like them, Drusilla represents the emotional cry for blood; as such she stands as one of the magnetic poles of *The Unvanquished,* the Southern-primitive code of physical heroism. She says to Bayard, "How beautiful: young, to be permitted to kill, to be permitted vengeance, to take into your bare hands the fire of heaven that cast down Lucifer" (p. 274). And certainly Bayard parallels Orestes and confronts Orestes' dilemma. He had already, as a boy, killed one man to exact revenge for the death of his grand-mother. Now his social code demands yet another murder to avenge his father's death. If the formal parallel to Orestes is not exact, the existential parallel is.

Yet, opposed to the social code is the religious one, the injunction "Thou shalt not kill" and its concomitant wisdom, "Who lives by the sword dies by it." Thus Bayard recognizes both the ultimate futility of revenge and the ethical nihilism of violence; but if this recognition can be transformed into action not even he knows. "At least," he thinks as he rides home from school on hearing that Redmond has killed his father, "this will be my chance to find out if I am what I think I am or if I just hope; if I am going to do what I have taught myself is right or if I am just going to wish I were" (p. 248).

If Drusilla stands at one extreme, demanding violence, Aunt Jenny stands at the other, seeking peace. Bayard need not act at all, she feels; he can end the cycle of violence by retreating from it. But Bayard wants neither to act violently nor to avoid acting. The cycle must be broken, for it is clear to him that if he does not deal with Redmond others will.

More important, however, than the two external demands made on Bay-ard is his inner need to maintain his own integrity. One sees this clearly in a significant exchange between him and his aunt:

Now it was Aunt Jenny who said "Bayard" twice before I heard her. "You are not going to kill him. All right."

"All right?" I said.

"Yes. All right. Don't let it be Drusilla, a poor hysterical young woman. And don't let it be him, Bayard, because he's dead now. And don't let it be George Wyatt and those others who will be waiting for you tomorrow morning. I know you are not afraid."

"But what good will that do?" I said. "What good will that do? . . . I must live with myself, you see."

"Then it's not just Drusilla? Not just him? Not just George Wyatt and Jefferson?"

"No," I said. (p. 276)

Faulkner, like Aeschylus, achieves resolution of the dilemma by rising above both demands in a symbolic gesture: Bayard goes to Jefferson to face his father's murderer unarmed. Redmond, faced with his moral courage, is unable to kill him and must admit the futility of further violence. He leaves town defeated. Thus Bayard acts, acts with courage, and, while maintaining his own self-respect, frees himself, Redmond and even his father's men from the necessity of further killing. He has done all that needs to be done.

Wyatt and Colonel Sartoris' men have functioned throughout like a Greek chorus, standing behind Drusilla with the demand for blood. ("I seemed . . . to watch myself enter the scene which she had postulated like another actor while in the background for a chorus Wyatt and the others stood . . .") (p. 269). But, like the Furies, they come to recognize not only the rightness of Bayard's action but its moral superiority. "I wouldn't have done it that way myself," Wyatt says to Bayard. "I'd a shot at him once anyway. But that's your way or you wouldn't have done it. . . . Maybe you're right, maybe there has been enough killing in your family without—Come on" (p. 289). And Drusilla, too, despite her insane desire for blood is forced to admit Bayard's superior courage. When he returns from Jefferson, he finds in his room a sprig of verbena, symbol of courage: "the single sprig of it . . . filling the room, the dusk, the evening with the odor which she said you could smell alone above the smell of horses" (p. 293). Thus Bayard has not rejected the demands of his society, but, as Cleanth Brooks says, has transcended them "in a complex action that honors the community's demand that he should call his father's assassin to account, while at the same time acknowledging the higher law embodied in 'Thou shalt not kill.' "[7] Like Aeschylus, Faulkner has harmonized antinomies: social and religious claims meet in morality.

Let me now return to Volpe's first statement that Faulkner has given *The Unvanquished* "the framework of Greek Tragedy." If the *Oresteia* were tragedy, so might be *The Unvanquished;* but, ultimately, neither is. The *Oresteia* begins in tragedy but ends as comedy, or, better, as a *commedia.* I use this term in Dante's sense, who justified calling his great work a *commedia* because it moved from darkness to light. The *Oresteia,* too, moves from darkness to light, so that its final affirmation is different from the starker, more defiant affirmation of tragedy.

The movement of *The Unvanquished* is more complicated. The novel is a *Bildungsroman* in which the style and tone of each episode fit the particular stage of Bayard's development: from the romantic, comic innocence of "Ambuscade" to the bitter realism of "Vendée." Through the penultimate episode, the movement is from light to dark, from the innocence of childhood to the knowledge of evil, violence and death. "An Odor of Verbena" reverses this movement: Bayard's courageous action leads out of the darkness of retributive violence into the light of a higher moral understanding. As the *Eumenides* transforms the *Oresteia* into a *divina commedia,* so "An Odor of Verbena" concludes *The Unvanquished* as a humanistic *commedia,* an affirmation of the

viability of non-violent courage to face and defeat the demand for a "succinct
and formal violence." This affirmation entitles it to be called Faulkner's
Oresteia.

1. *Selected Essays,* 3rd ed. (London, 1951), p. 15.
2. Cf. Werner Jaeger, *Paideia,* I (New York, 1943), p. 237.
3. Cf. *The Eumenides,* 490–565, tr. and ed. Richmond Lattimore (New York, 1942), pp. 170–72.
4. *Form and Meaning in Drama* (London, 1956), pp. 57–58.
5. *A Reader's Guide to William Faulkner* (New York, 1964), p. 83.
6. *The Unvanquished* (New York, 1938).
7. *William Faulkner: The Yoknapatawpha Country* (New Haven, Conn., 1963), p. 89. Cf. also Hyatt Waggoner, *William Faulkner: From Jefferson to the World* (Lexington, Ky., 1959), Ch. 8.

THE THEME AND STRUCTURE
OF FAULKNER'S *THE HAMLET*

T. Y. GREET

WILLIAM FAULKNER'S novel *The Hamlet* has received less critical attention
and, perhaps, less critical intelligence than any other of his major works. The
reasons for this neglect are rather easily stated. Published in 1940, Faulkner's
only significant novel between *Absalom, Absalom!* in 1936 and *Go Down,
Moses* in 1942, *The Hamlet* differs considerably from the novels of the "major
phase," 1929-1936. It comes at a point in the development of the Yoknapatawpha Cycle when the early conflict between legend and reality which so disturbed Quentin Compson had been largely resolved, and it is concerned with
themes that had earlier been of peripheral interest. It presents as protagonists
a class of Yoknapatawphans who are relative newcomers to the cycle. These
things together—the lessening of tension and the use of new material—are
reflected in the unique tone of *The Hamlet,* which led Malcolm Cowley to
entitle his review of the novel "Faulkner By Daylight."[1] Further, since the
novel is leisurely in its narrative method and relatively lucid in its style, it does

Reprinted with permission from *PMLA,* September, 1957, pp. 775-90.

not at first glance seem to demand or merit the sort of exhaustive readings which have been given, say, to *The Sound and the Fury*. Finally, with the major exception of Robert Penn Warren, almost none of the critics has been willing to recognize the book as a novel at all. Cowley speaks of its structure as that of "beads on a string."[2] John Arthos calls the book Faulkner's "most remarkable writing" but adds that it "falls into at least four separate stories . . . there is no real unity."[3] O'Connor, Howe, Campbell and Foster have all dealt with and appreciated various aspects of the novel but it remains the chief enigma of the cycle.[4]

This brief review of the criticism suggests some of the problems raised by *The Hamlet* and indicates the value, first, of attempting to place the novel in the geographical and thematic context of the Yoknapatawpha Cycle. To suggest that the dwellers of Frenchman's Bend have not been treated earlier in the cycle is to err in fact if not in principle. The Snopes family appears as early as the Civil War (Ab in *The Unvanquished*) and as late as 1929 (Senator Clarence in *Sanctuary*), so that the narrative of Flem Snopes's ascendancy in *The Hamlet* has ramifications extending both backward and forward into the cycle.[5] As for the setting, the state of *The Hamlet*, with its piney hills and red bluffs, is isolated almost as if by Snopesian design. The people of the Bend, with few exceptions, are "rednecks" and sharecroppers, ready victims of whichever Snopes or Varner is, for the season, providing them "furnishings." In Frenchman's Bend, Faulkner has created a "control condition" where Flem can practice his wiles before moving on to the less susceptible society of Jefferson.

The milieu of *The Hamlet*, though it differs from that of Faulkner's other works, is nonetheless part and parcel of Yoknapatawpha County, and the same is true of the novel as it relates thematically to the cycle. After disposing in *Absalom, Absalom!* of Quentin Compson's tortured search for reality, Faulkner turned from his major theme, that of man's relations with himself, to a minor aspect of that theme, the problem of man's relations to the land. The years from 1936 to "The Bear" in 1942 are in a sense transitional ones during which Faulkner seems to have been formulating the credo of Isaac McCaslin, many of whose ideas are implicit in *The Hamlet*. A sense of the richness and inviolability of the land pervades much of Faulkner's earlier work, especially the Indian stories, *Absalom, Absalom!* and *Old Man*, but not until *The Hamlet* does it become the dominant interest. Here, in the symbols of Eula and the cow, the conflict between Flem and Ratliff, Faulkner relates the minor theme most significantly to the major one. Only as he learns properly to value emotion, to venerate nature, will man recover his integrity and achieve a meaningful relationship with his fellows.

That the novel is itself a part of the greater unity of the cycle is thus clear, and it is now possible to refute such comments as those of Cowley and Arthos by relating the apparently diverse elements of the novel to each other. Robert Penn Warren in an early study of the book provides the first and, perhaps, most cogent defense of its structural integrity: "The structure of the book depends on the intricate patterning of contrasts, for instance the contrast of the Flem-Eula story with the Houston-wife story. . . . Flem stands outside the scale which runs from idiot to Houston, from groping animalism to secret poetry; in his cunning, he stands beyond appetite, passion, pride, fidelity, exploiting all of these things."[6] The development of the novel is governed, however, by a yet more significant contrast, that between reason and emotion. This conflict, of recurrent interest in American literature at least since Melville and Hawthorne, has been implicit in other works of Faulkner as well. Jason IV in *The Sound and the Fury* is made despicable largely because he possesses none of the compassion which gains our sympathy for the ineffectual Quentin. Even Isaac McCaslin fails at last because he has forgotten all he ever knew about love,[7] and again and again, as between Chick Mallison and Gavin Stevens, Faulkner's sympathies lie chiefly with children, with women, with "primitives" who retain in its most elemental degree the ability to respond with sincere emotion.

In still later works, especially *Requiem for a Nun* and *A Fable,* this theme has been so dominant as almost to obscure art, and it is in *The Hamlet* that it receives, though obliquely, its fullest and most effective treatment. One may think of the structure of the novel as a single, undeviating line opposed and crossed by many, always fore-shortened, lesser lines. The central line denotes Flem's rise, his progress along a coldly rational plane, "beyond appetite," from a clerkship in Varner's store to his victory over Ratliff. The opposing lines, ineffectual but sharply drawn, indicate those points at which Ratliff, Flem's only possible antagonist, attempts to forestall or mitigate the Snopes influence. Finally, the lines which rise from and return to the center denote actions stemming from passions foreign to Flem, actions which, nobly or violently conceived, prove futile when they come in contact with the rational plane. A concept of this sort leads, of course, to oversimplification, but the reading which follows will attempt to show how symbol, style, and tone serve to transform morality into art.

One of the primary sources of the critical confusion *The Hamlet* has caused is apparently its division into four books of approximately equal length and of rather sharply contrasting tones. Book I, which describes the arrival of Ab and Flem, the Varners' intimidation and Flem's symbolic ascension to

Will's barrel chair, is the lightest and most objectively written of the four. These qualities result from the predominance in the first book of the point of view of V.K. Ratliff, whose function in the novel is a double one, that of participant and observer-commentator. Faulkner's characterization of him as a man "affable, courteous, anecdotal and impenetrable" with his "shrewd brown face"[8] may well be supplemented by Constance Rourke's description of "Yankee peddlar": "The Yankee was never passive, not the cracker-box philosopher seated in some dim interior, uttering wisdom before a ring of quiet figures; he was noticeably out in the world; it was a prime part of his character to be 'a-doin'. But though he often pulled strings, always made shrewd or caustic comments . . . he was seldom deeply involved in situations; even his native background was meagerly drawn. . . . Though he talked increasingly his monologues still never brimmed over into personal revelation."[9]

That these details are so readily applicable to Ratliff makes him one with such classic American humorists as Sam Slick, Seba Smith, and Sut Lovingood. Critics have found him influenced chiefly by G.W. Harris' Sut and Augustus B. Longstreet's *Georgia Scenes*. Investigation of both these sources shows, however, that the influences are only general and suggests that attention might best be given to the nature rather than the genesis of Ratliff's humor.[10] In the first book of the novel he has two excellent opportunities to practice his forte, the humorous narrative, when he describes Ab's first triumph over Major de Spain and his later defeat at the hands of Pat Stamper in a horse trade. The first and more immediately significant story is related to Jody Varner as he rides confidently to Ab's with a rent contract. Ratliff is seeking to bait Jody and the structure and tone of the narrative are clearly purposeful.

As Jody glares down in "protuberant and speechless horror," Ratliff seizes on every detail which will dehumanize Ab. If his portrait of the Snopeses is no less "cruel" than his effort to intimidate Jody, it is continually lightened by comic devices of style and method. The circumlocution and litotes are harrowing: "Well . . . I don't know as I would go on record as saying he set ere a one of them afire. . . . You might say that fire seems to follow him around, like dogs follows some folks." Ab's daughters become grotesque, "strapping girls," not simply "like a pair of heifers," but in a comic extension and reversal of the figure, "like a pair of heifers just a little too valuable to hit hard with a stick" (14, 16). The pace of the narrative is slow, and Jody champs helplessly as Ratliff delights in his hyperboles, rustic comparisons, and comic juxtapositions. These and the other devices, characteristic of such humorists as Twain and Longstreet, are couched in an idiom reminiscent of Huck Finn's and Sut

Lovingood's, greatly moderated, of course. The whole tone of Ratliff's dis-
course is, in fact, colored by the vocabulary, the area of comparisons, and the
grammatical accuracy to which he is restricted in expressing his keen insights.
The manner of his speech as much as its matter lends to his reports and
comments the veracity which gives them value.

In his second anecdotal narrative, of Ab's being duped by Pat Stamper,
Ratliff, aware now of Flem's threat, seems almost regretful of his first characterization of Ab. Reminiscently, and in a tone different from that of the De
Spain story, Ratliff speaks of Ab in the days before he was "soured," when he
relished a sharp trade and was capable of a certain resignation when defeated.
This story has been related by O'Connor to "The Horse Swap" of *Georgia
Scenes,* but it is in tone and structure far superior to its possible source. The
second of many short stories to be incorporated into *The Hamlet,* this has
undergone less revision than any other and may well have provided the sharpest early conception of Ratliff's manner.[11] In its present context the story is
chiefly important for its introduction of at least two elements which later are
to be significant. At two points in the novel horses act to determine the actions
or fates of characters: Houston's wife is killed by a stallion, and the havoc of
Book IV is wrought by Flem's "spotted ponies." Here the horse is an object
purely of humor, free of menace, and of no symbolic value beyond that of
representing a dominant passion which sets up a conflict between Ab and his
wife. She herself is the second significant element. As Warren notes, much of
the novel is concerned with the lives of various pairs of "lovers," and Ab and
Mrs. Snopes are the first of them. Ab in his trading uses money which she has
set aside for a cream separator, just as Henry Armstid is later to use his wife's
meager savings to buy one of Flem's ponies; but not even a distaff Snopes can
be expected to show Mrs. Armstid's resignation, and Ab's wife caps the
comedy by swapping the cow for a separator which she can operate only with
borrowed milk. The pattern, then, is one of parallels and, more importantly,
contrasts. Flem's touch has yet to "sour" events. Only with his emergence does
the horse become a destroyer, the wife a helpless victim.

Ratliff is quick to perceive that it is not Ab's headstrong pride or his
vengefulness which must be feared. Rather it is Flem's utter lack of sensibility,
his irresistible and amoral logic. When he returns after an absence of some six
months to discover that a plague of Snopeses has descended on the Bend,
Ratliff seeks to counter Flem's wiles. If one pauses, however, to look at his
opponent, the fact of his only moderate success will be better understood.
Campbell and Foster have pointed out the significance of the Snopes names
(104-105), and in image after grotesque image Faulkner creates about Flem

and the rest an impression of animal greed and amorality. Flem "lurked among the ultimate shadows" of the store "with a good deal of the quality of a spider of that bulbous blond omnivorous though non-poisonous species" (66-67). I. O. has "a talkative weasel's face" and a "voice voluble and rapid and meaningless like something talking to itself about nothing in a deserted cavern" (74).

Such images, many of them extended to comic extremes, reveal the essential vacuousness of those to whom they apply. In his continual mention of Flem's costume, especially the machine-made bow tie, Faulkner seems to be striving for the same tone (66).[12] These things together, the brutality and depthlessness, suggest cardinal facts about the Snopeses with the exceptions of Eck, Ike, and Mink. One need not look to them for an awareness of conventional restraints or for any mode of conduct motivated by other than animal opportunism. Had Ratliff acknowledged these facts in time, he might have triumphed. Even Jody Varner, however, himself shrewd, is able to say as late as Book IV that St. Elmo Snopes, who may stand as a symbol for the tribe, is "worse than a goat," *likely* to devour the Bend, store, gin, and all (364).

Ratliff achieves little success with his first counterattack, which oddly enough utilizes goats. Thus Book I, dominated by his detached ironies, the arid setting, the sterile interplay of calculating minds, ends with Flem alone at the annual settlement, boarding at Varner's and, most importantly, symbolically enthroned in Will's barrel chair at Old Frenchman's Place. Already about his seat can be heard the distant rumble of the passions to which his advent will give rise. For the first time one learns that there is a conflict between Mink and Jack Houston over a cow that has wandered into the latter's fields. But we live in a rational world and are not greatly concerned. Flem has won, but so far he has broken only man's law; nature is still inviolate.

The undeviating line of Flem's rise is now fixed, but it is not until Book II that the full significance of his rational victory is made clear. Earlier Faulkner has mentioned Jody's sister, Eula, who impassively dominates the second book and, transformed into a symbol, becomes central to the meaning of the novel. At her second appearance she suggests "some symbology out of the old Dionysic times," and immediately the tone of the novel changes (107). Jody, his sister's and, unwittingly, nature's protector, says of her that "Soon as she passes anything in long pants she begins to give off something. You can smell it!" (112) And this aura of fecundity permeates not only the dry air of the Bend but the style of the novel.

Little summary of Eula's comatose career is necessary. When she is eight, Jody insists on the girl's entering the village school and persists in his endeavor until her quality, like that of "the very goddesses in Homer and Thucydides," has transformed the "wooden desks and benches" of the school "into a grove of Venus," the hapless teacher, Labove, into a satyr (128, 130). Eula in the schoolroom abrogates "the whole long sum of human thinking and suffering which is called knowledge, education, wisdom" (131). But Labove, even as late as his third year of teaching, hesitates to go with his graduating law class to a brothel because "He still believed . . . the white magic of Latin degrees, which was an actual counterpart of the old monk's faith in his wooden cross" (133). Irresistibly, though he knows it is to be his "Gethsemane . . . and his Golgotha too," Labove is drawn back by Eula to the Bend. Under her influence his transformation into satyr begins: his legs are described as "haired-over like those of a faun" (134).

His iron will does not break, however, until the end of the sixth year when Labove becomes aware of Eula's symbolic significance, seeing the "fine land rich and fecund and foul and eternal and impervious" deeded to a husband who will be "a dwarf, a gnome, without glands or desire" (134-135). Goaded by this sense of waste, Labove finally assaults Eula, but fails because at the instant of his act "something furious and cold, or [of?] repudiation and bereavement both, blew in him." Reason, morality, reassert themselves; his violence is made meaningless as Eula dismisses him: "Stop pawing me . . . You old headless horseman Ichabod Crane" (137-138).

This is in 1890 and for three years, the center of an ever more mature, more intensely watchful circle of admirers, she remains inviolate. Then appears Labove's antithesis, Hoake McCarron, the embodiment, in his dashing buggy, of the aggressive male principle. James G. Frazer points out that the earth goddess, "she who fertilizes nature must herself be fertile, and to be that she must necessarily have a male consort," and observes that the "marriage of the goddess is always a central rite."[13] Hoake is an admirably chosen consort, and Faulkner's treatment of Eula's seduction gives it certainly a central status. If rationality pervades the first book, then utter moon-struck madness is the tone of the second, where in passages rich with suggestive diction, assonance, and image Faulkner describes the frustration of Eula's suitors, who at last succeed in waylaying her with Hoake, breaking his arm in the melee. Later, symbolically, Eula must support his injured side to facilitate her ritual impregnation.

After the relief of a comic scene which reveals the Varners' total unawareness of the true nature of their tragedy, Flem's triumph ensues. Hoake, fearful of convention, has fled; the Varners, bound by it, must find a husband; and Will, in the central irony of the novel, chooses the sterile Flem, even deeding him Old Frenchman's Place and purchasing the wedding license. The earth goddess has been sacrificed to the pagan and from this point Eula's face is not only beautiful but "damned"—damned by the rational blindness which does not perceive, in the words of Ike McCaslin, that the land is no man's to bequeath to another, that as soon as anyone discovered "he could sell it for money, on that instant it ceased ever to have been his . . . and the man who bought it bought nothing."[14]

That Faulkner intends Eula's seduction to have great significance is clear from the elegiac lament which follows her marriage. The Bend becomes a village "without grace, forsaken, yet which wombed once by chance and accident one blind seed of the spendthrift Olympian ejaculation and did not even know it, without tumescence [the word hints at a miraculous birth] conceived and bore." The nymph and the symbolic buggies are departed and there remains only "the word, the dream and the wish of all male under the sun capable of harm" (169). This is the crux of the novel, that the favor of the gods—Love, Fertility—has been sacrificed to rational opportunism.

The union of Anchises with Venus produced Aeneas and inaugurated a golden age. The daughter of Eula and Hoake is barely mentioned in the novel, and of their union comes only tragedy. Ratliff, returning at the end of the "doomed and dying" summer of Eula's departure with Flem for Texas, enters a wasteland where "the very hot, vivid air . . . seemed to be filled with the slow laborious plaint of laden wagons." His regret is bitter that Eula could not have been "the unscalable sierra . . . for no man to conquer scot-free or even to conquer at all," and he is outraged at "the useless squandering . . . as though the gods themselves had funnelled all the concentrated bright wet-slanted unparadised June onto a dung-heap, breeding pismires" (181-182).

Ratliff's humorous detachment, under the pressure of this awareness, has deserted him; but Constance Rourke note that "humor bears the closest relation to emotion," often "rising like a rebirth of feeling from dead levels after turmoil."[15] Thus Ratliff's bitterness is suddenly transformed, and he conjures a vision of Flem in Hell, comically triumphant over Satan himself. But this humor is that of a new Ratliff, no longer gentle in his ironies. In his fantasy he seizes on the elements of the Snopes-Varner conflict and incorporates them with embellishments into an extended and accurate analogy which serves as a turning point on the humorous level as Eula's marriage does on the serious one.[16]

Flem's victory—from tenancy, to barrel chair, to Satan's throne—is now complete, and he disappears from the scene during the whole of Book II. The Fisher King is gone and life in the wasteland seeks to renew itself, but the passions which rise during the summer of his absence are perverse, virulent, destructive. The vague threat to sanity posed by the conflict between Mink Snopes and Jack Houston at the end of the first book breaks in Book III into violence, after Mink loses a suit for the recovery of his cow. Ratliff is at the store when I. O., Mink's self-styled attorney, emerges, offering him only the comfort of typically vapid aphorisms. Mink turns on him with a fierce obscenity, "—t," an epithet which suggests the heightened tone of the events that center about the cow.

For instance, Ratliff, still rankled by the sacrifice of Eula, seizes at once on I. O.'s idiom for the most scathing comment he has yet made: "Snopes can come and Snopes can go, but Will Varner looks like he is going to snopes forever. Or Varner will Snopes forever—take your pick. What is it the fellow says? off with the old and on with the new; the old job at the old stand, maybe a new fellow doing the jobbing but it's the same old stern getting reamed out?" (185). Here, in his first use of word play and sharp irony, Ratliff abandons humor and deliberately seizes on wit as his weapon. This form, forged by the critical intelligence, untempered by sympathy, now becomes his favorite mode, a fact which serves to guage his increasing bitterness and frustration. Thus all is now distorted, and when Ratliff's tirade is interrupted by a bid to watch some salacious occurrence in Mrs. Littlejohn's barn, our expectations are of the worst.

This event, the nature of which is revealed only slowly, has almost the significance of Eula's seduction and marriage in the thematic development of the novel. Hoake, the goddess' consort, is with sudden and tragic irony replaced by Ike Snopes, idiot; and the "shape of love" is transformed grotesquely into that of a cow. But the ironies here stem not only from diminution. As Faulkner develops one of his most brilliant symbols, Ike's relation with the cow becomes a metaphor of love, sharply contrasting with Flem's "courtship" of Eula.

Ike woos the cow at length, but only wins her after rescuing her from the inferno of a brush fire. Even in this, however, he is almost thwarted as a fear-crazed horse materializes out of the flames, "the wild eyes, the yellow teeth, the long gullet red with ravening gleeful triumph . . . the fierce dragon-reek of its passage, blasting at his hair and garments" (197). Four times, as Ike moans with pain, the horse rushes out at him, but he braves the monster, until he is finally discovered by Houston, who cries furiously to the cow, "Git on home, you damned whore!" The word shocks us into a rational perception and emphasizes by contrasts all that follows. On his way home Ike loses a coin which Houston has given him, but he refuses to search for it, this un-Snopes-like rejection marking him as a courtly lover who accepts no material compensation. Immediately afterward, however, he returns and leads the cow from her stall. He has braved the dragon and in the idyll which follows he rejoices in his reward.

Not only do these events suggest the medieval romance but so does the tone in which they are treated. Eula was often described in bovine terms, but the cow is Astarte, "maiden, meditant, shame-free"; and Ike, weaving for her clumsy garlands, is devout priest and swain together. The style, purple as any in modern prose, has the richness of Spenser. Campbell and Foster note this episode as being a striking example of Faulkner's "surrealistic" humor and point out that the style, so much richer than its objective content, adds much to this effect (97-98). But the style does even more. It elevates the lovers again into symbols, encouraging the reader to seek in myth and legend for its rationale. Indeed these two lovers, "orginal, in the womb-dimension, the unavoidable first and the inescapable last, eyeless," seem at times archetypes, but the style has a surer justification (212). In the wasteland any love, though it conventionally be a perverse one, is a promise of redemption, worth a prothalamion.

The quality and intent of this style are apparent as Faulkner describes Ike's walk to a farm from which he pilfers feed, when he observed

that dawn, light . . . is from the earth itself suspired. Roofed by the woven canopy of blind annealing grass-roots . . . dark in the blind dark of time's silt and rich refuse—the constant and unslumbering anonymous worm-glut . . . —Troy's Helen and the nymphs and the snoring mitred bishops . . . —it wakes, upseeping . . . first, root; then frond by frond, from whose escaping tips like gas it rises and disseminates and stains the sleep-fast earth with drowsy insect-murmur; then . . . it upward bursts . . . Far below, the gauzy hemisphere treads with herald cock . . . Vanes on steeples groove the southwest wind, and fields for plowing, since sunset married to the bedded and unhorsed plow, spring into half-furrowed sight . . . Then the sun itself . . . The silent copper roar fires the drenched grass and flings long before him his shadow prone for the vain eluded treading; the earth mirrors his antic and constant frustration . . . (207-208).

The poetic quality here—derived chiefly from parallelisms, repetitions, periods, and assonances—establishes the emotional rhythm of the entire idyll. The primordial quality of the moment before dawn is conveyed chiefly through evocations of darkness, lethargy, and enriching decay. The classical and medieval allusions especially suggest the permanence and fecundity of nature until, after the carefully wrought, richly detailed transition, they give way to the sun and bucolic reality. The implications of fertility are then made explicit, so that the progress is from slumbering potency to inchoate and, finally, aroused desire. The symbolic and objective levels of Ike's experience are perfectly merged.

But this love, the most elemental and pure emotion of the novel, is, like Eula's, truncated. After Houston recovers the cow, he takes it to Mrs. Littlejohn as a gift for Ike. It is not long until Lump, Ike's uncle, has pulled a plank off the barn and it is to this vantage point that Ratliff has ealier been invited. He shows deep concern, and Mrs. Littlejohn retorts, "So that's it . . . It's all right for it to be, but folks mustn't know it, see it?" Ratliff's reply epitomizes the conflict of the novel: "Was, . . . because it's finished now. . . . You don't need to tell me he aint got nothing else. I know that. . . . just as I know that the reason I aint going to leave him have what he does have is simply because I am strong enough to keep him from it. I am stronger than him. Not righter. Not any better, maybe. But just stronger" (226-227). Mrs. Littlejohn suggests that Ratliff is guilty of the same fear of convention whicn has sacrificed Eula; though acknowledging the injustice of his attitude, he nonetheless embraces it. Ratliff, the rational, the conventional, overbears Ike, the passionate, the natural. Ratliff is as humane, perhaps as good, as a man may be, but the ravished land will be redeemed by an act of love, not of righteousness.[17] Rain is described but once in *The Hamlet*: it falls on Ike and his beloved (210-211).

Ratliff achieves his purpose through I. O., who fears the effects of a family scandal on his position as teacher. In a comic travesty on the workings of the rational mind, one sees Snopes parrying Snopes in a ridiculous effort to preserve honor. More seriously, the cow, "the shape of love," has become merchandise to be haggled over, and we have on the comic level the same moral blindness Mrs. Littlejohn has condemned: "The Snopes name. . . . That's got to be kept pure as marble" (231-234).

This thwarting of Ike's passion has its parallel in the bitter outcome of Mink Snopes' murder of Jack Houston. Earlier, Ratliff has said of Mink "this here seems to be a different kind of Snopes like a cottonmouth is a different kind of snake" (104). But he is wrong. Mink, like Houston, is virile and proud; both men are capable of creative action, and it is only within a Snopesian context that their passions lead ironically to self-destruction. This episode is chiefly significant in that during Mink's ordeal, nature, twice violated, becomes actively hostile. It seeks not only to obstruct Mink but to inform against him. First, of course, there is the hound; then the shotgun is cast up from the slough into which Mink has thrown it; and, finally, after he believes the hound dead, circling buzzards seem intent on betraying him.

Still, there is a richness here, even though it be somber. After Mink's imprisonment to await trial, nature, in the bonds of winter, becomes sterile. At no other point in the novel is winter described, but now much is made of it. It is "the winter from which the people as they became older were to establish time and date events," and trains, unpeopled, rushed "without purpose through the white and rigid solitude" (296, 301).

Here the novel reaches its point of deepest negation. During the summer that follows, however, this bitterness is moderated by the injection, again, of frontier humor, by the lessening of tensions, and by Ratliff's admission of defeat at Flem's game. In May, Flem arrives from Texas with a string of wild ponies. These animals and their sale dominate the fourth book and are important because, given demonic proportions, they act as catalysts and serve to clarify two aspects of the theme: the destructive nature of purely acquisitive instincts and the susceptibility of acquisitive man to rational manipulation.

The horse has already been seen as a symbolic barrier between Ab and his wife, Ike and the cow. Lucy Pate has been killed by the stallion which Houston bought "as if for a wedding present to her," almost as if "that blood and bone and muscles represented that polygamous and bitless masculinity which he had relinquished" (246-247). Now these incidents become more meaningful. For every man in the Bend the ponies are a fatal temptation. Ratliff alone demurs, "You folks can buy them critters if you want to. But me, I'd just as soon buy a tiger or a rattlesnake."

Ratliff's skepticism is immediately justified as the ponies become a center of catastrophe. The most important injury, if we are finally to understand the horse as symbol, is done the Armstid family. Henry Armstid so desires one of the animals that he deprives his "chaps" of food that he may purchase it and cruelly flogs his wife for having failed in its capture. Later, when the ponies break free, Henry is trampled, his leg fractured; but his fate is less significant than the intensity of his desire. It is not necessary to see the horse, as do Russell Roth and Phyllis Hirshleifer, as a symbol of abnormal sexuality.[18] When one recalls how Henry and his wife, after the death of a mule, were forced to spell each other in the traces, he recognizes that in the economy of the Bend ownership of a horse represents not only affluence but a factor of survival as well. Further, to outwit one's opponents in a horse trade is to gain the immediate respect of one's peers. Corollary to this is the fact that to own and trade in horses is a purely masculine prerogative: that "bitless masculinity" which is relinquished not only in marriage but in subjugation of any sort. For these reasons, and not because they are a "symbolic disclosure of misdirected sexual energy," the horses are demonized as agents of destruction (Roth, 204).

The auction culminates in a violent competition for the possession of a pony, a last token of irresponsible individuality. Amid all the hysteria, however, the fecund imperturbability of setting serves continually to recall the symbolic values of Eula and the cow. The night of the ponies' escape is brilliant with moonlight which earlier, for Houston and Lucy, had possessed a magic quality: "they observed the old country belief that the full moon of April guaranteed the fertilizing act" (248). Near Mrs. Littlejohn's is a pear tree "now in full and frosty bloom, the twigs and branches . . . standing motionless and perpendicular above the horizontal boughs like the separated and upstreaming hair of a drowned woman" (316). After Armstid's accident, Ratliff and the others go to Varner's to fetch Will. There Eula opens an upstairs window and looks down upon them: "to those below what Brunhilde, what Rhinemaiden on what spurious river-rock of papier-mache, what Helen returned to what topless and shoddy Argos, waiting for no one." (349-350).

Later, returning to Mrs. Littlejohn's the men observe the pear tree: " 'Look at that tree,' Varner said. 'It ought to make this year, sho'." Then he adds that "A moon like this is good for every growing thing outen the full moon after she had done caught [as Mrs. Varner had when carrying Eula], it would be a gal" (351).

In the pear tree a "mockingbird's idiot reiteration pulsed and pearled," and with the addition of this detail Faulkner's intention becomes clear. In a series of synecdoches the whole theme of the novel seems to be implied. The moon pours its magic rays onto a land where, for the moment, man is given up to the pursuit of a bootless freedom. The pear tree is like a drowned woman sleeping, but it is sure to "make," suffer a sea change. Eula, however damned, remains inviolate, a goddess supreme over a sterile domain. The bird's song is an "idiot reiteration," to which the pear tree is insensible, just as Eula is insensible to "that man," just as the earth is insensible to the "thin and urgent cries and the brief and fading bursts of galloping hooves." Yet, Will pauses amid the chaos to remark on the burgeoning of nature, to recount a fertility legend, and we realize that the blight will somehow pass. the earth endures and in man's acknowledgment of this lies his hope for restoration.[19]

Essentially, *The Hamlet* culminates in the stampede of the ponies: from the ensuing chaos only Flem and the land emerge unaltered. The suit against Flem which is brought by Armstid and the Tulls miscarries because of a legal technicality and Lump's perjury. In sharp contrast Mink, who has proudly refused counsel, comes to trial in Jefferson and is convicted of murder. There is another sort of culmination, too, in Mink's words as he cries into the crowded courtroom, "Is Flem Snopes in this room? Tell that son of a bitch—" (382). Again an epithet crystallizes our reactions and, this time, prepares us for the final act, Ratliff's own fall.

So far in the novel Ratliff's involvement, which followed Eula's marriage, has been in minor "holding actions." After the injustice to Mrs. Armstid, Bookwright half expects Ratliff to return her money as he had Ike's, and his rejoinder is the bitterest of the novel: " 'I could have,' he said. 'But I didn't. . . . Besides, I wasn't protecting a Snopes from Snopeses; I wasn't even protecting a people from a Snopes. I was protecting something that . . . wouldn't know how to hurt no man even if it would . . . I never made them Snopeses and I never made the folks that can't wait to bare their backsides to them. I could do more, but I won't. I won't, I tell you!' " (367). Ratliff is making here his sharpest rejection of human sympathy. Later, Gavin Stevens' rational skepticism leads almost to tragedy, which is averted only by Charles Mallison's emotional intervention. Ratliff is a transitional figure; his faith in man shaken, he begins to abjure responsibility, foreshadowing, perhaps, Isaac McCaslin's withdrawal. Ratliff's pride, however, proves of a sort which precedes a fall. Himself ensnared, his sympathies will be renewed and deepened.

Ratliff's purchase of Old Frenchman's Place is made plausible not only by his loss of detachment. Afflicted already with a fatal acquisitiveness, he too readily trusts Will Varner's judgment. Varner formerly spent much of his time sitting alone at the Place, as if guarding something, and Ratliff "declined to believe that Varner ever had been or ever would be stuck with anything; that if . . . he kept it, it was too valuable to sell" (179). Also he had become infected by Henry's madness and the general atmosphere of irrational excitement. By his naïve negotiations with Flem, his superstitious use of a divining rod, his hysterical digging, Ratliff shows himself for a time transformed by money-lust and guilt: they "slept again . . . while noon came and the creeping and probing golden sun at whose touch they turned and shifted as though in impotent nightmare flight from that impalpable . . . burden" (411). It is this guilt, however, Ratliff's self-awareness, which permits reason once more to function. Perceiving Flem's arch deception and almost as if relieved that his turn has come and gone, Ratliff recovers his equanimity.

At the same time, thanks ironically to Ratliff's having deeded interest in a restaurant, Flem sets out for Jefferson, and only Henry remains as a grotesque reminder of the madness generated by the ponies. His emotion, perverted by deprivation and by Flem's injustice, has made him a notorious attraction. Henry digs himself "back into that earth which had produced him to be its born and fated thrall forever until he died," and as he does so, Flem pauses in his progress toward new conquests to contemplate the token of his first: Henry "got back into the trench and began to dig. Snopes turned his head and spat over the wagon wheel. He jerked the reins slightly. 'Come up,' he said" (420-421). This juxtaposition of Henry, the earth, and Flem objectifies the central irony toward which the novel has been directed: All men are thralls to the earth, but in his respect for his servitude lies man's chief hope of endurance through human sympathy and mutual respect.

This thesis is developed on two levels, the mythic and objective. On the primary level as major symbols stand Eula and the cow, while on the secondary are Flem and Ratliff; and out of the parallel and conflicting development of these levels the novel grows. Through the implication of symbolic event and style, Faulkner leads us to expect that Eula merits reverence as the embodiment of fertility. Proper understanding of this symbol demands, however, a sloughing off of such accretions as traditional morality and destructive individualism. Thus Labove fails because the instinctive rightness of his desire is repudiated by his overly developed rational will. Thus the horses rise again and again as barriers between man and woman, as sources of catastrophe.

The goddess is betrayed because she exists in a world predominantly self-conscious. Flem, whose utter lack of passion makes him irresistible on the rational level, can neither conceive of nor respect the values which Eula embodies. The Varners, though capable of pity and reverence, abet Flem in his corruption by sacrificing love on the sterile altar of conventional morality.

The result of this profanation is chaos. Eula is transformed into the cow and love becomes perverse; the fist fights of Eula's suitors become a murderous quarrel between Mink and Houston. Flem triumphs while Ike, Houston, and Mink, all capable of love, are deprived or destroyed. Even the earth, in the grip of winter, becomes sterile; and finally the humane, objective Ratliff shares the guilt of the Varners as he works the destruction of the cow, the last vestige in the land of "the shape of love."

These rich passions at rest, Flem returns to manipulate those which remain, offering the horse as a symbol of the self-respect which has been so damningly compromised. The consequent release of desire results in havoc, for Henry in madness. But now the moon-drenched earth gives promise of recovery, of endurance; the violence is but an "idiot repetition." With Ratliff's fall, justice, taking only Henry as its toll, seems to have worked itself out.

This didactic summary puts baldly ideas which Faulkner reveals only by indirection. Emphasis on theme and structure at the expense of the novel's many other facets has been the result of an effort to order apparent chaos. Most of all, Faulkner's humor has received less than due attention, though it is through humor—Ratliff's ironic comments, Faulkner's grandiose distortions —that the events of the novel are for the most part made acceptable. Humor states truth obliquely, leaving us to wonder whether it means what it says; it flanks our defenses so that often it is only later, with a degree of shock, that we concede its point. The development of *The Hamlet*, like that of *The Waste Land*, is contrapuntal. The myth gains immediacy from its juxtaposition with the contemporaneous, the rational; conversely, in a series of ironic contrasts, the contemporaneous derives meaning, universality, from its juxtaposition with myth. By indirection, Faulkner thus achieved in *The Hamlet*, to a higher degree than in any succeeding work, an effective union of art and morality.

1. *New Republic*, 102 (April 15, 1940), p. 510.

2. Introd., *The Portable Faulkner* (New York, 1949), p. 18.

3. "Ritual and Humor in the Writings of William Faulkner," *William Faulkner: Two Decades of Criticism*, Frederick J. Hoffman and Olga Vickery (eds) (East Lansing, Mich., 1951), p. 113.

4. Viola Hopkins, "Meaning and Form in Faulkner's *The Hamlet*," *Accent*, 15 (Spring 1955), pp. 125–144, provides an extended and provocative treatment.

5. Nor are the Snopeses the only persons from the Bend who are dealt with elsewhere. Suratt, who becomes Ratliff, is a companion of Bayard Sartoris and appears in several short stories. Cora and Vernon Tull, Bookwright, and the Armstids all play minor roles in other novels and, in a sense, the world of *As I Lay Dying* is that of *The Hamlet*. Faulkner's treatment of Flem and Eula in *The Town* has no appreciable bearing on my reading here of *The Hamlet*.

6. "The Snopes World," *Kenyon Review*, 3 (Spring 1941), p. 256.

7. "Delta Autumn," *Go Down, Moses* (New York, 1931), p. 363.

8. *The Hamlet* (New York, 1940), pp. 15–16. All subsequent references to the novel will appear in parentheses immediately following citations in the text.

9. *American Humor: A Study of the National Character* (New York, 1931), pp. 29–30.

10. William Van O'Connor, *The Tangled Fire of William Faulkner* (Minneapolis, 1954), is best on sources. John Arthos, "Ritual and Humor," and Harry M. Campbell and Ruel E. Foster, *William Faulkner* (Norman, Okla., 1951), are best on humor generally.

11. "Fool About a Horse," *Scribner's Magazine*, 100 (August 1936), pp. 80–86.

12. Suggestive also is Faulkner's description of I. O., who wears spectacles without lenses, a dickey, and a coat with shirt cuffs attached (229).

13. *The Golden Bough* (New York, 1937), I, p. 39; II, p. 129 ff.

14. "The Bear," *Go Down, Moses*, p. 257.

15. *American Humor*, p. 10.

16. It is worth noting that B. A. Botkin, *A Treasury of American Folk Humor* (New York, 1949), pp. 80–81, tells the story of a "Snopes" who went to Hell and was imprisoned under a washpot. Later, a visitor starting to lift it was stopped by the Devil's shouting. "Don't lift that pot! We have Old Man Cobb under there and if you let him out he'll foreclose a mortgage on all hell in the first crop season!"

17. Viola Hopkins views Ratliff's decision as an "act of conscience," which Faulkner sees as "one of the conditions of humanity." As she further points out, "Ratliff is certainly the chief spokesman and defendant of an ethical, humane tradition" ("Meaning and Form," pp. 135, 130); but I would suggest that his defensive attitude and Mrs. Littlejohn's comment justify my censure. Florence Leaver, "The Structure of *The Hamlet*," *Twentieth Century Literature*, (July 1955), pp. 77–84, holds Mrs, Littlejohn to be morally superior even to Ratliff.

18. "The Centaur and the Pear Tree," *Western Review*, 16 (Spring 1952), pp. 199–205; "As

Whirlwinds in the South," *Perspective,* 2 (Summer 1949), pp. 225–238.
  19. I have relied here, to some extent, on Roth. He, however, emphasizes the sexual implications of the symbolism, tending, perhaps, to distort its context. See also Harry M. Campbell, "Mr. Roth's Centaur and Faulkner's Symbolism," *Western Review,* 16 (Summer 1952), pp. 320–321.

THE "NORMALITY" OF SNOPESISM: UNIVERSAL THEMES IN FAULKNER'S *THE HAMLET*

JOSEPH GOLD

IN 1957 A literary scholar could write: "William Faulkner's novel *The Hamlet* has received less critical attention and, perhaps, less critical intelligence than any other of his major works."[1] Since that time little or nothing has appeared to alter the situation. All the criticism of *The Hamlet* that has so far appeared emphasizes either the symbolism and structure of the work, or the opposition of Flem and the villagers. It seems to me, however, that to see Snopesism as an alien and disastrous force of change in an otherwise sanguine world is to undermine the power of Faulkner's social criticism and the humanistic burden which I believe motivates the novel. It is necessary to see Snopesism as a product of its environment in order to comprehend the full significance of the Snopes idea wherever it occurs in Faulkner's fiction. The themes of *The Hamlet* are universal and we will miss them if we let our abhorrence of Flem blind us to the faults of those on whom he parasitically flourishes.

Although there has been ample criticism of Flem and his vices, there has been little said of Flem's compeers. To see Flem as a villainous exploiter of innocent country bumpkins is to misunderstand the novel. The people of Frenchman's Bend are basically self-interested. Although they are apparently strong in a sense of community, they are actually not prepared to involve themselves in the problems of others. This is made clear on several occasions. When Ratliff asks why the villagers have done nothing about Snopes, he receives the answer: " 'What could we do?' Tull said. 'It aint right. But it aint none of our business.' "[2] Later the villagers stand quietly by while Armstid and his wife are exploited by Flem and the Texan horse trader:

Reprinted with permission from *Wisconsin Studies in Contemporary Literature,* III (Winter 1962), 25–34.

"He aint no more despair than to buy one of them things," she said. "And us not but five dollars away from the poorhouse, he aint no more despair." The man turned upon her with the curious air of leashed, of dreamlike fury. *The others lounged along the fence in attitudes gravely inattentive, almost oblivious.*

(p. 332. Italics mine.)

But worse than their failure to act in opposition is their passive cooperation with Flem. This is illustrated by two events. Their own sublimated perversion enables Lump to use them in his exposure of Ike and the cow; their willingness to buy the Texas horses makes that business venture successful. Viola Hopkins is right in sensing some culmination of Flem's early career in the success of his horse auction, but she fails to point out that this is merely a symbolic revelation of his whole career.[3] Flem has finally become assured of the hamlet's weaknesses. The horse auction is a kind of chaotic pageant summarizing the whole history of social exploitation and divisiveness.

The evils revealed in the activities of the Snopeses are learned from the society out of which they grow. This is clearly understood by Ratliff who knew Ab when he was normal and kind and human. It is Ratliff who in the early part of *The Hamlet* persistently says of Ab, " 'He aint naturally mean. He's just soured.' " (p. 30) A variety of events have contributed to Ab's souring. He has not been strong enough to fully implement the evils he has learned. Ab is not evil or suspicious enough to outwit Pat Stamper in horse trading and he is defeated. The picture of society that is drawn by Ratliff in the retelling of "Fool About a Horse" is, in spite of the humor, one of cut-throat commercialism. Ab tries to cope with Stamper, but in a system of "democratic" capitalism only the fittest survive. Stamper is the representative of a society in which people are mainly occupied in dishonestly exchanging worthless objects. Materialism sets the standard for Ab and he learns his methods from his "betters." De Spain has built his big white house with "nigger sweat," and although this knowledge does not justify Ab's conduct in the matter of the expensive French rug, it at least explains it.

This account of Ab's history is more fully understood upon an examination of the Varners. The evil of the Snopeses is more formalized, more predictable than that of the Varners. The dehumanization of the race has gone one stage further with the ascendancy of Snopes, but the beginning of the process is clear in the tradition. The Varners are terrified and held thrall by the threat to their barn and this is some indication of their materialistic bondage. Pride and honor have disappeared here. The rise of Snopes and all the human suffering that follows can be directly attributed to Varner avarice. Will Varner's rise was presumably not very different from Flem's.

He was a farmer, a usurer, a veterinarian; Judge Benbow of Jefferson once said of him that a milder-mannered man never bled a mule or stuffed a ballot box. He owned most of the good land in the country and held mortgages on most of the rest. He owned the store and the cotton gin and the combined grist mill and blacksmith shop in the village proper and it was considered, to put it mildly, bad luck for a man of the neighborhood to do his trading or gin his cotton or grind his meal or shoe his stock anywhere else.

(pp. 5–6)

This account of Varner's character is further elaborated in *The Town*, where Will is described as "that tall lean choleric outrageous old brigand with his grim wife herself not church-ridden but herself running the local church she belonged to with the cold high-handedness of a wardboss, and his mulatto concubines. . . ."[4] He lives by only one principle, "that whatever Will Varner decided to do was right, and anybody in the way had damned well better beware."[5]

But the Varners make mistakes. Will Varner once bought a worthless piece of property, a mistake that Flem is never known to make. Varner makes a comment on the old Frenchman Place that is interesting in the light of Flem's subsequent use of it. He says, " 'But after all, I reckon I'll just keep what there is left of it, just to remind me of my one mistake. This is the only thing I ever bought in my life I couldn't sell to nobody.' " (p. 7) Flem is able to sell it because he is more capable than Will, not because Will does not want to resort to trickery. The salted mine is surely a piece of well-known chicanery, but it takes Flem to use it. The mistakes that Jody has always made in the store disappear when Flem takes over. This signifies the substitution of inhuman machine-like accuracy (with inhuman purposes) for human fallibility. The villagers prefer the errors of Jody, because they recognize the human bond between him and themselves. In Flem they are dealing with an uncontrollable and incomprehensible force.

Bur the Varners are not "good" men being exploited by "bad." They illustrate the process culminating in Flem and must take responsibility for engendering and assisting Snopesism. Flem is not a God-sent plague come as a judgment upon men. He is man-made, a curse that man brings upon himself like treeless land or worn-out soil, self-deprivation through greed. When Jody is trying to find some benefit in his enforced relationship with Flem, he makes some revealing comments on the Varner system:

'Say his benefits is the same benefits as the fellow that's paying some of his kinfolks a salary to protect his business; say it's a business where now and then (and you know it as well as I do,' Jody says) '—say benefits is always coming up that the fellow that's going to get the benefits just as lief not be actively mixed up in himself, . . .'

(p. 31)

Jody is right in sensing that he and Flem have a great deal in common, but he underestimates the Snopeses, who are too ambitious to remain mere assistants to the Varners.

The Varners are not alone in suffering Faulkner's indictment. Even Ratliff represents a society which is ripe for Snopes' plucking. He is the agent of finance capitalism, even though he is tempered by humane considerations. Ratliff himself is an agent for machines, somewhat ruthlessly involved in the business of making money.

The wholesaler made demand upon him for his (the wholesaler's) half of the outstanding twenty-dollar notes. Ratliff in his turn made a swift canvass of his own debtors. He was affable, bland, anecdotal and apparently unhurried as ever but he combed them thoroughly, not to be denied, although the cotton had just begun to bloom and it would be months yet before there would be any money in the land. (p. 63)

In spite of his being "affable" Ratliff is "not to be denied." He is caught up in a chain of commercial interactions and is forced to make demands of people who are easily beguiled by his eloquence and charm. There is something not quite right about this selling of sewing machines to people who are barely able to support their immediate needs on the cotton which the land almost reluctantly yields. Ratliff becomes the half-hearted champion of the hamlet, but his failure is predictable. His motives are largely noble, but his method is something of a contribution to Snopesism. Ratliff, like the Varners, tries to beat Snopeses on Snopeses' terms. It is he who seeks out Flem Snopes, thus causing his own defeat. He tries to trick Flem, to overcome evil with evil's own means. But on those terms Flem is unbeatable. Ratliff, like Will Varner, underestimates Snopes' degeneration and finds himself symbolically confronted with the idiot Ike Snopes at the end of the goat-transaction.

Materialism, the supreme value of the modern world, is not the only aspect of society that gives Snopeses both their standards and their foothold. Flem must also seek respectability; the hamlet (as well as the town) is more concerned with appearances than with anything else. This explains Flem's adoption of the neat little artificial black bow ties that have become so much a part of his "front" before he leaves the hamlet. On two separate occasions a general concern for "good name" permits Snopesism to make specific gains, and in both cases the events have a profound symbolic force. One is the sacrifice of Ike Snopes' cow (it *is* his property) and thereby his love affair, and the other is the parallel sacrifice of Eula Varner to Flem himself, in order that her child might appear to have an acknowledged father, even though the truth is well-known to all.

In the case of "Ike H-Mope" (his inability to say Snopes is significant) we are being presented with an antithesis to Snopesism. Not only is the episode an idyll and a tribute to love, which exists only in an idiot in a Snopes world, but it is also a portrait of the innocent, the anti-materialist:

The coin rang dully once on the dusty planks and perhaps glinted once, then vanished, though who to know what motion, infinitesimal and convulsive, of supreme repudiation there might have been, its impulse gone, vanished with the movement, because he even ceased to moan as he stood looking at his empty palm with quiet amazement, . . .

(p. 203)[6]

Ike commits himself totally and wholeheartedly to the cow, finally purchased for him with Ratliff's money. Ike goes through fire and water in attendance on the cow, symbol of the land and fertility. As a result, he becomes the acknowledged and accepted lover.

It is Ratliff who ends this love affair. He takes back his gift, eradicates his own generosity by forcing the Snopeses to kill the cow. He does this not out of sympathy with Ike, who has been made a public spectacle, nor even out of concern for the wrong, the perversion itself. Thomas Y. Greet has made the following comments on Ratliff's inadequacy:

Ratliff, the rational, the conventional, overbears Ike, the passionate, the natural. Ratliff is as humane, perhaps as good, as a man may be, but the ravished land will be redeemed by an act of love, not of righteousness. Rain is described but once in *The Hamlet:* it falls on Ike and his beloved.

(pp. 210–211)[7]

Ratliff goes against his best impulses when he deprives Ike. Mrs. Littlejohn says, " 'It aint that it is, that itches you. It's that somebody named Snopes, or that particular Snopes, is making something out of it and you don't know what it is.' " (p. 226), and Ratliff answers, " '. . . I know that the reason I aint going to leave him have what he does have is simply because I am strong enough to keep him from it. I am stronger than him. Not righter. Not any better, maybe. But just stronger.' " (p. 227). Love, not strength, must be the motive for action. Ratliff uses a Snopes to defeat a Snopes; he does not act from a concern with Ike himself.

Flem succeeds because there is no real opposition to him (in Faulkner's terms), and love is less significant than avarice and good name in Yoknapatawpha. The villagers are essentially human, and on the whole well-meaning, but their behavior has become formalized, their moral fiber weakened. They do not want to make trouble for themselves; they want only to live without fuss, to plod along untroubled. Faulkner's thesis, as we have seen it throughout this study, is that indifference is not enough to defeat Snopesism. Positive moral value and an insistence on a love ethic are essential to social salvation. Man must be helped, not merely ignored. Flem prospers because he adopts the material values of the world around him, and his efforts at "self-improvement" are not hampered by humane considerations. In a human world one must be for or against man; indifference leads to the success of those who, like Snopeses, are against man.

Whatever use others try to make of Flem always redounds to his advantage. One such attempt is the use of Flem as a husband for Eula Varner. Eula has been deserted by her lover, Hoake McCarron, and her pregnancy must be made respectable before the birth of her child. Here again a petty concern comes before truth and pride. The Varner name, with all its faults, must ironically be kept "good." Flem is the only person who will marry the sullied Eula. The Flem-Eula marriage has, of course, symbolic extension. Mr. Greet has pointed out that Eula is a sacrifice to Flem, and a sacrifice that in the light of Faulkner's description has great significance.[8] Eula symbolizes nature itself, the land, fertility, fecundity; "her entire appearance suggested some symbology out of the old Dionysic times—honey in sunlight and bursting grapes, the writhen bleeding of the crushed fecundated vine beneath the hard rapacious trampling goat-hoof." (p. 107) She represents that which antedates man. Man's attitude towards nature is symptomatic of his moral stature. The God-made naturally demands humility from man. Eula suffers at the hands of a Godless society. Marriage has replaced love. Eula symbolizes that which under the nurturing hands of man becomes regenerative, a divine fulfillment. Man, however, abdicates from his responsibility. Eula is left at the mercy of the most pernicious of man's considerations: social prestige, "good name," respectability, etc. Flem is thus further assisted in his rise to power.

The apparent chaos of *The Hamlet's* structure is actually a kaleidoscopic account of Flem's successes and the methods and opportunities that directly and indirectly assist his rise. In the same section with Ike and the cow we find the story of the conflict between Mink and Houston. It is interesting to note that Houston is deeply involved in both episodes and that his character in each is quite different, leading to different responses from the other protagonists. These differences might be viewed as one more summation of the meaning of the novel, like the horse auction, the Eula-Flem marriage and the purchase of the Frenchman Place. Each of these events reiterates a single theme. In his dealings with Ike, Houston is basically generous, even though he is driven to the bounds of his patience. He cleans the idiot's dirty overalls, gives him money as a futile but kindly gesture of recompense after Ike's bravery in the fire, and finally tries to give the cow to Ike, though Mrs. Littlejohn finally insists on making payment for it, knowing that Ratliff's money can never be put to better use. There are two direct results from Houston's generosity. At one and the same time he rids himself of the problem of Ike and the cow, and he brings intense happiness to Ike himself.

In his dealings with Mink Snopes, brother to Ike and Flem, Houston lowers himself to the level of petty wrangler. Here we have a picture of the chaotic divisiveness that is found in the story "Barn-Burning," where the source of Ab's alienation is revealed. An animal strays across a fence, from one man's land into another's. The event is repeated when Mink's yearling, a symbol of nature which abhors fences and knows no boundaries, tries to unite the wrongly divided land and men. But the pettiness and perversion of man's mind uses the event only for strife, and Houston and Mink, opposed to each other over the smallest of matters, are mutually destructive. Mink is no mad villain. He is victimized by the tenant-farmer system run by the Varners, and the three dollars awarded to Houston are the breaking point for the already impoverished Mink. In his struggle against overwhelming odds he even achieves a kind of nobility, but his amorality is recalled at the end of his story when he thinks, "Are they going to feed them niggers before they do a white man?" (p. 296) He is typical of his time and place.

The horse auction is interesting in several ways. In *The Town* we are told that Flem was not the first to import the ponies to Mississippi: " 'Because we did know about that, mainly because Flem Snopes had not been the first to import them. Every year or so someone brought into the county a string of wild unbroken plains ponies from somewhere in the west and auctioned them off.' "[9] This bears out my contention that Flem is merely using established practices to attain his ends. Many of the men who come to the auction are there by accident and are helplessly attracted. "Some of them did not have ropes. When they left home that morning, they had not heard about the horses, the auction. They had merely happened through the village by chance and learned of it and stopped." (p. 342) The task of the Texan is really very easy, and although he has difficulty in beginning the auction, he can readily arouse enthusiasm by giving away one horse at the start. This is the supreme temptation to the acquisitive instinct. It is irresistible. It not only begins the auction but attracts Armstid, who is driven by the degrading poverty and austerity of his life to buy something violent and useless. During the proceedings an interesting conversation takes place. Eck, furious at his boy Wallstreet for entering the lot and encountering the horses, is about to beat him:

'If you're going to whip him, you better whip the rest of us too and then one of us can frail hell out of you,' one of the others said.
'Or better still, take the rope and hang that durn fellow yonder,' the second said. The Texan was now standing in the wrecked door of the barn, taking the gingersnap carton from his hip pocket. 'Before he kills the rest of the Frenchman's Bend too.'
'You mean Flem Snopes,' the first said.

(p. 324)

The whole group, villagers, Texan and Flem are inextricably bound together. Each bears some responsibility; Flem could not function without the vulnerability of the others.

When the sale is over, someone accidentally leaves the gate open, and the horses all flee. They disappear in a wild flurry of excitement and color. The villagers have literally bought nothing but trouble. The innocent Tull is injured, Armstid is injured, Ratliff threatened, and Mrs. Littlejohn disturbed. The only horse caught is a dead one.

Arising out of the sale are two lawsuits representing a futile opposition to Snopesism. One is Mrs. Armstid's attempt to retrieve her five dollars, the other Mrs. Tull's attempt to get damages from Eck. Lump Snopes perjures himself to save Flem, and the law prevents Eck from making amends and opposes the natural impulse of his humanity. The implications of this should be clear, but they are made clearer by reference to the Snopes in hell scene, conjured up in the mind of Ratliff. There Flem is shown as the ethical man, demanding only his rights under a system that he himself did not set up. He cannot be bribed, he cannot be threatened. He is unapproachable. Ethics without spirit, the rational mind, is no answer to the Snopes system. Only in the heart, the emotions, can an alternative be found. Flem never breaks a contract, never makes a mistake with money, never "weakens," and likewise he expects no quarter. Only by discarding his entire system of values can society oppose him successfully. To possess (as in the case of the barns) is to lay oneself open to threat. Ratliff fails to see that means and ends are inextricable. He emerges most sympathetically when he stands off from Snopes activity, and this is surely substantiated by his wry and good humor on such occasions. His refusal to attend the horse auction is a positive anti-Snopes act, and the episode first becomes really humorous when the horse seeks out Ratliff in his private room. Humor is an admirable human attribute (totally missing in Flem) and Ratliff gradually loses it as he becomes more and more involved with Snopeses. This loss is part of Ratliff's growing confusion, the distortion of his once objective outlook, and the worsening chaos of his methods and objectives.

All this is made finally clear by the "salted mine." Ratliff's impetuousness, Armstid's insanity, and Bookwright's blind trust in Ratliff's reasoning power, lead to Flem's victory. Having overcome the last vestiges of opposition Flem can move on to the town, where he will find ground equally fertile. The only person totally unaffected by Flem's passage through Frenchman's Bend is Mrs. Littlejohn. She has refused to deal in Flem's terms, refused to accept his values, and so "only she is invulnerable."[10]

Robert Penn Warren has said of *The Hamlet* that "all stories and people in the novel finally refer to Flem, and in the end, the tribe of Snopes, with its violence, corruption, and cunning, has tainted Frenchman's Bend."[11] This seems to be an over-simplification of the Snopes role. Frenchman's Bend was "tainted" before Flem's arrival; it does not appear to have changed much by the time Flem leaves. His passage through Frenchman's Bend is catalytic. The inhabitants of the village have been confronted with their weaknesses, made active in Flem. Snopesism is a mirror that truthfully reflects the evils that permeate society.

1. Thomas Y. Greet, "The Theme and Structure of Faulkner's *The Hamlet*," *PMLA*, LXXII (September, 1957), 775.

2. *The Hamlet* (New York, 1940), 81. All subsequent page numbers in the text refer to this edition.

3. "William Faulkner's 'The Hamlet': A Study in Meaning and Form," *Accent*, XV (Spring, 1955), 125–144.

4. William Faulkner, *The Town* (New York, 1957), 276.

5. Ibid.

6. We should keep in mind that Ike is a Snopes, just as Eck is a Snopes. There should be little further proof needed that Snopeses are not merely inhuman exploiters of man, or even one class of men, but represent Faulkner's concept of every man, a method by which he may comment on and parody mankind.

7. Greet, p. 785.

8. *Ibid.,* pp. 775–790.
9. *The Town,* pp. 6–7.
10. Florence Leaver, "The Structure of *The Hamlet," Twentieth Century Literature,* I (July, 1955), 84. Miss Leaver has thoroughly explained the symbolism of Mrs. Littlejohn's conduct during the horse auction. The landlady busies herself with domestic concerns and pauses in her work to stare over the symbolic fence that separates her from the men who assist Snopes. However, being the minor character she is, it would be a distortion to make too much of her. She is merely a clue to the method for defeating Flem.
11. "The Snopes World," *Kenyon Review,* III (Spring 1941), 255.

THE UNITY
OF *GO DOWN, MOSES*

STANLEY TICK

AMONG THE CONTROVERSIAL issues in the Faulkner canon is that concerning the structure of *Go Down, Moses,* published in 1942. The Table of Contents, listing seven separate titles, makes it appear that the volume is a collection of short stories—with the final story lending its title to the volume. A first reading, however, assures us that at least three stories are intimately related, viz. "The Old People," "The Bear," and "Delta Autumn." Careful rereading establishes all the stories' interdependence, and the question of the volume's over-all structure becomes noteworthy: are six, or perhaps all seven, of these stories so significantly linked that we must judge them to be sections of a novel; or are these only more or less associated stories, each capable of being understood and analyzed independently?

Malcolm Cowley, reviewing *Go Down, Moses* in the *New Republic,* called the book "a hybrid: a loosely jointed but ambitious novel masquerading as a collection of short stories. . . ."[1] Similarly, Lionel Trilling, after excepting the story called "Pantaloon in Black," saw in the other six "a coherence strong enough to constitute, if not exactly a novel, then at least a narrative which begins, develops, and concludes."[2] The most recent reading of *Go Down, Moses* which affirms its novelistic structure is that of Olga Vickery: "All the stories in *Go Down, Moses* have certain unifying

Reprinted with permission from *Twentieth Century Literature,* VIII, No. 2 (July, 1962), 67–73.

features which give the book the character of a loosely constructed novel."³

Despite these conclusions, many critics evidently believe the seven stories in *Go Down, Moses* to be wholly independent. Thus there exist numerous articles dealing with one or several of the stories exclusive of the others. It is not deemed necessary by these commentators to understand individual stories in the context of the volume. An example would be R. W. B. Lewis, who, in *The Picaresque Saint*, writes at length about "The Bear" without once mentioning any of the other six stories.

Surely it is arguable that if *Go Down, Moses* is a novel or a continuous narrative, however "loosely jointed," then analyses of individual stories are doomed to be incomplete or possibly even erroneous. This being the case, any explication of "The Bear," for example, will be unsatisfactory at least to the degree that context is overlooked. It is my own belief that Cowley, Trilling, and Vickery have not overstated but, in fact, understated *Go Down, Moses*'s claims to be understood as a unified narrative—though this pertains to only six of the "sections." Furthermore, I feel that the architecture of this six-part novel is so compelling that no single section is fully explicable out of its context. For there is not only narrative development but thematic direction to the work; and what appears to be no more than careful chronological sequence ultimately reveals a profound moral commitment on the part of the author. Little of this, however, would emerge if the sections were thought to be autonomous structures.

Objection to my thesis on the record of publication history of these stories would be mistaken. Certainly versions of these stories appeared separately over a number of years: "Lion" (to be incorporated into "The Bear"), for example, as early as 1935; "Go Down, Moses" only in 1941. I realize, too, that Faulkner was working on various other material as well during these years. Yet the overruling fact is that Faulkner carefully expanded and revised the six separately fashioned stories so that they were not merely related but integrated for publication in novel form.⁴

On this subject, it is relevant to point out that at the time Faulkner was working on the elements of *Go Down, Moses*, his over-all method of composition was of a kind that could be called "blending." After the unquestionable and masterly unity of *Absalom, Absalom* in 1936, we get three consecutive, blended works. In 1938, *The Unvanquished*, seven chapters in the history of the Sartoris family. Like *Go Down, Moses*, this volume has provoked critical dispute concerning its structure: some refer to it as a novel, others call it a collection of short stories.⁵ In the following year, Faulkner produced *The Wild Palms*, an even more contentious work where the narrative relationship is contiguous rather than continuous. Then, in 1940, *The Hamlet* was published; the heretofore self-contained "Spotted Horses" had been expanded and revised for insertion into a larger structure. Most critics accord *The Hamlet* the title of novel and analyse it as such; indeed, it stands now as the first of a trilogy. Two years later, with no published volume intervening, *Go Down, Moses* appeared—another blended work. I believe that it is, in many ways, the most successful of these four blended works.

I do not intend the word *blend* to serve as a dodge for the nature of the issue it implies. If *The Unvanquished* (or *Go Down, Moses,* or any other work) is considered to be a collection of short stories—random or associated, but essentially independent—then critical judgment will receive and assess the volume on these terms. Faulkner has written numerous autonomous stories, and two volumes of them appeared in the early thirties. "A Rose for Emily," which appears in the first of these volumes, is an example of such a story. I feel certain that analysis of the tale as an independent unit is valid and can be fully effective. To be sure, this story, like any single piece of writing, can be related to some general aspect of its author's fiction. But the story, itself, does not demand such contextualizing; it is the critic who is taking upon himself the task of establishing relationships.

The gathering of diverse stories for publication in volume form is common practice, whereas blending is not. And if *The Unvanquished* (or the others) is considered to be a novel, or a blend—composed of units not essentially independent—then critical judgment can avail itself of other, more useful terms to evaluate the volume.

Of the seven stories in *Go Down, Moses,* "Pantaloon in Black" must be considered the unintegrated and therefore non-essential part of the structure. Both Cowley and Trilling recognized this, and I make the point here only because Miss Vickery, the most recent critic I know of to discuss the question, argues otherwise. She points to "unifying features" in all seven stories: "structurally, the framework of each individual story is a ritual hunt," she maintains. While this is a very astute observation, it cannot be applied quite the way Miss Vickery would have it. For one thing, Lucas' search for gold (in "The Fire and the Hearth") simply cannot be compared or even contrasted with Ike's ritual hunt; they are surely different in kind. More important, the final section of the volume, "Go Down, Moses," offers no hunt of any kind; and I am convinced that this section is of crucial importance. Even when Miss Vickery broadens —and thereby blurs—her focus to include "the nature of the hunted as well as the hunters," she fails to illuminate "Go Down, Moses." For this section is principally about the action of Gavin Stevens, not the grief of Molly or the fate of Samuel Beauchamp.

Miss Vickery's application of the hunger-hunted theme permits her to accommodate "Pantaloon in Black"; but any such accommodation will be either ingenious or accidental, for the story is largely irrelevant to the novel. Dissociated from the main narrative, "Pantaloon in Black" concerns no one with McCaslin blood (though it takes place on the McCaslin land)[6] And the central unifying theme in the six sections of *Go Down, Moses* is the fate of McCaslin blood, the fortunes of the McCaslin lineage. One must understand there that this implicates the Edmonds descendants as well as the Beauchamp mulattoes.

The generations of McCaslins are shown to be reaching to two features of their environment: the color-complex, and their natural heritage, of which some is owned and some merely used. Although I take this to be the major subject-matter of *Go Down, Moses,* I feel that it demands very little elaboration for purposes of this paper. I mean no paradox by this, only that my chief interest here is how Faulkner organized his material, not the kind of material he organized. Almost all the critics exploring *Go Down, Moses* have been compelled to treat the negro-white and Nature themes.

Let me give an instance of one of the relational ironies heretofore missed, as an indication of the extent of purposeful direction the full narrative possesses. The unnamed girl in "Delta Autumn" has borne a son to Carothers Edmonds; the time is 1940 (Ike, born in 1867, is here seventy-three). Edmonds repudiates both mother and child, though he leaves money to provide for them. Significantly, this fifth generation Edmonds is a "distaff" descendant of Lucius Quintus Carothers McCaslin, and the inheritor and possessor of the McCaslin land. Ironically, the girl reveals that she is a granddaughter of James Beauchamp (Tennie's Jim)—and thus even closer than Edmonds to the blood of old Lucius McCaslin, who is their common ancestor.

At this point, information provided in three previous sections of *Go Down, Moses*—"Was," "The Fire and the Hearth," and "The Bear"—allows the reader of "Delta Autumn" to grasp the full extent of this irony, which is nothing less than a closing of the circle of racial evil. Like his ancient ancestor, Edmonds has committed miscegenation; like Lucius McCaslin, again, Edmonds refuses to acknowledge the child but instead offers a legacy anonymously. (It is clear that Edmonds is under no illusions about the girl's color. On the drive to the hunting area, Legate explains to Ike what the situation is: "If it was just a buck he was coming all this distance for now. But he's got a doe in here. Of course a old man like Uncle Ike can't be interested in no doe, not one that walks on two legs—when she's standing up, that is. *Pretty light-colored, too.* The one he was after them nights last fall when he said he was coon-hunting, Uncle Ike." I have italicized the words whose meaning is undeniable. Not only is Edmonds as well as Ike, in the car when these words are spoken, but it is fair to assume that Legate could have no other source of information than Edmonds himself.)

The evil of the past concerned Nature as well as color, and in this too Edmonds is betrayed by his heritage.[7] He kills a doe using a shotgun, then disguises the fact by decapitating the animal. What the reader has learned in "The Old People" and "The Bear" teaches him that this action is a violation of all the true hunter's principles—which are virtues. At the start of "Delta Autumn," Ike sees in Carothers Edmonds "the face of his ancestor"; before this section ends, we have seen how the sinful deeds of this ancestor have been repeated.

"Delta Autumn" is the fifth of the six sections of *Go Down, Moses,* and its position in the over-all structure must be understood as such. This section, and most of "The Fire and the Hearth," are set in time-present, i.e. 1940–41: Edmonds is in his early forties, Lucas Beauchamp in his late sixties, and Ike in his early seventies. With the exception of "Go Down, Moses," the other sections are concerned with past events (whose importance, however, is not at all past). "Was" is set in 1859, "The Old People" between 1878–88. If I understand "Delta Autumn" properly, then, its contextual significance concerns the duplication of Lucius McCaslin's sins in the present day—i.e., when the *novel* was written.

The remainder of its context is the final section, called "Go Down, Moses." And as I shall try to make clear, this final section is the undeniable and essential context whose significance dictates our understanding of the entire novel. Directly relevant to "Delta Autumn" is the executed criminal in "Go Down, Moses"; his descent provides another relationship irony which must be comprehended. Samuel Worsham Beauchamp is a grandson of Lucas and Mollie, the child born to their eldest daughter, who, herself, did not survive the birth. Aware as the reader is now of the fate of the unnamed granddaughter of James Beauchamp, we can appreciate the irony of making the executed criminal her second cousin. The negro descendants of Eunice continue to be doomed. From the suicide of Eunice to the execution of Samuel and the rejection of the girl, none seems able to gain happiness. And the same is true for the white descendants that we know of. Only Lucas Beauchamp, in his isolating, Olympian pride, and Isaac in his Christ-like renunciation, are able to come to any sort of terms with their hostile environments.

Yet the full context of *Go Down, Moses* permits us to understand even more of the implications of Faulkner's moral position. We see, in the first five sections, the sins of the McCaslin father being visited on the children (negro and white) down to the fifth generation. In the final story, however, there is a notable change of mood, amounting to what I believe is a note of prophecy. No longer is the authority for action a McCaslin or an Edmonds—a doomed, however idiosyncratic, member of the old south. Now Gavin Stevens, "Phi Beta Kappa, Harvard, Ph.D., Heidelberg" takes over—a "new" southerner, aware of his heritage but personally free from its corrupting forces. I feel certain that Faulkner made "Go Down, Moses" the concluding section in order to emphasize its tone of futurity; equally revealing is the fact that this story, the only one which can be read as a moral for our time, is made to give its title to the volume.

The full consequence of reading "'Go Down, Moses" as prophetic is gained from understanding the actions of Gavin Stevens in the context of all the preceding sections. It is at this point that Miss Vickery's observation becomes most useful, though not as she applies it. For there is not merely an absence of any hunt in this final section, but the exact opposite of a hunt: the victim is not chased but instead brought home. Pathos rather than tension is the dominant chord. And what this means must be understood in the context of the full novel; it is only with that previous knowledge that we can appreciate the quality and sense of the prophetic in this concluding section.

The first McCaslin did not hunt for his negro mistress but merely took Eunice, and then Tomasina, with the arrogance of an unchallenged master dealing with slaves. That occurred in the 1830's. The next generation of McCaslins and Beauchamps appears in the first section of *Go Down, Moses,* "Was." Here Buck McCaslin hunts his slave, Tomey's Turl (who is, of course, Buck's half-brother). The narrator, Cass, recalls, Buck's language—that of the hunt: "You stay back where he won't see you and flush. I'll circle him through the woods and we will bay him at the creek ford." Later, Buck roars "He broke cover then," as though Turl were a deer or fox. Hounds are used to track Turl, and when they fail a fyce is tried. (Exactly like the order of dogs used in chasing Old Ben in "The Bear"—save for Lion, of course.) Though Buck and Buddy do not violate their slaves with the arrogance of their father, they nevertheless view the chase of Turl as a challenging hunt. This seems to me to be one of the reasons why Faulkner has a nine-year-old narrate the adventure—for the magnificent irony of the two levels of comprehension. To the boy, the chase is only an adventure; no social or moral considerations can be expected to occur to him. Yet the adults see the pursuit no differently; their interference with another human being, who is a negro, has for them no more significance than their dogs' pursuit of the fox which opens and ends this section.

The next hunt implicating McCaslin whites and negroes is Ike's search for Turl's children James and Fonsiba, and this is related in "The Bear." The nature of this hunt, however, is an extreme contrast with Buck's chase after Turl. For Ike seeks to give, not take; he wishes to pay his grandfather's legacy to these unacknowledged off-spring. Ike's good deed, nevertheless, is of only limited significance. For he is clearly saint-like, and his moral commitments are therefore idiosyncratic. His cousin McCaslin Edmonds, who is meant to speak for the cultural norm, cannot accept Ike's values; he cannot understand that the south is "cursed." Ike's sense of shame, therefore, implicates no other southerner; his sense of guilt as a white descendant of Lucius McCaslin leads him to atone as best he can for his grandfather's transgressions. But his community remains unrepentant.

In the time-present of "The Fire and the Hearth," the negro is more or less grudgingly accepted as an equal. But no atonement for past sins is in evidence. Not until the final section, "Go Down, Moses," does the white community perform what can be considered an act of expiation. And here it is Gavin Stevens, a highly educated, "new" southerner, who directs his fellow Jefferson townsfolk.

The actions of "the old time . . . the dark, corrupt and bloody time" are, in this final section, significantly reversed. The arrogance of the taker and the moral unconsciousness of the hunter have been the humility and sacrifice of Gavin Stevens and the newspaper editor, as well as the "merchant and clerk, proprietor and employee, doctor, dentist, lawyer and barber," who all donate money in order to have the corpse of a negro criminal returned for burial. Some come to the station to watch the casket being unloaded from the train; the others "watched quietly from doors and upstairs windows" as the funeral cortege slowly crossed the square and circled the Confederate Monument and the courthouse.

What these whites see, as the hearse passes, is the reflection of their inherited guilt. This final section looks back directly to "Was," and even to earlier time. "There is no such thing as *was*— only *is*. If *was* existed, there would be no grief or sorrow," Faulkner himself has said.[8] The concept of time as a dimension of moral consciousness is part of Faulkner's fundamental vision; history, for this artist, is continuous and the inevitable explanation of the present. As Gavin Stevens says in *Requiem for a Nun:* "The past is never dead. It's not even past." Or as Quentin, in *Absalom, Absalom,* reflects *"Maybe nothing ever happened once and is finished. Maybe happen is never once but like ripples moving on, and spreading. . . .*" Understood in this context, the implications of "Was" are enormous, just as the title, coming first in the volume, is indicative.

Ike alone, through his special moral awareness, could transcend time: he could shed his watch and compass, and then confront Old Ben—out of time. He invokes Keats' "Ode on a Grecian Urn" when debating with Cass. But Ike's powers are unique; no one else can shed the south's sinful heritage. Faulkner's point, however, is not merely that one cannot escape the past but that one should not, indeed must not. Moral stature can be attained only when one recognizes the moral claims such a past imposes. Denied the spiritual strength of an Isaac, one can aspire to the knowledge and integrity of a Gavin Stevens.

The continuum of time and the consquent growth of moral consciousness is of fundamental importance to Faulkner's fiction; the concept is a key to the novel *Go Down, Moses.* From "Was" to the future, the movement of events and the development of relationships are contained in a six-section narrative. No section is fully autonomous, and the tensions generated in these component parts are resolved only when one understands them in their full context.

1. Vol. 106 (29 June, 1942), p. 90.
2. *The Nation,* Vol. 154 (30 May, 1942), p. 632.
3. *The Novels of William Faulkner* (Louisiana State Universary Press, 1961), p. 124.
4. Compare, for example, "Gold is Not Always" in *Atlantic Monthly* (Nov. 1940), with the novel's "The Fire and the Hearth" to get some idea of the extensive changes Faulkner made.
5. See H. H. Waggoner's *William Faulkner* (Universary of Kentucy Press, 1959), p. 170 for a discussion of the structure of *The Unvanquished.*
6. W. V. O'Conner, in *The Tangled Fire of William Faulkner* (Minneapolis, 1954), argues that *Go Down, Moses* possesses "two loosely related strands of subject matter. . . ." (pl 125). Although the approach is sensible, the distinction is artificial; and O'Connor seriously undermines his terms by redefining them to allow for the inclusion of "Pantaloon in Black."
7. Whether or not Zack Edmonds, Carothers' father, committed miscegenation with Mollie Beauchamp is not made clear in "The Fire and the Hearth." But it is Carothers alone who is shown to violate the order of Nature as well as that of Man.
8. *Writers at Work: The Paris Review* Interviews (London, 1958), p. 127.

AN AMERICAN INTERPRETATION
OF EXISTENCE:
FAULKNER'S *A FABLE*

HEINRICH STRAUMANN

1

FOR THE EUROPEAN reader, William Faulkner's *A Fable* (1954) is the most important novel the American writer has written. At the same time it is the most significant work of an epic cast in English since the Second World War and belongs among those rare works to which the standard of a century may unhesitatingly be applied.

These are strong assertions, and it is proper to examine them more closely. First, it should be established that expressions such as "touching," "harmonious," "beautiful" have not been used. When *Robinson Crusoe* was published, no critic thought of regarding that work mainly as literature, much less of investing it with such attributes. Faulkner's novel is a powerful and moving book in the sense that Tolstoy's *War and Peace* is powerful and moving; it is also a philosophically loaded book, probably more difficult than *Moby-Dick*. And it confuses the reader because idea and event on the various levels of symbolic, allegorical, and imitative presentation appear now separated, now closely interwoven. Indeed, for precisely this reason its critical reception in America was not at all uniform. Certain skeptical voices made no secret of their uncertainty as to its meaning.[1]

This is, to be sure, nothing new for Faulkner and it is easily explicable. Perhaps one need only examine the antology of critical opinions about Faulkner's work, *William Faulkner: Two Decades of Criticism,* to get a picture of the astonishingly divergent interpretations and evaluation of the author. This is particularly true of the time between the two World Wars, while in the last ten years, especially since the Nobel Prize award of 1950, the attitude of the

Reprinted with permission from *Anglia*, 1955, pp. 484–515. Translated by Grace A. Goodman and Olga W. Vickery.

critics, though certainly no more uniform, has been in essence considerably more respectful. The striking increase of publications on Faulkner in recent years testifies to the growing desire for analysis of his work. Several books and dozens of articles, some very significant, have appeared in America; and Europe, especially France, is increasingly concerned with him.[2]

This can only mean that something is involved in Faulkner's presentation which only recently has been considered as particularly significant; in other words, the early Faulkner so far outstripped his time that he can only now be comprehended by criticism, while the present Faulkner is once more a considerable distance ahead. Thus, twenty years ago the discussion of *Light in August* (1932) was primarily concerned with what could be directly grasped of the story: the race question in the American South, the problem of the vagrant, the moral confusion of certain characters, the "trueness to life" of the presentation. Since then the critical approach has shifted decisively. The realistic, the psychological, the sociological facts are mentioned no longer or only incidentally. Instead the problem of the inner estrangement of the indivdual from society is regarded as essential; the position of the man of mixed blood, at first unrecognized, is interpreted as a symbol of the loneliness of man in general; the ethical question is focussed on the limits of human endurance; the complexity of the narrative is discussed as a necessity of form.[3] In short, the interpretation has shifted from the surface to the interior, thereby certainly doing more justice to the book and to Faulkner's earlier work in general.

Now, perhaps it is directly because of this shift in emphasis that recently *A Fable* could confuse critics. For neither a clear-cut structural analysis nor a radically symbolic interpretation can penetrate to the center of the work, although both are probably indispensable to the recognition of essential aspects of it. Rather, problems of mimesis, of allegory, of tone or level of style, and primarily of a certain world-view emerge in a way and to a degree scarcely found in Faulkner's earlier works.[4] Any attempt to comprehend the whole cannot evade the question of the nature of all these elements as well as their mutual interweavings.

2

It is usual to begin the consideration of a novel with the plot. In this case, that would be the events which center on the mutiny of a French and British unit on the Western front in the First World War, and which show a similarity, to be sure only remote, with the historical incident of General Nivelle's offensive in the spring of 1917. But this self-same point of departure, however much it claims and is supposed to claim the attention of the reader, is overshadowed by something else, that is, by the discussion among those who have to decide the fate of the mutineers. In these discussions is located the philosophical center of the work, and from this center the way leads to all other aspects of the novel, including the development of the action, characters, and levels of style. For this very reason it is something new in Faulkner—indeed, one can say that the author has never before taken up so meaningful a position on the problem of human existence as here. A clearly tragic world order is presented: tragic because it is shown in successive pairs of opposites each of which is absolutely irresolvable, and hence the whole allows room neither for the idea of completion nor for reconciliation.

The first and most important pair of opposites is that of the commander-in-chief of the Allied forces and the corporal who sets off the mutiny. If their relation to each other and to the total pattern is comprehended, the other problems almost solve themselves. Critics could say with ostensible justice that the commander-in-chief is almost inconceivable as a human being. He is a unique condensation of the most praiseworthy human characteristics: just, wise, serene, friendly, even loving. He has the highest intelligence and self-control, the keenest insight into the inner relationships of events, and in addition he is connected by birth with the most influential, most powerful, and wealthiest French families. His career brings him from the military academy first to a remote post in Morocco, then to Asia Minor, where, through a barely hinted at affair with a native girl, a son is born to him. He knows, of course, of his son's existence, but he never sees him until the decisive moment. The son is none other than the corporal who sets off the mutiny in the French regiment, is taken prisoner and faces execution. And incredible number of qualities are given to the son, as they are to the father, only this time they are those of the man who stands lowest in the social hierarchy: endless patience, the incomprehensible strength to endure and capacity to suffer, goodness, forbearance, and forgiveness. The son is brought by his half-sisters, Marya and Marthe, first to the coast of Asia Minor and then, through the marriage of Marthe to a French colonial soldier, to France. There the four manage a farm near St. Mihiel until the war breaks out and the son, after forming a relationship with a prostitute (Magdalena) in Marseille, is sent to the front as a corporal. In his extreme simplicity (he cannot even read) and anonymity he seems to be omnipresent in the army: superiors repeatedly identify him with soldiers who have been declared killed and buried.

From these short sketches it is immediately apparent that a purely realistic interpretation of the two main figures cannot do justice to the novel. Neither the piling up of the aforementioned qualities nor the position in which the antagonists find themselves is plausible by ordinary human standards. However, neither would a purely figurative interpretation succeed, even though the allegorical parallel with the events of Holy Week is made clear enough. For example, the corporal has in the regiment his twelve disciples: one, Polcheck, betrays him; another, Pierre Bouc, denies him; a third, Paul, represents him during a temporary absence. He is executed at the same time as a murderer and a thief; he has his crown of barbed wire, and his body is hidden by the three women, Marya, Marthe, and Magdalena. However, just as the commander-in-chief corresponds but little to the historical Marshal Foch or, despite certain similarities, to Pontius Pilate, so the corporal is far from being directly equated with Christ. Rather, these similarities are intended, on the one hand, to bring out the intensity of the basic concern, and, on the other hand, to establish the validity of the statements in relation to our own terrible reality and our own highest scale of values.

And this actually happens on the level of dialectic. First the commander-in-chief has to confer with the Allied generals and the German delegates about the events. What was impossible during four years of war has become possible through the mutiny of a French regiment: a conference between enemy commanders, who realize instantly that the war must not under any circumstances end in this way lest the whole significance of the military hierarchy and its concepts of honor break down. The French division commander in whose unit the mutiny occurred refuses to compromise: he demands the execution of the entire regiment and therefore of himself. This is the consequence, simultaneously exciting horror and working up to the grotesque, of a position which in itself is quite commendable, but which is carried to an extreme of rigidity. The shooting of the division commander, undertaken by three American volunteers since no French soldier can be expected to do it, is one of the most horrifying episodes in the book. It represents the conversion of the concept of honor into something subhuman.

In the talk between the Allied generals and the German delegates, the contrast is brought out in sociological terms. While the decision as such is scarcely mentioned, so much the more is said of British dilettantism as compared to German professionalism in warfare. The German general pays his respects to the concept of honor by shooting the German pilot who is ordered to set him down behind the enemy lines and who must therefore surrender his plane. Further, the human side of the affair is brought out and simultaneously connected with the metaphysical in the contrast between the commander-in-chief and the quartermaster-general, who have remained friends since their time together in the military academy. To the quartermaster-general, it is intolerable to know that one must make common cause with the enemy in order to finish off a group of honest compatriots. But he cannot get around the arguments of the commander-in-chief, who points out that among the mutineers themselves there is a traitor, that is, that something "bad" has crept into the "good" intentions; that the agreement with the enemy is the only alternative to certain chaos, and that it is precisely his execution that will prove the corporal neither lived nor died in vain. Here the dualistic nature of things is made so clear that it becomes a commentary on events which have already happened and been narrated and at the same time prepares us for the still higher plane of that which is to come.

This is the encounter between the commander-in-chief and the corporal, between the judge and the one who is to be judged, between father and son. In their long talk practically the only one to express himself is the commander-in-chief, whom we have known until now as a rather silent man: it is his most impressive attempt to persuade the corporal to yield his position. He casts all values into the scales to weigh them in his favor; he promises the corporal freedom, the possibility of moving unhindered through the universe; he offers him the whole world in the sense of a unique abundance of power; and finally he very simply presents to him the beauty of life itself as a temptation. All these offers are accompanied by cogent reasons, among which the statement that they both, commander-in-chief and corporal, are articulations of opposing terms of existence is the most important one. This is most concisely expressed in the commander's reference to himself as "champion of this mundane earth" (348) and to the corporal as, therefore, a champion "of an esoteric realm of man's baseless hopes and his infinite capacity—no: passion—for unfact" (348).[5] The corporal declines all these offers with the sole, scarcely articulated reason that the suffering of others would still not be helped. Although an unbridgeable gulf between the world of the commander-in-chief and that of the corporal does exist, they do have one important point of contact, namely, the conviction that mankind in its madness will continue to exist in spite of all horrors that the future may bring. For this future existence the commander-in-chief uses the word "prevail" and the corporal, "endure," whereby the distance between "prevailing" and "enduring" within the same existence is made clear.[6]

In the interpretation of this encounter one is first inclined to see the parallel with the temptation of Christ by Satan, and this is by no means to be rejected. However, for the comprehension of the whole, to do so would be an unjustified simplification, for in addition to the similarity there are the differences which cannot be disregarded. Of these only the most striking need be mentioned, namely, that the general is not only the corporal's father but also his highest superior. In fact, this very relationship is of particular significance for the further clarification of the underlying meaning. What is involved is a dualistic view of the world rooted in the profoundest depths and of literally Manichean proportions. A light and a dark principle is immanent in all the orders and values of existence. The commander-in-chief is none other than the origin and source of this double principle. He unites in himself qualities which can lead to the best as well as to the worst. He has godlike as well as satanic traits. He exercises the highest authority, which, on the one hand, means order and the confinement of chaos, but which, on the other hand, can destroy the lives of hundreds of thousands. He is the law, which seeks justice and simultaneously produces suffering. He has wisdom, which means not only knowledge but also temptation. Indeed, from him arise those very powers which directly challenge him and his principle: the powers of pure goodness, love, and hope, which, however, can only be expressed in rebellion against his control and which consequently have a dual nature. The essential point is that these powers can neither change anything of the original order nor effect any kind of deliverance from evil. There is suffering and endurance and perhaps hope but no question of the certainty of salvation. This constitutes a marked difference from Christian thought, which should be remembered in any consideration of Faulkner's pattern of ideas. Rather, we may speak of his intellectual affinity with the Stoics, for the very phenomenon of suffering and the ability to endure that gives outline to so many of Faulkner's works is here too in the foreground of all events and finds its ultimate significance in the corporal's final word "endure."[7]

It is not accidental that the two other most important characters in the book regard endurance as the highest value: the commander-in-chief, in an interior monologue immediately before the crucial decisions are made (239 and 242), and the British messenger, about whom we shall talk later, in his conversation with the Negro (203). For this reason alone one cannot speak of a really pessimistic world view, terrible as the separate events may be. But in addition there is that distinctive level of style, often approaching humor, which can also be found in Faulkner's other works. It is the direct accompaniment of a basically ironic mood which in its turn rests squarely on the knowledge of the inevitability of suffering and the conviction that mankind has the power to endure it. These intricate patterns are for many, especially American readers, the most pleasing side of the author, and their connection with the principle of the two-fold meaning of all things, a connection based as it were on natural laws, is evident. Indeed, most remaining aspects of the work follow from this basic attitude with conclusive logic.

3

From the sequence of events, the strongest formative element is the principle of duality, both in the sense of parallels and doubling and also of the interplay of persons, motives, and actions. Apart from the already mentioned pairs of opposites—commander-in-chief/corporal, commander-in-chief/quartermaster, German general/Allied generals—one is struck by the characteristic duality of the main theme, the mutiny. By the side of the French regiment for whose refusal to attack the corporal and his twelve followers are responsible, there is a British unit in which two days later something similar happens. The differences are, however, significant. While we learn almost no details of the past history of the French mutineers and outside of the war-weariness we know nothing of their reasons, there is in the British unit a quite definite and complex situation which requires some analysis.

The first decisive incident is the one in which the British soldiers, leaving their weapons behind, climb out of the trenches, with the idea of joining the German troops opposite them, who do the same thing. Instantly British and Germans are placed under concentric fire by the batteries which lie farther back, in accordance with the agreement of the troop leaders for this situation, so that the mutineers are completely annihilated. Therefore, while the mutiny among the French remains a mere "omission," it becomes with the British and Germans a definite "commission."

Furthermore, among the British, two contrasting characters play a special role: a runner and a sentry. The runner is a former officer, who has himself demoted to the ranks because he believes he can endure the wretchedness of war only by suffering with the anonymous mass. He forces his own demotion by committing an offense against public decency, that is, for the sake of a moral protest he must commit an immoral act—an example of the duality and irony of meaning. As a runner he hears not only of the passive resistance of the French regiment and the conference of the enemy army leaders, but he is also a witness to the strange authority which the sentry exercises over his comrades in the British unit. It consists of the fact that the sentry, through something that would normally be regarded as an insurance swindle, practically holds his comrads in bondage. He lends them small sums of money which they pay back in installments, and in return they appoint him beneficiary of their military insurance policies for the term of the loan. The sentry therefore speculates coldbloodedly on the highest possible casualty list for his unit. This is the obverse image of the sway that the French corporal has over his own comrades; on the one side brotherly kindness, on the other naked egotism. And it is grimly ironic that their effect is identical. For it is essentially this insane gambling that impels the runner to persuade the soldiers to mutiny. The fact that he also desperately though ineffectually tries to destroy their secret society by this means is again a reversal of the proceedings among the French, where an unspoken agreement already seems to exist among the mutineers. He is, further, in natural opposition to the sentry, who from the start has only curses for his reflections. Again we are confronted by an inversion of ethical values in that the humanly appealing but legally irresponsible act of the runner stands opposed to the humanly repugnant but legally permissible one of the sentry.

Of the numerous further examples of duality as a principle of structure we need only cite the following, which is at the same time related to the question of personal or professional honor. In the early stage of his career in Morocco the commander-in-chief sacrifices a Foreign Legionnaire in order to avert an armed conflict with an Arabian tribe. Although the author clearly states that the Legionnaire is a common criminal, even a murderer, it is nevertheless made evident that the commander-in-chief's action is shrewd and far-sighted since by it order and peace can be preserved though it cannot be approved from the standpoint of strict honor. What the commander-in-chief here performs in miniature is later repeated "in large" in his handling of the mutiny.

The concept of the ability to endure also is reversed in certain significant incidents connected with the problem of honor. One example is the episode of the young American pilot who, out of deepest conviction, has enlisted in the British air force. He is a witness as a German aircraft lands on the British airfield. His mission ought to be to attack this plane, and he tries to do so, only to perceive to his bewilderment that he is shooting blank ammunition. Other unusual events confirm his belief that this has been ordered by higher authorities. His bewilderment increases when he ultimately learns why the enemy plane is allowed to make a landing and for what purpose the troop commanders have met. He hears of the mutiny of the British battalion that was placed under bombardment; everything becomes mere appearance to him; the meaning of his existence, erected on a belief in honor and integrity of action, collapses; the values that alone give his life meaning do not exist; he seizes the pistol to put an end to his life. Here also is a significant detail: his flight dress is singed in one place by phosphorescent ammunition. It does only a little damage, but it goes on corroding slowly and constantly in the fabric, and causes an overpowering stench: a small leitmotif for the slow disintegration and destruction which recurs throughout the work.

The case of the priest is quite similar. His mission is to persuade the

French corporal, before his execution, to renounce the idea of personal suffering in connection with which the necessity of an order embodied in the institution of the Church becomes significant. Only here the collapse is enacted in the short span of a personal conversation. After the priest fails in his argument, including the appeal to life itself, his system of belief is shaken to its foundations. His whole existence has become meaningless and unbearable, and so he too chooses suicide.

In the fact that admirable, well-meaning men experience this collapse of meaning and are incapable of enduring it lies that irony which lends to the Faulkner world its dual nature and which is still to be discussed. First, however, a further essential element in the structure of the novel must be considered: the motif of "The Stranger in the Crowd."

4

Faulkner's novel begins and ends with mob scenes from which individuals emerge as strangers who have gone astray. This motif also recurs twice in the course of the story, so that it appears in quadruple variation, to which a fifth is added, enacted, to be sure, on an entirely different plane. The story begins with the description of the crowd which gathers in the French city where the Allied headquarters are located to see the arrival of the captive French mutineers as well as the troop commanders who are to decide their fate. An apathetic, shapeless, anonymous mass waits for an event unable to do more than just suspect its importance: "one vast tongueless brotherhood of dread and anxiety" (3)—a gigantic symbol for a passive mankind which has to accept happiness or disaster in speechless anxiety.

In this crowd is a young woman, whose strange individuality is noticed only because she almost collapses from exhaustion. She is, as is revealed later, the fiancée of the corporal, who himself appears as a stranger among strangers, as he moves past the crowd, chained in the lorry. The women is supported by another unknown, who gives her some bread and arouses the suspicion of a sergeant on duty because he has knowlege of the mutiny. No names are given. At the end of the scene, after the crowd has dispersed, the young woman stays behind in silent despair, alone.

These few indications already convey the tight interweaving of motifs, moods, and symbols which is so consistently carried out in this story. The fact that no names are given strengthens the impression of strangeness which emanates from these characters and simultaneously indicates their universal validity. Both are of significance for the comprehension of the whole. Above all, however, a feeling of unutterable isolation is produced through the events which take place around these few nameless people in the nameless mass. It is perhaps strongest here in the beginning of the story where it determines the level of style for the theme of suffering and the ability to endure which is articulated by the same events.

The same motif-groups and mood appear in varying strengths in the remaining four places in the story. The first elaborates the situation (120–39) in which the crowd continues to await the development of events silently and passively and only once turns purposelessly against that section of the camp where the mutineers are held captive. This time it is the crowd whose uncertain emotional impulses are noted; the strangers who appeared in the first scene are not mentioned here. Instead individual military figures are introduced into the story, but again only in such a way that the impression of indefiniteness is preserved: sentries are changed, couriers come and go, the arrival of the division commander and a staff officer is observed. But here too the element of strangeness is present: the prison compound is guarded by Senegalese, doing their duty carelessly, impenetrably, fatalistically.

The third time (212–23) the individuals emerge more distinctly from the same waiting crowd. A name, Marthe, is even given for one of the corporal's two half-sisters, and we learn of the other young nameless woman's relationship to the corporal. But this elucidation goes hand in hand with the stress on the foreign origin of the women, who are moreover threatened with actual violence by the crowd which has become hostile. The isolation of the individual is, as it were, replaced by his expulsion by a group whereupon the motif of suffering clearly assumes the meaning of "endure."

The fourth mob scene takes place in characteristic inversion in the completely different setting of a small city in the American South in connection with the story of the stolen racehorse. More about this later.

In a level of style once again entirely different basically the same motif group appears at the end of the novel as in the beginning. This is the fifth mob scene. Years after the end of the war, the commander-in-chief is carried to his grave in Paris, accompanied by the representatives of all the powers and the whole population of France. This time it is a respectful though as before anonymous crowd which has turned out in immense numbers for this event. At the instant that the funeral procession arrives at the grave of the Unknown Soldier, a stranger rushes out of the crowd, throws his war medal on the coffin, breaks into incoherent words about the fate of mankind and national slogans, until he is beaten down by the crowd and arrested by the police. A second unknown supports him, and then come the final sounds of laughter and tears with which the book closes.

This closing scene naturally contains a great deal more than merely a variation on the theme of "The Stranger in the Crowd," but characteristically this very motif is used once again in order to bring together the intellectual outlines of the work. There are the characteristic little brush strokes indicating the symbolic references which will be further discussed later: sabre, medal, blood on the corner of the mouth, scars, all point to what lies farther back in the story and establish the connection with the ideas of Power, Honor, Suffering, and Endurance. Slowly and with some effort we learn from certain signs that we should know both the strangers. One of them is the British runner who forced his own demotion; knowing about the proceedings at the front and hoping for a mystic brotherhood, he was about to call on his unit to lay down its arms, and was severely wounded in the barrage. The other, supporting him, is the quarter-master-general whose pleas to the commander-in-chief for an understanding of the mutineers were rejected. Together they have the last word in the work: the eternal, nameless rebel, the Man, who knows of our struggles, who knows how to renounce outward honor, who has suffered most terribly, who is not afraid to give expression to his confused truth, who spits blood and at the same time laughs—and the other, the helper, aware of duty, honestly anxious and conscientious, but always standing in second place, the eternal adjutant, so to speak, who is not concerned with laughter.

This is the dual image that appears most impressively once again in this most critical place: in effect, our existence cannot be interpreted from a single point of view but only as a duality. There will always be one power which wants order, and one which rebels against it; there will always be a crowd and an individual who is threatened by it; there will always be one who struggles and endures, and one who helps and reconciles; there will always be weeping and laughing, difficult though they are to distinguish now and then; the one, indeed, sometimes takes the place of the other inasmuch as he who endures knows how to laugh, and he who helps, weeps. And here also the irony becomes apparent in this huge and never resolved drama, though, to be sure, in such a way that only the reader is supposed to know of it: the corpse of the commander-in-chief is conveyed to the grave of the Unknown Soldier, the symbol of valor, sacrifice, and national honor. Who, however, lies in this grave? None other than the corporal who was responsible for the mutiny of the French regiment and who was executed on the order of the very same man whose remains are now being brought to him as the last, highest honor. Are we to laugh or cry?

5

Actually, in *A Fable* pain and laughter merge into one another in almost imperceptible fashion: just as, frequently, the incipient laughter suddenly sticks in the reader's throat, so the horror turns into laughter. One can probably say that Faulkner's irony attains its subtlest value in this work both as a structural element that conditions events and as a factor determining the level of style in numerous episodes.

Irony as an element which conditions events is most pronounced in the story of the sentry as a jockey and in the episodes after the death of the corporal. The former is perhaps the most difficult part of the book for the non-American. First of all, one is struck by its minuteness of detail. To the characterization and explanation of a mere subordinate figure are devoted about sixty pages, that is, a full seventh of the total length. At first the events related in it seem scarcely relevant for the whole. The jockey in the Southern states saves a famous racehorse out of a railroad accident and with the animal, healed but running on only three legs, wins numerous races in smaller towns; a Negro and a youth help him. Upon the urging of the legal owner the law finally intervenes and terminates the affair.

One might think this episode a mere digression intended mainly to do justice to the comic element. And indeed, as he himself informs us in his preface, Faulkner published this section first as a separate unit in a special edition. This demonstrates that the story is capable of standing alone. It is, however, also of significance for the novel as a whole, even if the relationships are not readily discernible. The quite special nature of these relationships can best be exprsssed in musical terms as "keeping close to the main theme in another key and instrumentation"—keeping in mind, of course, that it is scarcely probable that we have here a conscious principle of composition.

The jockey, an Englishman with a Cockney accent, is a stranger in America. This is noted several times both directly and with the veiled Faulkner humor: "A small bandy-legged foreigner who could barely speak English" (157, similarly farther on, 162, 189, etc.). He is a stranger, who, however, is successful in such an unusual and legally dubious manner that the mob favors him. Just as later in the deadly peril of war he speculates on the casualty list of his unit, thereby binding his comrades to him, so here he wins his races under the constant risk of being arrested with a stolen horse, and thus wins the admiration of the spectators so that even such groups as the Baptists and the Freemasons make him one of them. The motif of the Stranger and the Crowd is here given a comical variation. We are amused because something of intrinsic importance (a portion of mankind acting in accordance with high ideals) is directly connected with a slight and morally disreputable affair.

The same motif appears a second time. The police succeed in arresting the Negro and his boy, who have accompanied the jockey on his racing trips. A silent mob assembles in front of the prison of the small American town, giving the impression that the dangerous and alarming mood could develop which precedes an act of lynch-justice. But just the opposite happens. The crowd demands the release of the Negro, on condition, to be sure, that he leave town, since "rich negroes are unwelcome there" (189). This is a deliberately paradoxical variation of our motif of the Stranger in the Crowd, and its liberating effect rests on the familiar principle of the relaxation of a dramatically pointed situation.

It does not, however, happen by accident that the mob appears as a helper here. In reversing the expected manner of representation the motif undergoes a doubling. The jockey is taken in by the Freemasons and draws the Negro with him, and the Negro, who belongs to the Baptists, baptizes the jockey, so that both belong to two great organizations. From this, at the outbreak of war, comes the connection with the American relief organization in France, financed by an American woman whose son was killed as a volunteer at the front. The relief organization is finally named *Les Amis Myriades et Anonymes à la France de Tout le Monde,* and the Negro and his boy are active in it in Paris. This is actually a threatrically handled group sequence of the stranger-and-secret-society motif. In addition, technically the episode becomes a feasible part of the war front story.

Furthermore, the problem of the contrast of order and mutiny also has its parallel in the episode of the stolen horse. After the horse vanishes onto the small racetracks, the legal owner in New York sets the authorities in motion to regain possession of his property. But he does not succeed. Though the commissioned official of the American police department tries his hardest, he suddenly realizes the pursuit is hopeless in view of the popularity of the horse-thief, and tries to convince the owner of the uselessness of the undertaking. The owner, for his part, attempts to keep him on the job by offering to increase the reward, but the latter takes the side of the "persecuted." Here the author himself indicates a comparison with the British runner and subsequent mutineer (158). Also present in the official's discussion with the owner is the motif of temptation, reminiscent of the scene between the commander-in-chief and the corporal. However, because of the triviality of the object of the dispute, everything has a level of style which keeps the reader amused and amazed.

Finally, even a weak echo of the theme of suffering and the ability to endure can be noted, though transferred to a dumb animal. The racehorse, cause and occasion of the whole episode, before the beginning of his triumphal tour is so injured in a train accident that he remains lame in one leg even after his recovery. Nevertheless, he runs from victory to victory. The animal suffers, endures, and wins. The notion of a lame animal who is still able to run has something perplexing if not almost mad or grotesque about it, not unlike the impression which, at the end of the book, the British runner arouses with his gruesome scar and the threadbare dinner jacket. In addition to the parallel, however, there is also the contrast: the jockey kills the horse as it is on the point of being returned to the hands of the legal owner. He cannot endure the thought that it might be used as mere breeding material. What remains for me a lasting and eternally recurring state is for an animal a solitary event.

In contrast to the complexity of the jockey-and-racehorse episode, the irony connected with the events centering on the mortal remains of the corporal is grimly consistent in its level of style. It is a question of three separate crucial episodes which, however, all point directly to the corporal's death. The first shows how Marthe and Marya, the corporal's half-sisters, and his fiancée are given possession of his body after the execution, and bring him back by wagon and train to their farm in St. Mihiel near Verdun in order to bury him there under an old beech tree. The transportation takes place without hindrance, since it was so ordered by the supreme authority. The suspension of hostility still prevails as a consequence of the agreement among the opposing troop leaders. Finally, however, a day after the burial, a barrage of unheard of ferocity begins: the beech is shattered; a huge shell crater appears on the burial place; only splinters remain of the coffin; the body has disappeared. Again the analogy with the empty grave of Christ is evident, but the irony of the causal connection is just as important. The same supreme power which takes the greatest care to ensure in due order a grave for the executed man is also responsible for its destruction: from one and the same source come preservation and annihilation.

The second episode stands, in its turn, in a sort of inverse analogy to the first. After the start of the official truce, a non-commissioned officer and twelve soldiers carry out the order to bring a body out of the mass graves of Verdun to Paris for the projected grave of the Unknown Soldier. The first part of their assignment they carry out successfully. On the way back, however, a peasant woman, under the delusion that it is her dead son, demands the body from them in return for money and they agree to the proposition. The substitute which has become necessary is offered them by a peasant who has just ploughed up the body of a fallen Frenchman while cultivating his field in the neighborhood of St. Mihiel. No one knows that it is the mortal remains of the corporal and mutineer which now are laid to rest in the grave of the Unknown Soldier.

Again, the irony consists first of all in the fact that an order from the supreme authority, as it were, crosses itself up. What the men in unison with the state power honor as a symbol of resistance against the enemy and of the highest sacrifice for the Fatherland is in reality the incarnated pure brotherly love which has just been destroyed by precisely this power. Such an exchange becomes possible because the individual yields in crucial moments to some sort of weakness which in itself need not necessarily be a negative trait. In the double bargain concerning the corpse lies a macabre atrocity. We are not used to having people treat the remains of a human being as if it were some casual object. But the behavior of the soldiers is in complete harmony with what four years of a murderous war must evoke in a man: a sort of objective attitude to death, which almost appears as "gallows humor" and which together with other means serves to keep fear away. It is, then, no accident that the one place in the whole book where drunken soldiers are portrayed is connected with this exhuming episode. Indeed, the first bargain is really determined by a desire for alcohol. But just as important is the fact that the peasant woman who wants to get possession of the body suffers from the illusion that it is her son. Her illusion has for her become reality, and this constitutes an antithesis to the public's attitude concerning the grave of the Unknown Soldier. In handing over the corpse to her, the soldiers fulfill a humanly understandable even if completely foolish wish. Their deed is inextricably compounded from the best as well as lesser motives, thereby giving it that dual nature with which all important events in this work are endowed.

The third episode is concerned with the visit of two strange figures to the farm of the corporal's half-sisters. The one asks for a snack, tries to pay for it with thirty coins, and on departure stands for an instant in the doorway so that he looks as though we were hanging from a rope. We know it is Polchek, who belonged to the corporal's group and betrayed him. The other is an Englishman, badly injured in the war, in a tattered dinner jacket, who carries off in addition to his own two medals the third, which belonged to the corporal. We learn incidentally that the corporal's young fiancée has gone back to Marseille in order—once again as a prostitute—to earn money to support her mother; and that Marthe's husband has died.

Faulkner here once more takes up several threads, both to indicate the future fate of some important characters and to prepare us for the final scene beside the grave of the Unknown Soldier. Theme and level of style are matched. The corporal's fiancée suffers and endures as she has suffered and endured in the past. Marthe remains the provident, methodical, capable wife, accompanied by her simple-minded but clear-sighted sister, Marya. Marya recognizes the traitor without denying him the right to hospitality, since she knows that he cannot escape his own suffering and fate. This is one of the very few indications in the work which allows us to conclude that the author has a normative point of view about one of his characters. While deceit and blasphemy, swindling and prostitution, theft and even manslaughter must be accepted as part of the bargain and endured as phenomena of an immutably dualistic world order, the traitor is in a class by himself. He will put an end to his own life just as, at the other end of the scale, the airman and the priest can no longer endure their lives. In both cases the decision depends on a certain interpretation of honor which is here worked out reciprocally.

The Englishman is a strange figure. Only after he tells of his injury and of how he found the way to the sisters, do we know that he must be the runner, the same man who had himself demoted in order to be nearer to the suffering of his comrades and who was responsible for the outbreak of the mutiny in the British unit. It is almost more of a supposition than a certainty because what formerly was a strong, athletic figure is now a tattered cripple with only one eye, one ear, one leg, and with one corner of the mouth stiffened to a scar. He can, however, still laugh, and he laughs spontaneously with the simple and clear-sighted Marya, who gives him the corporal's medal. And then he sets out again on the road, painful and yet patient on his crutches: "not lonely: just solitary, invincible single" (431).

It is apparent that in this presentation mimetic and symbolic elements mingle in a unique way. The events themselves are on the very edge of the explicable and succeed each other, so to say, causelessly but still completely naturally. Marya knows why the stranger with the crutches comes although she has never seen him. The laughter of the two has no reference to anything tangible; the medal changes hands without our learning why. Inevitably the result is that we ponder more about the meaning of these actions than if they took place in a causal sequence. At the same time several essential traits emerge. Marya has the power of intuitive knowledge and in her simplicity she understands more than other people. She thus becomes a clear-cut symbol of absolute understanding. We already know the runner as one who rebels against force although he himself must use force, who struggles until he is mutilated and is willing to endure all suffering. Now he encounters for the first time absolute understanding, an intuition into the relationship of things, the "sancta simplicitas," and with it he can raise himself above the misery of the world.

He sees the irony of the way the world is ordered, and gains the power and the right to laugh. Only after this does he receive the medal, the badge of honor of one who had to die for his faith in the brotherhood of men. And now he will continue on his lonely way as stranger and as one who understands.

6

The details just observed belong to what may be called the network of symbolic references in *A Fable.* It consists of a great number of apparently unimportant elements, which together with the intellectual and motivational parts of the structure, nevertheless evoke an impression of a comprehensive unity of composition, a unity which is greater than in most other novels of Faulkner and his contemporaries. There are, moreover, two distinct layers to be distinguished, in which the specific elements take on more or less meaning as symbols according to the strength of their figurative nature.

Direct symbols, that is, symbols bound up with Christian and Western tradition, are the repeatedly mentioned names and events connected with the passion of Christ. These serve to place the aim of the author in the same human and metaphysical perspective, and at the same time to show in relief the complex of suffering and endurance. In addition there are signs which always embody certain values and which appear here in their natural role, namely, the sabre and the medal. But in certain situations these symbols achieve a new meaning through allusion. The division commander, Gragnon, in whose unit the mutiny occurs, hands over his sabre to his superior as a suitable expression of his demotion. This sabre appears several more times in the course of the story, most impressively perhaps when the anonymous crowd in the headquarters city awaits the arrival of the troop leader and recognizes "the longish object" (134) which the escorting staff officer carries under his arm. The crowd knows instantly what is involved when a division commander is under arrest, and it breaks out into a sound which carries its own symbolic meaning. The sabre is the recognized symbol not only of the honor of arms but also of the epitome of power, of rank, and of the war. And the fact that the division commander no longer commands it contains the concise theme of the collapse of order and its consequences.

In contrast to this uncomplicated symbol, the medal appears considerably more complex. In itself it is a military distinction, bestowed for bravery against the enemy. With Faulkner, however, it assumes still another meaning: it is the visible sign of injustice, suffering, and torment endured in the terror of war. A medal is first mentioned almost incidentally in the scene in which the division commander thinks of his past before he enters the headquarters. He recalls an incident in which one of his aides, at the sacrifice of his life, had warned the passengers in a coach of an artillery attack, and had been posthumously decorated. The theme of sacrifice is voiced and is characteristically connected immediately with the undertone of grim irony which anticipates a further theme: the medal can never be placed with the aide's corpse for the simple reason that it, as later that of the corporal, is not to be found. This episode, short as it is, has in addition its own special relevance, since among the passengers in the coach is the American woman in whose organization the Negro friend of the jockey works. Thus, the medal already serves to hold together several elements of the story.

The second mention of a military distinction occurs in the beginning of the story of the runner, who voluntarily has himself demoted and then conceals the decoration since he wants to remain an anonymous soldier (65). In this closer association with the group the first hint is given of the possible trouble which the runner could make in his new position, and which indeed later actually assumes the form of mutiny. Thus, here too the symbol is connected with elements which are crucial for the action.

The third medal is the corporal's, taken from him immediately before his execution by a non-commissioned officer who later gives it to Marthe (384). It is the tragic climax of the whole, once again sounding the disturbing note of irony: the sign of honor is removed at the instant when the passion attains its completion. And finally the same medal, which is saved by the two half-sisters in St. Mihiel, passes over into the hands of the British runner (431), who at the end of the story throws it on the coffin at the burial of the commander-in-chief. These two scenes, whose crucial significance we have already discussed, are thus prepared for not only through certain courses of action and intellectual concepts but equally through a slow and careful charging of the symbolic objects.

We have thus reached a second level of meaning, namely, those numerous examples of motives and plot divisions which first appear to be ordinary mimetic constructional elements and only through repetition assume by degrees the character of recurring motifs or symbols. The most easily recognizable motifs are perhaps the repeatedly mentioned mud-covered uniforms of the soldiers or, in contrast to this, the tattered tuxedo of the runner, symbol of his origin and rank in society, cast off by him but still not wholly to be denied. How the moldering airsuit of the young American officer, referred to time and again, in the end becomes a symbol of the decay and destruction of religious value has already been described. Similarly, the groaning noise which the waiting crowd raises at the appearance of the mutineers and later of the division commander gradually becomes an expression of that dull and silent suffering which in certain moments is heard not only by fellow men but also by those in authority without, however, the possibility of anything further being done about it.

The motif-group of food, drink, and spoon which appears repeatedly and which is given peculiar stress is far from easy to interpret. At the very beginning of the story we learn how the corporal's young fiancée obtains a piece of bread from an unknown person, which she spits out again while chewing as she sees her beloved, a prisoner, go by on the lorry (18). The three women are abused by the crowd as they approach a group to share a meal with it, and one of the crowd throws a spoon at them which mysteriously disappears. The next day the vanished spoon is the object of complaint that is even brought to the attention of the commander-in-chief, whereupon it reappears. The commander-in-chief, the division commander, the troop leaders, as well as the captured mutineers are depicted in detail while eating and drinking. This is also true of Polchek, the betrayer, and the British runner during their visit to the sisters, where, moreover, a spoon is once more mentioned, though knife and fork never appear in this context.

These examples affect all ranks, and there is in them something of the nature of Communion, which, according to the attitude of the participant, produces a redemptive or a hardening effect. The quality of Communion appears most unmistakably and in most direct analogy to Holy Week in the last common meal of the thirteen mutineers in prison where the treachery of Polchek becomes evident and Pierre denies the corporal. Amid tension and release and tinged with the grotesque, the mealtime of the troop leaders proceeds, as does that of the two visitors in St. Mihiel. An atmosphere of silence, loneliness, and also an awareness of their responsibility surrounds the means of the commander-in-chief and the division commander. Outspoken hardness, even hostility, confronts us in the attitude of part of the waiting crowd when a basket with foodstuffs is overthrown and the incident of the spoon occurs.[8] It seems as if, in their gross violation of the most elementary principles of decency, unique resources, at the very least, would have to be invoked to bring this group of human beings to order again. Here also the element of irony and the grotesque is not lacking. The commander-in-chief apparently attributes to the disappearance of the spoon such great significance that he sends out an adjutant with a whole company to search in the streets for it, knowing already that one of the sisters will produce it (273, 284). Perhaps it is going too far to think here of the concept of the wanton gods, but at least the notion of the highest being concerned with the smallest and most commonplace is present and this necessarily raises a serious matter in the sphere of humor.

In this connection one may also point to some of those elements of Faulkner's style which are especially close to the other aspects of his art. For a long time Faulkner's narrative technique and style were usually related to the allusions and associations of the stream of consciousness technique, and in fact his best known early works, especially *The Sound and the Fury* (1929), are strongly indebted to this manner of writing. In a greatly modified way, this is still the case even in *A Fable,* for here also are those feverish page-long sentences which set whole series of ideas in vibration. However, this time the ordering hand has become much more visible. What earlier often had a wearying effect because the relevance for the whole was not apparent has now been given direction and is filled with tension. The following example is taken from the scene at the beginning of the story when the crowd in the little French garrison city stands waiting for the arrival of the arrested mutineers and recognizes the thirteen ringleaders on the last truck:

Then you saw that four of the thirteen were really foreigners, alien not only by their gyves and isolation to the rest of the regiment but, against the whole panorama of city and soil across which the lorry was rushing them—the faces of four mountain men in a country which had no mountains, of peasants in a land which no longer had a peasantry; alien even among the other nine among whom they were chained and shackled, since where the other nine were grave and watchful and a little—not too much—concerned, three of the four who were not Frenchmen were merely a little puzzled, alert too, almost decorous, curious and interested: the mountain peasants whom they resembled, entering for the first time a strange valley market town, say; men overtaken suddenly by an uproar in a tongue which they had no hope of comprehending and, indeed, not much interest in, and therefore no concern in its significance—three of the four who were not Frenchmen, that is, because now the crowd itself had discerned that the fourth one was alien still somehow even to the other three, if only in being the sole object of its vituperation and terror and fury. (16–17)

The theme is that of the Crowd and the Stranger. The element of strangeness is expressed directly through words such as "alien," "foreigner," "strange," "not Frenchmen," "no hope of comprehending," etc; indirectly, though with equal force, through the opposites: land/city, peasantry/market-town; and finally through certain characteristic associations: "mountain men in a country which had no mountains, peasants in a land which no longer had a peasantry"; that is, concrete things in a surrounding to which they no longer belong. In this case, the alienation is indicated not only through the sharpness of the contrast but also through a special gradation. Relevant here is the just mentioned "no longer" that signifies a relation which is conceivable but no longer in existence, as well as (before the beginning of our quotation) the stress placed first on the thirteen out of the whole number of the regiment, then on the four out of the thirteen, and finally on the one out of the four. This gradation is further emphasized through the distinctions observed in the behavior of the captives. The nine are grave, attentive, and concerned; the four rather surprised by it all, a little puzzled, even curious and interested, so that the calm behavior of the one (the corporal) whose description is still to follow is then seen in really sharp contrast to the movement of the raging crowd. Appropriately the method of doubling and a kind of contrasted intensification is employed: doubling in the expressions "gyves and isolation," "city and soil," "chained and shackled," and in the already mentioned pairs of opposites; intensification in the expressions "grave and watchful and a little—not too much—concerned," and in the clear logical progression of "an uproar in a tongue which they had no hope of comprehending and, indeed, not much interest in, and therefore no concern in its significance." The successive qualifications in the style are achieved, among other things, by the introduction of negation-particles, that is, a positive is expressed by a negative. This is a stylistic device so striking in Faulkner that one can have scarcely any doubt about its reference to a basically dualistic world view.

7

The whole work combines extraordinary pertinence for our time with unusual validity in the statements. The world of the war, not only as a sequence of events to be regarded mimetically but also as a symbol for the eternal suffering of mankind, is by itself an idea whose power cannot be avoided by modern man. All our cares have here been put into epic form. No order without force, no justice without power, no power without destruction, no loyalty without betrayal, no faith without doubt, no union without loneliness, no constancy without weakness, no Christ without Judas, no God without Satan. The dualism that Faulkner attributes to the whole world order belongs to that concept of tragedy which rests on the irresolvable contrasts of existence, yet allows no room for a real despair. The collapse of the American flier and the suicide of the priest are actions which follow from the over-refining of an illusionary idealism. They are the catastrophes of those who cannot endure the irony of the dualistic scale of values. And indeed endurance is precisely the one single highest value that Faulkner does not question by a contrast to its own category. Endurance is terribly hard, but it is the solution of sensitive men in the incessant strife between the opposing forces. And he who can endure also learns to understand, and he who can understand can also laugh. The laughter may often be filled with bitterness and horror, but it is also the occasion for and the indication of a momentary liberation from the weight of existence. Faulkner's irony borders on humor as well as on pathos.

The intellectual conception of the whole would not alone establish the book as a literary masterpiece. What makes it this is the absolute fusion of the philosophical with the epic development. The techniques of doubling, inversion, parallel structure, and opposition, in plot, characters, and single motifs are omnipresent but so handled that one becomes conscious of them only through a close analysis of events. Otherwise one simply gains a forceful total impression of what was designated here as duality. Battlescene and armistice, front line and rear base, general and non-commissioned officer, crowd and individual, stranger and home, man and animal, communion and execution, burial and exhumation are contrasted in such a way that again and again an equilibrium of events is attained.

And finally we have to do with that rare form of action which is indebted to the real as well as to the symbolic in such a way that the two spheres merge almost imperceptibly. Parts of the action and characters such as the past history of the sentry as jockey, the execution of the French division commander, and the characterization of the American pilot at first appear to belong completely to mimesis and its crudest forms. In contrast, there are those elements of the same sort which can scarcely be interpreted mimetically, but must be regarded as openly symbolic, such as the encounter between the commander-in-chief and the corporal, their characterization, and all the episodes which are directly modelled on the events of the Passion. Between these two poles the rest revolve; that is, most of the events can be read either as a realistic account of a deeply moving war story or as an extensive allegory of the structure of existence held together by a whole network of real and symbolic references.

Faulkner's work confirms a trend which has become exceedingly significant in American intellectual life, and simultaneously gives it a new degree of projection. It is the remolding of the unalloyed realism of the period between the wars into something that could be called symbolic mimesis. It is found in numerous works of the younger authors such as Truman Capote, Wright Morris, Ralph Ellison, Jean Stafford, Paul Bowles, as well as in playwrights such as Tennessee Williams, Arthur Miller, and Robert Anderson, and in lyric poets such as Robert Lowell and Theodore Roethke. Hemingway's *The Old*

Man and the Sea also belongs here. Even in the American literary essay, the tendency to a synthesis of the concrete and the symbolic way of thinking can be seen. Furthermore, this goes hand in hand with a negative evaluation of all attitudes tending to illusion, of which the new concern with Scott Fitzgerald's work is characteristic. What raises Faulkner's book above all this, however, is the all-embracing nature of his subject-matter, the suspension of his intellectual magnetic field between Manichaeism, Stoicism, and Christianity, and the meaningful references which are thoroughly worked out down to the smallest detail. It is a milestone in the history of American literature.

1. One of the most understanding reviews up to this time is Philip Blair Rice's "Faulkner's Crucifixion," in the *Kenyon Reivew,* Autumn, 1954, p. 660 ff. In it among other things, remote connections with the theology of Reinhold Niebuhr and Paul Tillich are spoken of. Brilliant, but scarcely doing justice to the matter, is R. W. Flint's review in the *Hudson Review,* Winter, 1955, p. 602 ff.

After the completion of the present work, the article by the noted American lyric poet Delmore Schwartz appeared in *Perspectives,* No. 10, Winter, 1955, p. 126 ff. It contains a penetrating discussion of the novel, which is characterized as "a masterpiece, a unique fulfillment of Faulkner's genius." Schwartz also takes up several points which are considered as crucial in the present article, but his argument stresses the problem of a (monistically considered) belief in humanity and the conquest of fear.

2. See on this subject Maurice Edgar Coindreau, "William Faulkner in France," *Yale French Studies,* No. 10 (1953), p. 85 ff. as well as Thelma M. Smith and Ward L. Miner, *Transatlantic Migration: The Contemporary American Novel in France* (Durham, N.C., 1955).

3. Cf. Cleanth Brooks, "Notes on Faulkner's *Light in August,* " in the *Harvard Advocate,* 135, Nov. 1951, a number which contains several other noteworthy articles on Faulkner; further, see Richard Chase's "The Stone and the Crucifixion: Faulkner's *Light in August,* " in *Kenyon Review,* Autumn, 1948.

4. The expressions "mimesis" and "level of style" have been taken over, appropriately I hope, from Erich Auerbach's *Mimesis: Representation of Reality in Western Literature* (Bern, 1946).

5. The page numbers are those of the original American edition by Random House, New York, 1954.

6. The same expressions concluded the famous speech which Faulkner delivered on December 10, 1950, on the occasion of receiving the Nobel Prize.

7. Charles Anderson had already pointed to this before the publication of *A Fable* in his article "Faulkner's Moral Center," in *Études Anglaises,* January, 1954, p. 48 ff.

8. In the eastern Church the communion wine is taken with a spoon. Whether Faulkner knows of this custom is not certain.

THE REIVERS: FAULKNER'S TEMPEST

WILLIAM ROSSKY

WHETHER THEY APPROVED or not—and most approved—reviewers of William Faulkner's *The Reivers* generally regarded it as an easy, sometimes wild comedy with slight overtones of moral seriousness—an opinion which they shared, incidentally, with the dust-jacket blurb. And surely it is largely true that, as Irving Howe said in his thoughtful, rather representative review, "Faulkner does not strain as he has in his recent novels to compound a total vision of life," that *The Reivers* "is a comic novel more easy-spirited" and less "ponderous" than other late Faulkner novels.[1] But both in the early reviews and in the more recent books on Faulkner, repeatedly the implication has been, as in Howe's essay, that, since it is comedy and "does not strain," the book cannot evoke "a total vision of life" and is essentially escapist and minor— "deliberately minor," according to Howe.[2]

If, however, *The Reivers* is indeed minor, it must also be noted that it is most significant Faulkner and occupies a special place in the cannon of his works; that its thematic relationship to Faulkner's great tragedies of the 1920's and 1930's is something like the relationship of *The Tempest* to Shakespeare's major work.[3] In this light, the relaxed, sometimes amused, tolerant tone becomes perhaps the most important thing about the novel; for it is Faulkner viewing life with a Shakespeare-Prospero's perspective. Far from being his escape, it is precisely Faulkner's summing up—like Prospero's, his final, most complete acceptance of time, of the human condition.

Some such development we might well have anticipated from Faulkner's frequently expressed views of his art. Repeatedly he emphasized not only that every one of his novels was an attempt to capture on paper the whole of life and that this was his reason for writing—that he had "to tell all the truth in that one time,"[4] that even in his long sentences he was "trying to put the whole history of the human heart on the head of a pin"[5]—but also that "life is in constant flux and in constant change and the time that you don't learn some-

Reprinted with permission from *Mississippi Quarterly*, XVIII (Spring, 1965), 82–93.

thing new every day you are dead";[6] and he thus indicated that each novel was an attempt to communicate a newly evolved and evolving grasp of life, in a sense of summation to that point of his life. In his prefatory remarks to *The Mansion,* he spoke of "living" as "motion," which he called "change and alteration"; and "change and alteration" involved, for Faulkner, learning "more about the human heart and its dilemma than he knew thirty-four years ago."[7] From these comments, we may judge that in his work Faulkner felt he was expressing total visions, but visions constantly developing, changing. *The Reivers* fits this pattern.

But even were it not clear from Faulkner's own remarks that his every novel was an attempt at a final picture and for that moment of his time, surely in this novel he evokes the sense of a vision at the drawing to a close of the curtain. To a degree the very subtitle, *A Reminiscence,* suggests not only nostalgia, but also a *personal* review of life in old age. Earlier in *The Town,* Faulkner stands with Gavin Stevens on the ridge overlooking Jefferson, reviewing, trying for the final evaluation, not yet old but "old man, standing there," "detached as God Himself for this moment" above the vista of a land and a past "proffered for . . . perusal in ring by concentric ring like the ripples on living water."[8] In *The Reivers,* however, Faulkner views, not from the high ridge, but from the elevation of old age itself. A Grandfather Lucius speaks and a Grandfather Faulkner writes and upon this depends the particular mood and meaning of *The Reivers.*[9]

That the novel is the work of an aging Faulkner looking back, weighing life through his own past, is suggested not simply by the fact that Faulkner was at the time of the writing a grandfather, but perhaps more by the presence, to an unusual degree in his work, of such rather clearly autobiographical material as, for example, the facts that, like Lucius', Faulkner's father once ran a livery stable; that Faulkner's father's name also was Murray ("Maury" in *The Reivers*); that his grandfather, like Lucius', was a banker; that Faulkner had as childhood companion a man almost exactly like Boon who also worked for his father; that, indeed, on his farm outside Oxford, Faulkner employed an Uncle Ned, who, formerly like Ned of *The Reivers,* had been his grandfather's servant and who, from Robert Cantwell's description,[10] was the sort of person into whom the Uncle Ned of *The Reivers* might easily have turned. Even so small a thing as the satire on the hyprocrisy of citizens that elect a sheriff to enforce dry laws but express "the true will of the people" by buying bootleg liquor[11] reflects a personal interest—indeed has the same satirical point and tone as Faulkner's *Oxford Eagle* letter (Sept. 14, 1950) protesting the local dry vote.

However, that he is the grandfather, the aged author, reliving and review-ing his past is more strongly suggested by the ghosts of earlier fiction that float in the background of the novel like nostalgic echoes. It is not only that we have, in the familiar Faulknerian manner, those rather clear and often full references to characters and events of earlier novels, instances of which reviewers were quick to point out—the rewarding reappearance of Miss Reba and Mr. Binford from *Sancutary,* for instance, or the repeated anecdotes about Boon and his bad marksmanship, or even the references to the McCaslins and General Compson and the hunting and Lucius Quintus Carothers and his Negro de-scendants that appear earlier in *Go Down, Moses*—but that we hear as echoes only, casually, without elaboration, of the "baronial dream" of Sutpen from *Absalom, Absalom!* (p. 72); of Hiram Hightower, minister (p. 75), father to Gail Hightower from *Light in August;* of Christian's drugstore and Doc Pea-body and Judge Stevens (p. 15) from *As I Lay Dying, Knight's Gambit, The Town* and *The Mansion;* of Flem Snopes' "Hotel" and of Major Manfred de Spain and his "red E.M.F. racer" (pp. 24, 25) from *The Town;* of Colonel Sartoris and the Colonel (by courtesy) Bayard Sartoris of *Sartoris* and *The Unvanquished* (pp. 25, 74); of the Chickasaw chiefs—Issetibbeha, Moketubbe, and Ikkemotubbe, "who called himself Doom" (p. 73) from the Indian tales and the history of *Requiem for a Nun.* So too we encounter, almost sublimi-nally, any number of notes or ideas sounded before—for example, the idealistic freemasonry of the lovers of horses which appeared earlier in *A Fable,* the familiar Faulknerian view of the resiliency of women (pp. 111, 118), and echoes of the scene at the flooded river in *As I Lay Dying* as the "forked" animals struggle with their mired car (p. 87). Indeed, in the mule passage (pp. 121–123) Faulkner goes back to his novelistic beginnings, echoing the bravura section on the mule in *Sartoris,* even to describing the mule as the animal that copes with life. The world Faulkner created in his earlier fiction plays over *The Reivers* like the recurrent images of memory in day dreams. It is as if the old novelist were casually, almost unconsciously going back to touch charac-ters and events, ideas, and places of that fiction—the aged author surveying the past, his work.

Most of all, it is the grandfather note of past in present, the emphasis on age speaking to youth about growing up, of age trying to explain the meaning of life through its own past, that gives us the feeling of review and wise re-evaluation. Technically this sense of age revealing to youth is in part evoked by the little explanatory notes literally sprinkled through the novel: "Front seats didn't have doors in those days; you just walked up and got in" (p. 34), "Grandfather's house is now chopped into apartments" (p. 66), or "people took funerals seriously in those days. Not death: death was our constant familiar" (p. 44). In those days folks had to fill the car radiator at "creeks or barrow pits" (p. 65), and a hamlet consisted of "two or three stores" (p. 166). Always we are reminded of the age of the speaker interpreting the past for the present and for youth.

It is this grandfather emphasis which most of all gives to the book the tone of a man in his final relaxed vision, past the time of the personal agony, not forgetting it, indeed reliving it but also at ease, seeing it now as a part of the whole of life, and what life is. It is precisely this perspective, lacking in Faulkner's earlier novels, that helps to give *The Reivers* its *Tempest* flavor— the sense of a rich and final summing up, of life judged, of evil and difficulty sadly discovered as real and permanent but accepted with a complete faith in the regenerative power of difficulty itself, even with delight, therefore, in life. As *The Tempest* is often assumed to have been for Shakespeare, *The Reivers* is what Faulkner in the grandfather stage of life easily and spontaneously and ripely felt. As Prospero-Shakespeare reviewed his past magic—as he evoked in *The Tempest* echoes of *Macbeth* in "I have a bedimm'd/The noontide sun," of *King Lear* in "[I have] called forth the mutinous winds" and "to the dread rattling thunder/Have I given fire, and rifted Job's stout oak," or of *Macbeth* and *Hamlet* in "graves at my command/ Have wak'd their sleepers, op'd, and let 'em forth/By my so potent art" (V, i, 41–50)—so Faulkner, arriving in the logic of his development at his feeling about life in old age, surveys in passing *his* "rough magic," probably not knowing that his was the last time he would wield his staff, but, like Shakespeare, at the time and place of his life for the vision of age, as the sub-title prods us to understand, and thus in "motion," in the natural order of things, creating *his* final vision.

The Reivers, then, is Faulkner's reconciliation piece; the storm, "the sound and the fury" of earlier work is calmed by Prospero-Faulkner. To see this, we have only to examine Faulkner's use of the initiation experience. Repeatedly in working and re-working his basic grasp of experience, Faulkner has presented the impact of the difficult world upon opening consciousnesses, and thus indicated his constantly revised vision of experience. Frequently, as in *The Reivers,* youth emerges from the innocence and dream of Eden to the suffering of life, and the reaction to that suffering is an index to Faulkner's developing vision of how to "cope" with life. Even in those novels in which initiated youth is not the agency of Faulkner's vision, Faulkner often conveys a sense of initiation through an encounter with life. In his early work, although almost always there are the "accepters"[12] who can endure, generally the initiates suffer and fail, later they endure, and still later the compensation is that suffering helps them to come alive, to feel. But *The Reivers* conveys not only a sense of acceptance of the suffering because of the power of pain to rescue life from aridity, to give feeling, to give us our humanity, but also the value of suffering as a generative principle, as the essential basis of growth.

A brief review of the earlier work may serve to make this clear. Thus, as early as the sketches which appeared in 1925 in the New Orleans magazine, *The Double Dealer,* Faulkner presents characters who begin with the innocent dreams of childhood to end in the diminution of life and the disillusion that succeed the encounter. "When I was young" opens his sketch "The Cop"; "When I was a boy," begins "the Beggar." The second paragraph of his "Magdalen" starts, "I can remember when I found days of gold." Each finds, as the "Cop" tells us, that "life is not like that." But these are sketches and, despite occasional flashes of Faulknerian prose, rather conventionally sentimental reflections on the evanescence of the dreams and hopes of youth. So too the despairs of the early novels through most of *Sartoris* are commonly regarded as imitative Byronic or *fin de siecle* attitudes. But in *The Sound and the Fury* the harsh experience of the "loud world" shocks and disillusions the sensitive man, Quentin, much as it does Hamlet. Expelled by reality from the innocent paradise where Caddy's was Eve's "voice that breathed o'er Eden," he cannot learn to live with the evil of existence. For Quentin, living offers no compensations; everything in "time"—values included—is "temporary." Time is suffering, and Quentin's response, like Bayard's in *Sartoris,* is suicide. Indeed, if Dilsey goes on nobly, her compensation seems chiefly to be that she endures. If upon meeting the reality of death, Vardaman in *As I Lay Dying* is finally consoled by a banana, the encounter of the more sensitive Darl with the whirling world drives him mad. The Bundrens do "cope," says Faulkner;[13] but their coping is, after all, limited, not human, somewhat, indeed, like that of the mules of *Sartoris* or *The Reivers.* Horace Benbow in *Sanctuary,* again the sensitive man, is for the most part initiated into defeat. The child Joe Christmas, encountering in his orphaned childhood the hatreds of the adult world, is handed the cross upon which he is finally crucified. Repeatedly it is the child's lot to grow into suffering. "It ain't right. I be durned if it is. Because He said Suffer little children to come unto Me don't make it right, neither,"[14] is Tull's comment in *As I Lay Dying* on the inevitable course from childhood to manhood; and in *Absalom, Absalom!* Tull's point of view is echoed even in the poignant experience of a Rosa Coldfield, whose suffering seems to begin even with her birth and who lives, as she indicates, a silent, anguished little shade haunting the dark and empty corridors of her childhood. And Sutpen, just descended from his mountain Eden, stands innocently outside a plantation door; then the next moment is outraged by his encounter with a system that has grown out of man's cruelty and rapacity and is thus compressed into the new and blind "innocence" that drives him in another tragic waste along that reverberating hall of falling pillars which forms the last half of *Absalom, Absalom!* If in *The Unvanquished* Bayard, out of the experience of the arrogance, hatred, and violence that are the actual substance of the code of "honor" and vengeance, emerges to a recognition of the brutality and futility of that code, he wins the slender accolade of a sprig of verbena and, from George Wyatt, only a grudging admission that perhaps his point of view is right. Bayard has changed, and perhaps George Wyatt is beginning to change, but the effect is ultimately like that of *Go Down, Moses:* As Ike, perhaps the most famous of Faulkner's initiates, says, ". . . even from them the elected and chosen the best the very best He could expect . . . would be Bucks and Buddies and not even enough of them and in the third generation not even Bucks and Buddies. . . ."[15] And Ike is the only one in his own generation, and even he finally fails his own values in "Delta Autumn." Increasingly through his encounter the sensitive initiate learns more, becomes more human, and "copes" better; but the view of existence is still dim.

Somewhat earlier, in *The Wild Palms,* confronting, at the end, all the pain and all the "waste," the little that is asked by man and, despite the horror of "all the old graveyard-creeping," nevertheless denied, the once untutored Wilbourne finally faces the reality of how little man can expect and in assertion of life finally chooses *not* the "nothing" of death but "grief" which is at least living, feeling. But if there is life in grief, there is little promise. And this point of view reaches forward to that expressed in *Requiem for a Nun* in which suffering, Temple learns, is somehow, but very vaguely, man's salvation. The often bitter humor of *The Hamlet* modulates easily into the intense irony of Flem's success and into the immense tragic implications of the scene after the stampede as man, Armstid, lies screaming in pain while, vastly and silently, the spring night flowers and burgeons. As Varner says at this point, "Breathing is a sight-draft dated yesterday." To which Ratliff replies with the "fierce risibility" of the initiated man, "Even if there was time to take it." In contrast to Flem, every man in *The Hamlet* asserts his humanity in and through difficulty; he lives and feels. But ultimately in the novel generation and fertility are defeated.

Even in the three novels before *The Reivers,* novels in which it is generally felt that Faulkner pontificated solutions to the problems of life, the tone of the initiation remains more anguished than in *The Reivers.* At the end of *A Fable* the runner, who is here Faulkner's initiate and who of Faulkner's triumvirate in the novel ultimately represents the greatest hope, "knowing and caring,"[16] moves forward torturously, progressing only by excruciating effort. He will live—"I'm not going to die. Never," he asserts on the last page—but he is alone, crippled, and ends bloodily beaten by the mob. The corporal and his disciples of which there were only twelve—again not many "Bucks and Buddies"—have been executed. The faith in and promise of the endurance of the man who knows and cares is a slender hope. The best one can do—and it is, of course, not little—is to assert his own achieved humanity before the onslaught of existence. Even in *The Town,* not only is the Snopes humor on the whole rather grim, but, gazing over the town which becomes for a moment the world, the "old man," Stevens-as-Faulkner or Faulkner-as-Stevens, concedes man's rapacity and sees that his "dreams" are tortured (pp. 316–318): "Because the tragedy of life is, it must be premature, inconclusive and inconcludable in order to be life." So in symbolic moments at the end of *The Mansion* Stevens stands for a moment alone, dwarfed by the wheeling constellations in the first chill breaths of fall and oncoming winter, and Mink finally accepts, sinks to the "Old Moster" earth to lie "anonymous with" and "inextricable from" the glorious dead. If to a degree the passage exalts Mink, it also comments on the futility even of greatness—"Helen and the Bishops, the kings."

Repeatedly, to be sure, from Dilsey on, Faulkner presents values by which man "copes," but always the hope, though real and increasingly strong, remains comparatively tenuous, tentative, limited. Suffering is living, inescapably a part of life, indeed what helps us to feel, to be Man; "grief" is living and better than "nothing," and humor modifies anguish and man endures, shows courage, loyalty, even sometimes, out of the very anguish of his life, compassion for others, as in a Dilsey or Gail Hightower, or sometimes, out of the same suffering, a pride which helps him to endure before pain, although, again, that same pride, tangling and wrestling with other lives, itself creates pain and chaos for its possessors and a chain of others, as in a Sutpen, a Mink, or a Houston. Chiefly the view in the novels is tragic. All the way to *The Reivers* life is motion in time; and to live in time, to *be* in time, to be *is,* is to be in pain. Always we move from an innocent Eden into life's difficulty and the greatest compensation is our very humanization, our coming alive.

Even in *The Reivers* this view remains. It is hardly the hilarious romp that some critics have described, for Lucius learns that to live in time is to live in the world of broken promises and difficulty. Lucius, as grandfather, specifically recognizes this Faulknerian pattern in his past: "I was a child no longer now;

innocence and childhood were forever lost, forever gone from me" (p. 175). Not unlike Prospero's encounter with evil in Milan comes Lucius' exposure to the lying, the cruel unpitying lust of Butch, or, for that matter, even of Boon; to Butch's savage toying with Everbe, his delight in inflicting pain; to indignities offered to the truly dignified like Uncle Parsham; to human beings preying upon human beings, people like Otis and Butch and Aunt Fittie, who draws Everbe, still a child, into prostitution; and not only to Otis but to those whom Otis invites, at a price, to watch the shame of Everbe, a group very much like that which horrifies Ratliff and makes the reader seethe in *The Hamlet* when Lump utilizes for profit Ike's love for the cow. As so often in Faulkner, the index to the pain of time is once more the desire to be out of it. Knowing he is about to learn of evil from Otis and not wanting therefore "to be there at all" (p. 154), wishing he were in "another time: another life" (p. 156) and wishing even that he could stop, not asking the question which will destroy childhood paradise—"And already the thing inside me saying *No No Don't ask Leave it Leave it*" (p. 255)—but which, whatever the answer, he must ask and must somehow absorb, repeatedly Lucius wants to hold off the pain of knowledge, of the "things, circumstances, conditions in the world which should not be there but are, and you can't escape them" (p. 155). Even Minnie's gold tooth is a reminder of our mortal predicament. It is her talisman; restored to her, it makes her "once more immune, once more invulnerable to that extent which our frail webs of bone and flesh and coincidence ever hold or claim on Invulnerability" (p. 278). The very joy in the novel springs often out of frustration —Saturday night saturnalia end "in one last spumy upfling against the arduous humdrum of day-by-day for mere bread and shelter" (p. 139). And what Prospero sees in his great speech as he brings to a focal point a major Renaissance theme—that everything must "dissolve," that "We are such stuff/As dreams are made on, and our little life/Is rounded with a sleep" (IV, i, 156–158)—Lucius also learns: Life is brief, evanescent, a "quick leap in the dark" (p. 160).

But if in *The Reivers* Faulkner recognizes evil, he also sees not only the need to suffer in order to live, to become human, but also the regenerative power of the very difficulty of life. Here the stream of time is not to be anguished over but to be open to; not only to live in and to come alive in, but, in a more positive way than he has hitherto suggested, to learn from, to grow. Grief itself ends literally in a happy fertility; and even though it presents us with a comic Miranda and Ferdinand and even though, despite a kind of hard comedy which helps a little to cover the sentimentality, the episode may be described as "corny," the birth of Everbe's baby brings *The Reivers* to a close on a key note. If often the mood is less lighthearted than in this moment, the emphasis of the book remains, like that of *The Tempest*, on potential, growth, and ripeness in time.

Ripeness in time. If Lucius must leave his island Eden, his ultimate reward, like Prospero's, is a richness of understanding and development which leaves us soberly content as does *The Tempest*. Much of this feeling, of course, results from the Faulkner-grandfather perspective discussed earlier, a perspective which in its review of the past suggests Faulkner's own sense of the richness of the life lived and the creative work done. Even more it arises from the lambency of the kindly grandfather mind playing over the novel which in itself modifies the anguish. But most of all it lies in the Prospero-like vision of Lucius grown old. Clearly, young Lucius's initiation experiences are not all bitter; but, whatever the bitterness of his initiation, what must be remembered is that it ends in the vision of Lucius in old age, the harvest of a lifetime of initiation. Through the development of Lucius into sage grandfather, we feel chiefly the sense of ripeness in time; experience has been lived through and made valuable. Through Lucius' vision, we understand the fertility of time.

If, as kindly grandfather looking back upon youth, Lucius regrets sadly the difficulty of life, he goes beyond regret to an understanding of its promise. It is much like the mood conveyed by *The Tempest* when to Miranda's "O brave new world" (V, i, 183), Prospero replies, "Tis new to thee." His answer foreshadows the sad disillusion of every man, the pain of the inevitable encounter which lies in store for innocence leaving its island. But, in the context of the union of lovers, of regeneration and reconciliation, of the "increase, foison plenty" prophesied earlier by Ceres (IV, i, 110), this sad note fuses with and is almost overwhelmed by the sense of the potential fruitfulness of life. Thus if "Fortune" remains a "fickle jade, who never withholds but gives, either good or bad," she also, for the first time in Faulkner, gives "more of the former than you ever believe (perhaps with justice) that you deserve" as well as "more of the latter than you can handle" (p. 48). If fortune takes, she also gives copiously of the good. If there are "circumstances . . . which should not be there," it is also true that "you would not escape them even if you had the choice, since they too are a part of Motion, of participating in life, being alive" (p. 155). A combination of moods—humor, wryness, and seriousness—appears in the smilingly left-handed compliment of old Lucius' evaluation of the cleverness of mules and men; and out of the mingling of moods arises an edge of optimism in favor of "ignorant" man (p. 122), just as out of the mingled moods of *The*

Tempest arises an evaluation shaded optimistically in favor of man. If Saturday night joy springs out of frustration, it is also an "upfling," a surge of man's deep and rich being; if Minnie's gold tooth suggests our vulnerability, it is also a radiant hyperbole of dentistry that expresses warmly her human worth. And always man can help himself: God provides but man may use fruitfully what is provided. Uncle Parsham prays "briefly, courteously but with dignity, without abasement or cringing . . . notifying Heaven that we were about to eat and thanking It for the privilege, but at the same time reminding It that It had had some help too" (p. 247). Democracy itself is a fruit that arises out of the struggle with difficulty (p. 234). Earlier, Faulkner had seen the wilderness in "The Bear" as God's land which develops a man if he will let it; but then it develops only a single Ike, and the wilderness is vanishing. Here grandfather Lucius says, "But perhaps they—you—will find wilderness on the backside of Mars or the moon with maybe even bear and deer to run it" (p. 21). The wilderness expands, even beyond the world, into worlds, which expand into future time—the creative potential is almost infinite.

But the aged Lucius inherits from the child Lucius, and principally the regenerative hope of *The Reivers* comes from the initiation experience of Lucius as child. Parallel in many ways, his education nevertheless differs significantly from that of the other Faulkner figures examined above. Severe, trying, evil the experiences may often have been, but to quote Lucius:

I mean, if those four days—the lying and deceiving and tricking and decisions and undecisions, and the things I had done and seen and heard and learned that Mother and Father wouldn't have let me do and see and hear and learn —the things I had had to learn that I wasn't even ready for yet, had nowhere to store them nor even anywhere to lay them down; if all that had changed nothing, was the same as if it had never been—nothing smaller or larger or older or wiser or more pitying—then something had been wasted, thrown away, spent for nothing. . . . (pp. 299–300).

And what *The Reivers* makes clear is that it is not "wasted," that, indeed, the experience is creative. It is almost as if Lucius' grandfather were replying directly to the uncertainty which Lucius has expressed, when, a few pages later, he says, "Nothing is ever forgotten. Nothing is ever lost. It's too valuable" (p. 302).

The change about which Lucius is uncertain he finally begins to see has nothing to do with "your outside" because "your outside is just what you live in, sleep in, and has little connection with who you are and even less with what you do" (p. 304). It is not merely that Lucius has become acquainted with some of the basic "facts of life" (p. 196), as he has. Rather, like Ike McCaslin in the wilderness, Lucius through his experiences—tutored by Uncle Parsham's dignity, by Everbe's sacrifice of herself to keep the others free, by the sameness of man no matter what his color (Uncle Parsham is repeatedly compared with Lucius' grandfather), by the wiliness and appetites but more by the honor of Ned ("Because we never done it for money," p. 282), by the vicious egocentrism of a Butch or an Otis, by Sam's easy tolerance and efficiency, by the very need to go on for the sake of Ned and Boon, and, because he must accept "the responsibility of his actions" (p. 302), by his discovered need to finish a job, no matter how painful—tutored by all these, Lucius grows up. He lies and "sins" and meets sin, takes his "leaps in the dark," and, "hating" in the ambivalence of all our growth and change even the good who inflict decisions and pain upon us (p. 174), makes in the freedom of the will his Self-shaping choices. Like Ike in his encounter with the wilderness, Lucius, with the help of his rearing, learns and demonstrates the virtues of pity and pride, endurance, respect for the weak like Everbe, honor in defending it in an Everbe, and loyalty—which is severely tested yet confirmed by the demands placed upon it by the behavior of Boon, Everbe, and even Ned. However, although the wilderness may be said to represent God's basic world in "The Bear" and thus to offer some promise for any man's development, here in *The Reivers* the hope is greater: For in *The Reivers* the growth toward soul and manhood is possible not merely in a myth of the real world, but in the ordinary world; and the very ordinary conditions of existence do the developing. Whereas in "The Bear," moreover, our feeling is that Ike is a rare specimen, as Uncles Buck and Buddy were before him, here we are made to feel that anyone can become larger, more human.

Perhaps the fairly frequent allusions to Faustian damnation and the Fall[17] are, then, particularly significant; for Lucius' is yet another "fortunate Fall." In this life, Paradise must, for Faulkner, always be lost. As we have seen, always man moves from childhood innocence into the disillusioning sound and fury of maturity. But here, like Prospero, who also knows the difficult nature of existence and the nature of man both in its evil and in its promise, Lucius leaves his Eden and, like Prospero, leaves without the suffering of a Hamlet —or of a Quentin Compson. For, in *The Reivers*, we fall to rise, encounter evil and pain to grow. In this, Faulkner's fullest acceptance of time, the "leap in the dark" is made with hope. If it "is rounded with a sleep," our moment in time is nevertheless real, provides the ground and soil for our growth. Under the very impact of life, we sprout and ripen. Like Shakespeare's, this is Faulkner's final acceptance of the encounter with life.

1. "Time Out for Fun in Old Mississippi," *New York Times Book Review,* June 3, 1962.

2. "Minor Faulkner," said Granville Hicks in "Building Blocks of a Gentleman," *Saturday Review,* June 2, 1962, p. 27. Even so staunch an admirer of Faulkner as Warren Beck seemed to find few serious virtues and these chiefly in the typical Faulknerian indomitability of the characters and the assertion of "the code of gentleman" ("Told with Gusto," *Virginia Quarterly Review,* XXXVIII, Autumn 1962, 681–685). In recent books, Lawrance Thompson in *William Faulkner: An Introduction and Interpretation* (New York, 1963), found "only trivial forms of amusement" (p. 14), and Peter Swiggart, *The Art of Faulkner's Novels* (Austin, 1962), although favorably disposed, offered the restrained judgment of "satisfactory" (p. 207).

3. A review in *Time,* "Prospero in Yoknapatawpha," June 8, 1962, p. 92, comparing Faulkner to a "mellowed Prospero" who "proves an engaging fellow" after earlier tales of "human bestiality," makes a slender use of the *Tempest* parallel.

4. *Faulkner at Nagano,* ed. Robert A. Jelliffe (Tokyo, 1956), p. 35.

5. *Faulkner in the University,* ed. Frederick L. Gwynn and Joseph L. Blotner (Charlotteville, Va., 1959), p. 84.

6. *Ibid.,* p. 190.

7. Frederick J. Hoffman, in *William Faulkner* (New York, 1961), pp. 38–39, describes Faulkner's creations as "a succession of explorations of the varying and shifting nature of truth."

8. *The Town* (New York, 1957), pp. 316, 317. In *Man in Motion: Faulkner's Trilogy* (Madison, 1961), p. 70, Warren Beck, citing this passage, calls Gavin Stevens "Faulkner's *alter ego.* "

9. Warren Beck alone seems to have noticed this sense of reassessment "the perspective of a lifetime" ("Told with Gusto," p. 685).

10. "The Faulkners: Recollections of a Gifted Family," *William Faulkner: Three Decades of Criticism,* ed. Frederick J. Hoffman and Olga W. Vickery (East Lansing, 1960), p. 61.

11. *The Reivers* (New York, 1962), p. 72. All references in the text of this article are to this edition.

12. William Van O'Connor, "Faulkner's One-Sided Dialogue with Hemingway," *College English* XXIV (Dec., 1962), 213–215, lists some of the "accepters" and points up the existence of the theme of acceptance in *The Wild Palms.*

13. *Writers at Work: The Paris Review Interviews,* ed. Malcolm Cowley (New York, 1959), pp. 139–140.

14. *The Sound and the Fury* and *As I Lay Dying,* Mod. Library ed. (New York, 1945), p. 391.

15. Mod. Library ed. (New York, 1955), p. 283.

16. *Writers at Work,* p. 132.

17. See, for example, pp. 50, 53, 60–61, 66, 94.

Index

Adams, Henry, 63–6.
Aeschylus, 298–302.
Aiken, Conrad, 8–9, 57, 58, 173.
Aldington, Richard, 8.
allegory, 88–9.
Anderson, Robert, 356.
Anderson, Sherwood, 16–19, 20, 25, 28, 30–1, 259.
Appian, Lucius, 58.
Aquinas, Thomas, 59.
atmosphere, 192–8.
automobile, 65.

Baldwin, J. G., 38.
Balzac, Honoré de, 17, 18, 25–6, 39, 57, 60, 140.
Barr, Mammy Caroline, 110.
Basso, Hamilton, 59.
Bergson, Henri, 39–40, 56, 61–2.
Berman, Louis, 57.
Bell, Clive, 61.
Bible, King James version, 14, 25, 56.
blend, 328–34.
Blotner, Joseph, 55 ff.
Bourne, Randolph, 60.
Bowles, Paul, 356.
Brooks, Van Wyck, 60.

Caldwell, Taylor, 165.
Camus, Albert, 56.
Capote, Truman, 356.
Cather, Willa, 31, 59.
Catullus, 59.
Cézanne, Paul, 19–20.
characterization, 110.
Christianity (use of), 38–40, 100–102, 117–33, 339 ff.
Civil War, 97.

commedia, 301.
community, 258 ff., 298.
Conrad, Joseph, 16, 20–6, 56, 180.
Contempo, 49 ff.
Cooper, James Fenimore, 25–6.
Craft of Fiction, The, 57.
Crane, Stephen, 18

Defoe, Daniel, 58.
Dial, The, 8, 41.
Dickens, Charles, 30, 56.
Dilthey, Wilhelm, 60.
Doom, 116–7.
Don Quixote, 56.
Dos Passos, John, 165.
Dostoievski, Feodor, 30, 56.
Double Dealer, The, 8, 50–1, 59, 362.
dramatic imagery, 15.
dynamism, 64, 66.

Egoist, The, 8, 41.
Ellis, Havelock, 57.
Ellison, Ralph, 356.
Eliot, T.S., 10, 15, 38, 41, 51–2, 213, 298.
epic, 335.
epiphany, 240.
evil, 119–20 ff., 132.

family, 111–17, 214 ff., 244.
Faulkner, William
art, 191; biography, 359; criticism of his work, 335–6; development of, 7–44, 55; "Elmer," 61; humor, 16–7, 40, 68–82, 250–1, 358–68; locations, 17; as painter, 19; as poet, 44–54; as Southern writer, 51, 83–93, 94–109, 138, 196–7. Works of: *Absalom, Absalom!* 10, 14, 20, 22, 31,